'Metin Koca's book is a critique of the dominant perspective that places "values" at the heart of democratic transformation. Instead, Koca provocatively argues that what matters is the acknowledgement of disagreement over values. This insightful book is likely to initiate a fruitful debate.'

Asef Bayat, *Bastian Professor of Global and Transnational Studies, University of Illinois, Urbana-Champaign, USA*

'Koca's valuable and innovative study shows that democratization depends on recognizing that we *will* disagree about our values rather than on forging agreement on them. The author demonstrates this through exploring the dynamics of cultural change in contemporary Turkey in the areas of entertainment, women's clothing and Alevi religious ritual.'

Katerina Dalacoura, *Associate Professor in International Relations, London School of Economics and Political Science, UK*

'How can a democracy survive a strong ideological divide among its public opinion without falling into a civil war? Metin Koca offers an original and insightful approach, analyzing the ethic of debating that arose spontaneously in Turkish civil society when sensitive moral and religious issues are discussed in public.'

Olivier Roy, *Professor at the Robert Schuman Centre for Advanced Studies and the School of Transnational Governance, European University Institute, Italy*

Tracing Cultural Change in Turkey's Experience of Democratization

Does democracy require an agreement on specific foundational values? Bringing insights from Turkey to the study of democratization, this book argues that democracy may rather be about acknowledging the disagreement over values before negotiating over other concerns, such as rights, freedoms, capabilities, and duties.

It explores this idea by examining three landscapes of culture in Turkey, which have been the subjects of persistent stories regarding the unequal relationship between the *self* and the *other*. These include LGBT visibility and the entertainment sector, women and clothing, and Alevism and funerals. Through these case studies, the book analyses the remaking of (in)tolerance through the integration of LGBT representations into broader political struggles over values, the assertion of women's rights and freedoms from traditional values surrounding dress, and the conflict between essentialist intolerance and the syncretic traditions of Alevi identity.

Bringing these landscapes together with the surrounding cultural tensions in Turkey and the West, *Tracing Cultural Change in Turkey's Experience of Democratization* will be a valuable resource for students and scholars of Middle Eastern studies and politics, gender studies, and cultural studies.

Metin Koca works as a European Research Council postdoctoral researcher at Istanbul Bilgi University, Turkey. Koca received his Ph.D. in Social and Political Sciences from the European University Institute, Italy, in January 2020. He is interested in the dynamics of cultural change and reproduction, as well as the politics of recognition, tolerance, and difference.

Routledge Studies in Political Sociology

This series presents the latest research in political sociology. It welcomes both theoretical and empirical studies that pay close attention to the dynamics of power, popular protest and social movements, as well as work that engages in debates surrounding globalisation, democracy and political economy.

Titles in this series

Comparing and Contrasting the Impact of the COVID-19 Pandemic in the European Union
Linda Hantrais, Marie-Thérèse Letablier

The Political Attitudes of Divided European Citizens
Public Opinion and Social Inequalities in Comparative and Relational Perspective
Christian Lahusen

Technocratic Politics
Beyond Democratic Society?
Francesco Antonelli

Tracing Cultural Change in Turkey's Experience of Democratization
Unexpected Dialogues on Intolerance
Metin Koca

European Lobbying
An Occupational Field between Professionalism and Activism
Christian Lahusen

For more information about this series, please visit: https://www.routledge.com/Routledge-Studies-in-Political-Sociology/book-series/RSPS

Tracing Cultural Change in Turkey's Experience of Democratization

Unexpected Dialogues on Intolerance

Metin Koca

LONDON AND NEW YORK

First published 2023
by Routledge
4 Park Square, Milton Park, Abingdon, Oxon OX14 4RN

and by Routledge
605 Third Avenue, New York, NY 10158

Routledge is an imprint of the Taylor & Francis Group, an informa business

© 2023 Metin Koca

The right of Metin Koca to be identified as author of this work
has been asserted in accordance with sections 77 and 78 of the
Copyright, Designs and Patents Act 1988.

All rights reserved. No part of this book may be reprinted or
reproduced or utilised in any form or by any electronic, mechanical,
or other means, now known or hereafter invented, including
photocopying and recording, or in any information storage or
retrieval system, without permission in writing from the publishers.

Trademark notice: Product or corporate names may be trademarks
or registered trademarks, and are used only for identification and
explanation without intent to infringe.

British Library Cataloguing-in-Publication Data
A catalogue record for this book is available from the British Library

Library of Congress Cataloging-in-Publication Data
Names: Koca, Metin, author.
Title: Tracing cultural change in Turkey's experience of
democratization : unexpected dialogues on intolerance / Metin Koca.
Description: Milton Park, Abingdon, Oxon ; New York, NY :
Routledge, 2023. | Includes bibliographical references and index. |
Identifiers: LCCN 2022046688 (print) | LCCN 2022046689 (ebook) |
ISBN 9781032318684 (hardback) | ISBN 9781032318691 (paperback) |
ISBN 9781003311805 (ebook)
Subjects: LCSH: Social conflict—Turkey. | Social change—Turkey. |
Democratization—Turkey. | Sexual minorities—Turkey—Social
conditions. | Turkey—Social conditions—21st century.
Classification: LCC HN656.5.Z9 S6256 2023 (print) |
LCC HN656.5.Z9 (ebook) | DDC 303.609561—dc23/eng/20221007
LC record available at https://lccn.loc.gov/2022046688
LC ebook record available at https://lccn.loc.gov/2022046689

ISBN: 978-1-032-31868-4 (hbk)
ISBN: 978-1-032-31869-1 (pbk)
ISBN: 978-1-003-31180-5 (ebk)

DOI: 10.4324/9781003311805

Typeset in Times New Roman
by codeMantra

Contents

List of Figure	ix
Acknowledgments	xi
Preface	xiii
List of Abbreviations	xv

1	Introduction: Values and Others in Cultural Change	1
2	Democracy: Rethinking Cultural Prerequisites	22
3	LGBT and the Entertainment Sector	54
4	Women and Clothing	110
5	Alevis and Funerals	170
6	Conclusions	204
	Index	211

Figure

2.1 Correlation between each country's level of democracy and social hostilities involving religion according to a roughly considered map of the Middle East 41

Acknowledgments

This book is based on Ph.D. research I conducted at the European University Institute in Florence, Italy. My research would not have been possible without the intellectual contribution of Olivier Roy. While looking for my own voice, I learned a lot from Roy's guidance at all stages of my research, as well as his studies, seminars, and fantastic stories. Also, as a friend, I am grateful to him for being patient and understanding with me on the bumpy road.

In addition, I wish to acknowledge the help provided by Ann Swidler, who acted as my mentor during my stay at the University of California, Berkeley. Hopefully, my research carries the signs of her illuminating views on the mysterious matter of culture.

I would like to offer my special thanks to Asef Bayat, Élise Massicard, Erman Harun Karaduman, Ezgi Güler, Kayahan Cantekin, Anıl Kemal Aktaş, Nedra Cherif, Rián Tuathal Derrig, Lars Erik Berntzen, Katerina Dalacoura, Ayhan Kaya, Hanspeter Kriesi, Stefano Bartolini, Karen Barkey, Mojtaba Mahdavi, Stacey Gutkowski, Nil Şatana, Nihat Ali Özcan, and Ersel Aydınlı for their constructive feedback on various parts of my research. I am also indebted to the Routledge editors, Neil Jordan, Gemma Rogers, Kathrin Immanuel, and Andrew Leach, for their valuable assistance and guidance. Inadvertently, I may have left some names out, given that so many people directly or indirectly contributed to the research. To those whom I have not cited here, my apologies.

My special thanks are extended to the EUI colleagues in the Muslim World Working Group, the Middle East Working Group, the Middle East Directions, the Gender Project, the IR Working Group, and the A-Team of "Readings from the Underground."

On a more personal level, I am grateful for the unconditional support of my parents, sister, and brother. They always give me a safe and free space to think aloud, offering me solitude to recharge in times of stress.

Preface

The study of democracy is not immune to the tension between value-free and value-laden research expectations. Addressing this tension through various social research problems, this book problematizes the dominance of value expressions not only in defining democracy but also in the cultural clashes that appear in the making of political regimes. Having combined them, I refuse to see questioning the role of values in democratization merely as an area of scientific inquiry. The way researchers ask this question creates multifaceted social complications that situate them among their research objects. Situating myself as such, I think the central question is not (or not anymore) which values democracy should be built upon but how we can anticipate democratization within a plurality of values.

Like all else, researchers may employ a practical mind in their arguments instead of theoretical reason, and I see no problem in acknowledging that. Just as many philosophers and politicians came to admit at one point in their lives (credit given to Chris Brown), the realm of abstract principles and general laws should often be set aside to engage with the areas of morality. The latter evolves in the concrete and exceptional details of everyday life. Revolving around some of the most particular daily life interactions, the book aims to utilize this perspective.

Having recognized subjectivity as key to social research, I shall emphasize that I am not in a position to talk on behalf of all the social agents—the vulnerable or the strong, the narrator or the subaltern—covered in this book. However, I am convinced that imagining a world where one is entitled to talk only about oneself in isolation is incompatible with the history of our marked, unequal relationships. While seeking a change in the relationships between the *self* and the *other*, this book will also touch upon numerous conflicts between the representations of a shared identity. Describing the *self* in the form of owning a collective identity does not solve the problem of subjectivity. Moreover, one of the discussions in the book will be how forcing others to define their parochial identity can become a tool in the hands of the higher authority.

Questioning how democratization might be possible within value plurality requires sensing what is left after interlocutors speak with each other,

xiv *Preface*

not necessarily in peaceful terms, about each other's untouchables and non-negotiables. Therefore, my practical mind pushed me to take the burden of trying to translate the conversations between a great diversity of individuals into the democratization literature. It is a burden, given the discouragement of an Italian saying Olivier Roy told me during my Ph.D. research: "*Traduttore, traditore*" (en., translator, traitor). Although the phrase does not indicate a compelling equation in English and Turkish, I would not call the failure of this translation a betrayal. However, a universal audience would perhaps agree that mistranslation is a betrayal when ill-intentioned. My intention with this book is to take a step to shift the focus from value expressions to rights, freedoms, capabilities, and duties.

Metin Koca, 26 September 2022, Istanbul

Abbreviations

AABK	Avrupa Alevi Birlikleri Konfederasyonu (en. European Alevi Unions Confederation)
ABF	Alevi-Bektaşi Federasyonu (en. Alevi-Bektashi Federation)
AKP	Adalet ve Kalkınma Partisi (en. Justice and Development Party)
AVF	Alevi Vakıfları Federasyonu (en. The Federation of Alevi Associations)
BDP	Barış ve Demokrasi Partisi (en. Peace and Democracy Party)
CHP	Cumhuriyet Halk Partisi (en. Republican People's Party)
DBP	Demokratik Bölgeler Partisi (en. The Party of Democratic Regions)
DHKP-C	Devrimci Halk Kurtuluş Partisi-Cephesi (en. Revolutionary People's Liberation Front)
DISK	Devrimci İşçi Sendikaları Konf. (en. Confederation of Progressive Trade Unions)
Diyanet	Diyanet İşleri Başkanlığı (en. Directorate of Religious Affairs)
DTP	Demokratik Toplum Partisi (en. Democratic Society Party)
ECHR	European Convention on Human Rights
ECtHR	European Court of Human Rights
HADEP	Halkın Demokrasi Partisi (en. People's Democracy Party)
HDP	Halkların Demokratik Partisi (en. Peoples' Democratic Party)
İHD	İnsan Hakları Derneği (en. The Association of Human Rights)
ISIS	Islamic State of Iraq and the Levant (ar. Dawlat al-'Irāq al-'Islāmiyyah)
İŞKUR	Türkiye İş Kurumu (en. Turkish Employment Agency)
LGBT	Lezbiyen, Gey, Biseksüel, Transgender (en. Lesbian, Gay, Bisexual, Transgender)
METU	Middle East Technical University
PKK	Partiya Karkerên Kurdistanê (en. Kurdistan Workers' Party)
RTÜK	Radyo ve Televizyon Üst Kurulu (en. Radio and Television Supreme Council)
SHI	Social Hostilities Index

xvi   *Abbreviations*

TAF	Turkish Armed Forces (tr. Türk Silahlı Kuvvetleri, TSK)
TKP	Türkiye Komünist Partisi (en. Communist Party of Turkey)
TRT	Türkiye Radyo Televizyon Kurumu (en. Turkish Radio Television)
UN	United Nations
WVS	World Values Survey

1 Introduction

Values and Others in Cultural Change

How do values, beliefs, and their functions in making an ideology change in time? An inquiry into this question of cultural change requires going beyond values toward other cultural resources and different cultural periods that set these resources in motion. The value-based approach to culture takes "values"[1] as the core of "cultures." Therefore, its followers in the democratization literature have been keen to define a value system as the benchmark of transition to a democratic culture. Coupled with the understanding that democracy is foundationally dependent on shared values, advancements in the survey method like comprehensive cross-sectional and cross-temporal techniques have led value surveys to dominate the study of cultural change in this literature (*see* Hitlin and Piliavin 2004). Since then, some "cultures"—e.g., "Islamic culture"—have been labeled as exceptionally recalcitrant towards change (Inglehart and Baker 2000; Norris and Inglehart 2002), and some value systems—e.g., that of "progressives" and "conservatives," and the "sacred" and the "secular"—as irreconcilable competitors (Hunter 2009, 2014). In this book, I aim to problematize the understanding of change and democracy promoted by the value-based approach to culture.

This book places itself in an era of value demonstrativeness, where stakeholders validate their identities by accenting their non-negotiable values. Be these stakeholders the American evangelists, the Catholic Church, and the Muslim conservatives who constructed traditional family values in response to the post-1960s social changes, or the liberal democrats and the French laïcs championing sexual liberation and gender equality as a universal condition. Where expressing values has become an existential posture against the adversary, imposing on democracy a convergence criterion based on values becomes an obstacle against democratization. While addressing the democratization literature, the book focuses on Turkey, identified as a case of democratization, democratic backsliding, or at a standstill. Going beyond these markers, I take Turkey as an intersection of several landscapes where the voices raise to distinguish between the *self* and the *other* insistently in the name of "Islamic culture," "common values," "public decency," or "progress toward modernity."

DOI: 10.4324/9781003311805-1

2 Introduction: Values and Others in Cultural Change

Tracing change is an arduous task when continuities surround it. Beyond categorizing Turkey as a case of democratization, standstill, or democratic backsliding, I shall briefly highlight the culturally meaningful notions of change and reproduction. A primary way of seeking reproduction is to look at the state's attitude towards whom it defines as the other. Among others, Kaya argues that the state reproduces its othering mechanisms, no matter who spoke in its name over centuries:

> [T]here has been continuity between modern Turkey and the Ottoman Empire in terms of the management of ethno-cultural and religious diversity, and the tradition of tolerance since the imperial ascendancy of the 16th century [...] As long as these groups pay their tributes to the Turkish state and accept their subaltern and secondary position, they are tolerated.
>
> (Kaya 2013:3–14)

According to this position, a set of self-proclaimed or exogenously imposed identities, their antecedents and successors find their place in an inherently unequal system of tolerance. Also focusing on continuity, seasoned historian Halil İnalcık argues that "we" could not turn out to be entirely different despite the modernist project. This limited change further exacerbated the tension: "we are in the face of a culture and identity problem that is heavier than usual" (İnalcık 1998:13). İnalcık interpreted the most recent episode as a cultural contestation between the hegemonic Turk-Islam synthesis and its critiques.

In the last port of call, the reference points have become "Secularism," "Islamism," and others subordinated to their grand debate of values. Right before the third term of the Erdoğan government, Toprak *et al.* (2009:36–39) labeled "seculars" (tr. laikler) as the new others of Anatolia. Change was a central theme of controversy in this period: Erdoğan came to power in 2002, insisting that he took off the shirt of Islamism he previously carried. While his critiques discussed whether he had ever "changed," Erdoğan stressed that he did not change but made progress. In response, his opponents repeatedly referred to the free elections trap, which Erdoğan would use to overturn the democratic system.

Regarding how the grand debate has been reduced to the Islamism-Secularism dyad, Nuray Mert's (2013) position is noteworthy since it represents the formerly pro-government voices who saw a "post-Islamist" condition in the first AKP governments and then revised their positions in disappointment. According to Mert, the Islamists who once "reinvented themselves as conservative democrats under the roof of the AKP turned back to the Islamist ideology" (Mert2013:par3). Perceiving a similar revival of Islamism, Aygün (2016), Saraçoğlu (2017), and Soyer (2017) talked on behalf of the left-wing ideologies that did not previously self-identify with Secularism. Yıldızoğlu (2017) argued that there were many Turkeys in the past—e.g., that of labor and capital, LGBT people and LGBTphobes, men

Introduction: Values and Others in Cultural Change 3

and women. According to him, these multiple struggles have recently been pulled into a grand battle between only "two Turkeys"—that is, between "Secularism" and "Political Islam."

The notions of change presented so far are another name for illusion, between the loosening and the tightening of the reproduction mechanisms. Throughout the book, all chapters will suggest that cultural reproduction owes part of its power to repetitive explanations for the changing problems. For example, in the contestations introduced above, the primary way of promoting tolerance is to establish the argument on cherry-picked quotes from a selection of historical sources for the sake of legitimacy. Among these sources are Yusuf Has Hacip's (11th century) *Kutadgu Bilig*, Ahmet Yesevi (12th century), Babai Dervishes, Hacı Bektaş-ı Veli's (13th century) *Vilayet-name*, Yunus Emre and Rumi (13th century), and *Ehl-i Sünnet* (en., the followers of Prophet Muhammed's practice of Islam).[2] They have been retained as the principal reference points in intellectual statements, artistic expressions, political slogans, and the sense of humor. This dominating repetition blurs the scene of the culture that flows. Therefore, seeking cultural change requires paying attention to how these signifiers' representative functions may have fluctuated in the course of the value contestations.

As a case of value plurality, the Turkish case has much to offer against the value-based approach to democratization. The value-based democracy rests on value consensus by definition. Even when the agreement appears in the form of valuing the coexistence of juxtaposed parochial values, it imagines an overarching value to be shared by the clashing parties. While putting forward an image of democracy, this approach dismisses the possibility of democracy-building amid *persistent* expressions of clashing values. Connectedly, focusing exclusively on values, the democratization literature neglects the transformation of other cultural expressions, such as the ideology-making processes that operationalize unchanging values in different ways. In contrast, based on several empirical issues I will introduce, I argue that rights, freedoms, capabilities, and the rules of appropriateness may be disentangled from expectations of conceptual compromise in values. Hence, democracy may not require an agreement on values but acknowledging the disagreements over values before negotiating the rest.

A persistent expression of clashing values does not rule out the possibility of meaningful cultural change, as the expression of a value tends to be restrained, optimized, or entirely disconnected from action depending on the social context. Context—i.e., the situatedness of meanings—is read by the relational *self*, both a product and a re-maker of the culture. Therefore, this book will focus on social contexts dialogically formed between the *self* and the *other*. My starting point will be a set of conversational texts,[3] which shall hint at how *change*, as a theme, may appear in a dialogically formed social context. Conversations—exchanged (written or oral) texts—will constitute the building block of my methodological and theoretical approach to studying cultural reproduction. Methodologically, I will use the strength

4 *Introduction: Values and Others in Cultural Change*

of conversations to shed light on the weakness of value surveys in grasping social contexts and speech acts. Theoretically, I will demonstrate how a conversation's flow can manifest culture in action and, hence, as a process instead of an entity.

The Landscapes of Culture

I will focus on *change* by traveling through some landscapes where intolerance—in the shifting temporal, relational senses of the word—has been repeatedly rationalized, yet intended to say different *things*, negotiated in different terms, and given different responses. Starting with landscapes is an alternative to starting with pre-defined, abstract, decontextualized, and somewhat timeless concepts (e.g., "religious" and "secular" values). While explaining my choice in favor of the former, I will examine, in the course of the research, how the latter approach hinders the ability of value-survey researchers to read through some *natural* social contexts in which change appears in a culturally meaningful manner.

The book will specifically focus on three landscapes of culture in Turkey, which have persistently brought, for decades if not centuries, the authoritative claims of some (and often the same) hegemonic ideologies with social groups designated as *others*, who have dealt with these authorities in unique ways, commonly in an unequal relationship. I roughly identify these landscapes as follows: (i) "LGBT" and the entertainment sector, (ii) "women" and clothing, and (iii) "Alevis" and funerals. They bring together some of the most extensive illustrations of cultural change and reproduction while witnessing a persistently unequal relationship between the *self* and the *other*. My emphasis on them shall not de-emphasize the neighboring landscapes. On the contrary, I selected them as I think they contain some crystal-clear historical snapshots that shed light on the surrounding landscapes, which could (and should) be imagined.

Funeral

Consider Alevi students at school: their parents tend to oppose compulsory religion classes based on a form of Sunni Islam. Alongside, many of them also oppose the state funeral organizations at mosques for Alevi martyrs. The main fault lines in the two landscapes would be similar in terms of reflecting Alevis' struggle for a politics of recognition. However, the landscape of funerals can guide the content of a school textbook, especially because it includes an essential debate among Alevis on their in-group tolerance alongside the state's policies. Might an Alevi's funeral take place at a mosque? Should Alevis avoid praying behind Sunni religious personnel? Are mosque rituals exclusively Sunni? Alevis' discussions among themselves about their funeral rituals ultimately relate to the alternative definitions of the Alevi belief system.

Introduction: Values and Others in Cultural Change 5

Indeed, these questions shall be historicized to make sense. For centuries after the battle of Chaldiran (1514), some relatively unknown—yet stereotypically despised—religious rituals could survive in the isolation of certain villages in the mountains of Anatolia. As history progressed, the carriers of these different and also differentiating rituals were labeled by the *self* or the *other* as "Kızılbaş," "Rafizî," "Alevi," or as a "heterodox (Islamic) community." Following the urbanization processes after the 1950s, some Alevis' funeral rituals began to symbolize an acculturation process—i.e., the acculturation of the mosque funeral in urban settings. Alongside demanding tolerance of Sunni Muslims at mosques, the vast majority of Alevis began carrying the flag of "Secularism,"[4] together with Marxism(s), as part of great power politics. From the 1960s to the 1980s, many Alevis complained that they were not welcome at mosques, unlike Sunni Muslims. In the meantime, several incidents surfaced that were likely to offend them, for example, during their funeral organizations, a core activity that most people are involved in planning at least once in life.

As of the 1990s, some Alevi communities' expectations concerning mosques have fundamentally differed, as they concluded that their tolerance politics had failed. Accordingly, they re-configured their funerals, provoking a new tension between the belief system, *Alevilik*,[5] and the new identity politics, *Alevism*.[6] Through the landscape of funerals, one can follow where "we"—i.e., both the *self* and the *other*—have reached in "our" history of sectarianism.

Entertainment

Another landscape that always had a say over its neighbors is the entertainment sector. Some of the earliest visible representations of "LGBT" identity (alternatively, LGBTT, LGBTI, LGBTQ, LGBTI+) arguably appeared among performance artists—e.g., *köçek*, çengi, *kolbaşı*, *tavşan oğlanı*. In the face of a deadly attack in 1996, the trans sex workers of İstanbul's Ülker Street defended the legitimacy of their existence by amalgamating their identities with that of the Ottoman *köçeks* (Selek 2014). Their "entertainment" activities have been vital to their legitimacy since Ottoman times. As early as the 16th century, the sector began to represent a space in which these visible representations were occasionally needed as natural and appreciated as fabulous entities. After the paradigmatic shift to the initial modern understanding of sexualities and gender norms, this landscape became a haven for the outliers in the shrinking space of gender diversity.

However, at the same time, the sector represented a space of exclusion, which was realized by the members of the LGBT activism that developed after the 1990s. Accordingly, the industry crystallizes exclusion whenever it is organized and re-organized unilaterally by a higher authority. Moreover, the inclusivity of the sector indicates where tolerance ends in practice for LGBT people—e.g., a trans sex worker's willingness to leave the industry to

6   *Introduction: Values and Others in Cultural Change*

join another one, such as the public sector. It is through the landscape of the entertainment sector that one can follow how these boundaries have been pushed back and forth by the different visible representations of LGBT identity, as well as their interlocutors and the authoritative claims they advance.

Clothing

Clothing is another landscape I rambled through, at least because, for centuries, the dominant cultural mindset took clothing as an infallible indicator of personality. According to the Ottoman millet system, clothing materials were to act as the fundamental boundary markers between the pre-recognized religious communities (Barkey 2005). The personalities of garments were given and forcefully preserved by the state, or at least that was the commitment.

The clothing revolutions led by the Ottoman modernism and the Secularist Republic changed people's clothes several times. However, the competing ideology makers of these historical episodes shared the received wisdom about the formative role of clothing in constructing a society. In the ideological contestation that followed the foundation of the Republic, women's clothing was still perceived as a central moral issue, a very quickly-changing fashion, a symbol of social development or backwardness, and a reflection of women's "legitimate" environment.

Recently, however, this cultural mindset may have been challenged in unprecedented ways. After three decades of confrontation over the head-covering ban, many ideology makers who define and staunchly defend Secularism against Erdoğan have just recognized the agency of "türban wearers,"[7] together with the burden of responsibility that "türban" loads on its carrier. In other words, it is now discursively possible for a "türban-wearer" to defend human rights in the "Secular" sense of the term. Meanwhile, the Islamist intellectuals of "the old generation" are increasingly vocal about their disappointment with the new Islamic fashion. In other words, it is now discursively possible for a hijabi to be "immoral" in the "Islamist" sense of the term. Through the landscape of clothing, one can follow whether "we" re-made "our" relationship with the old ideals, and if so, at what expense.

Puzzle: Dialogues Illustrating Cultural Change

Beginning with some puzzling conversations in these historically significant landscapes, I will examine (1) the unchaining of "our" rights and freedoms from "our" parochial values; (2) the integration of a once-demonized group into the competing mass value systems; and (3) the clash between a minority belief system and the identity politics relating to it, with repercussions for the fault-line between tolerance and recognition.

My aim with these case selections is not to highlight the ideal examples of cultural change enabling pluralism and peaceful coexistence. Picking

Introduction: Values and Others in Cultural Change   7

such instances would be relatively easy elsewhere. On the contrary, I look at the three landscapes since they have been unique in persistently bringing together hegemonic ideologies with social groups designated as *others* and in new ways that push discursive boundaries. These landscapes, on the one hand, serve as key reference points during the broader ideological contestations over who owns the true religion, the purest form of morality, the ruling capacity, and the capital (e.g., financial, cultural). On the other hand, they include some of the most nuanced relationships of tolerance and some of the deadliest rationalizations of intolerance. Apart from informing each other and their neighbors as cultural reproduction locales, they point to limited yet decisive engagements, with prospects for further cultural change.

These sites crystallize many discontinuities as well. They relate to the sharing of public spaces (e.g., reappropriating clothing in a neighborhood), the re-operationalization of value systems (e.g., unchaining rights from values), the re-casting of belief systems (e.g., changing funeral rituals), the hyphenated identities (e.g., headscarved workers; religiously conservative LGBT people), and the new expressions of social classes (e.g., "anti-capitalist Muslims"; "middle-class Islamists"). It is also not uncommon for *others* to make their own others in the mix. Talking in the name of "women," "LGBT" people, and "Alevis" often mean an act of gatekeeping, which leads to tensions at the gate of identity. Combined, these landscapes expose the push and pull factors behind remaking ideologies. Scrutinizing them will contribute to "our" imagination of democracy.

"LGBT Pride" and Police Officers on Streets versus Erdoğan and Bülent Ersoy at Iftar

Having focused on some boundary moments in conversational texts, I will question, for example, how *unsettling* an unprecedented question may be for a government's ideology. The participants of a public parade, "LGBT Pride," asked the head of the government, Recep Tayyip Erdoğan, why he denounced them in moral terms and ordered the police to interfere with their parade while, on the same morally loaded Ramadan day, he and his wife Emine Erdoğan had *iftar*[8] with a "transsexual" singer, Bülent Ersoy, as known as the "trans-diva" of the country. Without the appearance of a voice to bring together these two snapshots, the tear gas that the police officers threw would do nothing more than underpin the already well-repeated argument that the ideology of the government, formed as an extension of the historical repertoire of Islamism, is undoubtedly antagonistic, and beyond antagonism, intolerant towards LGBT. However, by pointing out an exception to this narrative, some participants of the parade—no matter how vulnerable they may be within the given authority structure[9]—could push for re-evaluating a hegemonic ideology, "Islamism."

In response, the supporters of Erdoğan, his advisors, and the pro-government media organs had to devise a rationalization of tolerance.

8   *Introduction: Values and Others in Cultural Change*

Some denied seeing Bülent Ersoy as "a transsexual" on the basis that she was "much more" than that. Accordingly, she was taken as an indisputable talent, a religious conservative, or simply a "reality" of Turkey. Some other government defenders used the moment to "prove" that "transsexuals" have become freer under the rule of the AKP government. However, having problematized such explicit references to the gendered history of Ersoy, some other pro-government circles would be skeptical of any emphasis on LGBT as a marker of identity. Erdoğan kept his silence during this in-group discussion. Nevertheless, silence within this context should also be taken as an answer, albeit vague. As the (at least) two pro-Erdoğan claims did not overlap, a further contestation would occur: one between the pro- and anti-parade representations of LGBT and another between the clashing anti-parade claims.

Many who speak in the name of Islam will deny that they tolerate LGBT people. The cross-temporal value surveys continue to reach this intuitive conclusion,[10] just as the ideology makers keep repeating, "we cannot tolerate what Allah forbids."[11] However, the fundamental question here turns out to be more nuanced than these explicit uses of discourse. The following question must be asked: have the self-proclaimed Islamists begun to tolerate these people, *not* by putting up with their LGBT identity, but by ignoring or sidestepping their demonstration of some apparent markers of LGBT identity? If these authorities rationalize making such a distinction between "being only an LGBT person" and "being more than an LGBT person," what may be the implications of this *implicit tolerance* in the entertainment sector, which signifies the traditional labor sector of LGBT people? On the flip side, what may be the implications of this argument in, say, the public sector where LGBT employees cannot be easily visible? After all, Bülent Ersoy, who never hid her trans-identity but expressed it only in certain well-negotiated forms, was not marked as "a transsexual" in the abovementioned context. On the contrary, she was often appreciated for the foundational conservative values that she defended in the gaze of the authorities.

That said, under the given limits of appropriateness, which visible representatives of LGBT identity would consent, in the Gramscian sense of the term, to take on this role of acting as "more than an LGBT person"? After all, the question comes down to the first-order values one represents once s/he becomes visible. What opened a relatively safe space of tolerance for Ersoy is what fundamentally clashes with the aim of an "LGBT Pride" parade—i.e., the respectful recognition of a standalone LGBT identity. On the one hand, this process pushes the identity carriers to negotiate their in-group differences, especially regarding their alternative approaches to the broader ideological repertoires they face. On the other hand, it suggests that "LGBT" appears as a point of re-evaluation for the makers of hegemonic ideologies, such as those of "the right" and "the left," which, I will claim, previously blamed one another for being too soft on "sexual perversion." Having participated in these contestations, "LGBT" can no longer

Introduction: Values and Others in Cultural Change 9

be taken merely as a matter of sub-culture. Instead, I will offer a relational perspective that takes "LGBT" as a many-voiced identity, the alternative visible representations of which have been integrated into Turkey's mass political struggles over values.

Cübbeli Ahmet Hoca at His Daughter's Wedding

In the next landscape that I observed—i.e., women and clothing, the flow of the conversations went beyond the ideology makers' first-order values. What if, for example, the daughter of the most famous teacher of a religious community, *Ismailağa Cemaati*, wants to have her wedding in an allegedly "Western-style" wedding dress, contrary to what her father has preached for many decades? In this case, Ahmet Mahmut Ünlü, known as Cübbeli Ahmet Hoca, was challenged by the mismatch between his first-order values and the preferences of someone from his very close social circle. Sometime after the wedding ceremony, Ünlü publicized his disappointment with his daughter Yüsra's dress. That said, he emphasized that enforcement would not be a solution even if his daughter does not embrace "hijab"—i.e., the proper form of *tesettür*, the Islamic veil, according to Ünlü and the rest of *Ismailağa Cemaati*. Having dismissed the idea of forcing the youth to behave per "the Islamic values," Ünlü defined the main task as making young people embrace these values. Ultimately, in the face of her religious values, Yüsra would take the burden of her own behavior.

This conversation includes Ünlü's definition of his foundational values, but it goes beyond these values. Ünlü makes a normative, ethical claim when he puts forward what ought to be done in these cases. (1) He explained how he sadly turned his back on his daughter during the wedding. (2) He admitted that he was not entirely successful in educating his close social circle in this respect. (3) Having said that, he did not see enforcement as a solution since the practice of these values does not make sense as long as the practitioner does not fully internalize them. (4) By emphasizing the individual responsibility the belief-system places on its carriers, he reminded the public of his own "proper" wedding. (5) He preached that Muslims should "interfere with the wrong" if they can, utilizing a "balanced" action, such as conveying the message of Allah, or at least having an inward opposition. (6) Finally, Ünlü invited Muslims to pray for their fellow believers who have not yet embraced all the ideals of Islam.

As this context-dependent evaluation suggests, the expression of first-order values in a decontextualized setting tends to differ from the operationalization of these values in action. The survey method falls short in making sense of different social contexts. For example, according to the survey of the University of Michigan's Institute for Social Research, which is one of the most recent surveys on the subject, only half of the respondents agreed that "it is up to a woman to dress whichever way she wants" (Moaddel 2013:57, 97). However, the survey lacked a thorough examination

10   *Introduction: Values and Others in Cultural Change*

of the cognitive processes that the respondents may have undergone during their minimal speech acts. For example, in the responses, it remains unexplored what kind of an imagined authority it is that should restrict women's clothing—e.g., a court, a parent, a religious value of the self.

The survey conducted by Çarkoğlu and Toprak (2007) could construct more clear social contexts. The head-covering ban was posed as a straightforward legal question; the headscarf was presented as a command of religion; and interference with the others' clothing was asked as a potentially different social matter, which may be taken as an ethical question. Nevertheless, the cross-temporal approach of Toprak and Çarkoğlu examined change only by asking the same questions twice in a seven-year period. In other words, the survey was not made to examine how each of these questions may have lost or gained significance in time. This is part of my aim in delving into a history of conversations. This history should demonstrate how the formulation of some critical questions differed in time.

For example, the ethical question that was available in Ünlü's speech has prevailed in some mass debates. Recently, many religious conservatives of the old generation mentioned their disappointment with the most recent generation's conduct of tesettür. Given the new fashion and style that influenced the appearance of tesettür, they shared their doubts regarding the sincerity of some fellow practitioners of religion—e.g., those that bring together "style," "fashion," and tesettür. Accordingly, the critiques have diagnosed the problem as fake conduct of certain practices without the accompaniment of the necessary element of belief. However, the flow of these conversations obliged them to re-evaluate their approach to those who do not share the value system they put forward in the name of Islam. If the problem is the lack of sincere belief, to what extent and in which form should "pressure" be an option? In this way, it turns out to be a question of tolerance, though the form of tolerance that emanates from these strong expressions of first-order values would be, at most, a *tolerance without relativism*.

A similar ethical concern, which necessitates going beyond one's first-order values without renouncing these values, also leads to the re-making of Secularism. In late 2013, CHP[12] did not oppose the parliament's de-facto lifting of the head-covering ban. In the parliamentary session on the subject, CHP MP Şafak Pavey made a historic speech aimed at carrying Secularism beyond one's and others' already irreconcilable first-order values. Pavey did not hide her values in this speech but implied that Secularism should go beyond parochial value systems. Accordingly, Pavey's concern was "oppression" instead of others' clothes. After many years of defending the head-covering ban staunchly, CHP ceased its opposition to lifting the ban.

Moreover, the women whose clothing any want-to-be authority has intervened to alter have begun campaigning with the slogan, "do not meddle with my outfit" (tr. kıyafetime karışma). Clearly, the tension lies between the agency of these women and the hegemonic ideologies that imagine an ideal-type woman with ideal clothes representing her personality coherently.

Introduction: Values and Others in Cultural Change 11

Bringing them together, I will discuss how these conversations challenge a dominant cultural mindset on women's clothing. Surviving the Ottoman *millet* system as well as various clothing revolutions, this prevailing mindset objectified clothing as an infallible precursor of personality. For the first time in "our" history, clothes may have been deposed from this position.

Alevis Reformulating Funeral Rituals

Thirdly, I will focus on a landscape that exemplifies the self-conscious re-operationalization of one's rituals in the face of an existential threat. For the sake of a politics of recognition, one might attempt to deconstruct and reconstruct a cultural institution that was once pretty much habitualized in one's mind. What would happen, for example, if some members of a religious community raise their voices to ask the other believers to stop having their funerals in the way to which they have been accustomed? Such disagreements happened in the Alevi community in the aftermath of the identity turn of the early-1990s.

Approximately four decades before this moment, the community's urbanization process made a substantial part of the urban Alevis accustomed to mosque funerals. Many Alevis, among whom were the active politicians and some of the most vocal thinkers of their time, settled for this acculturation in the large cities, as they did not think of institutionalizing their funerals in any unique way—i.e., any way alternative to that of Sunni Muslims. Among the other options were holding the funeral in the hometown or in front of one's apartment in the city. However, many Alevis did not see mosque funerals as a theological problem. Meanwhile, they followed a politics of tolerance, through which they demanded their funeral proceedings to be undertaken by the religious personnel in the same way Sunni Muslims could require (e.g., washing and enshrouding the body, performing a funeral prayer, reading salâ[13] for the funeral). At the time, the ideology makers who spoke in the name of Alevis often reiterated that the mosque was also their place of worship, as they were also Muslims. Their criticism was instead that the official Diyanet[14] personnel consisted of Sunni Muslims. During mosque funerals, Alevis were occasionally harassed by religious personnel. In response, many Alevis called for the state, in the name of Secularism, to re-structure Diyanet so that *Alevilik* could be institutionally recognized as a "sect of Islam."

Though Alevis did not experience a contradiction between the ongoing practice of mosque funerals and their belief system, an unprecedented wave of identity mindfulness triggered their fears of assimilation at the outset of the 1990s. Thereafter, for many, demanding and bestowing tolerance were to be taken as the two faces of the same assimilationism. Among other attempts to "revive" Alevilik, the new institutions of *Alevism* (e.g., civic foundations and associations) configured a place of worship, *cemevi*,[15] to function in urban settings. Even though the historical legitimacy of

12   *Introduction: Values and Others in Cultural Change*

cemevi has been defended by all the mainstream organizations that Alevis established, some of the re-cast cemevi rituals brought these organizations into thorny contestation between the new politics of identity and the essence of the belief system.

The tension in this setting is twofold. Firstly, the state institutions pressured Alevis to come up with a single definition of Alevilik. Merged with a wide range of ideological positions,[16] the traditional claim of the state is that Alevilik should have a clear-cut definition for it to be recognized. Connectedly, this pressure further exacerbates the internal contestations of Alevilik that the Alevi communities had experienced following the identity turn. Challenging one another as to the definition of the true Alevilik, Alevis enter debates about their self-identification. Often poisoned, the arguments include derogatory labels, with "assimilationism," "statism," and "separatism" being primary keywords.

The Alevi citizens of Turkey have been organizing their funerals in ways that may easily challenge these clear-cut differences. Mosque has become the place of worship for the assimilated Alevis, and cemevi has become the place of worship for the Alevis who managed to differentiate their sacred space from others in urban centers. There is a third group between the cleavage. This group includes those who want to have their funerals at a cemevi, while requesting a mosque read only a salâ for these funerals. It also welcomes those who have two separate funeral ceremonies, one at a mosque and one at a cemevi. Their mutation is as natural as the urbanization history of Turkey. What kind of a democratic structure will keep them alongside others: the politics of recognition or tolerance? Will they be the ones who destroy the binary opposition or the ones to become the black sheep? The cultural process Alevis underwent demonstrates how the turn from a settled cultural period to a period of ideology-making may create some very different senses of the same practice (e.g., having requests from mosques).

The Role of Dialectics in Cultural Change

Common to all the cultural processes I have so far described is the indispensable role that *dialectics* play in cultural change, but also in "our" (un) awareness of change and continuity. The relationship of one with the other determines the properties of the process they undergo. They may proceed together in the route of a settled cultural period, where their everyday actions make meaningful change, willingly or not (Bayat 2013). Alternatively, one would wake the other up from the habit, unsettling the ground for the "good" or "bad" and provoking the cognitive capacity of the *self* or the *other* for more ideological thought. Cultural change surfaces in "our" dialogues by the time "we" pass from one period to another.

During these periods, one uses one's cultural resources as parts of a "toolkit" (Swidler 1986). However, the use of the tools differs significantly from one period to another. As the toolkit components are subject to

Introduction: Values and Others in Cultural Change 13

assembly, disassembly, and transformation, culture operates as a *process* where meanings, repertoires, scripts, and the discourses of activities are intrinsically linked to historical time (Greenfield 1997:303–04). The transition from one period to another is not merely an introspective and conscious choice. It is an essential consequence of one's access to structural (material) "resources" (*see* Sewell Jr, 1992) and, at an ideational level, one's perception of social context—i.e., that of the relational *self*.[17]

Cultural Periods: Change and Continuity as Mental Challenges

The book traces *change* in *continuity*. This mental event is challenging, as continuity refers to the consistent existence of something over time, whereas change signifies newness that suddenly or gradually appears. One is processual reproduction; the other is an interruption, a pause, or a juncture, and hence the re-casting of some pre-existing structures. That said, continuity and change are not necessarily mutually exclusive. On the contrary, they may go together in remarkable or subtle ways.

It is subtle if, for instance, a traditional form of expression settles on differentiated meanings under differentiated conditions. This process may underpin what Eco referred to as the widening discrepancy between "the order of words" and "the order of things:"

> Our universe is in full crisis. The order of words no longer corresponds to the order of things: whereas the former still insists on following a traditional system, the latter seems to be mostly characterized by disorder and discontinuity, or so science tells us. Our feelings and emotions have been frozen into stereotypical expressions that have nothing to do with our reality.
>
> (Eco 1989:141)

Aristotle referred to this process in his critique of sophism, as he described a fundamental reasoning error that arises "from an unnoticed shift in the meaning of terms used within an argument" (Eemeren 2015:8). Accordingly, the meanings may change without notice that a statement, utterance, or expression may be used to signify things that are different from those it signified previously.

In a *settled* cultural period (Swidler 2003:89–111), however, the participants tend to be too undisturbed to feel any need to review their dispositions. Such dispositions appear in the form of habits, in a manner so that their doers will comfortably miss their shifting representative functions. Deleuze was among those who argued that habit never leads to a true repetition since, in some situations, the same action comes with a different intent. In others, a different action comes with the same intent (Deleuze 1994:5). Even though variation hides beneath unquestioned repetition, the process obscures one's awareness of the element of change.

14   *Introduction: Values and Others in Cultural Change*

Another element that hinders one's awareness of change might be reliance on an exterior formalization while making sense of repetitive language (Wittgenstein 2009:par11–12, par66). Reliance on such preset reasoning misses the point that everything in the language, including repetitions, may signify change: the meaning is only in the present, hidden only in ordinary uses, and beyond the reach of any exogenous technical, scientistic specialty (De Certeau 1984:8–12). Moreover, the words one uses may be from others, but the "evaluative tone" of these words reflects one's own way of assimilating, reworking, and re-accentuating—i.e., polyphony (many-voicedness), according to Bakhtin (1986:89). Analogously, Phelan (2003) argued that "performance" is only in the present and, therefore, cannot be represented, recorded, or reproduced.

Questioning some of the most "serious" speech acts (Dreyfus and Rabinow 2013:20), Foucault had a similar interest in discontinuities in language. In his explanation of the many discontinuities that "Western culture" experienced during its shift to modernity, Foucault's key argument was that language was displaced away from its "representative functions," as the mode of the word was transformed by the "sounds" that composed it (Foucault 2002:305–30). The process indicated a de-coupling of the word and its very being. In other words, this transformation did not originate in some discursive quality intrinsic to the language itself but was led by the power relations beyond it. Relatedly, Foucault argued that the birth of philology was initially hidden to "Western consciousness"— unlike the well-noticed shifts in biology and economics. It was because of the inevitability of thinking through the discourse of one's language, which raises its barrier against one's awareness of what might have appeared beyond it:

> As one is in the act of discoursing, how is one to know – unless by means of some obscure indices that can interpret only with difficulty and badly – that language (the very language one is using) is acquiring a dimension irreducible to pure discursivity?
>
> (Foucault 2002:307)

This unawareness brings me to another transitory mental process, where discourse begins to lose its significance in the human mind. During a repetition, the tie between the practice and the discourse behind it may loosen. A once-conscious act may turn out as a habit, hence losing the reflexive tone behind it. In this case, no more thought would be needed in the repetition of the practice: "you do it, you do it, and you do it; then you become it," as Catharine MacKinnon (1989:123) quoted from a woman coerced into pornography (*see* also, Chambers 2005). Perceived continuities, routines, and the lack of threat tend to create habitual cultural periods. When culture is entirely in place—i.e., undoubted and undisturbed—it is more difficult to notice how it functions, which is why it remains a methodological challenge

Introduction: Values and Others in Cultural Change 15

for any student of culture. If "the order of things" is re-cast through such pre-reflexive (Bourdieu 1990:108) or tacitly reflexive processes (*see* "practical consciousness" in Giddens 1979:57), it means that the occurrence of cultural change is beyond one's idea of things. This is how an agent might lose awareness, or at the very least, one's vision of change in and around oneself. Though this process beyond reflexivity is missed by the realist notions of agency, among them that of Margaret Archer, it was captured by the *habitus* of Bourdieu (Akram 2013).

Such processes may indicate solid cultural institutions, such as a latent ideology, the meanings of which would not be accessible to those whose performances are likely to appear in the form of habits. Because the ambiguities that underlie habitual periods tend to be meaningful only to a few, it should be these few who trigger a moment to wake the others from the habit (Patterson 2010:141–42). In other words, one provokes one's interlocutors to develop an insight into the cultural institutions functioning in the background of their minds. Once in a simultaneous public debate in Turkey and Egypt ("Mass" 2014), this provocation was depicted in a famous slogan: "Muslim, don't sleep!" Accordingly, one would not be an "Islamist," but at most a Muslim if s/he lost ideological alertness.

All moral crises are triggered at a key moment when one realizes the direction or need for a cultural change. For example, MacKinnon's interviewee reached a stage of self-awareness somewhere before or during the dialogue with MacKinnon, which pulled her back to a conscious examination of herself, through which she could explicitly evaluate her own experience of undergoing a pre-reflexive or tacitly reflexive process. This motif is how a settled cultural period may be problematized for the first time. In itself, one's awareness of the problem indicates cultural change, as it indicates a boundary moment between indifference and care.

As opposed to the structuralist approach, Rose argued that these cultural periods are triggered by the agents who actively manipulate the symbols behind them (Rose 1999:221–22). Certainly, there are moments that wake one up despite one's willingness to continue sleeping, but these boundary moments are not passively reflected. As an example, I shall take the study of the history of sectarianism in Islam—i.e., a case in which either the element of temporality or the key role of the social agency has often been missed. The Ottoman state refused to tolerate Seyyid (Battal) Gazi shrine[18] after the 16th century, even though it had shared "some kind" of *Gaza spirit*[19] since its foundation. What has changed then at this moment in which it was problematized? Cemal Kafadar demonstrated that the Ottoman state became unprecedentedly self-conscious in the making of its ideological formation of Sunni Orthodoxy. In the same (17th) century, this dialogic context that nurtured sectarianism was also a contribution of the dervishes of the Seyyid Shrine, who represented "Shia Bektaşi," which they had not explicitly named back in the 13th century (Kafadar 1995:92).

16   Introduction: Values and Others in Cultural Change

Even though various *Gaza spirits* existed long before this moment, they did not take the unsettling shape they took later. On the contrary, the Ottoman state and the Bektaşi order had "started this adventure in some harmony and cooperation but ended up as the two opposing poles of the Ottoman religio-political culture" (Kafadar 1995:98). The new disagreement was relevant to the geopolitical clash of the "Sunni" Ottoman and the "Shia" Safavid. That said, this process was not led by some self-structured cultural symbols but by the transitory stages of consciousness, through which the agents formed some historically contingent understandings of being Sunni and Shia.

At such boundary moments, a previously used expression may be consciously reiterated for new purposes (Prager 1987). To exemplify this moment that challenges the "immobilization" of the text, Deleuze invoked Borges' ability to describe "a real book," Don Quixote, as though it was written by Pierre Menard, an imaginary author (Deleuze 1994:xxii). A calculation of this kind may be described as part of an explicit ideology-making process—i.e., "doing philosophy" in Deleuze's terminology (Neil 1998). Feeling disturbed in the face of a situation triggers the need to develop new strategies. Therefore, it may trigger one's formulation of the inherited ideological repertoire differently. Change and continuity would go hand in hand at this moment when a new strategy of action is produced for the latest chapter of a seemingly ongoing problem. This stage of re-evaluation is inevitably a self-conscious, reflexive mental process.

Finally, the element of change may also be overlooked in these explicit ideology-making processes, at least because the speakers may be so busy with a lasting stalemate in which they lack the means to evaluate what may have changed in the common playing field. At the very least, their mental state may not be ready to face any cognitive dissonance amid the flowing contestation over some of their staunchly embraced knowledge claims. In the course of a conversation, the interlocutors may not realize how many things they take from one another. This situation may be relevant to Eco's description because the "order of words" may not be ready to face the puzzling "order of things."

In all the situations I have described, the speakers have to *explore, evaluate*, and *retroact* to deal with the change within and around themselves. They explore the new conditions by entering a boundary moment. They assess these moments, respond to others' evaluations, refer to past occurrences, and bring together the past, the current, the self, and the other. These meetings with *change* will constitute the building blocks of my methodological approach.

Research Design and Aims

Having analyzed some unique ways in which change may unfold in the flow of a conversation, I will argue in the next chapter that value surveys

Introduction: Values and Others in Cultural Change   17

fail to grasp these changes. Their failure is notably due to their reliance on exogenously imposed social contexts, limited speech acts, and the explicit expression of cultural resources prior to social action. Moreover, research based on cross-temporal value surveys has specific problems due to its tendency to seek change through pre-defined concepts and directions (e.g., a teleology of democratization). Instead, this study will delve into a history of conversational texts, which are endogenously grounded within culture, capable of demonstrating culture in action, and reflecting what is collective about culture as it operates through dialectical encounters.

My methodological approach will be a qualitative event-based approach, which allows for (1) cross-checking the multiple accounts of *incidents*, (2) keeping track of some references to meaningful silences in these accounts, (3) making cross-temporal comparisons in dialogue with the meanings in texts or silences, and (4) distinguishing between *exploratory, evaluative*, and *retroactive* conversations, which tend to differ in terms of participants, conversational settings, and outputs. As a part of my methodological explanations, I will also employ a negative heuristic—i.e., a "quantitative" event-based approach.

After all, this book has four goals. First, and most broadly, it aims to offer insight into the ongoing disputes on the cultural prerequisites of democracy. In the light of my analysis regarding the different ways values may be translated into ideology, I conclude that democracy may not require agreement on a set of foundational values; but an acknowledgment of disagreement on values before negotiating the rest—e.g., rules of appropriateness, rights, and freedoms. Secondly and relatedly, this research describes some historically contingent representations of recognition and tolerance. In the meantime, it points to various points of intersection and cleavages between the very ideas of recognition and tolerance. The necessary acknowledgment of disagreement on values indicates the merit of recognition. That said, while clarifying some limitations and risks based on my case studies, I will conclude that replacing tolerance with recognition would lead to its own crisis in "our" unequal relationships.

Thirdly, by re-configuring some archival sources in accordance with their conversational qualities, this research aims to offer a new approach to the transdisciplinary study of cultural change in Turkey. Amid the dominance of great power politics in research agendas concerning the region, I was greatly motivated by the many rarely-heard speakers whom I believe can be more thoroughly followed in the literature, with all the constraints, opportunities, and confusions they reveal. Finally, by demonstrating how micro-level conversations might hinge upon the most powerful, authoritative speeches, this research addresses a relatively new—i.e., post-linguistic turn—research agenda of Cultural Sociology. In this vein, it pays attention to cultures in action, as they fascinatingly turn "what otherwise might be a babble of cultural voices into a semiotically coherent and politically ordered field of differences" (Sewell Jr 2005:92).

18   *Introduction: Values and Others in Cultural Change*

Notes

1 Though there are different definitions of "values" in the literature, these definitions are commonly centered on what people want. Therefore, according to the value-based approach to culture, values signify desires towards which actions are oriented.

2 See Kula (2011) for an exhaustive collection of such cross-references in defense of tolerance.

3 A conversational interaction may be defined as "the voices and actions that constitute the relational space among actors" (Watkins and Swidler 2006:2, 2009).

4 I will use the capital "S" to refer to state secularism at a given moment. The alternative understandings of secularism, which may or may not be critical of the former, will be denoted with the lowercase "s."

5 Alevilik signifies the belief system of Alevis, in the form of a religion, sect, or philosophy.

6 Alevism indicates extraordinary political consciousness attached to Alevilik (see Massicard 2007).

7 Türban is a somewhat pejorative term that many Secularists used to distinguish between a "modern" and a "traditional" headscarf. According to them, only the latter, which "our mothers" used, was tolerable in the public space.

8 "The evening meal eaten by Muslims after the sun has gone down during Ramadan" ("Iftar" 2008).

9 Making the question heard was possible amidst the broader social polarization and some, albeit limited, open communication channels. The speakers of a broader "left-wing" opposition made sure that their interlocutor—i.e., government circles—paid attention to the contradiction.

10 See Inglehart and Welzel (2005:133) on World Values Surveys:

> We do not have time-series data on attitudes toward homosexuality from any Islamic society because our Islamic colleagues were extremely reluctant to even ask about this topic. With considerable effort, we were able to obtain readings at a single time point for ten Islamic societies and found the following percentages saying that homosexuality is never justifiable: Bangladesh, 99; Egypt, 99; Jordan, 98; Pakistan, 96; Indonesia, 95; Iran, 94; Algeria, 93; Azerbaijan, 89; Turkey, 84; and Albania, 68. [...] [it] is clear that there cannot have been much movement toward growing tolerance of homosexuality in most of these countries.

11 This phrase was used by Hayrettin Karaman and Ahmet Mahmut Ünlü among others.

12 Cumhuriyet Halk Partisi (en. Republican People's Party).

13 Salâ is a form in Turkish religious music. The word originates from the Arabic word for the Islamic prayer, salat or salah. In the literature of Turkish music, alongside being a representation of mosque music, salâ may be read in tasavvufî lodges such as tekkes. Depending on its time and place, salâ may take different forms. Among them may be exemplified morning salâ, Friday salâ, and funeral salâ (Özcan 2009).

14 I will use the name as an abbreviation for Diyanet İşleri Başkanlığı (en. Directorate of Religious Affairs).

15 Pronounced as "djemevi," and literally means "a house of gathering."

16 In this regard, an argument in the name of nationalism, such as that of Yusuf Halaçoğlu, might not differ in essence from an argument in the name of Islamism, such as that of Abdülaziz Bayındır. Halaçoğlu, who served as Milliyetçi Hareket Partisi (en. Nationalist Action Party) MP and the chairman of Türk Tarih Kurumu (en. Turkish Historical Society), argues that recognizing Alevilik

Introduction: Values and Others in Cultural Change 19

as "a separate religion" would be a matter of "fitne" (en. unrest). Abdülaziz Bayındır, who is a professor of Islamic law at İstanbul University, asked Alevis to define if they are an Islamic sect, a separate religion, or else: "then we can talk [about recognition]" (Bayındır 2011). In both cases, Alevis are pushed to come up with a single definition (Avundukluoglu 2014).

17 This understanding of social context does not match the way the concept has been defined, for example, in Social Sequence Analysis, which limits the social context to "the phenomena surrounding a case" (see Abbott 1995:94). In the way I have used the term in the introduction, it extends into the reflexive processes within which a participant construes these surroundings. Reflexivity is key to one's understanding of one's position in a social structure and one's ability to develop action strategies (i.e., making ideology) in response.

18 Seyyid Battal Ghazi was a mythical warrior who campaigned against the Byzantines.

19 "Ghaza [tr. Gazi] spirit" signifies a mythical belief in holy war.

References

Abbott, Andrew. 1995. "Sequence Analysis: New Methods for Old Ideas." *Annual Review of Sociology* 21(1):93–113.

Akram, Sadiya. 2013. "Fully Unconscious and Prone to Habit: The Characteristics Akram of Agency in the Structure and Agency Dialectic." *Journal for the Theory of Social Behaviour* 43(1):45–65. doi: 10.1111/jtsb.12002.

Avundukluoğlu, Emin. 2014. "Fitne Sokmaya Çalışıyorlar." *Anadolu Ajansı*, October 25. Retrieved (https://www.aa.com.tr/tr/politika/bremenin-alevilik-karari-tamamen-siyasi/107706).

Aygün, Hüseyin. 2016. "Laiklik." *BirGün*, April 28.

Bakhtin, Mikhail. 1986. *Speech Genres and Other Late Essays. Trans. Vern W. McGee.* Austin: University of Texas Press.

Barkey, Karen. 2005. "Islam and Toleration: Studying the Ottoman Imperial Model." *International Journal of Politics, Culture, and Society* 19(1–2):5–19.

Bayat, Asef. 2013. *Life as Politics: How Ordinary People Change the Middle East,* Second Edition. Stanford, CA: Stanford University Press.

Bayındır, Abdulaziz. 2011. *Alevilik.* Süleymaniye Vakfı, March 27. Retrieved (https://www.youtube.com/watch?v=oR1DyWCR00o).

Bourdieu, Pierre. 1990. *In Other Words: Essays Towards a Reflexive Sociology.* Stanford, CA: Stanford University Press.

Çarkoğlu, Ali, and Binnaz Toprak. 2007. *Religion, Society and Politics in a Changing Turkey.* İstanbul: TESEV Publications.

Chambers, Clare. 2005. "Masculine Domination, Radical Feminism and Change." *Feminist Theory* 6(3):325–46.

De Certeau, Michel. 1984. *The Practice of Everyday Life.* Berkeley: University of California Press.

Deleuze, Gilles. 1994. *Difference and Repetition.* London and New York: Continuum.

Dreyfus, Hubert L., and Paul Rabinow. 2013. *Michel Foucault: Beyond Structuralism and Hermeneutics.* New York: Routledge.

Eco, Umberto. 1989. *Opera Aperta.* Cambridge, MA: Harvard University Press.

Eemeren, Frans H. van. 2015. *Reasonableness and Effectiveness in Argumentative Discourse: Fifty Contributions to the Development of Pragma-Dialectics.* Amsterdam: Springer.

20 Introduction: Values and Others in Cultural Change

Foucault, Michel. 2002. *The Order of Things: An Archaeology of the Human Sciences.* London: Routledge.

Giddens, Anthony. 1979. "Agency, Structure." Pp. 49–95 in *Central Problems in Social Theory.* Berkeley and Los Angeles: University of California Press.

Greenfield, Patricia M. 1997. "Culture as Process: Empirical Methods for Cultural Psychology." Pp. 301–46 in *Handbook of Cross-Cultural Psychology: Theory and Method.* Boston, MA: Allyn & Bacon.

Hitlin, Steven, and Jane Allyn Piliavin. 2004. "Values: Reviving a Dormant Concept." *Annual Review of Sociology* 30(1):359–93. doi: 10.1146/annurev. soc.30.012703.110640.

Hunter, James Davison. 2009. "The Culture War and the Sacred/Secular Divide: The Problem of Pluralism and Weak Hegemony." *Social Research* 76(4):1307–22.

Hunter, James Davison. 2014. "An Uneasy Coexistence." *Society* 51(2):120–25. doi: 10.1007/s12115-014-9750-9.

"Iftar." 2008. *Cambridge Online Dictionary.* Retrieved (https://dictionary. cambridge.org/dictionary/english/iftar).

İnalcık, Halil. 1998. "Türkiye Cumhuriyeti ve Osmanlı." *Doğu Batı* (5):11–21.

Inglehart, Ronald, and Wayne E. Baker. 2000. "Modernization, Cultural Change, and the Persistence of Traditional Values." *American Sociological Review* 65(1):19–51.

Inglehart, Ronald, and Christian Welzel. 2005. *Modernization, Cultural Change, and Democracy: The Human Development Sequence.* Cambridge: Cambridge University Press.

Kafadar, Cemal. 1995. *Between Two Worlds: The Construction of the Ottoman State.* London: University of California Press.

Kaya, Ayhan. 2013. *Europeanization and Tolerance in Turkey: The Myth of Toleration.* Basingstoke: Palgrave Macmillan.

Kula, Onur Bilge. 2011. *Anadolu'da çoğulculuk ve tolerans.* İstanbul: Türkiye İş Bankası Kültür Yayınları.

MacKinnon, Catharine A. 1989. *Toward a Feminist Theory of the State.* Cambridge: Harvard University Press.

"Mass Protests in Turkey against Egypt Death Sentences." 2014. *İnsani Yardım Vakfı,* April 29. Retrieved (http://www.ihh.org.tr/en/main/activity/volunteer-activities/3/ mass-protests-in-turkey-against-egypt-death-s/2281).

Massicard, Elise. 2007. *Alevi Hareketinin Siyasallaşması.* İstanbul: İletişim Yayınları.

Mert, Nuray. 2013. "The Demise of Post-Islamist Politics." *Hürriyet Daily News.* Retrieved June 6, 2018 (http://www.hurriyetdailynews.com/opinion/nuray-mert/ the-demise-of-post-islamist-politics-51133).

Moaddel, Mansoor. 2013. "The Birthplace of the Arab Spring: Values and Perceptions of Tunisians and A Comparative Assessment of Egyptian, Iraqi, Lebanese, Pakistani, Saudi, Tunisian, and Turkish Publics." *Middle Eastern Values Study, University of Maryland.* Retrieved (https://mevs.umd.edu/sites/mevs.umd.edu/ files/2021-03/Tunisia_FinalReport.pdf).

Neil, David. 1998. "The Uses of Anachronism: Deleuze's History of the Subject." *Philosophy Today.* Retrieved November 9, 2018 (https://www.pdcnet.org/pdc/bvdb.nsf/ purchase?openform&fp=philtoday&id=philtoday_1998_0042_0004_0418_0431).

Norris, Pippa, and Ronald Inglehart. 2002. "Islamic Culture and Democracy: Testing the Clash of Civilizations Thesis." *Comparative Sociology* 1(3):235–63. doi: 10.1163/156913302100418592.

Introduction: Values and Others in Cultural Change   21

Özcan, Nuri. 2009. "Salâ الصل." *İslam Ansiklopedisi* 36:15–16.
Patterson, Orlando. 2010. "The Mechanisms of Cultural Reproduction: Explaining the Puzzle of Persistence." Pp 139–51 in *Handbook of Cultural Sociology*. New York: Routledge.
Phelan, Peggy. 2003. *Unmarked: The Politics of Performance*. London: Routledge.
Prager, Jeffrey. 1987. "American Political Culture and the Shifting Meaning of Race." *Ethnic and Racial Studies* 10(1):62–81. doi: 10.1080/01419870.1987.9993556.
Rose, Sonya O. 1999. "Cultural Analysis and Moral Discourses: Episodes, Continuities, and Transformations." Pp.217–40 in *Beyond the Cultural Turn: New Directions in the Study of Society and Culture*, edited by Victoria E. Bonnell and Lynn Hunt. Berkeley, CA: University of California Press.
Saraçoglu, Cenk. 2017. "2016 Türkiyesi'nde Solun Laiklikle İmtihanı." Pp. 107–14 in *İleri Yazılar - Türkiye'nin Laiklik Kavgası*, edited by C. Soyer. İstanbul: İleri Kitaplığı Yayınevi.
Selek, Pınar. 2014. *Maskeler Süvariler Gacılar. Ülker Sokak: Bir Alt Kültürün Dışlanma Mekanı*. İstanbul: Ayizi Kitap.
Sewell Jr, William H. 1992. "A Theory of Structure: Duality, Agency, and Transformation." *American Journal of Sociology* 98(1):1–29.
Sewell Jr, William H. 2005. "The Concep(s) of Culture." Pp.76–96 in *Practicing History: New Directions in Historical Writing after the Linguistic Turn*. New York: Routledge.
Soyer, Can. 2017. "Türkiye'nin Laiklik Kavgası." Pp. 7–21 in *İleri Yazılar - Türkiye'nin Laiklik Kavgası*, edited by C. Soyer. İstanbul: İleri Kitaplığı Yayınevi.
Swidler, Ann. 1986. "Culture in Action: Symbols and Strategies." *American Sociological Review* 51(2):273–86. doi: 10.2307/2095521.
Swidler, Ann. 2003. *Talk of Love: How Culture Matters*. Chicago, IL: University of Chicago Press.
Toprak, Binnaz, İrfan Bozan, Tan Morgül, and Nedim Şener. 2009. *Türkiye'de Farklı Olmak:Din ve Muhafazakarlık Ekseninde Ötekileştirilenler. İstanbul: Metis Yayınları*.
Watkins, Susan Cotts, and Ann Swidler. 2006. "Conversations Into Texts: A Method for Studying Public Culture." *California Center for Population Research*.
Watkins, Susan Cotts, and Ann Swidler. 2009. "Hearsay Ethnography: Conversational Journals as a Method for Studying Culture in Action." *Poetics (Hague, Netherlands)* 37(2):162–84. doi: 10.1016/j.poetic.2009.03.002.
Wittgenstein, Ludwig. 2009. *Philosophical Investigations*. Hoboken, NJ: Wiley-Blackwell.
Yıldızoğlu, Ergin. 2017. "İki Türkiye Var." *Cumhuriyet*, July 27.

2 Democracy
Rethinking Cultural Prerequisites

Concurrently with the respective cultural turns in social and political sciences, the democratization literature began to revisit *culture* after the 1990s. This period, which followed the Cold War, marks the alleged slowdown of the third wave of democratization, the opening of pandora's ethnocultural box (Juergensmeyer 1996), rising identity politics (Bang 2009),[1] and an "Islam question" in post-industrial democracies (Bayat 2007). In this section, I will analyze the value-based approach to culture that has been instantiated in this transnational political climate. My focal point will be the research designs that (1) take "culture" as an entity that facilitates/inhibits a democratization process and (2) measure "cultural change" through value surveys by reducing culture into certain value expressions.

Before discussing what the value-based approach has become in combination with the survey techniques, I shall start by overviewing original debates over the value of democracy and the values a democracy may require. Despite having divergent emphases on values and lacking shared intuitions on democracy (Ziliotti 2020), competing branches of the value-based approach to democracy agree on the necessity of shared value expressions, including various ranges of tolerable disagreements.

For proceduralists, a democrat should see democracy as *intrinsically* valuable, whereas, for instrumentalists, democracy is *extrinsically* valuable. The latter refers to democracy as a means for *something else* (Arneson 2003), such as redistributive ideological programs for the left and stability for the right. Around these alternative philosophical starting points are democrats with adjectives (Schedler and Sarsfield 2007). They have numerous substantive, aggregative, deliberative, epistemic, and populist demands for democracy. Each of them sees the feasibility of democracy in the ability to form shared overarching values that isolate and regulate partial disagreements, albeit different ones and with varying success.

Once introduced, the value-based approach has an all-encompassing narrative power, given that any institution-building process excluding values implies some form of coercive attempt. The only possibility of democracy that ever emerged outside the scope of shared higher values is "democracy without democrats" (Salamé 1994:15).[2] While this phrase continues to rely on a prescribed

DOI: 10.4324/9781003311805-2

value-based definition of democrat, its emphasis uncouples values from institutional outcomes or, at the very least, externalizes the value of democracy in the way instrumentalists propose. Accordingly, democracy does not owe its first steps to democrats, even though it may later produce them (Somer 2011:512).

Considering the transnational cultural contentions introduced above and elaborated below, I argue that imposing a convergence criterion based on values has become part of the problem against democratization. Even when it appears in the form of valuing the coexistence of juxtaposed parochial values, the value-based approach continues to rest on value consensus at a higher level. In other words, seeking an ultimate point of convergence by its very definition, this approach dismisses the possibility of democracy-building amid *persistent* expressions of clashing values.

Connectedly, as a study of cultural change, the democratization literature neglects the transformation of other cultural expressions by focusing exclusively on values. In this research, I aim to demonstrate that rules of appropriateness, rights, and freedoms may be and, considering the empirical cases I will analyze, should be disentangled from expectations of overarching value consensus. For democratization, parties do not have to value diversity in the same manner, nor do they have to treat diversity and the procedures that sustain it as an expression of value. Value expressions might not be the only way of naturalizing diversity and challenging the *other* within the confines of rules. Despite being close to Mouffe's (2000) *antagonistic democracy*, the cross-temporal cultural study I offer shall differ in that it seeks part of democracy in antagonism's shifting boundaries, with individuals and repertoires changing position over time. Such changes may indicate unique democratization opportunities or possible escapes from non-democratic foundations.

This argument does not mean that values play no role in understanding others' rights and freedoms. Hence, I distinguish between interlocutors' first-order and second-order values to question this role. The first-order values denote one's foundational values on one's universe, whereas second-order values are those we infer concerning differences of values. Second-order values tend to play a significant role in shaping others' rights. However, while acknowledging the role that values may play, my framework suggests that one's values do not necessarily converge with others' values, even at the highest-order levels. Therefore, simply put, disagreeing parties do not have to respond to a value-survey question in the same way to contribute to a process of democratization. This cultural element remains a fundamental challenge for survey researchers. In this vein, I will scrutinize parochial values of coexistence among other sources of cultural expression, which I elaborated on before.

Counterproductive Arguments over Values and Tolerable Disagreements

Other schools that follow the value-based approach criticize populist and epistemic accounts for ignoring social cleavages (Rokkan 1999; Saffon and

24 *Democracy: Rethinking Cultural Prerequisites*

Urbinati 2013). The argument is valid, given that they dismiss the diversity of values to pursue the most "efficient" or "popular" decisions. Nevertheless, in practice, even various manifestations of populist politics have adopted a proceduralist language that welcomes *some* disagreements while, on the other hand, emphasizing the "instrumental ineffectiveness" of elite-based democracies (Kitschelt 2002). Populist movements join others to decide where to delegitimize diversity. In doing so, they use a value-laden language, which exhibits the limits of the value-based approach, regardless of its form within the ongoing wave of identity politics.

The debate on democracy has become a cultural contestation on substantive concepts such as gender equality, sexual freedom, human rights, secularism, and procedural concepts such as equal political liberty and direct mass participation. Simply put, the very concept of democracy has been politicized (Somer and McCoy 2018). Pursuing a "direct" rule by a social construct called "people," several populist movements have gained weight in the value talks fixated on the Islam question. Unlike the former representations of right-wing populism in the West, the new-right refashioned the notions of fundamental human rights and liberal values "against Islam" (Pelinka 2013:12). As Wilders calls it "the time for a liberal jihad" (Hirsi Ali and Wilders 2003), the new-right populism welcomes many value disagreements except those that include specific symbols associated with Islam. What precedes this strategy is a widespread disappointment with migrant-origin Europeans, primarily Muslims, who are said to have not embraced the value labels I listed above.

It is not just the populists who refer to them as an essential threat to the values that define democracy. The Macron government's bill on "Islamist separatism" targeted a series of practices which it deems contrary to the essentially liberal "values of the French republic" (Rieker 2018). In addition to extended bans on burkini and restrictions against refusing handshaking in public space, the government targeted homeschooling and gendered swimming pools. Taken together with the way it operationalizes freedom of expression, the bill indicated a broader yet masked conflict between conservative religious versus liberal values (Roy 2021). Therefore, liberal Muslims within and outside France support such measures ("A Call" 2020; Manea 2020), whereas many religious Catholics and Calvinists express their frustration about the popularized mockery of faiths (Allen 2020).

The latter, however, seems to settle for a democracy that will identify with the Christian identity, even if it has been secularized (Roy 2020).[3] So far, the National Rally has led the public debate's concentration on Muslims by toning down its past Catholic traditionalist, homophobic, racist, and anti-semitic outbursts. Engaging with this fragile balance between liberal and authoritarian values (Berntzen 2019), many seasoned liberals end up near the populist camp in public debates concerning the illiberal forms of Islam (*see* Koopmans in "Migrationsforscher" 2021). According to Stepan and Taylor (2014:3–4), "the liberal zealotry" has created its own short-sightedness after the cultural turn.

On the flip side, a promotion of Islamist democracy in the Middle East embraced the same motto, *whose realm, their values.* The AKP in Turkey, the Muslim Brotherhood in Egypt, and until it turned from its claims in 2016, Ennahda in Tunisia made similar arguments in constitution-making processes (Koca 2017; Somer 2017; Meddeb 2019). By claiming co-authorship in the democracy book, they put forward their own range of acceptable disagreements based on values—*e.g.*, competing traditional rituals in the name of Islam, various profane traditions allegedly against Islam, rights of other Abrahamic religions, differences among the four Sunni sects, and some ethnic cleavages.[4]

Indeed, the "LGBT rights" were not in the range of these acceptable disagreements. As I will discuss, the Erdoğan government deemed some transgender representations more tolerable. The problem is that the rights of LGBT individuals were limited by the Erdoğan government's understanding of tolerance, as we all assume that values and rights have to go together. In a similar vein, symmetrical oppositions between value expressions, such as "gender equality" versus "gender justice," have been formed in this period as keywords to represent exclusive cultural identities. As such, the counter-position makes pretty much all previously stated values parochial and renders higher-order values not so high in the face of a recalcitrant politics of cultural identity.

While liberal and religious nationalists tend towards assimilation policies in different geographies, proponents of constitutional patriotism, such as Habermas and Rorty, acknowledged how their contribution to the value-based approach might also fail to stop the majority culture's domination. Notwithstanding his defense of constitutional patriotism, Müller states, "there is no guarantee that patriotism centered on values [...] could not deteriorate in this manner" (Müller 2009:23). Habermas (2018:225) aimed to overcome the risk by making a more apparent distinction between procedural and substantive values. Accordingly, in the ideal deliberative condition, a substantial consensus on values shall not be sought, although an agreement on some procedural values would still be required to maintain differences peacefully.

Despite distinguishing the two value levels similarly, Laclau argues that agreement on procedural values would be impossible without agreement on some substantive values. That said, instead of prescribing the content of values required for a substantial consensus, Laclau leaves the question open with the prediction that "a plurality of subject positions" (i.e., multiple selves) in separate cultural groups will subvert the particularistic group demands (Laclau 2005a:199). Forming such an "equivalential chain" will weaken the political institutions' connection with particularistic demands (Laclau 2005b:40). While populism in Laclau's framework acts as an essential component of democracy that requires a "people," its discursive creation

26   *Democracy: Rethinking Cultural Prerequisites*

of shared values is nothing more than a matter of empty signifiers. As no one shall have a privileged claim to fill in them, the center of democracy is supposed to remain empty (Gasché 2004; Laclau and Mouffe 2014:170).

Democratic Culture as Entity or Process

The bulk of the democratization literature is preoccupied with listing down and filling in these signifiers. A repercussion of the search for overarching values is the concept of "democratic culture," representing a blueprint for the ideal culture. This concept took many forms in the literature: a success/ failure story of religions[5] and "cultural nations" (Abizadeh 2002); a passport where only some cultures of proper Westernized experience can enter;[6] or a set of de-contextualized labels attached to the ideals of the concept of democracy and its opposite, authoritarianism, on timeless grounds. As such, democratic culture is an entity, not a process. Accordingly, a democratic culture should be, among other things, "modern," "liberal," "generous," "tolerant," "autonomous," "secular-rational," and "emancipative."[7] Because processes are not of interest in this act of tagging democratic culture, what each of these labels may have meant in any spatiotemporal setting tends to remain unquestioned—hence taken as given—in the literature.

Despite definitional limits, the need for a definition is commonly accepted in the literature. Accordingly, several democracy indices aim to quantify and measure the key components of democracy, whereas the academic studies rely on their varying (e.g., maximalist and minimalist) operational definitions of the concept. For example, comparativists tend to make sense of the data they take from indices by processing it with a cross-sectional comparative logic of inference. This means comparing less democratic cases (*i.e.,* state-level) with more democratic ones and then making sense of the "democracy gap" by emphasizing countries' remaining characteristic differences. Among these characteristic differences, students take into account some predefined "cultural variables" (Midlarsky 1998; Fish 2002; Lane and Ersson 2016). The so-called "Islamic" or "Middle Eastern" cultural exceptionalism in the literature has resulted from this form of research design (*see* Hinnebusch 2000:125).

Comparativism does not help very much in adding motion to the democratic culture. The democratization literature is—or ought to be—a literature of cultural change, as it examines some profoundly changing structures, modes of thought, and behavior. That said, any questioning of progress beyond the annually awarded labels of "democratic," "semi-democratic," and "authoritarian" remains rare in the comparativist section of the literature. It is paradigmatically taken for granted that "democratic" is the illustration of excellence, "semi-democratic" means being stuck somewhere on the road, and "authoritarian" represents a dead-end. Even though a case at hand may be considered *a process*, this process is predominantly based on a linear continuum that ranges from progression to backsliding. Culture is

Democracy: Rethinking Cultural Prerequisites 27

taken as a process only for those (e.g., countries) that continuously follow the predefined teleology (*see* Carothers 2002). The cases stuck between some two points on the continuum are mainly taken as the cases at a "standstill" (Sorensen 2008:55–78)—*i.e.*, a condition in which all movement has stopped.

To overcome this inability to take into account any kind of change other than the ones that fit into the predefined notions of democratization, many discussions which I will not scrutinize have been initiated. For example, Schlumberger (2000), among others, called for new typologies so that students can make sense of the transitions from one non-democracy to another. The idea of "liberalization without democracy" was introduced as part of similar efforts. Going further beyond this call, Hinnebusch criticized current operationalizations of the concept of democracy on the basis that the use of the democracy-autocracy dichotomy "obscures" both the variations and the similarities between regimes (Hinnebusch 2010:201).

The limit of the cross-sectional comparative design is primarily in its use of culture as a synchronic marker, which undermines the cultural experience of societies by naming their cultures as *entities*. This synchronic use of concepts as part of the comparative method was seldom disputed (Bartolini 1993). In this vein, "Islamic" often meant Islamic everywhere anytime in an *aggregatable* sense, just because its carriers could be denoted identically as "Islamic,"[8] or the in-group differences in "Islamic" were assumed to be *comparable* at any given point in time because being "Islamic" should have been a strong enough common denominator for them to lead to the same consequences (Fox 2000). For example, within this context, Turkey was commonly regarded as the exception of an exception—i.e., the exception as a democracy of "Muslims," contrary to the exceptional resistance of "Muslims" to democracy (Lewis 1994; Gülalp 2005:358; Hinnebusch 2010:210). In all these cases, culture acts as a synchronic entity that should be named before being studied.

Indeed, research agendas have a significant role in the way culture is understood. A cultural element was recognized in the functioning of democracies long ago (Dahl 1986:49). However, the focal point of this more recent cultural turn was not to understand change but persistence. In this context, culture was taken as "persistence," "return," "revival," or "resurgence." These terms have often been used interchangeably to refer to the reappearance of certain phenomena in their old, but also somehow timeless format. Therefore, this turn to "culture" was meant to be the answer for reproduction processes in the aftermath of the cold war. Accordingly, change fitted well into rational-choice theories that relied on structural patterns (e.g., urbanization, industrialization), whereas reproduction was left to culturalism. In this reasoning, the premise is as follows: if the structural variables do not demonstrate any clear progress towards democratization, it must be a cultural variable that led to the failure. Therefore, the "persistence of authoritarianism," in which the rational-choice theories seemed to have lost their explanatory power, was to be associated with "survival,"

28   *Democracy: Rethinking Cultural Prerequisites*

"traditional values," and other similar cultural entities (Inglehart and Baker 2000; Norris and Inglehart 2002). In sum, for explanations of the failure of democratic teleology, the cultural markers were to be emphasized as a last resort (Huntington 1997:5–6). Therefore, the idea of culture has been introduced into the literature not to explain the change but persistence.

Therefore, the "culture" of this school falls short of accounting for any of the debates in which these labels acquire a temporal dimension. For instance, it could not help students question the state of "the secular age" in Western Democracies, which has been taken by Charles Taylor (2007) as the social imaginary of an era and not a naked truth beyond time. In the same vein, it did not help them engage with the argument of Habermas that "the secular Western society" has entered a phase of "post-secularity"—an episode where people remain secular, but religion becomes relevant in unprecedented ways (Habermas 2008).

In both Habermas' and Taylor's senses of the new moment, the question of democracy has been rendered as one of *tolerance*—i.e., an old concept in a unique setting. In this new setting, many actors, from courts to parliaments, have rationalized intolerance by sticking to an alternative idea of democracy. According to some ideology makers, the democratic regimes shall be more assertive to put a clear limit on tolerance: "Democracy and autonomy go together [...] these considerations set limits to toleration" (Arneson and Shapiro 1996:137). On the one hand, many students emphasize that tolerance is offensive to the ideals of liberal democracy in an age of differences (Vainio and Visala 2016). On the other hand, their interlocutors stress that democracy cannot survive without tolerance (Roy 2007). As the flow of these conversations suggests, culture—i.e., "democratic" or not—is *not* a Leibnizian monad (Lapid and Kratochwil 1996:7), such that its components (e.g., tolerance as a value, autonomy as a capacity) are *not* indivisible.

Democratic Culture: Terms of Disagreement

The indivisibility of democratic culture provokes the question of whether such a culture requires a single package of values. Without assuming that democracy requires agreement on values, it would already be meaningless to focus on "democratic culture" based on values. In unity with this assumption, students study the relationship between democracy and various value sets, such as "postmaterialist values," which seem to go hand in hand with the core values of liberalism (*see* Inglehart 2006).

As a part of these efforts to sketch out the value system that is conducive to democracy, the students of the World Values Survey (WVS) have come up with "self-expression values" as opposed to "survival values." According to Inglehart and Welzel, the self-expression values are "extremely important in the emergence and flourishing of democracy" ("Findings" 2015).

Nearly two decades before the cultural turn that I have described, Almond and Verba (1989:6) argued that the meeting of "traditional" and

Democracy: Rethinking Cultural Prerequisites 29

"modern" cultures in Britain paved the way for a third culture, which was one of diversity and persuasion. Although their argument was centered on "attitudes," they occasionally combined attitudes with "values" without making a detailed description of the relationship between the two. Their research suggested that "shared social values and attitudes" underpinned the British and the US democracies in contrast with Germany, Italy, and Mexico, which suffered from partisanship, apparently due to the lack of such values (Almond and Verba 1989:243).

Their aim was neither to make an exhaustive list of values required by the concept of democracy nor to examine the ideational and the material sources of those values. Instead, they compared these five countries to figure out some cultural characteristics specific to the relatively democratic ones. Consequently, they emphasized the interpersonal value of generosity as conducive to a participant, "civic culture" that favors democracy. In Almond and Verba's narrative, the values such as generosity and trust must have acted as second-order values which constitute a common culture. As such, these second-order values were supposed to help the "modern" and the "traditional" coexist despite their contradicting foundational values (Almond and Verba 1989:23–28). The limit of this narrative is that it does not address a persistent contradiction, given the homogenizing role assigned to generosity and trust. The clash is not sustained if these values are already present to solve the problem. Hence, the social outcome they create shall be named a "concord," or "fellow feeling," instead of a "consensus" (for a similar scenario, *see* Schlueter 2009).

Research that relies on the WVS categories, such as "self-expression" and "survival," challenged this narrative, which Almond and Verba revisited as well (Dalton and Welzel 2014). Nevertheless, while doing so, the researchers did not consider how values might be processed in the light of other cultural resources. Instead, they were content to focus on changes in certain value expressions against changing material conditions and different democratic outcomes (Inglehart and Abramson 1999; Ng and Diener 2014).

In this endeavor, the studies that rely on the self-expression/survival dichotomy blend values that possibly act as second-order values with values that their carriers might recognize as foundational ones. For example, on the axis of survival versus self-expression values, the respondents are claimed to clash depending on their levels of (dis)agreement on the statements such as, "a woman does not have to have children to be fulfilled"; "I favour emphasis on the development of technology"; "I have signed a petition to protect the environment"; "homosexuality is sometimes justifiable." As such, according to Inglehart and Welzel, carrying self-expression values meant taking the democratic culture through "tolerance of foreigners, gays, and lesbians," "gender equality," and "environmental protection" (Inglehart and Welzel 2010:564; "Cultural" 2015:par6).

This interpretation suggests that one is not likely to rationalize a kind of tolerance towards "homosexuals"[9] if s/he does not agree with the statement

30   Democracy: Rethinking Cultural Prerequisites

that "homosexuality is justifiable." Similarly, it does not consider whether the same person can come to terms with "a homosexual" based on another value, a norm, or an interest. Its range of scenarios also ignores the possibility that a social context in which the *exclusionary other* will not define "a homosexual" as such can turn around and influence different situations. It also assumes that one will not accommodate childless women, who s/he labels as "unfulfilled" in a particular social context. To conclude, the narrative built on these restricted choices will leave no room to imagine a society where democracy could be possible despite such instances of persistent disagreement on values. In the way it has been argued, the self-expression values do not resolve this puzzle of heterogeneity since a democracy based on this argument would not leave any space for *any other way* of agreeing to disagree.

Cultural Change through Value Surveys

The arguments I built above bring me to the status of continuity in value surveys. Researchers prefer the survey method to make sense of the labels mentioned above. Some of the most popularly used datasets are, in Social Psychology, Hofstede's Values Survey Module and Rokeach Value Survey, and in Sociology and Political Science, WVS led principally by Inglehart. By adding time to the aforementioned conceptual baggage, cross-temporal and cross-sectional value surveys became popular as a primary source behind the indices of democracy, a source for conducting cross-cultural comparisons, and a unit for measuring "cultures" in the light of an ideal, democratic culture.

Recently, value surveys have been used in the literature to explain if cultures can be compatible with the prerequisites of democracy (Tessler 2002), or whether a given culture is changing in the direction of democracy or its derivatives (Norris and Inglehart 2002; Jamal 2006; Inglehart and Welzel 2010). In a manner complementary to the use of labels I examined in the previous section, these surveys claim to measure the extent to which "tolerance of foreigners," "gender equality," or some other "democratic convictions" are desired in societies. This mode of inquiry is often encouraged in the concluding sections of the synchronic comparative configurations—e.g., "the question of why Islamic regimes tend to be disproportionally autocratic remains open" (Fox 2000:16).

In this search for cultural change, the terms of change do not emanate from inside the studied cultures. On the contrary, they are "known" beforehand from outside—hence the criticism of "Eurocentrism" and "strict linearity" (Wallerstein 1997:25; Wang 2015:183). For example, using the WVS, Norris and Inglehart questioned which cultures were more resistant to change towards "gender equality." As a result, they argued that "Muslim countries not only lag behind the West but behind all other societies as well" (Inglehart and Norris 2003:68). According to their conclusion, the industrialized "Islamic societies" were changing more quickly than the other Islamic societies, but the change was still slow compared to "South Asia."

Given the contestations on the marker gender equality, which I elaborated on previously, this research outcome might be more about learned speech acts than about promises and practices. The term has acquired a dimension such that many speakers feel the need to express their "strong support" for it, even though they do not necessarily put this support into actual practice.[10] In contrast, many others reject the term when they hear it, predominantly because the discourse seems to have been imposed from "the West" (*see* Fernandez 2009).

Among other problems with this use of the survey method (Hurtienne and Kaufmann 2011:22), the broadest problem I shall emphasize is the idea that cultural change is measurable by repeating a standard forced-choice survey across various times and locations. For the sake of producing quantifiable data, value surveys consist of some so-called de-contextualized questions with severely restrict speech acts, despite including a vocabulary that cannot carry any context-independent meaning. Just as no conversation can ever be context-free (Schegloff 1997), in this case, it is the conduct of the survey which imposes a context of its own. The setting in which respondents express themselves is never de-contextualized. On the contrary, they are contextualized through the impositions of the questioner.

In surveys, the social context is imposed primarily by researchers: the configuration of the questions, the order of them, the way they are asked, and the pre-determined response limits are among the constitutive factors. All these factors potentially distort the meanings that the respondent draws from the questions and the meanings that the researcher draws from the responses. Contrary to the assumption that there is a "social contract" (Cicourel 1982:12) between researchers and respondents, questions and answers are never self-explanatory. The highly restricted speech acts tend to leave their meanings immature. Mainly because value surveys are intended to deal with highly abstract concepts instead of some simply comprehensible statements (e.g., the name of the political party one votes for), their validity relies heavily on the approximations of a group of so-called "cultural experts" (Peng et al. 1997:329)—e.g., academics, journalists, translators, research centers, survey companies. They are the ones who negotiate the cross-cultural content of surveys bethween one another, translate questions, convert arguments to fit the different storage formats of different societies, communicate with the respondents, and give feedback to a broader community.

Despite such experts being the ones who do surveys in practice, and hence ultimately the ones who impose the social context—i.e., the universe of meanings in which the respondents are situated to talk—very little has so far been written to critically assess their status or that of the intermediaries with whom they work. By going beyond the de-politicizing technocratic references to their *expertise*, their role in the meaning-making of cultural

32   Democracy: Rethinking Cultural Prerequisites

representations should be considered. In this sense, their undertaking of sociological research is not different from that of an anthropologist in terms of having a personal role in making the research outcome.

However, whereas the auto-biographic dimension of anthropological writing is well-emphasized and disputed (Hofer 1968; Ahmed 1986:26), the so-called context-free tone blurs this dimension of the role of survey researchers. In this vein, Cicourel discusses how "culture" matters in surveys:

> Sociologists are sensitive to the fact that many problems are associated with the way questionnaires are administered, coded, and organized for analysis. But they are insensitive to the information processing problems associated with these tasks. Because so many surveys are done in the same culture in which the researchers also are native, and because we gradually have socialized our respondents to be fairly docile to the demands of surveys [...] we have little knowledge about the social practices of survey research within field settings and within research centers where the analysis takes place.
>
> (Cicourel 1982:16)

Even though Cicourel well-described sociologists' tendency to see little point in challenging the routine use of the survey method, he may have exaggerated the benefits of being native. What matters is not just having more or less knowledge of the social conditions in "the same culture," but also the culture-bound relations in which this knowledge is embedded. In this vein, the power relations are not overcome when the survey researchers are native in any sense of the term. On the contrary, given that the response patterns are highly dependent on, for example, the wording of questions (Foddy 1994:5–6; Page and Shapiro 2010:29–31), a local questioner who is familiar with the ties between the cognitive processes and the speech acts of the "native" may be inclined, intentionally or not, to take the answers in a particular targeted way. The assumption that questioners are "cooperative communicators" (Schwarz 1994) is yet to be disputed in survey research.

Based on these arguments, I suggest an approach that does not ignore the potentially toxic relationship between questioners and respondents. In the next section, I will defend a process capable of observing conversational settings configured during the *natural* operation of culture, with its own restrictions and opportunities for interlocutors. To elaborate on this point, I ask the following questions to illustrate some possibilities in a dialogic social context, where value surveys turn a blind eye: How differently will the interlocutor approach *something* if it is not marked for them explicitly in a specific manner? How might a group of people approach differences in an environment where their value orientations are not explicitly counter-posed? How differently might a value be expressed? Which tools, alongside or apart

Democracy: Rethinking Cultural Prerequisites   33

from values, may one take from one's toolkit of culture? Beginning with the next part, I will pay attention to these questions in the course of the book.

An Introduction to the Context: Surveys, Values, and the Periods Beyond

Before laying down my research methodology, I will clarify some limits of the value-based approach in various social contexts. Firstly, considering a social context where values do not serve as the chief drivers of culture, I will touch upon some moments of (dis)connection between the expression of values and the culture in action. Secondly, I will argue that the survey setting, in which values have been conveyed explicitly, may not necessarily represent their operationalization elsewhere.

As to how differently values may interact with the other cultural resources, I shall begin with a specific social context, such as the one in which "Islamists" sacrificed some of their values in the face of modern technology. In 2015 at the picnic of the Ensar Foundation, a government-linked religious association, Professor of Islamic Law Hayrettin Karaman, known as one of the most highly and consistently praised guides of the AKP leadership, recalled his dialogue with his grandfather many decades before (Karaman 2015) "My grandfather once told me that he would kill me if I ever went to the cinema—not simply beat me, but kill me!" Karaman quoted his grandfather as he saw the cellphones and tablets in the hands of the younger participants of the picnic.

At this moment, he shared the way he revised his grandfather's intolerance on this issue:

> [B]ut we cannot make you leave them. If I tried [to force you on that], you would leave me alone instead of leaving these devices. I know it from myself [...] I always found a way to go to the cinema.
>
> (Karaman 2015)

In his speech, despite having described "these devices" as "the inventions of dajjal,"[11] Karaman told the participants to instrumentalize them for ideological ends: "make them full of the words of Allah, given that you cannot leave them." In this position, the ideology was to be re-configured under compelling new circumstances, which Karaman described as the appetite for using new technological devices.

Karaman's view that technology should be instrumentalized even though it is evil has been shared by many other famous teachers of Islam in Turkey and elsewhere, who do not necessarily make peace with Karaman on other issues. For instance, Ahmet Mahmut Ünlü, also known as Cübbeli Ahmet Hoca of *Ismailağa Cemaati* (*en.* The Religious Community of Ismailağa), has occasionally been criticized within and outside his religious community for heavily using TV programs and the internet-based channels to send his

34   Democracy: Rethinking Cultural Prerequisites

messages. Having noted that technology became "a religious duty against irreligious propaganda," Ünlü has justified the ideological change as follows:

> We have been compelled [by the evil] to use these devices [...]. By using these channels, we have to reach people looking for a cure to their problems; otherwise, they will not find us on their own.

Even though Ünlü refused to see any intrinsic virtue in technology, he stressed that it has turned out to be necessary to prevent more of "the vice." Similarly, *Fatih Medreseleri* (en. Fatih Muslim Seminaries), a group that has also associated itself with İsmailağa Cemaati,[12] justified technology for their followers with the following words: "a Muslim should be able to overturn the projects that, while nobody is noticing, invite people to secularization" ("Teknoloji" 2015). These arguments were in line with a massive trend in the making of Islamism. In this vein, Yavuz explained how the five largest communities of the *Nakşibendi* Islamist Strand[13] used technology effectively in Turkey, such that they owned some of the largest media channels (Yavuz 2005:141–43). Invoking those he called "Sunni Arab Fundamentalists," Bassam Tibi defined this massive revision as one that de-couples the use of technology from its underlying values (Tibi 1993:74). Though technology does not represent any value, they have begun to justify its use in ideological terms. The context-dependent ideology-making processes occurring at the expense of values may be sought elsewhere, from the decreasing fertility rates to the rising average age of marriage, to the increasing levels of education among Muslim women. They all suggest that de-contextualized value orders suggest little about the operation of cultural practice.

In this vein, the approach that takes values as the core of culture misses some crucial aspects of cognition. I will elaborate on this point with the following study on sectarianism. Immediately after the execution of so-called Iran-backed Shia leader Nimr al-Nimr by the Saudi Government, a survey conducted in five Middle Eastern countries asked how "favorable" the sample population felt Saudi Arabia and Iran were towards them. According to the finding, most respondents labeled the country from their sect as "more favorable" to them (Poushter 2016). That said, it remains ambiguous what favorability may imply in terms of the existence of sectarianism in the region, at least because the setting in which the respondents spoke did not suffice to clarify its definition.

It remains unknown at which point in time the forced choices in this survey will meet a respondent's real-life conditions: what does it mean to choose between "Saudi Arabia" and "Iran"? It may mean that there is "a sectarian divide" in the region, as suggested by the survey's interpreter, but then, what this sectarianism indicates in a given spatiotemporal setting will remain unexplored. What kind of situations that fit the design of the survey may one ever face in life—i.e., (a) detecting what counts as "Saudi Arabia" and "Iran"; (b) expressing an opinion on them, and (c) practicing it in a

Democracy: Rethinking Cultural Prerequisites 35

manner that contributes to "a sectarian divide"? How do we practice the words we are pushed to choose in the survey—*e.g.,* in which way will we make use of "favor"? After the survey project, these questions were matters of pure speculation.

It is the survey researcher who pulls the respondent onto the playing field. In the case exemplified above, the survey design invites respondents to play with the vocabulary of sectarianism. In this case, people who may never have anything to do with "Iran" or "Saudi Arabia" have been kept busy with these words and pushed to form and express an opinion on them. As Bourdieu (2014) reiterated many times in his College de France lectures, this imposition of the discursive framing is not specific to this particular value survey but is inherent in the survey approach. WVS does not have a different function when it pushes the respondents to deal with the discourse, "homosexuality is never justifiable" (Inglehart 2018:88). The same problem appears when survey researchers ask people to tell which clothing style from six representations is "appropriate for women in public."[14] By asking this question, the survey researchers pushed the respondents to form and express opinions in favor of exclusion. Ignoring this aspect of the method means ignoring the ultimately exogenous social context imposed by the research design on the cognitive processes that the respondents go through.

Alternative Analytical Framework: Cultural Change through Conversational Texts

Based on the critique I have so far made, the primary sources I choose for my research are conversations. Conversational texts are endogenously grounded and are therefore capable of reflecting social contexts from the point of view of the *insiders* of a culture (Watkins and Swidler 2006, 2009). In a conversational text, the interlocutors talk in a dialogically informed social context, wherein they present their agendas in their own ways with no artificial interference.

This approach does not exclude surveys or interviews, given that they should also be taken as conversations—albeit possibly within limited parameters. Every piece of social research relies on a social context, but many do not pay attention to the context formed endogenously in the studied culture (Schegloff 1997). As I have already argued, the survey approach cannot escape from the question of whose context researchers should consider. Interviews also rely on a social context. Accordingly, an able interviewer can exploit an interview by simulating a particular situation reliably. In such a case, the interviewee can follow the conversational implicature and talk more or less accurately concerning the research subject of the interviewer. That said, the flow of interviews is also likely to be ultimately determined following the interviewer's agenda, which is not necessarily the agenda of the interviewee.

Exogenous context is also a challenge for students of conversational texts, but this challenge occurs differently and, I believe, in a less problematic

36   Democracy: Rethinking Cultural Prerequisites

manner. For example, there may be some shared elements in a conversation that only the participants will know and not mention explicitly within the confines of that conversation. Even though these elements may be evident for a person overhearing, s/he shall still attempt to impose a context to make meaning. Otherwise, s/he would miss a vital component of the conversation. This limitation, however, is less problematic than the previously mentioned impositions of exogenous context because it is a challenge only for the analyst, not for the participants in the conversation (Turnbull 2003:176).

As opposed to alternatives, conversational texts allow students to delve into the local players' conversations as their culture operates. Though the difficulty of this approach lies in the lack of means to push the interlocutors to keep conversing along the track of one's research agenda, I claim that this may be a fruitful difficulty. It is productive, at least because a research problem that the insiders of a culture care about is likely to be meaningful for their culture. Entering this natural flow of culture seems to be the only way to reach some parameters within which *change* and *continuity* begin to make sense. Thus, a study of conversations can pave the way for new talks in the culture from which it originates.

Relatedly, going beyond the atomistic notions of culture, conversational texts capture culture's collective dimension (Watkins and Swidler 2009). So far, I have repeatedly argued that a social context is always dialogically formed. This argument has been digested from an enormous body of literature, starting from Hegelian idealism in philosophy, Adorno's *Negative Dialectics* in political science, Martin Buber's *I-Thou* theme in psychotherapy, Bakhtin's *dialogism*, Ricoeur's hermeneutic phenomenology, and the poststructuralist critique of Saussure's *langue*. Apart from their differences, common to all is the understanding that consciousness lies in *the between* (Buber 1947; Ricoeur 1978:101) instead of in one's isolated psyches.[15] Conversational texts represent this social link between different voices that otherwise seem noise-proof and impenetrable to one another.

Indifference to these social links is a common misconception in the study of culture(s), as suggested by the exclusive imagining of "cultural zones," "civilizations," and a world of "multiculturalism" where cultures are commonly taken as separate entities in isolated locations. The contemporary narrative of "culture wars" tends to rely on this notion of clear-cut cultural monoliths that meet one another only to remain the same. Ideologically, the modernist paradigm has advanced a teleological image that made sense of the contact as a conflictual one between the pre-modern and the modern. In contrast, some so-called postmodernist counterarguments tend to see *everyone* making their claims on the grounds of irresolvable relativity, implying that engagement is meaningless (Eagleton 2013:3–4).

The medium of a conversation can project this common playing field where seemingly different worlds operate in interaction. The encounter occurs in the making of conflicts and subsequent power relations and in sharing spaces, in which intended and unintended transmissions occur. The markers are not fixed in such a dialogical relationship. In Amira Mitter-maier's words, "thinking Islam dialogically means proceeding from neither Islam nor the secular as a given" (Mittermaier 2015:280).

Methodology

There are two fundamental methodological questions I shall address in this part. These are: (1) how to select snapshots that include conversations involving (in)tolerance; and (2) how to connect these conversations. While the starting point of my data collection is events, my main source is what I describe as conversational texts, which take place *within* or *over* events. I will develop a qualitative event-based approach, which allows multiple accounts of incidents to be cross-checked, keeping track of references to meaningful silences in these accounts, and making cross-temporal comparisons in dia-logue with these meanings in texts or silences. In conclusion, based on my previous analysis of *change* and *continuity* as mental challenges, I will focus on three types of conversations—notably, *exploratory, evaluative,* and *retro-active* conversations.

Event-Based Approach

I choose to follow an event-based approach since events embody the shortest time scale in which cultural practice occurs (Butts 2008). In selecting those moments, I relied primarily on incident records, which constitute a funda-mental part of collective memory (*see* Nixon and Henry 1991; Maharaj et al. 2005; Tomsen and Markwell 2009; Triandafyllidou and Kouki 2013). These records have limits. For example, I rarely had access to the entirety of an incident. And even though I obtained full transcripts, camera footage, or sound recordings, I would oppose the idea of taking them and myself as disengaged observers (*see* Ricoeur 2004:162). Therefore, I relied on the indi-vidual or collective impressions/memories (Hirst and Echterhoff 2012), pri-marily of the conversing parties and secondarily those participating in the same incident by overhearing. I focused on the ideology-making processes during and in the aftermath of these incidents.

In order to examine these processes of knowledge production and ver-ification, the book rests on a variety of sources such as police and court records, newspapers, magazines, and, if available, personal records. The sites of culture I have chosen—i.e., "women" and clothing, "Alevis" and funerals, "LGBT" and the entertainment sector—have witnessed contesta-tion over a long period. The ideological polarization in these sites provokes the speakers to make the incidents be heard and cross-checked more con-sistently. Social polarization is of assistance here, if nowhere else, because it ensures that any action that may refer to the dispute is likely to be explic-itly problematized. In this endeavor, it was essential for me to follow the

38   Democracy: Rethinking Cultural Prerequisites

'heretics' of their time—e.g., the Islamist magazines of the early-1950s, the LGBT magazines published after the late-1980s, or the social media channels critical of the AKP government throughout the 2010s.

Among the three landscapes, a noteworthy exception is the relatively late advent of public awareness about the problems of "LGBT" people. This development in itself is a significant indication of cultural change. In this case, my focal point is those incidents that have been problematized in the new, unsettled cultural period. Among them are the cases of murder after sex workers have become visible in the gaze of civilians and the dismissal of LGBT people in the public sector, which turned out to be a matter of legal as well as a social dispute. That said, recent oral history studies gave me an insight into the way some undocumented incidents of the past may be recalled and problematized by virtue of the recently accessible ideological repertoires (*see* Gürsu 2012; Cingöz and Gürsu 2013).

Even in an unsettled cultural period where, for example, women's clothing attracts watchful eyes in public, the incidents may not always be well-documented. This lack of data may be due to the privacy of matters in some social contexts (e.g., the bonds in a family). It may also be due to the one-sided reporting of what happened (e.g., the murdered trans sex workers often lacked the means to document their account of the incidents of murder). Given these limitations, I aimed to take some snapshots from all available incidents that enter the mass debate without claiming that these incidents are exhaustive of the experience in society.

Nevertheless, they should be exhaustive of the experience that could explicitly or implicitly be mentioned in the mass debate. Therefore, my horizon is limited by the cultural horizon of contesting parties, who have an idea of what to problematize in public. In this vein, I will keep track of the changing problematization of allegedly similar issues. The starting point of my approach was to flesh out the critical matters of dispute, which I have already elaborated on at the very outset of the research.

The introduction should have also provided an insight into the boundary moments on which I focus. Accordingly, my analysis in the chapter entitled women and clothing relies on the incidents documented after the *de-facto* lifting of the head-covering ban (2013), which also corresponds to the political climate after the third term of the AKP government. The chapter entitled Alevis and funerals is based on the incidents documented after the late-2000s, which follows the spread of *cemevleri*, the intensification of the thorny controversies over the true definition of Alevilik, the changed authority structures prompted by Alevism, and the varied relationship of Alevis with the institutions through which Islam is practiced. Lastly, my analysis in the chapter entitled LGBT and the entertainment sector covers the incidents throughout the late-2000s and the 2010s, which displayed some new cleavages between the alternative visible representations of LGBT identity in the form of sex workers, entertainers, or public employees.

Cross-Checking the Multiple Accounts

The diversity of accounts on an incident does not necessarily damage the reliability of any of these accounts. On the contrary, it helps researchers follow how the parties participating in the incident make their meanings. My aim here is neither to say whether testimony is trustworthy nor which of the multiple accounts is correct. The conversing parties conduct enough of these fact-checking efforts, despite the confines of authority structures. Instead, I aim to present how differently they form discourse over the same practice. Because one cannot perform intolerance without meaning it, such an act is always dependent on being explained by the parties involved.

Incidents display the practices of intolerance, but they are also actively recalled as reference points. Among those incidents relating to women's clothing in the 1880s, the 1950s, and the 2010s, the most recent provoked "us" to recall what had happened in the past, despite the very different social conditions surrounding them. Given that the ideology-making processes are actively in place to make sense of incidents as parts of a wholly meaningful universe, an incident rarely remains a standalone matter. For instance, support for the head-covering ban was based on the *amalgamation* of the prohibition with a set of other incidents. It includes the people who were attacked for not fasting, those who were demonized for having "open" clothing, and those who, in Former President Demirel's account, could not enjoy their freedom and capability to *not* pray alongside those who performed their freedom of religion. Whereas the proponents of the head-covering ban perceived the incidents mentioned above in connection with one another, many opponents of the ban (e.g., the "liberal" argument) saw no relationship between these sets of incidents.

Relatedly, ideology makers often do not categorize incidents in the same way, even across different times. Because I aim to capture changes in these interrelationships between ideology-making processes, I refuse to implement any exogenous categorization standard on incidents. Concomitantly, I do not take the incidents as though they always stand in the same way in "our" collective memory. These shifting meanings of an incident hint at cultural change. In this vein, I will discuss the changing place of the concept of agency (vis-à-vis responsibility) in the re-making of Secularism.

Negative Heuristics: Cultural Analysis Based on Quantification

A pitfall in this event-based approach would be attempting to measure intolerance based on a quantification of incidents. It would be a pitfall for the study of culture, not only because the incidents may not always be recorded but also because the absence of incidents may not mean that the experience is simply one of a settled cultural period. Pew Research Center's Social Hostilities Index (SHI) is a helpful example within this context. The index aims to measure the level of social hostilities involving religion by counting

40   Democracy: Rethinking Cultural Prerequisites

incidents based on some categories deemed relevant to the notion of social hostility. The index does not fall into the pitfall of trying to count how many of which incidents occurred. However, it still aims to quantify the data from each country based on whether some *types* of incidents happened within a given period. The mistaken assumption of SHI is that it claims to measure the levels of social hostilities based on the occurrence of incidents.

To begin with, the research team is confident that, irrespective of the differences between countries in terms of transparency, they can collect data from 198 countries by relying on "more than a dozen published cross-national sources" ("Latest" 2015:34). When complemented with a democracy index, SHI indicates that "full democracies" are less prone to "social hostilities" ("Five Key" 2015:20). This conclusion suggests that SHI successfully gathered sufficient data from "authoritarian" countries, where the incidents may have otherwise been missed due to a lack of transparency.

That said, my implementation of the same data (2007–2013) on 20 countries in a roughly sketched map of the Middle East demonstrated a more questionable result in terms of the operation of culture. According to the result, the relatively democratic/democratizing[16] ones among 20 Middle Eastern countries—i.e., Turkey, Israel, Lebanon, and post-uprising Tunisia—could not get close to the threshold that signifies a "low" level of social hostility (*see* Figure 2.1). On the contrary, many authoritarian countries in the region were on the "low" side. In other words, according to the correlation, the more democratic a state is in the Middle East, the more "social hostilities" from which it tends to suffer.

Eschewing any search for a causal link in this correlation, I shall demonstrate why the quantitative event-based approach will not capture how culture operates. This example rests on data that covers before and after the uprisings in Tunisia and Libya. The rates of social hostility in both countries were among the lowest in 2010—i.e., one year before the uprisings. Suddenly, within a year, both countries seemed to have moved towards the high end of the chart.

After the new constitution, Tunisia's democracy did not lead to any notable decrease in its social hostility ratings. On the contrary, the Ben Ali era looks like an unreachable goal in retrospect. This finding is unreliable, at least because Tunisia did not develop these "social hostilities involving religion," including their ideational or material roots, within only one year (Boulby 1988; Marzouki 2011; Cavatorta and Merone 2013:861). The correlation suggests instead that the social hostilities were not made explicit before the uprisings. The event-based quantitative approach misses some decades-long incubation periods, which constitute some of Tunisia's most fundamental cultural tensions (Mas 2006; Merone 2015).

Meanings in Silences

The challenge of silences appears in the last example. I think this challenge partly stems from the lack of means of making sense of silences.

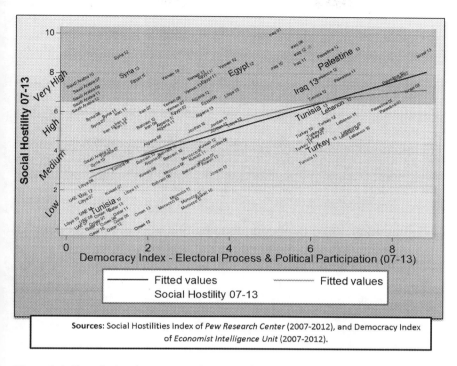

Figure 2.1 Correlation between each country's level of democracy and social hostilities involving religion according to a roughly considered map of the Middle East

A fundamental methodological challenge in historiography is that the records of non-problematized processes—be them the relationships of "tolerance," "peace," or "coexistence"—are not as accessible as the sources of *negative* incidents—e.g., "intolerance," "war," or any other kind of conflict. Simply put, it is often the lack of incidents—i.e., routines and habits—which signifies harmony. As Bryant (2016:5) puts it in the context of the Ottoman society, the everyday life practices are likely to be absent in the records, "as opposed to the 'events' that construct archives and define historical study." With an awareness of this limit, I aim to capture the instances where silence means a lot to the conversing parties.

Silence does not necessarily represent an absence of meaning. They are empirical materials—just as sounds are—to indicate peaceful routines or some relatively subtle relationships of power, which appear "most often as silence or muffled subtext" (Mazzei 2003). In this study, I suggest exploring silences through their meanings in some surrounding conversational texts. I engaged in such an exploration when I underlined the question of those who asked Erdoğan why he was silent towards a visible representation of

42 Democracy: Rethinking Cultural Prerequisites

LGBT identity in one case (i.e., the iftar with Ersoy), whereas he was loudly opposed to another visible representation (i.e., the LGBT Pride parade in Taksim square). Was this silence wholly meaningless, or was it aimed at promoting the visibility of the *other* in one particular way, which is not supposed to be spoken to function? In any case, I shall analyze the implications of silence for tolerance.

The case of Gözde Kansu illustrates how I do that in this study. Kansu lost her job when Minister Hüseyin Çelik denigrated her "open cloth" on a TV show. After the incident, when conversing with journalist Ayşe Arman, Kansu agreed with Arman's argument that she was cherry-picked in a media landscape where many others were wearing "more open clothes" without interference. Based on this conversation, the silence in these other cases became meaningful and even a prerequisite to exploring what happened to trigger Kansu's dismissal.

Moreover, intolerance may be hidden in silence as well. Many Alevi citizens recently complained that the mosque personnel did not read salâ for their deceased family members. In fact, they meant that this officer refused to use the word "cemevi" as a part of the salâ, even though he read the salâ. The families insisted that the word be used because their funeral would take place at a cemevi. With a complementary function, they perceive the mosque as the place to announce this funeral for their fellow Muslims in a religious musical form. In these cases, the Diyanet officers defined the border of tolerance as the beginning of silence.

Cross-Temporal Comparisons

A fundamental task underpinning the comparative method is the necessity to establish a thorough understanding of comparability. Because the comparative configuration risks imposing the categories of one particular case onto another, it is criticized by seasoned field experts and anthropologists and heavily cautioned against by some comparativists who also conduct field research (Roy 1996:8–12; Bayat 2001:154; Whitehead 2002:191). My study rests on the comparative skills of conversing parties, who often express a view on today versus the past, here versus there, and the *self* versus the *other*. Therefore, the research travels in time, constantly going to the past and coming back to the moment. Because what gives an event its historicity is not just its occurrence but also its later representations, it was through the representations that I decided where to seek cultural change.

I have already explained that it seems rational for many people to perceive a process of cultural reproduction, "given" that the same things seem to happen again and again. For example, I clarified how the Ticanis remain essential in 'our' conversations after 70 years, especially when the matter of dispute turns out to be aggression against women for their clothing preferences. This repetition obliged me to go back to the archives to check the extent to which what happened in the early-1950s is similar to what happens today. What did the women who were attacked for their clothing preferences say back at the time, and what do they say now? How did the ideology makers of the past discuss the matter, and how do they discuss it at the moment?

In this endeavor, I accessed conversational texts from the early-1950s through the newspapers where the incidents were covered, narrated, and argued over (e.g., Akşam, Milliyet, Cumhuriyet, Yeni Sabah). Additionally, I used court records (e.g., the Ticani files), the minutes of parliamentary debates (e.g., over the law on the protection of Atatürk), declarations from public protests (e.g., the parades against Ticani aggression, organized by women and student associations), the first so-called "women's magazines" (e.g., Resimli Hayat), and the Islamist magazines of the time (e.g., Büyük Doğu, Sebilürreşad).

I could not conduct fully systematic research in the sense that some of the sources are easier to follow than others (e.g., Cumhuriyet and Milliyet have well-coded search databases, whereas Akşam and Yeni Sabah must be searched manually). That said, despite not being wholly exhaustive, the available snapshots allowed me to figure out some critical contradictions between then and now, especially in terms of who speaks in the name of women; how s/he speaks; which ideological repertoire s/he adopts; and how s/he makes use of the cultural resources s/he has.

Though the contexts, structures, and agents differ in fundamental ways between these episodes —arguably in a manner that renders them incomparable—what makes them parts of comparison is those interlocutors who see some corresponding patterns in them. Given that the idea of cultural reproduction relies on these arguments and the explicit or implicit agreements upon them, the idea of cultural change can make sense only in dialogue with them.

My position as a researcher is no different than that of any of the parties conversing on the subject: we all make arguments over change and continuity, in part based on a historiographical approach and partly on 'our' individual or collective memory. My effort, within this context, is to bring to the forefront more of the relevant data so that the ongoing contestations make a new sense in terms of signifying cultural change.

Exploratory, Evaluative, and Retroactive Conversations

Based on my theoretical and methodological explanations, I consider three types of conversation separate yet interrelated. The participants, the settings, or the outputs tend to vary in accordance with the kind of conversation. I will first take into account *exploratory conversations*, which take place in a discrete setting where "intolerance"—i.e., perceived as such by the 'intolerant,' the addressee, or both—is put into action. These conversations are likely to appear during micro-level *incidents*, where the interlocutors share a relatively narrow physical environment.

The interlocutors in these conversations are often unknown to one another. Usually, the speakers of an exploratory conversation must deal with

44   *Democracy: Rethinking Cultural Prerequisites*

some extraordinary circumstances for which they are not well-prepared. A key defining feature of these conversations is that they include some initial reactions to situations, such as frustration, anger, and sudden physical or verbal tension.

Because the strategies of action in this speech type are likely to be developed in a hurry, the thought processes tend to be unstable, unexpected, and possibly disconnected from prior thinking. In this sense, they serve as the imperfect representations of some widely accessible ideological repertoires. Additionally, in exploratory conversations, the speakers exercise disruptive role performances. Employing a spoken language, they have to argue in an interruptive manner, which arguably constitutes social action in its very natural form (Nikulin 2010; Goffman 2017).

By contrast, *evaluative conversations* are not limited to a narrowly delimited environment. These conversations may take place in books, presentations, or detailed, prepared speeches on an issue. This setting may be called dialectical instead of dialogical, given that the conversing parties do not have disruptive role performances, even though they respond to one another. These conversations are the products of some conscious thought processes, in which the conversing parties have enough time and space to make their most coherent arguments.

Though everyone may participate in an evaluative conversation, the more significant examples of these conversations are those between some relatively powerful actors that make, re-make, and represent ideologies in public—e.g., civil society movements, academics, journalists, politicians, or courts. In these conversations, the conversing parties tend to combine their arguments with those of like-minded others. By examining such conversations, I aimed to follow the fusion and the polarization of arguments in public debates.

In this research design, I aim for the exploratory conversations to be exhaustive of all broadly communicated incidents and their (alleged) content. Ideally, there should be no selection bias in the exploratory conversations on which I focused. However, I shall admit that this is an arduous task to undertake in archival research. In order to keep the selection bias at an insignificant level, I used a wide array of archival material, as I explained before. Arguments over each incident, in which the speakers tend to make cross-references between the past and the present, helped me implement a snowball technique to reach more and more incidents.

On the other hand, throughout the research, I had to question which set of evaluative conversations I should be scrutinizing. During this dynamic process, I prioritized conversations about the boundary moments I laid down in the introduction of this research—e.g. (1) which arguments the 'vanguards' of Secularism used when they stopped opposing the lifting of the head-covering ban; (2) how the religious communities reacted to the generational change in the operationalization of Islamic veil; (3) how the Alevi communities discussed their changing funeral rituals, between one

Democracy: Rethinking Cultural Prerequisites 45

another and together with the state institutions; (4) how the pro-government "Islamists" distinguished between some different visible representations of LGBT identity.

In the case of evaluative conversations, I focused on relatively influential ideology-making circles. Given this limitation, I took into account another type of conversation between, on the one hand, rather 'ordinary' speakers of exploratory conversations, and on the other hand, knowledge claims put forward during evaluative conversations. As I noted above, speakers are likely to be unprepared for an exploratory conversation. However, they can re-consider their positions in time, as the others' claims on the subject matter tend to provoke them. I categorized these re-considerations of the past as retroactive conversations. Thanks to them, I could observe the actors who participated in exploratory conversations with their more detailed, revised arguments.

Naming the Identities

My study does not aim to find out the most proper name for any group of identities or classify them under specific categories. I am interested in the clashing claims of ownership over any identity marker as they appear in the landscapes I identified. My objective was to capture the disagreements over the definitions of the *self* and the *other*.

Many of the talks I focused on already provided an insight into the identity markers. For example, based on their claims on Islam at a critical juncture, the following actors may easily be differentiated: an "Islamist"[17] politician who sees in Islam a modern political ideology but not a constant armed struggle; the "Jihadist" attacker of a nightclub who sees physical violence and militancy in Islam; and a "secular Muslim" who may not problematize going to this nightclub. They do not have to be classified in this research to make sense within the context of the attack on Reina Nightclub. In the same vein, during the parliamentary debates over the lifting of the head-covering ban in late 2013, the "secularists" whose defense of Secularism was more akin to "Anglo-model secularism" could be distinguished from the "secularists" whose views are more in line with "French Laïcité." After all, they all have a claim of ownership over Secularism.

My policy of naming also applies to "LGBT," "women," and "Alevis," including their arguable sub-identities, derivatives, antecedents, successors, and possible extensions. A transgender sex worker who associates oneself with Ottoman *köçeks* constructs their relationship with history. In contrast, many other transgender people may not see any tie between this past and the present. In this vein, my approach differs from that of a historian searching for the archives' answers.

Finally, identities are not always taken by the *self*. The Alevis who had problems in mosques throughout the Cold War did not necessarily state that they were Alevis. For example, during the funeral of Bektaş, the imam

46 *Democracy: Rethinking Cultural Prerequisites*

suspected that Bektaş might have been an Alevi due to his name, originating from the mystic philosopher Haji Bektaş Veli. Similarly, many "knew" that legendary folk musician Neşet Ertaş was an "Abdal," which signifies a cultural identity closely related to Alevilik. Nevertheless, Ertaş did not take an identity due to his lifelong effort not to arrest the *other* while defining the *self*. He was just a *garip* (literal eng. strange, abandoned, lonely) on the mountain of *gönül* (literal eng. heart). Because many of "us" were sure that this was a unique representation of the Abdal tradition, his state-led mosque funeral turned out to be a mass controversy.

Notes

1 Bang (2009) is particularly helpful as a criticism of identity politics in Almond and Verba's civic culture, Putnam's social capital framework, and Norris's cause-oriented politics.
2 *See* Somer (2011) specifically on Turkey.
3 *See* Cremer (2021) for the German exception.
4 Figures that are both political and religious, such as Qaradawi, Hayrettin Karaman, and Ghannouchi led simultaneous processes in these countries.
5 An early representation of this effort was made by Griffith et al. (1956:103) who referred to the theological corpuses of Christianity and Judaism, which they regarded to be "not only desirable, but perhaps even necessary to democratic survival."
6 This claim was based on the argument that democracy is impossible to fully replicate with "no Feudalism, no Renaissance, no Reformation, no Enlightenment, French Revolution, [and] liberalism" (Huntington 1991:299).
7 Some of these labels that have been attached to democracy and democratic culture may be summarized as follows: "modern" (Griffith et al. 1956); "Secular political culture" (Lipset 1959); "generosity" (Almond and Verba 1965); "Secular-rational" and "self-expression values" (Inglehart and Norris 2003); "a healthy dose of tolerance" (Gibson et al. 1992).
8 For example, Fish (2011) relies on this marker of identity in his comparisons between "Muslims" and "non-Muslims."
9 Beyond all these limitations, "homosexuality" as a discourse has become archaic for many LGBT individuals who developed more inclusive terms, and media organs such as the Associated Press and the New York Times, which restrict the usage of the word. These developments hint at a significant sociolinguistic challenge for cross-temporal value surveys.
10 In many Western contexts, women still need to "undo" gender to be accepted in male-dominated environments (Powell et al. 2009).
11 An evil figure in Islamic eschatology.
12 This group has been excluded by other İsmailağa members.
13 Some notable examples are the religious communities of Süleymancılar, İskenderpaşa, Erenköy, İsmailağa, and Menzil.
14 These six representations were described by the research design extrinsically on a scale of "conservatism" (Poushter 2014).
15 This route to consciousness depends, (1) according to Adorno, on non-identitarian thought in "contradictions" against the reality of "suffering," (2) according to Hegel, on the dialectical structure of "experience," and (3) according to Bakhtin, on the "dialogic context" between voices.

16 I use this connotation with the caveat that, for once, I have to set aside my previous critique on the teleological implications and the definitional problems in the democratization literature. For the sake of following SHI's other couplings with democracy indices, I relied on two democracy indices: Economist Intelligence Unit (EIU) and V-Dem. Although the values depicted in Figure 2.1 are based on EIU, I did not find any noteworthy difference between the two results.

17 Many Islamists did not initially like the term "Islamism"—they wanted simply to be called "Muslims." Nevertheless, having recognized that all Muslims do not make the same political ideology out of Islam, they later decided to embrace "Islamism" in the long run. Today, many leading ideology makers organize marches and panels, and write books in the name of Islamism.

References

Gürsu, Erdem, ed. 2012. *80'lerde Lubunya Olmak. İzmir: Siyah Pembe Üçgen.*

Cingöz, Yavuz, and Erdem Gürsu, eds. 2013. *90'larda Lubunya Olmak.* Izmir: Siyah Pembe Üçgen.

Abizadeh, Arash. 2002. "Does Liberal Democracy Presuppose a Cultural Nation? Four Arguments." *American Political Science Review* 96(3):495–509. doi: 10.1017/S000305540200028X.

"A Call from Muslim Intellectuals : 'The boycott of France must stop '." 2020. *Le Monde.fr*, November 3.

Ahmed, Akbar S. 1986. *Toward Islamic Anthropology: Definition, Dogma, and Directions.* International Institute of Islamic Thought (IIIT).

Allen, Elise Ann. 2020. "Bishops Condemn Terrorist Attacks, Lament Mockery of Faith." *Crux.* Retrieved November 30, 2020 (https://cruxnow.com/church-in-europe/2020/11/bishops-condemn-terrorist-attacks-lament-mockery-of-faith/).

Almond, Gabriel A., and Sidney Verba. 1965. *The Civic Culture: Political Attitudes and Democracy in Five Nations.* Abridged edition. Boston, MA: Little, Brown.

Almond, Gabriel A., and Sidney Verba. 1989. *The Civic Culture: Political Attitudes and Democracy in Five Nations.* Newbury Park, CA: Sage Publications.

Arneson, Richard J. 2003. "Defending the Purely Instrumental Account of Democratic Legitimacy." *Journal of Political Philosophy* 11(1):122–32.

Arneson, Richard J., and Ian Shapiro. 1996. "Democratic Autonomy and Religious Freedom: A Critique of Wisconsin v. Yoder." Pp.137–74 in *Democracy's Place*, edited by I. Shapiro. New York: Cornell University Press.

Bang, Henrik P. 2009. "'Yes We Can': Identity Politics and Project Politics for a Late-Modern World." *Urban Research & Practice* 2(2):117–37. doi: 10.1080/17535060902979022.

Bartolini, Stefano. 1993. "On Time and Comparative Research." *Journal of Theoretical Politics* 5(2):131–67.

Bayat, Asef. 2007. *Islam and Democracy: What Is the Real Question?* Vol. 8. Leiden: Amsterdam University Press.

Bayat, Asef. 2001. "Studying Middle Eastern Societies: Imperatives and Modalities of Thinking Comparatively." *Middle East Studies Association Bulletin* 35(2):151–58.

Berntzen, Lars Erik. 2019. *Liberal Roots of Far Right Activism: The Anti-Islamic Movement in the 21st Century.* London: Routledge.

48 *Democracy: Rethinking Cultural Prerequisites*

Boulby, Marion. 1988. "The Islamic Challenge: Tunisia since Independence." *Third World Quarterly* 10(2):590–614. doi: 10.1080/01436598808420073.

Bourdieu, Pierre. 2014. "Lecture of 1 February 1990." Pp.44–64 in *On the State: Lectures at the Collège de France, 1989–1992*, edited by Patrick Champagne, Remi Lenoir, Franck Poupeau and Marie-Christine Riviere. Cambridge: Polity.

Bryant, Rebecca. 2016. "Introduction: Everyday Coexistence in the Post-Ottoman Space."Pp. 1–38 in *Post-Ottoman Coexistence: Sharing Space in the Shadow of Conflict*, edited by R. Bryant. New York: Berghahn Books.

Buber, Martin. 1947. *Between Man and Man*. London: Routledge.

Butts, Carter T. 2008. "A Relational Event Framework for Social Action." *Sociological Methodology* 38:155–200.

Carothers, Thomas. 2002. "The End of the Transition Paradigm." *Journal of Democracy* 13(1):5–21. doi: 10.1353/jod.2002.0003.

Cavatorta, Francesco, and Fabio Merone. 2013. "Moderation through Exclusion? The Journey of the Tunisian Ennahda from Fundamentalist to Conservative Party." *Democratization* 20(5):857–75. doi: 10.1080/13510347.2013.801255.

Cicourel, Aaron V. 1982. "Interviews, Surveys, and the Problem of Ecological Validity." *The American Sociologist* 17(1):11–20.

Cremer, Tobias. 2021. "Why Are Christians in Germany More Immune to Far-Right Populism than in the US?" *OpenDemocracy*, July 12.

"Cultural Map: Findings and Insights." 2015. *World Values Survey*. Retrieved November 6, 2019 (http://www.worldvaluessurvey.org/WVSContents.jsp).

Dahl, Robert Alan. 1986. *A Preface to Economic Democracy*. Berkeley: University of California Press.

Dalton, Russell J., and Christian Welzel. 2014. *The Civic Culture Transformed: From Allegiant to Assertive Citizens*. New York: Cambridge University Press.

Eagleton, Terry. 2013. *The Idea of Culture*. Oxford: Wiley-Blackwell.

Fernandez, Sonya. 2009. "The Crusade over the Bodies of Women." *Patterns of Prejudice* 43(3–4):269–86. doi: 10.1080/00313220903109185.

"Findings and Insights: Aspirations for Democracy." 2015. *World Values Survey*. Retrieved November 6, 2019 (http://www.worldvaluessurvey.org/WVSContents.jsp).

Fish, M. Steven. 2002. "Islam and Authoritarianism." *World Politics* 55(1):4–37.

Fish, M. Steven. 2011. *Are Muslims Distinctive? A Look at the Evidence*. Oxford University Press.

"Five Key Questions Answered on the Link between Peace & Religion." 2015. *Institute for Economics & Peace*. Retrieved (http://economicsandpeace.org/wp-content/uploads/2015/06/Peace-and-Religion-Report.pdf).

Foddy, William. 1994. *Constructing Questions for Interviews and Questionnaires: Theory and Practice in Social Research*. Cambridge: Cambridge University Press.

Fox, Jonathan. 2000. "Is Islam More Conflict Prone than Other Religions? A Cross-sectional Study of Ethnoreligious Conflict." *Nationalism and Ethnic Politics* 6(2):1–24. doi: 10.1080/13537110008428593.

Gasché, Rodolphe. 2004. "How Empty Can Empty Be? On the Place of the Universal." Pp.17–34 in *Laclau: A Critical Reader*, edited by Simon Critchley and Oliver Marchart. Abingdon: Routledge.

Gibson, James L., Raymond M. Duch, and Kent L. Tedin. 1992. "Democratic Values and the Transformation of the Soviet Union." *The Journal of Politics* 54(2):329–71. doi: 10.2307/2132030.

Goffman, Erving. 2017. *Interaction Ritual: Essays in Face-to-Face Behavior*. Routledge.

Democracy: Rethinking Cultural Prerequisites 49

Griffith, Ernest S., John Plamenatz, and J. Roland Pennock. 1956. "Cultural Prerequisites to a Successfully Functioning Democracy: A Symposium." *American Political Science Review* 50(01):101–37. doi: 10.2307/1951601.

Gülalp, Haldun. 2005. "Enlightenment by Fiat: Secularization and Democracy in Turkey." *Middle Eastern Studies* 41(3):351–72. doi: 10.1080/00263200500105984.

Habermas, Jürgen. 2008. "Notes on a Post-Secular Society." *Signandsight*, June 18.

Habermas, Jürgen. 2018. "Struggles for Recognition in the Democratic Constitutional State." Pp.203–38 in *Inclusion of the Other: Studies in Political Theory*, edited by Ciaran Cronin and Pablo De Greiff. New York: John Wiley & Sons.

Karaman, Hayrettin. 2015. "Teknoloji Bağımlılığı ve İmam-Hatipli Bilinci." *Ensar Pikniği Konuşması*. Retrieved (https://www.youtube.com/watch?v=cwsiybaiLTs).

Hinnebusch, Raymond. 2000. "Political Culture, Modernization, and Islam." Pp.123–45 in *Citizenship and the State in the Middle East: Approaches and Applications*, edited by N. A. Butenschøn, U. Davis, and M. S. Hassassian. New York: Syracuse University Press.

Hinnebusch, Raymond. 2010. "Toward a Historical Sociology of State Formation in the Middle East." *Middle East Critique* 19(3):201–16. doi: 10.1080/19436149.2010.514470.

Hirsi Ali, Ayaan, and Geert Wilders. 2003. "Het Is Tijd Voor Een Liberale Jihad." *NRC Handelsblad* 12. Retrieved (https://www.nrc.nl/nieuws/2003/04/12/het-is-tijd-voor-een-liberale-jihad-7634743-a224126).

Hirst, William, and Gerald Echterhoff. 2012. "Remembering in Conversations: The Social Sharing and Reshaping of Memories." *Annual Review of Psychology* 63(1):55–79. doi: 10.1146/annurev-psych-120710-100340.

Hofer, Tamas. 1968. "Anthropologists and Native Ethnographers in Central European Villages: Comparative Notes on the Professional Personality of Two Disciplines." *Current Anthropology* 9(4):311–15. doi: 10.1086/200902.

Huntington, Samuel P. 1991. *The Third Wave: Democratization in the Late Twentieth Century*. Norman: University of Oklahoma Press.

Huntington, Samuel P. 1997. "After Twenty Years: The Future of the Third Wave." *Journal of Democracy* 8(4):3–12. doi: 10.1353/jod.1997.0059.

Hurtienne, Thomas, and Götz Kaufmann. 2011. "Methodological Biases. Inglehart's World Value Survey and Q Methodology." *Journal of Human Subjectivity* 9(2):2011.

Inglehart, Ronald. 2006. "Mapping Global Values." *Comparative Sociology* 5(2–3):115–36. doi: 10.1163/156913306778667401.

Inglehart, Ronald. 2018. *Cultural Evolution: People's Motivations Are Changing, and Reshaping the World*. Cambridge University Press.

Inglehart, Ronald, and Christian Welzel. 2010. "Changing Mass Priorities: The Link between Modernization and Democracy." *Perspectives on Politics* 8(2):551–67.

Inglehart, Ronald, and Paul R. Abramson. 1999. "Measuring Postmaterialism." *American Political Science Review* 93(3):665–77. doi: 10.2307/2585581.

Inglehart, Ronald, and Pippa Norris. 2003. "The True Clash of Civilizations." *Foreign Policy* 135(2):63–70.

Inglehart, Ronald, and Wayne E. Baker. 2000. "Modernization, Cultural Change, and the Persistence of Traditional Values." *American Sociological Review* 65(1):19–51.

Jamal, Amaney A. 2006. "Reassessing Support for Islam and Democracy in the Arab World? Evidence from Egypt and Jordan." *World Affairs* 169(2):51–63.

50   *Democracy: Rethinking Cultural Prerequisites*

Juergensmeyer, Mark. 1996. "The Worldwide Rise of Religious Nationalism." *Journal of International Affairs* 50(1):1–20.

Kitschelt, Herbert. 2002. "Popular Dissatisfaction with Democracy: Populism and Party Systems." Pp. 179–96 in *Democracies and the Populist Challenge*, edited by Y. Mény and Y. Surel. London: Palgrave Macmillan UK.

Koca, Metin. 2017. "On the Borders of Cultural Relativism, Nativism, and International Society: A Promotion of Islamist Democracy in the Middle East after the Arab Uprisings." *All Azimuth: A Journal of Foreign Policy and Peace* 6(2):43–63.

Laclau, Ernesto. 2005a. *On Populist Reason*. London: Verso.

Laclau, Ernesto. 2005b. "Populism: What's in a Name?" in *Populism and the Mirror of Democracy*. Vol. 48, edited by F. Panizza. London: Verso.

Laclau, Ernesto, and Chantal Mouffe. 2014. *Hegemony and Socialist Strategy: Towards a Radical Democratic Politics*. London: Verso.

Lane, Jan-Erik, and Svante Ersson. 2016. *Culture and Politics: A Comparative Approach*. London: Routledge.

Lapid, Yosef, and Friedrich V. Kratochwil, eds. 1996. *The Return of Culture and Identity in IR Theory*. Boulder, CO; London: Lynne Rienner.

"Latest Trends in Religious Restrictions and Hostilities." 2015. *Pew Research Center*. February 26.

Lewis, Bernard. 1994. "Why Turkey Is the Only Muslim Democracy." *Middle East Quarterly* 1(1): 41–9.

Lipset, Seymour Martin. 1959. "Some Social Requisites of Democracy: Economic Development and Political Legitimacy." *The American Political Science Review* 53(1):69–105. doi: 10.2307/1951731.

Maharaj, R. G., J. Rampersad, J. Henry, K. V. Khan, B. Koonj-Beharry, J. Moham-med, U. Rajhbeharrysingh, F. Ramkissoon, M. Sriranganathan, B. Brathwaite, and S. Barclay. 2005. "Critical Incidents Contributing to the Initiation of Sub-stance Use and Abuse among Women Attending Drug Rehabilitation Centres in Trinidad and Tobago." *West Indian Medical Journal* 54(1):51–58. doi: 10.1590/S0043-31442005000100011.

Manea, Elham. 2020. "The Case for Supporting Macron's Stance on 'Islamist Separatism.'" *SWI Swissinfo.Ch*. Retrieved November 26, 2020 (https://www.swissinfo.ch/eng/the-case-for-supporting-macron-s-stance-on--islamist-separatism-/46179236).

Marzouki, Nadia. 2011. "From People to Citizens in Tunisia." *Middle East Report* 259:16–19.

Mas, Ruth. 2006. "Compelling the Muslim Subject: Memory as Post-Colonial Violence and the Public Performativity of 'Secular and Cultural Islam.'" *The Muslim World* 96(4):585–616. doi: 10.1111/j.1478-1913.2006.00149.x.

Mazzei, Lisa A. 2003. "Inhabited Silences: In Pursuit of a Muffled Subtext." *Qualitative Inquiry* 9(3):355–68. doi: 10.1177/1077800403009003002.

Meddeb, Hamza. 2019. "Ennahda's Uneasy Exit from Political Islam." *Carnegie Middle East Center*. Retrieved July 1, 2021 (https://carnegie-mec.org/2019/09/05/ennahda-s-uneasy-exit-from-political-islam-pub-79789).

Merone, Fabio. 2015. "Enduring Class Struggle in Tunisia: The Fight for Identity beyond Political Islam." *British Journal of Middle Eastern Studies* 42(1):74–87. doi: 10.1080/13530194.2015.973188.

Midlarsky, Manus I. 1998. "Democracy and Islam: Implications for Civilizational Conflict and the Democratic Peace." *International Studies Quarterly* 42(3):485–511.

"Migrationsforscher Erklärt Ziele Des Expertenkreises Islamismus." 2021. *Domradio.De*, June 23.

Mittermaier, Amira. 2015. "Trading with God: Islam, Calculation, Excess." Pp.274–93 in *A Companion to the Anthropology of Religion*. West Sussex: John Wiley & Sons.

Mouffe, Chantal. 2000. *The Democratic Paradox*. Verso.

Müller, Jan-Werner. 2009. "Seven Ways to Misunderstand Constitutional Patriotism." *Notizie Di POLITEIA* 25(96):20–24.

Ng, Weiting, and Ed Diener. 2014. "What Matters to the Rich and the Poor? Subjective Well-Being, Financial Satisfaction, and Postmaterialist Needs across the World." *Journal of Personality and Social Psychology* 107(2):326–38. doi: 10.1037/a0036856.

Nikulin, Dmitri. 2010. *Dialectic and Dialogue*. Stanford: Stanford University Press.

Nixon, Harold L., and Wilma J. Henry. 1991. "White Students at the Black University: Their Experiences Regarding Acts of Racial Intolerance." *Equity & Excellence in Education* 25(2–4):121–23.

Norris, Pippa, and Ronald Inglehart. 2002. "Islamic Culture and Democracy: Testing the 'Clash of Civilizations' Thesis." *Comparative Sociology* 1(3):235–63. doi: 10.1163/156913302100418592.

Page, Benjamin I., and Robert Y. Shapiro. 2010. *The Rational Public: Fifty Years of Trends in Americans' Policy Preferences*. Chicago, IL: University of Chicago Press.

Pelinka, Anton. 2013. "Right-Wing Populism: Concept and Typology." Pp.3–22 in *Right-Wing Populism in Europe: Politics and Discourse,* edited by Ruth Wodak, Majid KhosraviNik and Brigitte Mral. London: Bloomsbury Academic,

Peng, Kaiping, Richard E. Nisbett, and Nancy YC Wong. 1997. "Validity Problems Comparing Values across Cultures and Possible Solutions." *Psychological Methods* 2(4):329–44.

Poushter, Jacob. 2016. "The Middle East's Sectarian Divide on Views of Saudi Arabia, Iran." *Pew Research Center*. Retrieved March 11, 2018 (http://www.pewresearch.org/fact-tank/2016/01/07/the-middle-easts-sectarian-divide-on-views-of-saudi-arabia-iran/).

Powell, Abigail, Barbara Bagilhole, and Andrew Dainty. 2009. "How Women Engineers Do and Undo Gender: Consequences for Gender Equality." *Gender, Work & Organization* 16(4):411–28. doi: 10.1111/j.1468-0432.2008.00406.x.

Ricoeur, Paul. 1978. "Existence and Hermeneutics." Pp.97–108 in *The Philosophy of Paul Ricoeur: An Anthology of His Work*. Vol. 567, edited by C. E. Reagan and D. Stewart. Boston, MA: Beacon Press.

Ricoeur, Paul. 2004. *Memory, History, Forgetting*. Chicago, IL: University of Chicago Press.

Rieker, Pernille. 2018. "French Status Seeking in a Changing World: Taking on the Role as the Guardian of the Liberal Order." *French Politics* 16(4):419–38. doi: 10.1057/s41253-018-0078-5.

Rokkan, Stein. 1999. *State Formation, Nation-Building, and Mass Politics in Europe: The Theory of Stein Rokkan: Based on His Collected Works*. Clarendon Press.

Roy, Olivier. 1996. *The Failure of Political Islam*. Cambridge, MA: Harvard University Press.

Roy, Olivier. 2007. *Secularism Confronts Islam*. New York: Columbia University Press.

Roy, Olivier. 2020. *Is Europe Christian?* New York: Oxford University Press.

Roy, Olivier. 2021. "Religion and the State: Unintended Effects of Anti-Radicalisation Policies." *OpenDemocracy*. Retrieved July 19, 2021 (https://www.opendemocracy.net/en/global-extremes/religion-and-state-unintended-effects-anti-radicalisation-policies/).

52 Democracy: Rethinking Cultural Prerequisites

Saffon, Maria Paula, and Nadia Urbinati. 2013. "Procedural Democracy, the Bulwark of Equal Liberty." *Political Theory* 41(3):441–81.

Salamé, Ghassane, ed. 1994. *Democracy without Democrats? The Renewal of Politics in the Muslim World.* London; New York: I.B. Tauris.

Schedler, Andreas, and Rodolfo Sarsfield. 2007. "Democrats with Adjectives: Linking Direct and Indirect Measures of Democratic Support." *European Journal of Political Research* 46(5):637–59. doi: 10.1111/j.1475-6765.2007.00708.x.

Schegloff, Emanuel A. 1997. "Whose Text? Whose Context?" *Discourse & Society* 8(2):165–87.

Schlueter, John. 2009. "The Art of Debate: Disagreement, Consensus, and Democratic Association." *Soundings: An Interdisciplinary Journal* 92(3/4):279–302.

Schlumberger, Oliver. 2000. "The Arab Middle East and the Question of Democratization: Some Critical Remarks." *Democratization* 7(4):104–32. doi: 10.1080/13510340008403686.

Schwarz, Norbert. 1994. "Judgment in a Social Context: Biases, Shortcomings, and the Logic of Conversation." Pp. 123–62 in *Advances in Experimental Social Psychology.* Vol. 26, edited by M. P. Zanna. Academic Press.

Somer, Murat. 2011. "Does It Take Democrats to Democratize? Lessons from Islamic and Secular Elite Values in Turkey." *Comparative Political Studies* 44(5):511–45. doi: 10.1177/0010414010397751.

Somer, Murat. 2017. "Conquering versus Democratizing the State: Political Islamists and Fourth Wave Democratization in Turkey and Tunisia." *Democratization* 24(6):1025–43. doi: 10.1080/13510347.2016.1259216.

Somer, Murat, and Jennifer McCoy. 2018. "Déjà vu? Polarization and Endangered Democracies in the 21st Century." *American Behavioral Scientist* 62(1):3–15. doi: 10.1177/0002764218760371.

Sorensen, Georg. 2008. *Democracy and Democratization: Processes and Prospects in a Changing World.* Third edition. Boulder, CO: Westview Press.

Stepan, Alfred, and Charles Taylor. 2014. *Boundaries of Toleration.* New York: Columbia University Press.

Taylor, Charles. 2007. *A Secular Age.* Cambridge, MA: Harvard University Press.

"Teknoloji ve Müslüman." 2015. *Ismailaga.Com.Tr.* Retrieved August 27, 2015 (http://www.ismailaga.com.tr/teknoloji-ve-musluman.html).

Tessler, Mark. 2002. "Islam and Democracy in the Middle East: The Impact of Religious Orientations on Attitudes toward Democracy in Four Arab Countries." *Comparative Politics* 34(3):337–54. doi: 10.2307/4146957.

Tibi, Bassam. 1993. "The Worldview of Sunni Arab Fundamentalists: Attitudes toward Modern Science and Technology." Pp.73–102 in *Fundumentalisms and Society,* edited by Martin E. Marty, R. Scott Appleby. Chicago, IL: University of Chicago Press.

Triandafyllidou, Anna, and Hara Kouki. 2013. "Muslim Immigrants and the Greek Nation: The Emergence of Nationalist Intolerance." *Ethnicities* 13(6):709–28. doi: 10.1177/1468796813483287.

Tomsen, Stephen, and Kevin Markwell. 2009. "Violence, Cultural Display and the Suspension of Sexual Prejudice." *Sexuality & Culture* 13(4):201–17.

Turnbull, William. 2003. *Language in Action: Psychological Models of Conversation.* New York: Psychology Press.

Vainio, Olli-Pekka, and Aku Visala. 2016. "Tolerance or Recognition? What Can We Expect?" *Open Theology* 2(1):553–65.

Democracy: Rethinking Cultural Prerequisites   53

Wallerstein, Immanuel. 1997. "Eurocentrism and Its Avatars: The Dilemmas of Social Science." *Sociological Bulletin* 46(1):21–39.

Wang, Zi. 2015. "Modernization, Value-Change, and Gender Inequality in Japan: Japanese Exceptionalism or Theoretical Inadequacy?" Pp. 181–204 in *Multi-faced Transformations: Challenges and Studies*, edited by E. Danilova, M. Makarovic, and A. Zubkovych. Newcastle upon Tyne: Cambridge Scholars Publishing.

Watkins, Susan Cotts, and Ann Swidler. 2006. "Conversations Into Texts: A Method for Studying Public Culture." *California Center for Population Research: Online Working Paper Series*. Retrieved (https://escholarship.org/uc/item/3zx0t0j5).

Watkins, Susan Cotts, and Ann Swidler. 2009. "Hearsay Ethnography: Conversational Journals as a Method for Studying Culture in Action." *Poetics (Hague, Netherlands)* 37(2):162–84. doi: 10.1016/j.poetic.2009.03.002.

Whitehead, Laurence. 2002. *Democratization*. Oxford: Oxford University Press.

Yavuz, M. Hakan. 2005. *Islamic Political Identity in Turkey*. Oxford: Oxford University Press.

Ziliotti, Elena. 2020. "Democracy's Value: A Conceptual Map." *The Journal of Value Inquiry* 54(3):407–27. doi: 10.1007/s10790-019-09717-1.

3 LGBT and the Entertainment Sector

This chapter analyzes how the visible representations of the LGBT identity integrate with the mass political struggles over "our" values. In contemporary Turkey, what a "pro-LGBT" narrative opposes is likely what many others, including some of the strongest narrators, also oppose. Among the local competitors that these narrators problematize is the Islamic traditionalism that could not reach modernity and the heteronormative Kemalism that could not surpass modernity. On the broader political-economic front, the alternative structures to be charged are, on the one hand, the capitalist commodification of the LGBT people in sex and show businesses, and on the other, Marxism's identity blindness, which extends to the trans-exclusionary form of orthodox feminism. Many identify one or a combination of them as the root cause of the daily evils, such as the militarist state, the gender binary, the Ottoman-Roman hammam culture, and the patriarchal microcosmic authority of shopkeepers (tr. "esnaf kültürü"). Nonetheless, the same ideologies serve as parts of a solution for others, including those who speak for an LGBT existence. Taking them all in one milieu, I argue that the reservoir of arguments through which LGBT individuals can claim their visibility has diversified unprecedentedly. Their varying approaches to an authoritative claim receive very different responses, from implicit tolerance to direct interference.

This diversification drifts the LGBT presence away from being a determinant of hierarchical relationships. In the landscapes of the entertainment and public sectors, the outcome of the dialogue tends to be dependent on the variety of identities that may become visible alongside "LGBT." In other words, what matters is the subject's properties that become visible: Alongside carrying the markers of a sexuality or gender identity, what other symbols does s/he carry? What is the subject's approach to the authoritative institutions that s/he faces, from the notion of "common values" to the judgments of state institutions? In the face of these institutions, how do they express themselves—*e.g.,* as a carrier of a private or a public identity, as a sinner or a proud activist? Do they follow the "traditional route" and work as an entertainer in the best-case scenario, or do they try to make their way as civil servants? As employees or citizens, how do they interact with the

DOI: 10.4324/9781003311805-3

authoritative claims—notably, the *meritocratic, identitarian,* or *secretive* claims—that rule over the public sphere?

After demonstrating how these questions have begun to draw the borders of tolerance, I will conclude that the cultural process entails a shift from what "LGBT" is to what it is against. On the one hand, the process renders the constructions of the "LGBT community" less cohesive and more visible than ever; on the other hand, it helps the conflicting visible representations obtain some agency in mass political struggles taking place in the country. Instead of focusing on the LGBT community merely as an isolated sub-culture, future studies should focus on the broader social links that LGBT people have established.

Before proceeding with my analysis, I will introduce the concept of visible representation, which, I claim, should be disentangled from the assumption that more visibility brings more political power and self-representation. At the outset, based on a cross-temporal analysis of the visible representations of LGBT sex workers, I will hint at how increased visibility also brought challenges. For instance, the ongoing contestation over the meaning of prostitution: will the hitherto hidden and later visible sex workers define it, or will the eyes that once objectify them reproduce their kind? Contrary to the understanding of visibility as political agency, these eyes exploited sex workers' visibility to target, kidnap, and murder them more effortlessly. Utilizing sex workers' visibility, the adversaries developed new clear-cut frames that rationalized all these acts. Uncanny stories nourished by the invisibility of sex workers in the wider society have been replaced by the transparency that reveals their vulnerability. Within this context, I will problematize the role several stereotypical narratives have played in the recent court proceedings, especially in the legal interpretations of "unjust provocation."

A set of exploratory conversations will follow this discussion. The conversations will focus on the transgender applicants to the Turkish Employment Agency (tr. İŞKUR), whom the authority labeled as inappropriate for any work other than sex work. The negative stereotypes about them, coupled with their almost uncontrollable visibility, tend to disqualify them at the earliest job interview. However, others could make it to the negotiation table, including lesbians, gays, and bisexuals who seem "normal" to the authority at first glance. In this context, I will examine the interactions between three major authoritative claims—notably, the *identitarian, meritocratic,* and *secretive* claims, based on which the visible representations of LGBT have been negotiated in the public sector.

The section will suggest that the anti-LGBT identitarian claim has lost ground in legal interpretations. Having said that, I will also demonstrate how the courts continue to rely on administrative disciplinary actions to measure the potentially negative impact of one's sexual activity on one's work. Accordingly, in most cases, *being an LGBT person* can no longer constitute the legal basis for the dismissal of an employee, but *acting as an LGBT person* may well be considered a "justifiable" reason. At the end of this part,

56 *LGBT and the Entertainment Sector*

I will conclude that the public sector employees align their merit-based, public, and secret qualities differently, depending on their branches of government and the opportunity structures they access.

In the final set of exploratory conversations, I will examine how the visibility of the LGBT identity has been negotiated in the entertainment sector, which traditionally includes the most "tolerable" representations. This section will map the entertainment sector to manifest the fault lines between clashing LGBT representations. Some of these representations were banned, whereas others remain visible. Regarding the discrepancy, I argue that the AKP government primarily tends to restrict those critical to its value politics rather than its value expressions. The value expressions remain there to otherize all LGBT representations, whereas the value politics open space for those compatible with the system. Beginning with the case of *Boston Gay Men's Chorus*, my analysis will distinguish between those voices that challenge the hierarchical implications of tolerance and others that periodically negotiate their visibility with the higher authorities of the sector. This negotiation process requires one either to theatrically obscure one's already well-known identity or privatize this identity explicitly as opposed to the public claims of "LGBT activism."

In the first evaluative conversations, I analyze how "Islamists" have begun rationalizing tolerance towards some visible LGBT representations. Though the leading ideology makers reiterate that "which Allah forbids can never be tolerated," I will argue that their approach to these visible representations radically differs from one case to another. Before deciding how to react to an LGBT person, they focus on the multiple identities this person carries alongside one's sexuality and gender identity. This person's visibility may be justifiable, depending primarily on one's lip service to authoritative institutions such as the notions of "common values" and "public morals." The mainstream current of Islamism has developed a kind of *implicit tolerance*, characterized by refusing to see an LGBT person as a carrier of the LGBT identity under some circumstances. This way, a theatrically obscured LGBT identity could receive a positive response from the theatrically blind authority. On the one hand, this approach is not offering tolerance to "LGBT" on a textual level. On the other hand, it requires a discursive practical examination of who is to be marked as "LGBT." In most cases, "LGBT" is used in synonymity with "Islamophobic," with the latter shifting from representing a government to a tiny minority to be governed.

The fifth part will focus on the retroactive conversations between these "tolerable" and "intolerable" visible representations. Indeed, they have fundamentally different approaches to authority and society. The former has fulfilled the pre-conditions of tolerance, whereas the latter has problematized the idea of remaining at the bottom of a hierarchical relationship for reward. This section highlights how the interlocutors share the understanding that the former fits into religious conservatism, whereas the latter aligns with left-wing revolutionism. In more depth, I will seek the critical aspects of this divergence in alternative recognition politics, alternative approaches to "common values," and alternative visibility policies. Though the two camps have been counter-posed, this part also touches upon the relatively subtle clashes at the core of each. The section will emphasize those who, despite not using the repertoire of conservatism, expressed skepticism about the strategic use of uncompromising visibility. This doubt has turned out to be a debate in which a larger group of "left-wing" activists participate within the context of resistance and activism.

Finally, I analyze a series of conversations about integrating LGBT activism into fractured left-wing politics. The ultimate common concern manifests as a conservative neoliberal hegemony that imposes its first-order values as ascendant for all. Therefore, this coalition of the "otherized" factions envisioned the active participation of LGBT activists in the left-wing opposition parties, some of which previously closed their doors to LGBT activism. In due course, the activists have become an indispensable part of university clubs, various civil society organizations, and the mass protests such as the May 1 marches. On the other hand, this integration also brings the existential crisis of "left-wing politics" into LGBT activism. The crisis primarily relates to the divided ideological priorities and the common confusion about the most effective ways to cope with an aggressive yet popularly supported conservative hegemony. Amid the disappointment led by the successive AKP governments, the mainstream opposition parties had to re-visit their "weak spots" in the electorate's eyes. Accordingly, one of the first things to hide was LGBT candidates. Let alone challenging "the culture of shopkeepers," this policy entails a vow to establish a ministry of shopkeepers.

Center-Right, Center-Left, and the Underground: The Whereabouts of Subjectivity

This section aims to problematize the assumption that increased visibility brings enhanced self-representation. In this endeavor, Peggy Phelan developed a noteworthy framework after re-visiting cultural theory, feminist theories of representation, and psychic theory. Phelan considers the relationship between a "looker" and a "given to be seen" as one between the *self* and the *other*. In such relationships, capturing more frames about the hitherto underrepresented may serve to arrest it in a fixed position as the "other":

> [T]here is a dismaying similarity in the beliefs generated about the political efficacy of visible representation. The dangerous complicity between progressives dedicated to visibility politics and conservatives patrolling the borders of museums, movie houses, and mainstream broadcasting is based on their mutual belief that representations can be treated as "real truths" and guarded or championed accordingly. Both sides believe that

58   *LGBT and the Entertainment Sector*

greater visibility of the hitherto under-represented leads to enhanced political power [...] [B]oth groups [...] mistake the relation between real and representational.

(Phelan 1993:2)

A representation can never match the "real" in the sense that it can never become totalizing as such. One's view of the other will not represent the reality, for multiple readings are possible over the visible representation of the other. However, amid such a proliferation of discourses, the real world— i.e., one of the historically unequal and marked relationships—will push the visible representation to face a master narrative, which tests the ability of the underrepresented to escape from the power of the fixed definition. In this relationship, *subjectivity* can only lie in one's ability to disappear from the authority's gaze when necessary. Self-representation requires subjectivity, and being visible does not necessarily mean representing oneself.

Upon this starting point, I shall put the visible "LGBT" representations into historical context. While disentangling *subjectivity*, *visibility*, and *representation*, I will rely on some key snapshots from the history of Turkey. For example, in 1966, writer Halit Çapın humorously classified the nightclubs of Istanbul as follows: (I) the ones on the center-right, (II) the ones on the center-left, and (III) the ones forced to go underground. The ones on the right were playing some American-style "brainwashers" in English. In contrast, the ones on the left played Turkish folk songs predominantly about the collectivization of farms for brothers and sisters. As to those in the third category—i.e., those below the ground, Çapın underlined that they were not predictable at all (tr idiom. "sağı solu belli olmayanlar"). This last category consisted of some groups understood neither by the left nor the right. They are "third-class artists," "second-class brothel girls," "first-class homosexuals," and "the low-income policemen" (Çapın 1966a, 1966b).

Though the "homosexuals" were invisible to many civilian eyes in daily life, they were there in terms of representation since (1) they were unable to vanish from the sight of the low-income policemen (*see* Çapın 1966c), and (2) the mainstream media channels were interested in their "mysterious" stories. In other words, the hegemonic ideologies of the bipolar world did not let them speak for themselves, but the gaze of the authorities had already marked them. Those authorities, who talk through the language of "the right" and "the left," claimed to know what these groups consisted of and where they originated from. Accordingly, the leading ideology-makers commonly considered "homosexuals," which indicated pretty much anyone who did not fit the norms, including trans individuals self-identifying as heterosexual, to be an evil consequence of the rival ideology.

One group who spoke in the name of Secularism held the Ottoman pre-modernity and its residues of religious bigotry responsible for "homosexuality." Historian Refik Ahmet Sevengil often touched upon the subject, criticizing the Ottoman rulers for their soft measures against the spread of

LGBT and the Entertainment Sector   59

"uranism"—an old term that referred to (especially male) homosexuality (Sevengil 1985:71). Back then, the performance arts were the primary livelihood for a group whose later representations were to be marked as homosexuals. Between the 16th and the 19th centuries, it was the field of life where, in the lately imported sense of the term, the "non-hetero" sexuality had a visible representation in the form of "*tavşan oğlanı*," "*köçek*," "*çengi*," or "*kolbaşı.*" They were actors, if not identities, in the 21st-century senses of the term (Vance 2007:57–74).

Tolerance was not the matter of debate about these representations, for they were openly needed and frequently appreciated, at least within the context of artisanry. Therefore, in the cosmopolitan setting of Istanbul, the groups could remain well-organized for a period enough to render them an element of the settled culture. The çengis (en. women dancers) had their unions in Ayvansaray and the Hammam of Tahtakale (Hiçyılmaz 1991:28). Some subtle or apparent markers of "homosexual" relationship were later inferred by historians, politicians, or storytellers, who relied on the artistic repertoire of çengi groups in entertainment activities such as bridal showers (tr. kına geceleri), weddings, bear dances, drinking parties featuring music (tr. oturak alemleri) and women's hammam meetings (e.g., the 40th-day bath after childbirth).

Köçeks, male belly dancers in traditional women's clothes,[1] were also interchangeably called çengi (*see* Enderunlu Fazıl's "çenginame" in Bardakçı 2005:146). The famous *köçek groups* were well-organized as the regular employees of *Gedikli Meyhaneler* (sing. meyhane/en. literal, regular winehouses), which operated based on a special permit issued by the state (Koçu 2002:14–18). While some of these köçek groups were hired by a single meyhane, the most talented often toured between these places (Melek 1953:2705–29). They also acted as an essential part of the Ottoman rulers' entertainment activities to welcome visitors. Some rulers, such as Sultan Aziz, established köçek/çengi cadres for such important days (Hiçyılmaz 1991:26).

Based on the records of a *subaşı*, an officer in charge of the security of the Ottoman cities, Evliya Çelebi wrote that Istanbul had 500 "*esnâf-ı hîzan-ı dilberan*" (en. passive male homosexuals) as of 1633. Alongside the members of some *tekke* (en. religious lodge) organizations, this group allegedly included some Janissaries, young (tr. *civelekler*) and old, whom Mehmet Halife (1986:12) accused of publicly engaging in homosexual intercourse. Many other writings from the time suggest that *livâta,* a conventional connotation for homosexual activity, was clearly considered a sin,[2] but in "the age of beloveds" (Andrews and Kalpaklı 2005:174, 270), only occasionally surveilled in the flow of the settled culture. After all, life in the school of Enderun—i.e., devoid of women—and *Harem*—i.e., devoid of men—relied upon the daily routine of same-sex relations.

Among the post-1923 manifestos on the virtues of the Republic, many held these Ottoman practices responsible for making "homosexuality"

60 LGBT and the Entertainment Sector

natural and inevitable. These thinkers thought it was preventable with a social re-configuration led by the principles of Secularism. According to Çetin Altan, who guided the masses with his columns in several newspapers as well as his activity in the parliament, homosexuality was more common in religiously conservative towns. It was because the microcosmic authorities of these towns did not let men and women freely show their "natural feelings" (Altan 1960). If women were given the power to be visible, homosexuality would become extinct. After making the same claim, Ilhan Selçuk added that many people "chose" homosexuality due to their economic needs (Selçuk 1981). Therefore, the barriers against a welfare state were supposed to be lifted, so that homosexual people would return to their "normal" condition.

In response to the arguments about the Ottoman "perversion," the media that glorified the past defended the Ottoman harem culture, despite admitting that some "problematic" incidents may have taken place in the harem (Çabuk 1977; Bardakçı 1983; Şenlikoğlu 1996). In this vein, the thinkers on "the right" staunchly opposed the allegations of homosexuality against the Ottoman rulers. For example, Peyami Safa reacted against a professor who argued that Ottoman statesman Baltacı Mehmet Pasha was a "passive homosexual." Safa got especially angry at the professor's use of this "dirty word" to label such a "significant" historical figure (Safa 1955). According to Safa, homosexuality resulted from a moral decay caused by neglecting religious education after the 1930s (Safa 1956). He was not the only one who problematized the "superficial" religious education in the Republic. Others criticized Secularism more openly by making the causal claim that "secular democracies" raised undomesticated generations unaware of moral values ("Federal" 1973; Yıldırım 1985; Kayacan 1990; Yavuz 1990; "Kavramlar" 1993; Emiroğlu 1997; Bulaç 2012).

Demonized by "the left" and "the right," the remnants of köçek and çengi could become occasionally visible only in parts of rural Anatolia (Özen 2000:88–96) if not in the urban undergrounds. Metin And, who wrote extensively and authoritatively on köçek and çengi groups in modern Turkey, defined this visible representation as one which is to be carried out in rural areas for the lower classes (And 1968:25–29; see also Haynes 2014:3–11). On the other hand, the 1980s travesties later conveyed how they watched, from below the ground, the proud and unstoppable appearances of Zeki Müren and Bülent Ersoy in the entertainment sector in front of millions.[3] The two historic figures represented "homosexuals" in a new fashion. Notwithstanding their newness, they were not alien to those who carried the marks of the old performance arts. Within this context, writer Pınar Selek conveyed how the oldest travesti of the Ülker Street[4] often recalled her childhood memory of performing the köçek dance in a small central-Anatolian city, Kırşehir (Selek 2014:90).[5] By the 1990s, the mainstream media became concerned with the stars of the "post-köçek era": Fatih Ürek, Aydın, Serdar Ortaç, Rober Hatemo (Baştürk 1998:27–29).

The debate outside the mainstream media was much broader. Many "homosexuals" did not see any possibility of subjectivity in being the *köçeks* of a post-köçek era. They were keen to declare their independence from the historical baggage of this sector. Accordingly, they desired to (1) become visible outside rural environments, or the underground, (2) leave the cage of the entertainment sector, and (3) deconstruct the hammam and harem stories. Meanwhile, they aimed to develop a public voice to challenge violence committed mainly by the police and not the civilians, who were deprived of the visibility of a lonely and vulnerable prostitute and had plenty of horror stories about the "homosexual terror." In the aftermath of the 1980s identity turn, these agents, who would later constitute clashing visible representations of "LGBT," manifested and negotiated their in-group differences for the first time. With this, I refer to "LGBT" as a by-product of the efforts to construct one comprehensive identity marker needed to represent a joint political and social movement.

Apart from signifying this particular context of identity formation, "LGBT" can rarely be taken as a monolithic body. It is not either the only way to name the collective identity it signifies. The following part will begin examining the many-voicedness of the LGBT identity. In the course of the chapter, I will highlight how some individuals in the movement refused a subject-centered approach and instead idealized the move as one against homophobia, biphobia, and transphobia. Meanwhile, others refused to identify their individual stories with a collective struggle.

"You know these homos": Trans Sex Workers' Changing Visible Representations

The first portion of exploratory conversations includes LGBT sex workers who have turned out to be unprecedentedly visible in the gaze of civilians. Between 2008 and 2021, at least 63 trans and gender-diverse people have reportedly been murdered in Turkey (Kaos GL 2016a, 2016b; Pembe Hayat and Kaos GL 2017; Öz 2019, 2020; "TMM" 2021; Dikmen 2022). Most of the murdered were sex workers marked (and sometimes self-identify) as "travesti" and "transsexual." Of all these cases, very few reliable conversations were left, given that the only witnesses to these conversations are likely to be the murderers. Moreover, the lawyers of the murdered often argued that the state officials did not work hard enough to double-check the murderers' accounts, let alone the other cases of unidentified murder.

The discourses of action, including dialogues and individual perceptions, are of utmost importance in such court processes, as they often lead to legal consequences. If the analysis lacks a solid material, theoretical, and ideological ground, a set of stereotypical narratives may dominate the process. As the legal cases on the murder of Ahmet Öztürk and Abdülbaki Koşar suggest, the stereotypes help the murderers convince the authorities of the existence of an "unjust provocation" behind aggression. These narratives

62   LGBT and the Entertainment Sector

take impetus from the predominantly despised visible representations of transgender sex workers. In order to convince the legal practitioners of their goodwill, the aggressors rationalized their acts by relying on the vocabulary concerning how dangerous and promiscuous "these travesti prostitutes" can be.

The aggressors' almost carbon-copied accounts of their attacks reveal deep-rooted confidence in the usefulness of a shared vocabulary. Common to the 63 mortal attacks recorded after 2008 was that the aggressors demanded sentence reductions by making almost identical statements. Among their well-regurgitated sentences were the following: (1) "he offered me homosexual intercourse"; (2) "I got angry as I realized that he was a man only after he undressed"; (3) "when I saw he was a man, I wanted my money back, but he refused"; (4) "during the sexual intercourse, he told me that it was his turn to be active." Furthermore, the aggressors often justified their fatal attacks based on yet another commonsense knowledge-claim, that transgender people are dangerous people by definition: "I did not mean to kill him, but the fight went bad."

Contrary to this monotony, some decades ago—i.e., when sex workers were not as visible, such cases of murder were likely to have highly mysterious and somewhat unexpected causes ("Bir Kahveci" 1953; "Bir Cinayet" 1957; "Bir Kaatil" 1968; "Büyükada'da" 1972), such as jealousy ("Kan Çekti" 1959), financial disagreement ("Bir Cinsî" 1963) and in-group conflict ("Dolmabahçe" 1952; "İzmir'de" 1966). This variety signals a period in which the murderers did not have access to clear-cut frames helpful in justifying their acts.

Indeed, the survivors of similar attacks can make their counterclaims against these stereotypical narratives. The threats they receive are predominantly based on the value expression that sex work is degrading enough to necessitate submitting to any order. According to the survivors' accounts, an attack is likely to be triggered after unsuccessful rape attempts. For example, Bahar, the survivor of an attack in the Maltepe district of Istanbul, claimed that she was attacked because she refused to follow the orders of a group of rapists ("Maltepe'deki" 2012). Similarly, a sex worker, Yeliz, made a deal with Mehmet C. but was then beaten and raped by three of Mehmet's friends (Kocaer 2011). Serap, also a sex worker, was attacked by a former customer since she stopped answering his calls ("Çorum'da" 2014). Avşa argued that she was heavily beaten by an officer who had sexually harassed her in the past (Tar 2014). In another recorded attack, Selahattin G. kidnapped E.K. by threatening her life. In the meantime, he attempted to rape E.K. and seized her money and ring ("Şizofreni" 2014).

These victims reported that the threats they received were consistently based on a set of roles or characteristic features associated with their identities. Some survivors shared the impression that LGBT people are especially targeted, since it is much easier to develop a narrative that renders them guilty. As an illustration, Bihter, a trans woman from Ankara, was asked

LGBT and the Entertainment Sector   63

by a group of strangers to give some "money for fuel." When she refused
to give away her wallet, the man leaned towards Bihter's lips and gasped:
"I will give you 20 liras, f. you and kill you [and take it all back]" (Akpınar
2015). Just like Bihter, A.O. was threatened by a gang on the basis of her
visible representation as a travesti: "you are a travesti, so you must have lots
of money." Kemal Ördek, the founder of Red Umbrella for Sexual Health
and Human Rights Association, described how a gang, which not only sexually assaulted Ördek but also forced him to go to a cash machine, tried to
bargain with the police officers while in custody:

> Sir, he invited us to his home, you know these homos [tr. ibneler] [...]
> You and I understand each other, right?
>
> (Tahaoğlu 2015)

In order to deter transgender groups from living in certain neighborhoods,
some gangs targeted them exclusively ("Transları" 2017). Throughout the
2000s, many transgender individuals reported that they were fined by the
police whenever they were visible on the streets. Because their appearance is
invariably associated with sex work—which is outlawed except for a group
of licensed biological women—the police officers rarely need to prove that a
trans individual is in fact caught in action.

The speech acts based on such stereotypes are likely to bring special treat-
ment. As an illustration, on the one hand, Cem B., who killed Derya during his extortion attempt, was sentenced to life imprisonment ("Travestiyi"
2011); on the other hand, Ramazan S., who killed Seda and later claimed
that he got angry for being offered homosexual intercourse, had a reduced
sentence due to "the possibility that [his story] is true" ("Öldürülen" 2014).
The very same justification helped Fikret O. have a reduced sentence for the
murder of Saim Kayhanmete, a businessman of queer identity somewhat
ambivalently treated by public opinion.[6] The court considered the victim's
offer of homosexual intercourse an unjust provocation, even though the
killer was proven to have registered himself on a gay dating site, where he
finally met Kayhanmete after meeting some other gay men. As the highest
legal interpretation regarding the foundations of unjust provocation, some
decisions of the Court of Cassation were problematized by LGBT associations (*see* the case Abdülbaki K. in *"SpoD" 2012:78*). These associations
contend that many LGBT people do not appeal to the courts, as they do not
have faith in the value-laden legal system.

Nevertheless, the records also demonstrate that some recent court decisions were not disappointing from the victims' perspectives. Despite the
aggressors consistently relying on the courts' traditional take on "unjust
provocation" or "sexual intercourse in its natural form," the court processes
do not always meet their expectations. For example, although Selahattin
G. was set free one day after the incident on the basis that he had chronic
schizophrenia, he was later sentenced to 16 years in prison. After describing

64   LGBT and the Entertainment Sector

the verdict as a "fair" one, E.K.'s lawyer Ahmet Toköz stressed that this decision would be "a response to those who do not consider trans women as equal citizens" ("Trans kadın" 2015). The gang members who attacked A.O. during their extortion attempt were sentenced to up to 12 years in prison. In her evaluation, A.O. wittily stated that, for the first time in her life, it was not her who was to be punished by the court (Tar 2016a). A.O.'s lawyer Ahmet Çevik expressed his appreciation of the legal process, as it was not distorted by the perception that "travesties lie."

There are other similarly satisfying cases for the LGBT associations. The gang members who attacked Kemal Ördek were found guilty of sexual assault, theft, threat, insult, and deprivation of liberty, which amounted to a 20-year sentence. Ördek described the court decision as an impartial one: "[the criminals] tried to devalue me with my 'LGBT activist' and 'sex worker' identities," but their strategy failed (Tar 2016b). Roşin's father and two uncles, who killed Roşin for his homosexual orientation, were sentenced to life imprisonment. They appealed to the Court of Cassation, but the latter approved the local court's decision. The murderers of Melek K. and Çağla Ç., who argued that they committed the crime due to the "unjust provocation" of being offered homosexual intercourse, were sentenced to life imprisonment as well (SPoD 2012:77). In the same vein, the Court of Cassation corrected a local court's problematic interpretation of unjust provocation (Yargıtay 1. Ceza 2012). Taken together with other cases, the interpretations developed for these cases do not indicate a systematic change.

Examining these court decisions per their dates suggests that the legal interpretation of unjust provocation has not changed consistently in one direction. These decisions are not only random, but they also lack a common logic, the establishment of which would require a comprehensive ideology-making process. On the flip side, I shall note that the increased visibility of travesti and trans sex workers helped the civilian aggressors develop common ways to target them more systematically. Their repetition of the same stereotypes reveals that they have a clear idea of what to say and what not to say against their victims. I will come back to this point with a group of sex workers' retroactive conversations concerning the drawbacks associated with the policy of uncompromising visibility.

Negotiation Tables in the Public Sector: Identitarian, Meritocratic, and Secretive Approaches

Having realized that their visible representations are not in their control, a group of transgender individuals raised their voices in an unprecedented manner:

> Everyone thought we were prostituting for easy money and that we were constantly kicking up a fuss. As the Association of *Pembe Hayat*, we

LGBT and the Entertainment Sector   65

organize events to destroy these perceptions. We said, "we want to be public employees."

("Merhaba" 2007:1)

With their public declaration in front of the Turkish Employment Agency (tr. İŞKUR), Buse Kılıçkaya and her friends "confused" many people, including the policemen who formed a barricade in front of the building (Kılıçkaya 2010:18). Even though the Agency never responded to any of their applications, they were keen to register for the preparatory courses that the Agency opened. They were motivated, such that one of them managed to be the first-ranking student in a course program. She was not offered a job in return. Obviously, no transparent mechanism has been established to prevent such identity-based discrimination in selection procedures. However, after being accepted for a career in the public sector, some LGBT people could negotiate the conditions in which they worked. This part explores various interactions between the claims—notably, the identitarian, meritocratic, and secretive claims, based on which some visible representations of LGBT have been negotiated in the public sector.

Those whom the authority marks as LGBT at first glance are likely to lose their opportunity to negotiate the borders of tolerance. Exploring the LGBT public officers' work experiences, a recent (2017) survey of Kaos-GL could reach only five trans individuals in a sample of 80 LGBT people (Göregenli 2018). Transgender individuals' low chance of being employed in the public sector is relevant to the uncontrollable visibility of some images—e.g., related to one's physical appearance, voice, medical records, or identity card—which, in the eyes of the authorities, tend to represent an indefensible personality. The very few trans respondents to the annually conducted Kaos-GL surveys commonly mentioned their fear of being noticed in the office. A career employee recalls how his colleagues always made fun of transgender people: "I don't know what may happen if they notice that I am a trans" (Göregenli 2018:24).

The public sector has turned out to be the theater for a set of authoritative claims about who and how to become visible. Though these claims have some oblique points of intersection that the following parts shall hint at, they may be differentiated as follows: (1) the identitarian claim—i.e. the individuals whose identity threaten the "public morals" (tr. genel ahlak) should be dismissed, as they will sooner or later toxify the workplace; (2) the meritocratic claim—i.e., one who likes one's country most is the one who does one's job best (popularly phrased in tr. "vatanını en çok seven işini en iyi yapandır"); (3) the secretive claim—i.e., those who do not offend the eye must not be cherry-picked. Depending on the conversational settings (e.g., a legal dispute, an administrative conflict, an ordinary chat) as well as the cultural resources of the interacting parties, any of these basic categories may prevail over the others.

The identitarian claim has recently lost ground in legal interpretations concerning the visibility of LGBT identity. Instead, meritocratic and

66 LGBT and the Entertainment Sector

secretive claims tend to prevail in accordance with these interpretations. Accordingly, the recent court decisions have made it clear that an employee cannot be dismissed on the basis of one's sexual orientation. That said, they have ruled that one's dismissal can be legally justified if s/he had an administrative (disciplinary) punishment for sexual activity with negative repercussions on one's work. In short, "being LGBT" is no longer regarded as a sufficient reason for dismissal, but "acting as LGBT" may well be considered a reason. Aware of this nuance, some administrations have re-operationalized their disciplinary precautions regarding LGBT employees to circumvent the new legal constraints against discrimination. Their popular method is to trigger a dismissal process by imposing fines under the label of disorderly activity instead of sexual orientation.

A fundamental pillar of the identitarian claim lost ground when the Council of State revised the law on elementary and middle school teachers. This law from the 1930s stipulates that any teacher should be dismissed in cases of "unchastity" (tr. iffetsizlik), irrespective of whether it appears at school ("Ilk ve Orta" 1930). It remains a reference point behind the dismissal of many teachers, including some, due to their sexuality, sexual orientation, or gender identity. Nonetheless, in 2014, a teacher who was dismissed from their teaching position due to their sexual orientation won a lawsuit in the 12th Chamber of the Council of State. In its reasoning, the court refused to focus on the teacher's sexual orientation or private sexual activity. Instead, it questioned whether the teacher's sexual orientation interfered with his work. For that matter, it scrutinized the teacher's activity, firstly at school and secondly in the off-hours with one's students. On the basis that there was no such evidence against the teacher, the court argued that the administrative action and the local court decision violated the principle of respect for family and private life (Danıştay 2014).

Including those in which the courts made their decisions in favor of dismissal, other cases from this period suggest that the meritocratic claim prevails. While the administrative court approved the dismissal of a gay worker in 2006, it emphasized that the worker was dismissed not for his sexual orientation but for sexual activity that affected the work negatively (Aydın 2006). Similarly, an investigation was opened against an allegedly gay professor at Tunceli University on account that he had homosexual intercourse with some of his students in exchange for higher grades. With an official declaration, Tunceli Education and Science Workers Union summarized the basis of the investigation as the professor's exploitation of the hierarchical relationship between him and his students.

In several court decisions, "sexual orientation" has been explicitly mentioned among the grounds to be protected against discrimination (Anayasa 2014a, 2014b, 2015). Also overriding the identitarian claim, the Constitutional Court ruled that the category of hate speeches includes labeling any sexual orientation as "perversion" (Anayasa 2014c). These arguments were based on a wide array of national and international sources, such as the fundamental principles of the Constitution of 1982 (i.e., Articles 10, 13, 20), the European Convention on Human Rights (i.e., Articles 8, 14), more than 50 ECtHR decisions concerning "sexual orientation," the International Covenant on Civil and Political Rights (i.e., Articles 2, 26), the interpretations of the UN Human Rights Council, and the general comments of the Committee on Economic, Social and Cultural Rights (i.e., Comments 14, 15, 18).

Bypassing the legal jargon mentioned above, a breach of the secretive claim risks poisoning relations at the workplace. Given that the courts reject the cases based merely on the identitarian claim, some LGBT-hostile administrations began re-framing their arguments around incidents. Therefore, many ongoing cases have revolved around incidents (e.g., acting as LGBT) instead of identities (e.g., being LGBT). Among them are (1) the soldiers who were dismissed from the military due to being involved in "unnatural sexual intercourse" (tr. gayri tabii mukarenet), (2) the four municipal workers who were fired for having homosexual intercourse in their off-hours, and for the same reason, (3) the two workers who were dismissed from the credit and dormitories institution. In short, the secretive claim expects one to consent that one can work as an LGBT person only if they do not get caught "in action."

Breaching the secretive claim had grave consequences for many. For example, a teacher who offered homosexual intercourse to the school janitor was fired due to his "unchastity." Upon the teacher's appeal, the Constitutional Court concluded that he could not return to his teaching position because he "carelessly" publicized the elements of his sexual life (Anayasa 2017). In another case, a police officer was first fined and then fired due to uncovering his sexual orientation, which, contrary to the teacher mentioned above, he did not publicize himself. His account of the disciplinary fine imposed on him was as follows:

> The inspectors told me, "we know that homosexuality does not happen after birth. Allah created you this way[7] [...] [But] we will downgrade you [...] Otherwise, some people might try to dismiss you later. We make this endeavor for you." [They said it] but this is a sham fight [tr. danışıklı dövüş]. The same things happened to all the friends who have been dismissed.
>
> (Karakaş 2014)

The officer was not fired straightforwardly since, in this case, the court would have to return him to his former position due to his clear disciplinary record. Instead, before dismissing him, the inspectors penalized him on the basis that his gay identity became an action. On this ground, his application to the administrative court was also rejected. In these two decisions, the courts also concluded that the teaching and law enforcement institutions require more strict limitations on employees' privacy.

Consequently, surveillance has become a weapon in the hands of rival factions at these institutions. In 2010, numerous unsigned reports mentioned

68   LGBT and the Entertainment Sector

a group of Naval Academy students engaging in homosexual activity. Considering them a conspiracy, Türker Ertürk, the Commander of the Academy, refused to investigate these reports (Akkaya 2010; Dağlar 2010). These reports were made public when the military institutions were under heavy pressure from politically driven legal cases, namely *Ergenekon* and *Sledgehammer*. Within this context, the media channels of the then pro-investigation coalition, *Akit*'s *Habervaktim* and the Gülen Movement's *Zaman* Website, published accompanying private documents about these soldiers they marked as "immoral," "pro-coup," and "irreligious" ("LGBTT" 2010). Some years later, Türker Ertürk talked to the *Akit TV* members who had initially accused Ertürk but then turned against the Gülen movement:

> After we checked these students' academic and social standings, we noticed that they were our best students [...] The aim [of the reporters] was clear: it was a purge [led by the Gülenists].
>
> ("Ankebut" 2019)

Ertürk underlined that they fired a student who was involved in homosexual activity. However, having considered the report that it was not an individual case but one that relates to the whole group of 40 students, Ertürk did not allow further investigation into who is gay: "I will not ask, and I will not let anyone ask that kind of a question to my students."

What ultimately determines the repercussions of such identities, orientations, or behaviors is the dialogue between administrators and employees. During a conference on the limits of LGBT visibility, a public employee at the Ministry of Culture recalled her experience of sharing her sexual orientation at the office: "everybody remained silent, and the subject was never opened again" (Öztop 2009:28). Depending on one's take on this dialogue, the attitude of the colleagues was either non-recognition or tolerance through ignoring. In any case, it was less troubling than facing dismissal. At least, those like Mine who, sometime in the mid-1990s, lost her accountancy job due to her lesbian identity make this argument: "when I look at the situation now, [I think] the ones [that came after us] are so comfortable" ("Ve hayat" 2013:48–49).

In conclusion, the LGBT-hostile identitarian claim has lost ground in legal interpretations. Nonetheless, the courts continue to rely on administrative disciplinary actions to measure the potentially negative impact of sexual activity on one's work. Therefore, depending on the branch of the public sector in which they work and the communicative possibilities they have, the public employees align their merit-based and secretive qualities differently. The accompanying surveillance environment leads to a conspiratorial climate in the bureaucracy, damaging the institutions. In the next part, I will examine how the visibility of LGBT identity has been negotiated in the entertainment sector. It is not only the sector that has traditionally been the most tolerant of all towards LGBT employees, but also the sector that demonstrates how LGBT people may clash with one another in terms of approaching an authoritative claim.

Flags and Identity Cards: The Visible Representations of LGBT Entertainers

The following exploratory conversations include the recent cases of (in)tolerance within the landscape of the entertainment sector. As AKP gradually dominated the authoritative institutions of the industry, many commentators argued that this domination on the part of "Islamists" would lead to some unprecedentedly severe restrictions against LGBT people. This part suggests that this argument needs refinement. Accordingly, I argue that the AKP government tends to restrict only the representations it finds critical of its political establishment. These binding representations primarily consisted of the 'flag-carriers' of LGBT, who followed an explicit politics of recognition that consciously challenged the hierarchical implications of tolerance. On the other hand, those others who personalized or 'theatrically' obscured their visible representations of LGBT could combine the tolerance of the authoritative institutions with a unique politics of recognition, albeit limited by their individual identities. However, they could find a balance between tolerance and recognition only by negotiating periodically re-adjusted tolerance prerequisites with authority.

Firstly, I will elaborate on the difference between the concerts of the Boston Gay Men's Chorus and Elton John. While the former faced the authority's gaze, the latter passed the scene pretty much unnoticed. In this context, I will demonstrate how the selective perception of the authority relies on the proactive discourse of the other. Then, I will assess how the personalized or *theatrically obscured* visible representations of LGBT settle in the sector as the "tolerable" ones. With this aim, the section contrasts the visibilities of critical figures, such as *Fatih Ürek, Huysuz Virjin, VJ Bülent, Kerimcan Durmaz, Nil Makaracı,* and the *Avlu TV* series, *among others.* In particular, I will distinguish between the voices openly critical of the establishment versus those that send subtly critical or explicitly laudatory messages to these institutions.

Boston Gay Men's Chorus versus Elton John

I take the Istanbul concert of the Boston Gay Men's Chorus as a key example of the contrast between the intolerable and tolerable visible representations of LGBT identity. In response to the Chorus, which declared itself "the first gay chorus to perform across the Middle East" ("2015 Middle East Tour" 2015), some newspapers, such as *Yeni Şafak, Yeni Akit,* and *Vahdet,* launched a campaign against the event. The campaign underlined that the program opposes the "values," "history," and the "culture" of the society. It would be provocative in "a Muslim country," especially "during the month of Ramadan," they argued ("PSM'deki" 2015). The problem for *Group*

70 LGBT and the Entertainment Sector

Zorlu, the organizer of the concert, was its reputation in the watchful eyes of the Erdoğan government it relied on for the bulk of its businesses. As a result, Zorlu contacted the Chorus to inform them about some new conditions. According to these conditions, which the Chorus later publicized, the concert was not to take place during Ramadan. Moreover, the Chorus would have to drop "Gay" from its title ("İptal edilen" 2015).

At least because appearing as the "Boston Men's Chorus" would not sound as fascinating, the Chorus members refused these conditions. Eventually, Zorlu terminated the contract at the expense of a significant amount of compensation. Later, the Chorus accepted another invitation from Boğaziçi University LGBTI Group for a free concert on the day the Zorlu concert was initially scheduled. Although the financial supporter of this "immoral" activity was searched for by the likes of Director Ihsan Karaman of Medeniyet University ("M. İhsan Karaman on Twitter [1]" 2015), it became clear later that the organization was made possible by the compensation fee Zorlu would have to pay. The following address of İhsan Karaman was to the followers of Boğaziçi University: "say NO to the gay concert at Boğaziçi!" ("M. İhsan Karaman on Twitter [2]" 2015). Karaman's call mobilized a group of students from Boğaziçi University. Having made the argument that Islam forbids interference with anyone's privacy, they described what they opposed as the visibility of the Chorus in "the public space" ("Boğaziçi'li" 2015). With a similar claim on the public space, Karaman stressed that he did not intend to target any gay individual in their privacy: "Personally, I can only pray for them to recover from this disease" ("Boğaziçi" 2015). Eventually, the concert took place. However, because it happened without a clear rationalization of tolerance, it did not give comfort to potential organizers of future similar events.

A key question in this context is what kind of activities may be deemed similar to this one. The selective perception of the pro-cancellation campaign was based on its obsession with the label "gay" as a standalone marker of collective identity. Just as the authorities have been intolerant bothering the appearance of LGBT flags on Taksim Square—i.e., "the heart of Istanbul" ("Bülent Arınç" 2015), they considered the marker "gay" to be existentially dangerous for the ascendancy of their values. Including potentially aggressive groups, many reproduced this claim during the 2022 Pride Parade, with anti-LGBT demonstrations being held to reclaim dominance over the public space. Nevertheless, this act of grabbing corners, by definition, rests on selective perception. Therefore, when nobody pressed their buttons, these groups did not pay attention to previous events of well-known gay artists, such as Elton John and George Michael, as these artists did not appear only and explicitly as "gay" in their announcements. At least by not carrying a flag in the name of LGBT, many well-known Turkish LGBT people, from the self-identified conservative gay fashion designer Cemil Ipekçi to the trans diva Bülent Ersoy, have secured their places in the entertainment sector.

For the same reason, the authorities did not pay attention to the broadcasting of *Avlu*, an adaptation of the famous American web-TV series, *Orange is the New Black*, exploring, among other things, lesbian relationships in a women's prison. However, actress Nil Makaracı was dismissed from this project by the time she, as a self-declared lesbian, explicitly marked the series as an LGBT-friendly one. After her dismissal, Makaracı reported what the producer told her:

> They say, "you talked to the LGBTs, shared photos [and] wrote something about lesbianness. I told you not to talk about this matter."
>
> (Salik 2018)

According to Makaracı, the markers of LGBT were already apparent in the project, from the short hair of the characters to the selection of a women's prison as the central place where the story takes place ("Nil" 2018). Makaracı did not distinguish between producing an explicit discourse and putting on display images without a clear sub-text. The latter would be obscure, fluid, and unfinalizable.

These cases shed light on the reason behind the problematization of the Boston Gay Men's Chorus concert. Contrary to the manifestoes of adversaries that like to imagine timeless rivalries, the authoritative claim arose after it was declared—collectively by the official account of the Chorus and then the Turkish media—that a chorus with the word "gay" in its title would have its first concert, interchangeably in "the Muslim world" or "the Middle East" at "the month of Ramadan." These keywords denoted an intersubjectively shared remoteness. The narrative was meant to do more than challenge the authority; before that episode, it was meant to consolidate some babble of voices into a semiotically coherent, self-conscious authority. It brought the authority to light to deconstruct it.

Theatrically Obscured Visible Representations

Turkey has had many trans artists labeled "the first trans star." It is because, on the one hand, it is always sensational to be the "first" in the sector, and on the other hand, their identities were somehow re-adjusted in the course of their careers. Contrary to the experience of the Boston Gay Men's Chorus, the entertainment sector represents more of a landscape of tolerance than any other. Accordingly, the most tolerable visible representations of LGBT identity appear as singers, makeup models, dancers, showpeople, publicity agents, or fashion designers. Those professions, primarily aimed at entertaining customers, have been considered "gay jobs." Therefore, the entertainment sector remains ideal for LGBT people who settled for this stereotyped visible representation. However, in order to maintain their positions as objects of tolerance, these entertainers must re-adjust their performances periodically according to the authoritative feedback they receive. Recently, some have begun to refuse to comply with some of the commands, whereas the other great pretenders continue to dance with authority.

72   LGBT and the Entertainment Sector

After many years of stereotypically "feminine" performance (e.g., low-neck, slim-fit, and transparent dresses, a stereotypically feminine body posture, and hand gestures), Fatih Ürek appeared in his next project as a stereotypical 'masculine' man (e.g., formal suit and full-beard in a macho posture). This man was bored with "geisha" women's submissive attitudes ("Fatih Ürek'i" 2009). Çiğdem Sonkurt, his image-maker for the project, stated that Ürek himself proposed the main idea. According to Ürek, all these appearances meant nothing other than different theatrical roles he undertook based on customers' demands.

On the flip side, even in this moment of traditional masculinity, he did not hesitate to associate his appearance with those whom one may classify in the gay club: "they say I look like Elton John" ("En harbi" 2008). Ürek's visibility relied on this obscure depiction of his identity, which he often revealed but never decisively confirmed. Complementary sources from this period suggest that Ürek was negotiating his visibility with the Radio and Television Supreme Council (RTÜK) and the state-led Turkish Radio Television (TRT). The period in which he changed his appearance was also one in which RTÜK began fining some popular TV programs more heavily for the appearance of their participants. This was especially the case for programs that included "bad" role models for children.

Concurrently, in 2007, Seyfi Dursunoğlu's seasoned performances as a zenne[8] (en. drag-queen) named *Huysuz Virjin*, were eventually removed from TV on the basis that he was wearing women's clothes and making obscene jokes ("RTÜK'ten" 2007). In the following years, he was supposed to act as *Seyfi* instead of *Huysuz* to take part in advertisements (Eyüboğlu 2007). Moreover, known for his "feminine" acts very similar to those of Fatih Ürek, the singer Aydın had to end his TV program in 2008 (Çağlayan 2015). Meanwhile, actor Tuğrul Tülek declared that he was fired from his position at TRT's channel for children, *TRT Çocuk*, on the basis that he acted as "a gay man" on a TV series at *Kanal D* ("Gay karakteri" 2010). The famous video jockey of *Kral TV*, VJ Bülent, was fired because he did not follow the "advice" of the managers to grow a beard to mask his sexual orientation. He later declared that he sacrificed his job to keep his free will: "Probably I am hairier than everybody else, but I had to tell [them] that I have no beard" (Avşar 2009).

This context of pressure reveals the difference between Ürek and others mentioned above. Also suffering from this climate of censorship, Ürek questioned during a conversation on *Star TV* why *TRT* was not showing his activities:

> I do not understand why I do not appear on TRT. I want to know which standards I do not fit into. [I want to know] why they think I am dangerous [...] I work in this country; I pay my taxes!
>
> ("Fatih Ürek" 2009)

Contrary to VJ Bülent, Ürek looked for the authority to negotiate its rules of appropriateness with him. By wearing a veil of ignorance, Ürek made clear that he did not intend to challenge the power but to learn the conditions under which it would tolerate his visibility.

Therefore, Fatih Ürek could continue to participate in the traditional mass media by keeping an eye on the periodically re-negotiated limits, unlike Seyfi Dursunoğlu, who, as an artist that already "hung up his boots" (Ulusum 2016), continued to criticize the authoritative claims on his appearance. In 2018, with his popular TV show on *Kanal D*, Ürek won the best morning-show award in the 45th *Pantene Golden Butterfly Awards.* Meanwhile, he managed to carry on with the fluidity of his performative acts. He kept moving back and forth between "gay" and "masculine" men— or maybe some altogether different social types that the narrow-minded observers missed. Some commentators tried to understand why Ürek occasionally returned to his "garish" femininity during this period ("Fatih Ürek imajını" 2015). A commentator, Melis Alphan, expressed this confusion with a question (Alphan 2016): "Does everybody eventually return to one's essence?" Before everyone else, one of the first image-makers of Ürek was puzzled about his unstoppable shifts: "I do not understand why he returned to his previous appearance" ("Fatih neden" 2008).

Contrary to Alphan's wording of the question, Ürek's activity conveyed the message that gender is not a matter of essence but, as Bayramoğlu (2009) read through Judith Butler's terms, an imitation of the enforced social conventions. Ürek's approach to gender was very different from that of, for example, Rüzgar Erkoçlar, who had sex reassignment surgery after attaining popularity as a woman actress. Unlike Ürek's continuously fluid gender performances, Erkoçlar directly embraced a stereotypical man's vocabulary after his sex reassignment—e.g., "one should not trust women" ("Rüzgar" 2017). Even though Ürek's gay identity is well-known, his visible representation remains fluid, such that he publicizes his desire to be a "father," and in the following speech act, he describes his identity as "asexual" and "nongendered" ("Fatih Ürek'ten" 2016).

Although, like Ürek, Aydın tried to perform "the masculine man" in some of his newer projects, he had to end his TV career. Instead of the intolerance of any cultural claim-owner, however, this outcome was primarily due to Aydın's gradually decreased market value ("Kuşum Aydın" 2018). His followers in the mainstream media did not appreciate his new appearance. Although meeting the conditions of tolerance seems to be a necessary condition to enter the market, it is not a sufficient condition to succeed in it. In this case, the cultural authority acts as the sieve, which one should pass through before facing the authority of the market. On the flip side, the actors have to align what may attract the attention of a target population with the cultural boundary of tolerable attractions.

Market and Culture: The Case of Acun Ilıcalı

There is a compromising relationship between the authoritative claims in the name of the culture and the market. This entanglement often brings

74   LGBT and the Entertainment Sector

these fields' gatekeepers together. In the entertainment sector, Acun Ilıcalı, the owner of the relatively new "entertainment TV" named TV8, and the most steadily rising media icon of the AKP-era, coupled his success in getting high ratings with his special ties with Erdoğan. Despite voting for him openly, Ilıcalı described his relationship with Erdoğan as a personal one rather than a political one:

> He likes me a lot. I like him a lot too [...] we see each other a few times a year. I sometimes ask for his opinion.
>
> ("Acun Ilıcalı" 2011)

Exceptionally, TV8 stopped its dance show on the day President Erdoğan's mother, Tenzile Erdoğan, passed away.

Having been approached on the matter repeatedly, Ilıcalı argued that he did not get any reward for being close to Erdoğan. He said, "they treat all TV channels equally" (CNN Türk 2018). Moreover, the records suggest that TV8 stands at the top regarding RTÜK's fines. As a matter of fact, RTÜK heavily fined TV8 due to the clothes of a group of children who participated in the dance show mentioned above. It was also fined for the appearance of a belly dancer after a whirling dervish due to the sequence's "incompatibility with the values of the society" ("Acun Ilıcalı'ya" 2016). For the same reason, the talent show on TV8 was fined because of a participant's use of the phrase "Allah Baba," God the Father.

In his argument, however, Ilıcalı overlooked the point that RTÜK's symbolic significance does not lie in the amount of its fines but in its claim of legitimacy behind these fines. Ilıcalı never put into doubt RTÜK's legitimacy, but for the sake of high ratings, he *mistakenly* breached RTÜK's rules on an occasional basis. Being treated "equally," he readily complied with these imposed rules of appropriateness. Previously, when Ilıcalı's show on STAR TV was fined, he reportedly visited RTÜK to negotiate the decision with the board members ("Acun rekor" 2013). Stressing that the producers should take into account "these rules" set by the regulatory institutions, he agreed with the criticism that some dancers' clothes were too "sexy" and "erotic" in the dance show on TV8: "[We] should address people without pushing the boundaries" ("Acun Ilıcalı" 2011:par14). Upon the question of why the music show on TV8 never included a Kurdish song, Ilıcalı admitted that they deliberately prevented it since "our shows [...] should be distanced to these controversial subjects" ("Acun Ilıcalı" 2011:par15). Unlike other mass TV channels, Ilıcalı's TV8 also dodged such controversial subjects by not broadcasting any news.

Striving to Be Tolerated: The Case of Kerimcan Durmaz

Having accepted the legitimacy behind "these rules," Ilıcalı led several projects that included some visible representations of LGBT. Accordingly, Ilıcalı shares a notion of common sense: customers want to see LGBT people

LGBT and the Entertainment Sector   75

on their screens, but not as teachers, doctors, lawyers, or police officers.[9] For example, since the establishment of the first private channels, trans people appeared on TV series predominantly in the form of hitchhiking sex workers ("Medyanın Lanetlileri: İlkim" 2013:267). As the received wisdom allows, Kerimcan Durmaz, whose appearance contradicts the heteronormative stereotypes about men—e.g., men's distaste for eyebrow plucking, make-up, and plastic surgery—turned out to be a popular figure as a jury member in a fashion show on TV8. As of 2017, Durmaz not only reached more than 2 million Instagram followers but also began earning a monthly income of nearly 500,000 Turkish Liras ("Kerimcan Durmaz'ın" 2017)—i.e., some ten times more than that of a senior engineer.

Like many other carriers of this identity in the entertainment sector, Durmaz was careful with the given boundaries. He re-adjusted his visibility several times during his career to appease the authorities. He even stopped spreading the videos of his "twerk" dance, which he initially became famous for:

[T]werk is now [associated with] eroticism... I do not have such a life.
(Gence 2017:par2)

When the interviewer asked what had changed in the meantime, Durmaz concluded that one must "get a grip on oneself in order to live in this country" (Gence 2017:par3), which may be an inappropriate statement to overtly articulate. Regarding his articulations, Durmaz was constantly guided, and sometimes warned by his more experienced forerunners. For example, Fatih Ürek reproached Durmaz on account that he had not been careful enough in public (Oktay 2017): "I [repeatedly] tell him, 'a few words that may come out of your mouth will sink you!'"

After a mob attacked him in the city of Samsun, Durmaz was careful enough to avoid politicizing the attack as a matter of LGBT visibility. He did not generalize the attack as a representation of "homophobia" or any other concept prioritized in the repertoire of LGBT activism. Instead, following the incident, Durmaz disappeared for several weeks. In response to the speculations, he declared that he moved to Milano for a couple of weeks to recover psychologically. While explaining what hurt his mental health, he did not place the blame on the justice system, heteronormative social codes, or the conservative identity of the inhabitants of the Black Sea region. Instead, he blamed the aggressors for their misrepresentation of the public values ("Kerimcan Durmaz Samsun'daki" 2016). In his later summary of the attack, Durmaz mentioned how some people were jealous of his success. Alongside his success, thanks partly to the depoliticizing way he handled this attack, he could keep up with his music and fashion shows at nightclubs and on TVs.

Every mistake Kerimcan made against authority required a new concession to the notion of shared values. In the summer of 2019, Durmaz made a mistake by pushing the wrong button and uploading his masturbation

76 LGBT and the Entertainment Sector

video on Instagram. He was quick enough to declare that it was a grave mistake that taught him "the importance of the concept of family" (Magazin Burada 2019). Although he did not elaborate on how the incident was about family, this statement was yet another representation of Durmaz's negotiation with conservatism.

Islamism's Implicit Tolerance

On one of these days that the police tear-gassed the participants of the LGBT Pride Parade (i.e., 2016 Summer), President Tayyip Erdoğan and his wife Emine Erdoğan were to have dinner with the famous "trans diva," Bülent Ersoy. Undoubtedly, Bülent Ersoy had many different stories, statuses, and identities, but this particular context has led to cherry-picking her very well-known transgender background. Many have inferred a contradiction between, on the one hand, the ideology of Erdoğan's political regime, which interfered with an LGBT parade for the sake of "public decency," and on the other hand, Erdoğan's choice to share the same table with Ersoy during the *iftar* of a Ramadan day.

Erdoğan's choice was not necessarily an ideologically minded act unless the supporters of the LGBT parade ideologized it for their Islamist interlocutors. In this context, their questions relied on an intersubjectively shared sense of incompatibility. The interlocutors share some sense of contradiction since they are not ignorant of each other's ideological repertoires. On this matter, Islamism's repertoire is so well-known that even the conductors of value surveys have been afraid to ask questions on sexuality in "Islamic Societies" (Inglehart and Welzel 2005). Before asking their interlocutors to explain what was different between Ersoy and the participants in the LGBT Pride parade, the critics surely knew that it was not unsurprising for a person who talks in the name of Islamism to perceive some incoherence in Bülent Ersoy's valued position within the government circles.

Here came the in-group contestations: when Ersoy wore a headscarf for her TV show's program on the Night of Destiny,[10] anchorman Erkan Tan of Beyaz TV reproached "the religious and conservatives" from within their group:

> This is really enough [...] [for] conservatives. I do not tell you to condemn [Ersoy], but at least do not applaud this! By applauding, you make it legitimate and reasonable [...] There is a verse in the Quran about her situation, but neither does the Diyanet nor the leaders talk about it! I cannot believe it is only me who is saying these words.
>
> (Beyaz TV 2014)

Various circles in the media disputed Ersoy's ties with the "conservative democratic" government several times. However, Erdoğan has not stepped back. In Erdoğan's speeches, Ersoy was an alternative role model against

LGBT and the Entertainment Sector 77

the artists who participated in the Gezi Protests. This appreciation suggests that she could convince others of the variety of her identities over decades. Among other identities, her religious personality was stressed by her emotional reciting of the call for prayer. She declared that she prays five times a day, visits shrines, fasts openly during Ramadan, and promises that she will bequeath half of her estate to the Turkish Religious Foundation (tr. Türk Diyanet Vakfı). In the process, Ersoy could frequently attend the Ramadan meetings that the government organized.

While the opposition media channels were disputing the dinner, Erdoğan preferred not to talk about the matter. Nevertheless, the hardliners had to develop an account of this case to rationalize Erdoğan's act. Mahmut Övür defended it as a sign that Erdoğan's Turkey would be "Everybody's Turkey" (Övür 2014). Daily Sabah, the English-speaking edition of Sabah, described Ersoy as "a symbol for the increased tolerance for LGBT figures in Turkey over the years" ("Transsexual singer" 2016). This explanation not only puzzled the participants in the parade but also bewildered some of those pro-government ideologues that have been supporting Erdoğan for his religious conservatism. Among them, *Habervaktim* approached the interpretation of Daily Sabah with a grain of salt: "it is remarkable how Daily Sabah especially emphasized Ersoy's transsexuality" ("Daily Sabah'tan" 2016). The problem for *Habervaktim* did not seem to be that "a transsexual" was invited to the iftar organization. Instead, the problem was that Ersoy was labeled as "a transsexual" by Daily Sabah. Although of the Islamist newspapers, *Yeni Akit* remained the most distanced from Ersoy, even this newspaper defended Ersoy against the "obsession" of her left-wing critics, such as Cumhuriyet Newspaper ("Cumhuriyet'in" 2018).

Like *Habervaktim*, many others consciously preferred not to see Ersoy as a "transsexual." In this context, seeing does not refer to the ability to discern visually but relates to the meaning-making processes after reflection. A journalist and the former spokesperson of Erdoğan's prime ministry, Akif Beki, underlined that Ersoy is "much more than a 'trans star'" (Beki 2016). This is one of those meritocratic claims that have become a competing argument in the public sector landscape. As an illustration of the fault line between Ersoy and others, Beki later expressed his frustration with the "LGBT propaganda" on Netflix (Beki 2019).

As these speech acts suggest, the primary way of justifying Erdoğan's action without falling into any ideological contradiction was by stressing that Ersoy is not *simply* a "transsexual." Alongside her fantastic career, which she began as a biological man and continued as a trans woman, Ersoy's management of her visible representation served as a source of rationalization for tolerance. Her dialogue with the authorities made it possible that, for example, Sabah Newspaper labeled her news of marriage as a disgrace. In contrast, on the very same day, ATV (owned by the same group) was to broadcast a movie in which Ersoy acted (Düzgören 1998). All in all, the tolerant Islamists prioritized Ersoy's other, more desirable markers of identity.

78   *LGBT and the Entertainment Sector*

Although the mainstream channels of Islamism are full of zero-tolerance manifestos against LGBT sexualities (Karaman 2017), it has become justifiable for many to implicitly tolerate an LGBT figure as long as one does not leave the moral ground that their hegemonic ideology prescribes. In this context, Özlem Albayrak from *Yeni Şafak,* which disperses the agenda of the mainstream current of Islamism, wrote that the "conservative" LGBT voters of AKP are more virtuous than those who vote for the party merely due to its neoliberal economic policies (Albayrak 2008a). After analyzing the "interestingly contradictory" personalities of Bülent Ersoy, Albayrak admitted that many citizens who appreciate Ersoy do not want to rent their houses to transgender people (Albayrak 2008b). Her solution to this hypocrisy was inconclusive because she was also frustrated by Ersoy's contradictions.

Professor Hayrettin Karaman, whose religious knowledge has been influential among government members, responded to a mail from a "Muslim homosexual" firstly by noting that his interlocutor seemed pious. Then, Karaman continued: "There are issues, events, attitudes, deficiencies, and possibilities that test everyone in this life" (Karaman n.d.). Then, he encouraged his interlocutor to be patient enough to refrain from homosexual intercourse, just as all other Muslims try to refrain from committing the sin of *zina* (en. adultery).

In due course, many preachers reiterate that one should not despise a Muslim LGBT person who is aware that they are in a test. Among the teachers in the Ismailağa religious community, Cübbeli Ahmet Hoca repeatedly preached that Islam commands one not to exclude any fellow believer for their sins. According to Ünlü, one can have a "neighborly" or a "friendly" relationship with an LGBT person as long as this person admits the religious boundaries:

> They are just like the normal society. Whatever your relationship is with those who commit adultery or take alcohol, it is the same [with LGBT]. You pay a visit to them to offer your condolences in times of death, to support in times of sickness, [...] bring food to their home [...] They are not lepers whom you should not get close to [...].
>
> (Flash TV 2013)

During another speech to a mosque community, Ünlü told a story that had allegedly taken place between "a taxi driver" and "a travesti." According to the report, the taxi driver, who was listening to Ünlü's speech on the radio, turned off the radio he realized that the passenger was "a travesti." Suddenly, the travesti got angry: "why have you turned it off?! Am I an infidel?!" ("Travesti anısı" 2016). The main point of this narrative, according to Ünlü, was that one must never despise another since nobody could ever know who would end up being a better Muslim at the end of the divine test. On the other hand, this call for tolerance merges with Ünlü's rationalization of intolerance against those LGBTs who refuse to see any shame in their status. In this context, Ünlü concludes that the border of tolerable diversity shall be drawn between the LGBT who admits one's sin and the LGBT that is proud to attend a public parade with an LGBT flag. The latter is not tolerable at all: "may Allah make them extinct!" (Ünlü 2017).

In the same vein, writer Ismail Kılıçarslan of the *Yeni Şafak* newspaper advised religious people to hate "the sins instead of the sinners." Until he saw the slogans and the placards, which he called purely Islamophobic, Kılıçarslan was against police intervention in the LGBT Pride parade. Harshly criticized by some of his followers for his tolerance, he reiterated what Emine Şenlikoğlu (2013) had been saying for many years: fellow believers should not exclude the LGBT "sinners" in order not to push these sinners to the "enemies of Islam" (Kılıçarslan 2015). With the latter, Kılıçarslan meant the organizers of the LGBT Pride parade. Therefore, Kılıçarslan is particularly interested in the changing approach to gender among conservative youth. One case is an Imam Hatip class in which half of the students are fanatics of the South Korean pop band, *BTS*, which symbolizes a non-gendered appearance (Kılıçarslan 2019). Having paid attention to similar developments, Diyanet encouraged its "spiritual advisors" in prisons and student dormitories not to discriminate against their advisees based on "sexual orientation" (Özgenç 2018).

In those eyes, the ideological stance of the parade and the perspective of the likes of Ersoy were fundamentally different, as the former seemed anti-religious in terms of method (i.e., uncompromising visibility) and rhetoric ("whose public morals?"). In this vein, Mevlüt Tezel from Sabah Newspaper appreciated Ersoy for distancing herself from the LGBT Pride parades while "being honest" about her sexual orientation (Tezel 2016). Erdoğan rationalized a conditional, negative tolerance:

> These radicals [tr. "marjinaller"] whom, we observe, come around from time to time on the streets of Beyoğlu as well [...] [if they] keep their propriety [tr. "edepleriyle durdukları sürece"], they can remain one of the colors of this country. But if they resort to pressure, aggression, violence, and intolerance [tr. tahammülsüzlük] against those who are not like them, sorry but [in this case] we will hold them by their ears and throw them where they belong.
>
> ("Erdoğan: Beyoğlu'ndaki" 2018)

According to this authoritative position, the participants in the parade represented themselves as a bunch of LGBT people, contrary to Ersoy's multidimensional visible representation. Therefore, the authority was unwilling to open any room that would normalize their visibility. Despite not normalizing them, it opened a limited and surrounded space for their existence: the courts have not closed the LGBT associations on the precondition that they will not "encourage homosexuality." This precondition was a funny

80   *LGBT and the Entertainment Sector*

misapprehension before a threat to LGBT associations, given that they do not see sexual orientation as a matter of persuasion.

The want-to-be authority has not (yet) "thrown them where they belong." This decision may naïvely be considered a result of the pluralist convictions of the government. Alternatively, based on its populist record, the decision may have stemmed from a calculation about the negative public image of LGBT activism. According to this calculation, the visibility of LGBT activists will decrease the widespread support for AKP's main opposition. Following the conclusive victory of Erdoğan in his claim on being the authority, a more-extensive purge would be imaginable. Intolerance has already defined this relationship, given that the government's desire to tolerate receives a negative response from the activists. Plain and simple, activism in this context means opposing any form of tolerance. On the contrary, activists have many things to say against the normative ruling order tolerance rests on.

Appearing as Other in "This Culture"

> If the people, who pave the way for all these [bad] experiences [of transgender individuals], see me as a fantastic [character]; if they designate me, make me feel my monstrosity [tr. ucubeliğimi] and wretchedness [tr. zavallılığımı]; if they approach to me abhorringly, [...] then, indeed, I must be the queen of this fantastic world. Then I will be the goddess of beauty, the queen, the princess, the duchess, the madam, Aphrodite. You are already not giving me another chance.
>
> (Gani Met 2012: 33–36)

In her evaluation, Gani Met describes how she ended up being herself. Her experience includes imprisonment in sex work and an obligation to fit into certain stereotypical forms of being travesti. In the face of these constraints, she admittedly resigned herself to the performative roles imposed on her identity by the authorities. Despite having suspicions as to whether she can be called an activist (Kılıçkaya 2011:16), Gani Met found her own ways to challenge the authorities that deny seeing her as a woman:

> Then, on the streets, I will shout at your face "ayol abla…ayol abla"[11] in a manner to multiply the behaviors specific to women with 3, so that [my performance] reaches a fantastic level.

Dealing with men who aim to prove their "manliness" to sex workers, she explains how she copes daily with violence. She criticizes many who ignore her experience, including some "activist individuals that talk and write nonsense" without paying attention to what transgender individuals feel under the given constraints. Finally, she calls on others to learn that "travesties and transsexuals" are at the bottom of the hierarchy, even in the LGBT community.

As the variety of outcomes in the entertainment and public sectors demonstrate, the contestation has not just been one of LGBT versus others. On the contrary, it has been primarily between the divergent expressions of being LGBT. From Ersoy to the hijabi transgender people living in the so-called ultra-conservative Keçiören district of Ankara, some *sui generis* visible representations of LGBT seem to have fitted into the repertoire of Islamism. Based on these divergent takes on the visibility of LGBT, this part analyzes a series of retroactive conversations. Accordingly, I argue that the disagreements are no longer centered on what LGBT stands for but on what it should be against. Some crystallized disputes regarding this issue of contention render the "LGBT community" less cohesive than ever. Therefore, the identity-building processes have inevitably become target-centered rather than subject-centered.

In 2010, "a gay man" wrote an open letter in reaction to Bülent Ersoy: "if Ersoy had been defending gay rights for 35 years, we would not be in a miserable situation today" ("Bülent Ersoy'a" 2010). After the marriage of Bülent Ersoy, writer Can Çavuşoğlu (2014) asked why it would be necessary for gay people to undergo a physical operation to marry: "if it is available for Ersoy, why not available for us?" Despite having won her own recognition struggles, firstly for a pink identity card—i.e., the card for legally recognized women—and secondly for trans individuals' right to marry, Ersoy did not develop a far-reaching vocabulary of activism on behalf of a broader LGBT community.

Her sharing of the same photo frames with the right-wing leaders, from Özal to Erdoğan, has damaged Ersoy's image among many activists whose organizations have been speaking in the name of left-wing ideologies. Journalist Michelle Demisevich, also a seasoned LGBT activist, suggested that Erdoğan would never have dinner with a trans other than Ersoy: "they have something in common—they are both rulers in their own domains" (Arman 2016). Esmeray, who, after five years of sex work, became a vendor of stuffed mussels and a stand-up comedian, made the nuclear claim: "Bülent Ersoy is transsexual up to the extent that Michael Jackson is black" (Öğünç 2007a).

Alternative Politics of Recognition

As a memory of appreciation or ingratitude, Ersoy affected all imaginations of the community by fighting for her own recognition. Many trans women like Asya Özgür dislike Ersoy because she ignores "her fellow beings." Meanwhile, it is doubtful whether Ersoy sees her trans background as a public identity. Only in this case could it have been voiced in reference to a larger community. She was already very famous when she decided on her sex reassignment. Therefore, she admitted that it would be a significant subject in the country.[12] Her medical record and well-publicized efforts to redefine her clothing, voice, and language in the aftermath of the operation made her a "trans" in the eyes of the trans communities. However, she

82   LGBT and the Entertainment Sector

never associated her own identity with any publicly shared label. She did not participate in any in-group debates over the title "LGBT." If she had a decades-long effort for a public identity, it was an effort to be known as a conservative, upper-class Ottoman woman (Altınay 2008:219). Ersoy was the crystal-clear illustration of the in-group cleavage: "what we name as *we* is not one-piece" (Öğünç 2007a, 2007b:38).

Though the LGBT associations have criticized her for not saying a single word in favor of their struggle, Ersoy raised her voice for recognition by developing a delicate way of doing so. As Ertur and Lebow (2014:3) put it eloquently, she "destabilized categories, both real and textual." In the aftermath of her sex reassignment in 1981, she was subject to harsh criticism. This spotlight effect resulted in two short-term prison sentences: one for insulting a judge and one for attacking a journalist. In this period, Ersoy attended some court hearings and public interviews with her new skirts and high-heel shoes. In an interview, Ersoy noted that she was so happy to be put into the women's ward that she almost forgot that she had been sentenced ("Bülent Ersoy hapishaneyi" 1982). When she wanted her "pink identity" as a part of her politics of recognition, the 2nd Chamber of the Court of Cassation rejected it with the following statement:

> It is not right to seek a solution on grounds of emotions, because the law [...] is intolerant [*tr.* müsamahasız] in case of mistakes. The desperation of a person who lost one's virility, yet could not become a woman, [should be] pitied by all. But no opportunities can be created by leaving aside the law.
>
> (Yargıtay 2. Daire 1986)

Judge Erdoğan Gökçe warned Ersoy's lawyer more bluntly ("Bülent Ersoy'un" 1982): "the rule *laissez faire laissez passer* does not apply here!" In June 1981, among other transgender artists of the time, the military leadership banned Ersoy from acting onstage ("Eşcinsel şarkıcıların" 1981). The ban lasted for seven years. Concerning these lost years, she asked (Capa 2017): "what can be more important than a person's freedom? Who will seek my rights?" Before all else, some LGBT—then "homosexual"—artists got angry with Ersoy, whom they criticized for intimidating the authorities ("Eşcinsel şarkıcılar" 1981; Kemal 1981; Som 1981). With the first legal arrangement concerning transgender people, Ersoy could acquire her pink card in 1988 thanks to another figure behind conservatism, President Turgut Özal (Will and Oztan 1993).

In the following decades, Ersoy did not refrain from seeking her rights in her unique methods. She sued those who used stereotypes about her gender identity, like singer Eylül Metin who called her "hepatitis B." She has been outspoken in the AKP era as well as in the past: when she declared for the first time that she voted for AKP, her main reason was the promise of the government to "take revenge from Kenan Evren," the head of the

LGBT and the Entertainment Sector   83

1980 military coup ("Bülent Ersoy intikam" 2012). At the time, her defense of AKP was not unconditional either. For instance, AKP's formerly leftist minister of culture, Ertuğrul Günay, described in 2009 how "confusing" the 1980s were:

> Bülent Ersoy was awarded as the best woman singer [...]; it was that kind of an absurd, dramatic, confusing period.

By describing Günay's words as "zealotry," Ersoy called him to resign from his ministerial post. She added:

> I would also like to remind the philosophy of Rumi: "come whoever you are."
>
> ("Bülent Ersoy, Ertuğrul" 2009)

The Rumi quotes, which have become autonomous from the literary debate over what Rumi actually meant, are used in contemporary Turkey to demand tolerance toward unorthodox ways of life. Ersoy's politics of recognition did not rule out the idea of tolerance.

Calling for tolerance with a Rumi quote is quite a contrast with calling for recognition with an LGBT parade. With this reference, Ersoy explicitly recognized the hierarchical position between the one to tolerate and the one to be tolerated, given that being able to say "come whoever you are" implies the power not to say it.[13] Connectedly, by directing this quote to those powerful ones in a position to welcome or threaten differences, the speaker also recognizes that her identity may be incompatible with some fundamentals. In this call for tolerance, the authority should accept the difference as long as it does not threaten the dominant value system.

For many years, Ersoy claimed that the visibility of people with different sexual orientations would never threaten the broader society *per se*. The threat within this context was defined by Ersoy as tempting others to question their sexual orientations:

> If I gave you trillions [...] and asked you to put yourself into this position, [...] would any heterosexual man attempt to do it? [...] If you pretend to be affected, it means that you carry these feelings inside.
>
> (Tulgar 2004)

Because the sexual orientation of a minority cannot put the dominant heteronormative structures in danger, these sexual orientations should be tolerated. In this call for tolerance, the one entitled to be tolerated would, in return, be supposed to come to terms with the "common values" in a way: "our common denominator is the existence of music."[14] Obviously, another commonality Ersoy considered was the religious repertoire. She commented openly about what would be a sin and a good deed; she repeatedly

84   *LGBT and the Entertainment Sector*

mentioned her fear of Allah; she prayed several times in public, and she broke her Ramadan fast on TV even though, on one occasion, it was not the right time for Istanbul ("Paris" 2007).

Alternative Approaches to "Common Values"

Her critics' defense of LGBT activism starkly contrasts Ersoy's position in approaching the notion of shared values and the hierarchy it implies. Kaos-GL asked a group of "trans activists" about Ersoy's publicized intention to bequeath her assets to the Turkish Religious Foundation (tr. Türk Diyanet Vakfı) (Güner 2014). In response, Tuna Şahin argued that Ersoy was in love with her murderer. Şahin added, "[Ersoy] confesses her sins because she is afraid of death."

Şahin's point that Ersoy was confessing her sins may have been grounded in a constant pressure Ersoy acknowledged. Ersoy stressed in an interview that she was afraid of death, firstly because she did not know whether people would speak about her sex reassignment or her music after her death. This is a fear that Ersoy says she developed in the aftermath of the death of an iconic drag queen, Zeki Müren: "they attacked him when he was not in a position to defend himself." Secondly, on a more transcendental level, Ersoy has constantly been suspicious of whether she sins (Capa 2017).

Suppose Ersoy shares the moral claims of the Turkish Religious Foundation, which unequivocally describes sex reassignment as a sin. In that case, it is possible to infer that Ersoy sees herself as a sinner. Within this context, Doğa Asi Çevik commented on Ersoy's decision: "this institution, which Ersoy feeds with money, will strengthen its LGBTphobia." Halil Kandok (2014), a blogger who wrote extensively on the problems of LGBT, questioned what Ersoy's act symbolizes: "does not it [i.e., Ersoy's testament] mean saying [...] you can curse us?"

This alternative expression either dismisses the existence of shared values or refuses to respect the dominant public values. Its primary aim is instead to construct a political agency against the otherwise untouchable, overriding narrative. Hayat Kırbaş, a sex worker who nicknamed herself "dishonorable," wrote in this vein:

> [...] where is my honor, who is honorable? [...] the honor did not employ us. I could not be a burglar either [...] SO, SHOULD I HAVE REMAINED HUNGRY? [*sic*] [...] I lost my honor, [and] I will not find it. I will not be the honor of anyone!
>
> (Kırbaş 2009:1)

Self-identifying with socially despised markers has become a common approach among LGBT activists. Kırbaş no longer looks for a relationship of tolerance, in which she may be tolerated at the expense of being condemned. Just like Kırbaş, the speakers in the Kaos-GL project mentioned

LGBT and the Entertainment Sector   85

above did not problematize their "shamelessness" in a social structure they opposed. With this aim in mind, many activists join or organize street protests with slogans that explicitly challenge the moral claims that they think nurture heteronormativity: "Gay-Trans hand in hand, towards the immoral revolution."[15] These elements should be fully publicized since the ruling homophobia, biphobia, and transphobia can be challenged only by facing and resisting them.

Ersoy's engagement with the notion of shared values often put her against LGBT activists. While using a consistently religious repertoire, Ersoy never tried to justify her sex reassignment in the name of Islam. Furthermore, she occasionally politicized her religious repertoire to position herself alongside the orthodoxy as opposed to the *other*. For example, after the assassination of the Armenian journalist, Hrant Dink, she reacted against those who made a campaign around the slogan "we are all Hrant, we are all Armenians." "I am the Muslim daughter of a Muslim family; I am not Armenian," Ersoy said. Those eager to reproduce this slogan quoted Ersoy numerous times, such that they would stop questioning, at least for once, whether she could have ever become a "daughter." When Ersoy was differentiating herself from Hrant Dink, the activists of *Pembe Hayat, Lambda-Istanbul,* and *Kaos-GL* were mourning Dink's loss.

Ersoy intermingled her deviance with her other, more acceptable or even desirable identities. She occasionally appeared as an "Ottoman" thanks to her musical and conversational performances. Often in tandem, she was a religious conservative. When some activists criticized her for wearing fur, she responded:

> Quran orders us to benefit from animals' meat, milk and skin [...] Who are these animal lovers?!
>
> ("Bülent Ersoy'dan Ömür" 2016)

However, above all, she acted as a woman with maternal sensibilities. Bouncing between these identities, she depicted an incoherent picture of herself, arguably as a sign of honesty. For example, she played the nationalist with her claim to not being an Armenian. Still, after a while, her motherhood prevailed over her nationalism when a group of soldiers returned dead or wounded from the military operations in South-East Turkey. At this emotional moment, she declared that she would not send her son to the military service if she had one. In response, the then minister, Binali Yıldırım, mocked Ersoy with a smile: "No worries, there is no such possibility" (Selvi 2008).

Alternatives for the Religious LGBT People

Even though Ersoy's stance seems uniquely individual at first glance, it would be a mistake to think that this moral position is an outlier among the many expressions of LGBT in Turkey. According to a local survey conducted

86 LGBT and the Entertainment Sector

with 116 transgender participants from Istanbul, 56% of these respondents recognized their identity as a "sin," and 39.7% reported that they thought at one point in their life that they would go to "the hell" ("İt iti ısırmaz" 2010:17–18).[16] Many of them had a moral consciousness that pushed them to find a balance between being an LGBT person and following a life in accordance with their beliefs, including their knowledge of religion. As a result, some move to atheism as they learn to lose the faith that curses them, whereas others deal with their sins through their unique ways of communicating with the divine rule as they see it (*see* Bereket and Adam 2008).

As an example of the latter, Utku Uysal, a famous "trans singer" of Istanbul nightlife, explained how she made her only mistake "against Allah":

> It was a religious mistake [...] it should not have happened, but it happened. I feel very good in the way I am [...] I asked the greatest Islamic scholars. They said that even a nose surgery would be a great sin [...], but we have our own will.
>
> (Sever 2010)

The argumentation is less unstable than it may seem at first glance. Uysal admits that her sex reassignment was wrong in religious terms but, at the same time, stresses that she is pleased with some other virtues that her sin brought. Uysal makes the distinction shared by most of the survey participants mentioned above: they believe they are sinners but do not accept that they are sick. Having uncovered the dissonance between being happy with the way she exists and feeling guilty about its religious consequences, Uysal explained why she does not want to have a sexual life anymore:

> [This is] because I believe that it is not right! [...] From now on, a little bit of work must be done for Allah.

As a trade-off, losing one's sexual life is a prerequisite for enjoying one's gender identity as a believer. Similarly, Mustafa, from the "Muslim homosexuals'" association called Meşcid, warned the LGBT associations: "to be a homosexual is not a preference, but to live a homosexual life is a preference" (Açıkgöz 2013). These two arguments were in unity with the previously discussed advice of Professor Hayrettin Karaman, who called for the LGBT "sinners" not to let their sexual desires push them to sin. Uysal's explanation is also very similar to that of Kerimcan Durmaz who, also as discussed before, removed his twerk videos from his social media accounts.

In his appearances after the attack, Kerimcan Durmaz made his moral position clear: he has put on display his appreciation of President Erdoğan his boss, Acun Ilıcalı ("Kerimcan Durmaz'dan" 2018). Durmaz declared that he prays, fasts, and reads Quran in his free time: "I won't let anybody say anything against my conservatism" ("Namaz kılıp" 2016). He underlined that he has a delicate "policy of morality," through which he keeps

LGBT and the Entertainment Sector 87

checking where to control his expressions. In response to a commentator who blamed him for playing around with society's values, Durmaz reacted ("Kerimcan Durmaz Canlı" 2018): "do not confuse me with the others [other LGBT people] on social media!"

In response to the critique that LGBT associations did not support Durmaz, Yunus Emre Demir explained why Kaos-GL would never defend "capitalism's rusted approach to art," which polishes the likes of Durmaz. According to Demir, Durmaz is nothing but a visible representation of obedience:

> Kerimcan will stand up [...] In the worst-case scenario, with the money he saved, he will stay in America for three months [...] But the issue is much greater than Kerimcan. The problem is the possibility that this _lubunya_ [en. Slang, passive male homosexual] waiter, who works where Kerimcan takes the stage, may be beaten and unable to stand up as easily as Kerimcan will do [...] Kerimcan's homosexuality does not make him one of us.
>
> (Demir 2016)

Demir emphasizes that the "conservative make-up" of Durmaz does not justify the attack against him. However, he concludes, they should defend the gayness of Durmaz, not only from the aggressors but also from the reactionary (tr. "gerici") capitalist system that Durmaz represents. Fashion designer Barbaros Şansal generalized the same argument:

> It is still almost impossible for two gays to hold their hands [...] on Istiklal Street. Hate killing and homophobia do not stop at all. But there is no problem if you are rich and famous with powerful friends.
>
> (Şansal 2014:52–53)

The subject-centered identity (e.g., the "LGBT Movement") misleadingly counted the likes of Durmaz in the group, alienating the non-LGBT defenders of the anti-capitalist and anti-heteronormative ideology. Therefore, the Kaos-GL team has begun defining their movement not as an LGBT movement but as a movement against homophobia, biphobia, and transphobia.

A famous friend of Durmaz from "Capitalism's rusted" entertainment sector, Selin Ciğerci, who had sex reassignment surgery, made public her morality statement similarly. In her explanation, Ciğerci mentioned her city of origin, Konya, which is known for its ultra-conservative outlook:

> I am from Konya. Just like them, I do not like wearing revealing clothes and exhibitionism. For this reason, women like me so much. Some mothers [...] write to me, "my child follows you. I did not initially let him/her do so, but then, I watched you as well, and I like you too."
>
> (Semercioğlu 2017)

88 *LGBT and the Entertainment Sector*

Emphasizing the same moral sensitivity, Nedim Uzun, a trans woman singer known as Madam Marika, harshly criticized the LGBT Pride parades and their organizers. In a spontaneous pop-up interview in the Beyoğlu district of Istanbul, Uzun explained the reason behind her defense of Erdoğan's restriction of the LGBT Pride parades:

> If you give lots of freedom, these transsexuals will go to Istiklal Street [i.e., a central location where LGBT Pride parades take place] and have sex there in public. Look at the Gay Pride marches; they open their breasts and arses [...] This is not the freedom I want. This is immoral.

While condemning them, Uzun also condemned her record. "Trans queen" Seyhan Soylu was probably the first to consider the idea of wandering naked in public so that she could become undeniably visible in the gaze of the authority ("Yılmaz'a" 1991). Some decades later, a group of activists put this idea into practice.

As "an Ottoman woman" like Ersoy, Nedim Uzun stressed that many of those who speak in the name of LGBT insult her during her concerts: "they ask me like, 'you are despised by [the AKP], how can you support them?'" Uzun claimed that she was beaten by a pro-CHP group just because she asked them if any president before Erdoğan ever had dinner with a "transsexual." She recalled: "I remember how the CHP members were running away from us!" Belgin, a trans sex worker on Abanoz Street in the 1970s, insisted on the same point: "Abanoz was closed for the first time under the rule of [CHP leader] Ecevit" ("80'lerde" 2012:70–71).

In one of her later speeches, Uzun declared that she became a member of "AK LGBT," formed by a group of LGBT people who sympathize with AKP. The interviewers on Ahsen TV very much appreciated Marika's moralist claims. The producers have become famous for their provocative approach during street interviews, pushing their interviewees to be convinced of the ascendancy of what they claim to be the rule of Islam. After Madam Marika finished her ten-minute-long speech with little interruption, the interviewer told her: "I really appreciate your attitude here!"

A couple of weeks before the Municipal Elections of 2019, Madam Marika and the LGBT activists she criticizes faced off again. A day after a TV debate in which the CHP candidate for the Beyoğlu Municipality (Istanbul) promised "equal rights" for the LGBT people, the presenter of this TV program, journalist Çağlar Cilara, had to resign from TV5—i.e., the TV channel of Saadet Party, which is the descendant of Refah Party. This resignation was forced by a campaign led by some AKP supporters who blamed the Saadet Party for "selling out" the Islamism of the Refah tradition. Interestingly, a week later, Madam Marika appeared as the announcer on the election stand of AKP in the Beyoğlu district. With another trans fellow,[17] she asked the citizens to vote for the AKP. Given that the AKP members on the stand let her talk, Çağlar Cilara reacted ("Çağlar" 2019): "why have you put me in trouble if you would do something like that?"

LGBT and the Entertainment Sector   89

Alternative Politics of Visibility

Without breaching the confines of "common values," Ersoy has defended the meritocratic claim in favor of LGBT people in her field of work. In the TV program *Popstar Alaturka*, Ersoy had a severe verbal conflict with her colleague, Ebru Gündeş, due to her identitarian claim, which led to the elimination of a possibly gay contestant:

ERSOY: If Allah gave him these feelings, what is it to you? Are we here to deal with what is below the contestants' belts?

GÜNDEŞ: He would have been a wrong role model for the Turkish society [...] It does not seem right to me, given that we have so many young people.

   [...]

ERSOY: You are a role model as well!

GÜNDEŞ: Yes, we are! [...] We are also role models with our good and bad behaviors.

ERSOY: Okay! So, everyone has characteristic features, some of which are to be taken as a guide, whereas others are not [...] That guy was treated unfairly here! [...] He was singing very well! Are you able to sleep well after refusing him?! [*yelling*]

GÜNDEŞ: Vallahi, I sleep very well.

ERSOY: How come you sleep well?! I cannot! [*throws the microphone away*] (Star TV 2006)

In this defense of the merit-based approach, Ersoy did not dismiss the concept of shared values. Instead, she argued that everyone has benevolent and malevolent features judged by shared values. Those who fulfill their tasks at their workplaces should not be dismissed due to potentially improper, secondary aspects of their personality.

This claim on meritocracy hints at an alternative politics of visibility as well. Accordingly, one may not put forward the markers of one's LGBT identity as a priority in the workplace, even if s/he does not hide them either. The contestant, whom Ersoy defends, did not limit his visibility, but at the same time, he exhibited other marks that closely relate to his work—e.g., "singing very well." His multivocal appearance made possible a conservative religious defense of his career. The way Ersoy defends this contestant merges with several in-group criticisms of the politics of uncompromising visibility.

A series of interviews conducted by Aysun Öner revealed that some LGBT employees consciously oppose forming a visible representation based on their sexualities or gender identity. For example, an interviewee, Bora, reproached fellow gays and lesbians who do not prioritize their expertise in their workplaces (Öner 2017:32). He emphasized that, otherwise, LGBT people would never be able to overcome minority pressure. This argument is not reducible to the secretive claim in the sense that it does not require an LGBT

90 *LGBT and the Entertainment Sector*

person to hide one's LGBTness. Instead, it calls for the LGBT person to be "professional enough" to not keep becoming visible based on the markers of this single identity. Concomitantly, the annual surveys of Kaos-GL suggest that many LGBT public employees think their jobs were described to them in gender-neutral terms. In other words, they did not notice any overt or covert criteria which may discourage LGBT people from applying (Göregenli 2018:17).

In a broader study, Öner examined the strategies through which LGBT employees cope with discrimination based on sexual orientation at their workplaces. In this context, she described a group of LGBT employees as indirectly open. According to the analysis, those indirectly open employees become visible as LGBT people only when they think a relevant subject is triggered in their conversations. In most other instances, they prefer not to expose any details of their "private" lives, within which they also tend to consider their sexualities and sexual orientations. Öner suggests that this policy of indirect visibility is "like a preliminary preparation" for uninterrupted openness (Öner 2015:182–83).

Contrary to Öner's approximation, these visibility policies do not necessarily represent the somewhat coordinated stages of a single struggle. LGBT people talk about very different political purposes by virtue of which they follow these policies. The same policy of visibility may be practiced with different aims—e.g., the aim of resistance, appropriation, or accommodation. For the LGBT employees whose ultimate goal is to resist the authority structures around themselves, "indirect openness" is likely to be followed as a matter of compulsion (Güner 2016). In contrast, it seems to be an ideal choice for those like Bora, who oppose the idea of resistance. The problem Bora faces is that he can become an open target for the authorities due to the activities of more woke LGBT people. At its best, such actions were illustrated by a gay member of the online forum *memurlar.net*, where thousands of public employees meet. Refusing to be "careful" with the visibility of his sexuality at his workplace, the forum member wrote: "I do not care what anybody thinks [of me]. On the contrary, I will hit them in the eye" (Koseku 2016).

Ersoy repeatedly dismissed the idea of resistance. She never preferred to participate in any kind of street activism, about which most members of the LGBT associations have been passionate. When the Gezi Protests erupted with the participation of LGBT associations alongside others, Ersoy asked them: "don't we feel uncomfortable about many things in life?" In her following sentence, she gave her advice to the protesters:

> Some things may seem wrong to you. Seek your rights in the ballot box, not in laying waste [to the streets].
>
> ("Bülent Ersoy'dan Gezi" 2013)

This emphasis on the ballot box is one of the most stereotypical arguments of center-right politicians. Legitimizing oneself with the same argument, then PM Erdoğan publicly appreciated Ersoy's speech ("Erdoğan, Bülent" 2013).

LGBT and the Entertainment Sector 91

Seeking one's rights at the ballot box also implied seeking one's rights through peaceful negotiation with those who succeed at the ballot box. Beginning with President Turgut Özal and the Özal brothers' TV channel in the early-1990s, Ersoy's good relations with the governments have proven the usefulness of this strategy on her side. Belgin explained how the Özal government behaved differently to Ersoy and other trans people at that time: "there was torture and beating under the rule of Özal [...] Mrs. Özal [i.e., Turgut Özal's wife Semra Özal] protected her daughter [i.e., Ersoy], but she crushed us" ("80'lerde" 2012:84).

The new implicit toleration, which requires one to have some desirable identities alongside LGBT, emanates from a model relationship. It rests on the visible representation of an inward-looking LGBT person who has tension within oneself instead of tension with society. If they are a sex worker, they should be the ones who have admittedly been in moral decay. If they are working in the entertainment sector, they should be the ones that respect the legitimacy of the likes of RTÜK, TRT, and other higher authorities. As a national, they should know that national security is and will always be of utmost importance.

Fashion designer Cemil Ipekçi could continue to appear on the pro-government TV channels, even after he began to criticize the government in some respects. On the other hand, fashion-designer Barbaros Şansal, whose sharp tongue intersected with his gay identity, had to leave the country. When Şansal was asked on a social media platform about this alleged discrepancy between his and Ipekçi's living conditions, Şansal explained: "he is a conservative, whereas I am a revolutionary gay" ("Barbaros Şansal" 2018). Social psychologist Melek Göregenli, who has also been an advisor for Kaos-GL, diagnoses the core problem behind sexism as "conservatism," which, she claims, nurtures "nationalism" and "religious fundamentalism" among other perils. According to Göregenli, this conservatism represents a clichéd film in which the leading man is "always Turkish, Sunni, male and heterosexual" (Erol 2018a). The struggles frequently set up those who aim to negotiate and follow the rules of appropriateness against those who aspire to breach, resist, and ultimately de-construct these rules.

Some disagreements, albeit relatively subtle, over visibility have appeared within the context of resistance. Many LGBT people, especially trans sex workers, have begun to re-evaluate the strategic use of the policy of uncompromising visibility. This revision is at least because their increased visibility has led them to suffer from unprecedentedly dangerous surveillance and target acquisition methods. Accordingly, uncompromising visibility may not be a helpful form of resistance, as it may uncover the fragility of the hitherto unseen agent, who may have owed some of their power to their mysterious position. Three members of the *Lubunya* magazine—"S," "D," and "I"—had an illuminating discussion on this matter:

D: There was no violence in the past. I have been a travesti for 16 years. There was no such violence [in Ankara] when I began working as a sex worker [...]. There was no killing.

92   LGBT and the Entertainment Sector

[...]

S: There was always police violence, but you are right that there was no social violence [...] After we established our associations, [...] we said, "let's go to the police and make a complaint" whenever someone raised his hand against us. Those who were frightened of us began seeing us as weak, and [therefore] they started attacking us [...] They have learned that we are so fragile. I think this is very dangerous. ("Zaman Cinnet" 2009:11–14)

Ironically, in the aftermath of the RTÜK fines, such negative representations have also been limited in the mainstream media. Before RTÜK's recent restrictions on the visibility of transgender individuals, many TV programs, such as those of Reha Muhtar and Savaş Ay, publicized these people for their "degraded," "dirty," but also "interesting" lives ("Medyanın Lanetlileri: Esmeray" 2013:269–70). Most importantly, these broadcastings disclosed the vulnerability of a community after many years of storytelling based on members of this community being seen as dangerous. Before the age of transparency, "homosexuals" appeared only as serial killers (see "Çumra" 1967), mobsters (see "Homoseksüel gangster" 1969:7), psychopaths (Doksat 1958; Dümen 1965), bandits (see "Taşkışla" 1963; "Cinsi" 1958; "1962'nin" 1962), or rapists ("2'si kardeş" 1971) that no one—including murderers—would like to face.

At a conference on the opportunities and the risks of visibility, the participants shared the sense that, in the given circumstances, it is strategically best to be visible only in some cases—e.g., only to some people ("Kadın" 2009:30). In her conversation with journalist Zeynep Ekim Elbaşı (2013), Esmeray admitted that their increased visibility could not be translated into legal rights. During a debate between the activists of different LGBT associations, Belgin Çelik, from *Pembe Hayat*, recalled her friend who was not hired despite having succeeded in attaining the highest rank in the İŞKUR course:

[we] encourage them to [...] attend these exams, but the state deceives us. And it turns out that we deceive the trans people [with false promises].

Decades after learning as part of collective memory that secrecy brought alienation and violence (see Nil 2003:13–18), many activists have begun to acknowledge that visibility also facilitated a specific mode of violence. In this vein, researcher Volkan Yılmaz mentioned an unprecedented danger that looms as a side effect of LGBT people's increased visibility. The risk is that LGBTphobia, which has become more vocal in the face of a more visible LGBT advocacy, might also try to re-cast the legal mechanisms for its interests (Yılmaz 2012).

Erdem Gür, from *Siyah Pembe Üçgen*, described how they were lost in the "vicious cycle" of press releases, parades, and protests with placards. Gür made the following point, which, he emphasized, all "opposition groups" should consider:

> We hesitate to be active in places dominated by shopkeepers' culture (tr. esnaf kültürü). This is because we fear they may react as if [...] we struggle against them [...] When we say, "our struggle is against masculinity in these places," we fear that it may be misunderstood and turn out to mean, "our struggle is against you."
>
> (Kılıçkaya 2011)

In the face of the given power imbalance between them and "this culture" they resist, the methods of activism have been at a deadlock, admittedly, for more than a decade. These strategic calculations by LGBT activists may bridge some of their visibility policies with those of the LGBT people who settled for negotiating with authority. Even though their political motivations ultimately diverge, these different approaches to visibility may have to be combined in unique ways. This prospect would have consequences for anti-government activism. In the following section, I shall analyze such broader ideological channels into which LGBT activism has gradually been integrated.

All Together or None of Us: the Left and the Like-Minded LGBT People

This section elaborates on the activists' evaluations of developing party networks, grassroots groups, and coalitions. In the previous evaluative conversations (I), I analyzed how the visible representation of Bülent Ersoy pushed the "Islamists" to fine-tune their approach to the LGBT "sinners." Similarly, in this part, I examine how the visible representation of the activists encouraged the development of a shared sensitivity in fractured "left-wing" politics. These activists, who began their activities at home and continued in the university campuses and the corridors of "left-wing" parties,[18] pushed all these circles to re-evaluate their ideological repertoires, from Marxism to Secularism. However, this re-making process prompted significant problems concerning the perceived hegemony of the "culture of shopkeepers" and the contested priorities in left-wing politics against this culture.

In 1986, Ahmet Necdet Sezer was among the members of the 2nd Chamber of the Court of Cassation, which denied the "pink identity" to Ersoy. Later, Sezer would not only become the president of the Republic of Turkey (2000–2007), but he would also become, as a president, a primary defendant of Secularism (i.e., state secularism) in response to the AKP revisionism. As a fundamental part of Sezer's ideological thought, his value-laden understanding of Secularism never included a reaction against what many self-proclaimed secularists of the young generation began problematizing as "heteronormativity."

94 LGBT and the Entertainment Sector

These new ideology makers hold the conservative hegemony responsible for many evils, including heteronormativity. Their narrative does not threaten the traditional line of Secularism, problematizing women's lack of rights and the perils of religious bigotry. Nevertheless, another part of this narrative, the question of gender, reconfigures the received wisdom. Accordingly, what brought them together with the LGBT activists against "this culture" is their realization of the possibility that a homosexual couple, as well as a heterosexual one, may be beaten for holding hands on the street. Just like a biological woman, a trans woman may be dismissed from her job due to her "unchastity." A homosexual man may also be condemned publicly for his extra-marital affair—i.e., his "private life." Meanwhile, the LGBT activists clarified that the rainbow has many colors, from those who struggle against poverty (Yılmaz 2010:20–21) to the student labeled as an "infidel" by his classmate for not attending the Quran course (Saygun 2017:10–11).[19] The adversary is the shopkeepers' culture, intersecting "aggression" and "bigotry."

In 2004, MP Orhan Eraslan became one of the first CHP members—if not the first—to publicly meet the members of an LGBT association, *Lambda-Istanbul*. In this meeting, their demands included lifting the obstacles that pushed them into sex work and the re-consideration of the legal interpretation of "unjust provocation" ("Eşcinseller Taleplerini" 2004). When the AKP MPs and the pro-government media denigrated Eraslan for hosting LGBT people, Eraslan defended himself with a cautious statement:

> Being a democrat means, however, listening to those who are different and reflecting on them. The fact that I agreed to meet them does not mean I agree with their demands.
>
> (Ilkkaracan 2016:59)

Then the leader of the party, Deniz Baykal, remained silent on this matter. However, one year later, Baykal responded to an allegation made by Bülent Ersoy by mocking her medical record: "This is a hormone-fed lie" (Arıkan 2005). Using a similarly derogatory language, Kemal Anadol, a senior member of CHP, labeled the politics of AKP as that of a "political travesti," in the sense that the AKP leaders kept wearing the dresses of ideologies that they did not represent. At the time, such negative connotations provoked many LGBT activists to discuss whether CHP was their friend in a two-party parliament or just another foe alongside AKP. As a humorous part of the 2007 LGBT Pride parade, the activists declared Deniz Baykal the "hormone-fed tomato award" winner ("Eşcinseller Ayrımcılığa" 2007).

Refreshed by a group of younger members in the aftermath of the 2011 parliamentary elections, CHP demanded sexualities, sexual orientations, and gender identities be explicitly written into the constitutional clause on the principle of equality ("BDP ve CHP" 2012). When the LGBT associations, *Kaos-GL* and *Pembe Hayat*, visited the parliament in January 2012,

CHP greeted them with eight MPs and a more explicit political will ("LGBT Dernek" 2012). Alongside a senior member, Rıza Türmen, the group predominantly consisted of the MPs of the new generation, like Şafak Pavey who, in the parliament, would later deliver an attention-grabbing defense of Secularism in the name of the "minority" (*see* Chapter 4). CHP members never missed subsequent LGBT Pride parades. During the LGBT Pride parade of 2015, MP Mahmut Tanal of CHP climbed atop the police water cannon vehicle to try to stop the intervention in the parade. In the following years, this scene became traditional.

As has been acknowledged by the Kaos-GL team, the Gezi Protests (2013) acted as the primary catalyst for the LGBT activists' integration into this broader political spectrum (Cantek 2013:225). Before Gezi, the association had been organized only in Ankara, Istanbul, İzmir, Eskişehir, and Diyarbakır, whereas after Gezi, its activity expanded to many other cities, from Edirne to Kars. From its emphasis on union rights to labor-centered street activism, the association's action strategies were already very similar to left-wing organizations (Kaos GL 2018). A long way has been traveled since the late-1980s. Since then, the LGBT activists were gradually welcome into broader left-wing politics:

> When I attended a meeting of the Association of Human Rights (tr. İHD) for the first time, they reacted against me, "what are these homos [tr. ibneler] doing here?" But maybe, we were much more revolutionary compared to them.
>
> (Günçıkan 2006:5)

In May 2001, neither the labor unions nor the left-wing groups were happy when the members of LGBT associations attended the march (Cantek 2013). A decade later, the anarchists are carrying the LGBT flags alongside others in the front row.

Nonetheless, orthodox Marxists maintained their stances against sex work. In these marches, the visible representation of "the sex worker" has still been the least acceptable of all. Şevval, a trans activist, was highly disappointed after they met with the labor union DISK, which she criticizes for reproducing radical feminist and orthodox Marxist language ("Bütün Lubunyalar Toplandık: Şevval" 2013:149). Even though those admittedly forced into sex work are taken as the victims to be saved in this language, the other "liberal" sex workers are among the enemies that commodify the woman's body. Considering the feminist contribution to the cross-ideological demonization of sex work, Erdem (2011:34) suggested that LGBT activists should not take feminism as a "natural ally."

A decade after Erdem's argument, new ideological cleavages fuel this deepseated tension, eventually making it difficult even to consider femicides and trans murders under the same umbrella. On this front, a group of socialist feminists denigrates queer feminism as the liberal, pro-US ally of market-oriented

96 LGBT and the Entertainment Sector

postmodernism. According to them, Islamism is nothing more than a pillar of this grand alliance. Meanwhile, they complain about the cancel culture that "LGBT lobbies" produce against them. During the 2022 Women's Day marches, these fractions looked for each other's involvement before that of the state authority in the provocations: "This ugliness does not come from the police, it comes from the women we walk side by side" ("Peki" 2022). While the already-vulnerable feminists and LGBT activists are targeting each other, they know that this is perhaps the most profound struggle for rulership, which only a new global order would resolve.

Apart from these tensions, a group of LGBT activists became candidates to stand as MPs. In 2017, the CHP members of the Avcılar district of Istanbul elected their first "openly trans delegate," Niler Albayrak, who was also an MP candidate from the same political party (Dörtkardeş 2017). Albayrak declared that CHP's policy would be centered on defending the "otherized" groups, which include the victims of what they define as the heterosexist ideology or the heteronormative system. In the same vein, trans woman Deva Özenen became an MP candidate from the newly founded political party of Emine Ülker Tarhan, a former investigating judge of the Court of Cassation. Barış Sulu, who openly identifies as gay, became an MP candidate for HDP. Sulu noted that he chose HDP as the members of this party had been with the LGBT activists "since the beginning" ("LGBTİ Aday" 2015). For their uncompromising visibility, the LGBT associations refused to be subsumed by any political party but were always open to bilateral agreements and side deals.

Alongside its focus on the "Kurdish Problem" (tr. Kürt Sorunu), HDP prioritized LGBT activism and feminism, as it aimed to transform into "the party of Turkey" for all disadvantaged groups. It did not take long for many LGBT activists to enter the city organizations of HDP, with which they had already collaborated in the past, in *HADEP, DTP,* and *BDP.* At its best, an indication of this agreement was the conversation between Elçin Kurbanoğlu and Buse Kılıçkaya from *Lubunya*:

> As a result, I am a human rights activist [and not just a trans] [...] I am a Kurdish trans, an Alevi trans, a socialist trans [...] Just as we said "we are all Hrant Dink" [and] "we are all Alevis" when their time came, it is essential, today, to be able to say "we are all trans."
>
> (Kurbanoğlu 2011)

Despite some conservative critiques of this agreement from within HDP ("LGBT: Altan Tan" 2015) and PKK (Çakır 2014; "HDP'den PKK'lı" 2014), the activists could develop their dialogue with the party offices in the metropolitan areas, as well as the leading members of the party, such as former president Selahattin Demirtaş and MP Ertuğrul Kürkçü.

LGBT activists' visibility in the Kurdish political movement or relationship with PKK has long been problematized by the mainstream political

LGBT and the Entertainment Sector   97

circles. More noteworthy are the objections coming from others in the opposition LGBT community (*see* Eğin 2018). Some have been seeking the chief role in the external funders of the LGBT associations, such as the Soros Foundations and some foreign countries' embassies. Indeed, this is not a new cleavage. In the mid-1990s, the idea of struggling alongside the "Kurdish separatists" became a hotly contested topic in LGBT activism. Ibrahim Eren, an openly gay man who aimed to form a green party in Turkey, was at the center of these contestations. Eren was highly praised at the time, as he was the one who used his club *Yeşil Bizans* to bring together many gay, lesbian, and bisexual activists for the first time ("Bütün Lubunyalar Toplandık: Şevval" 2013:244). Eren was the only visible gay activist for some time, whereas others masked themselves (Engindeniz 2011). His party was to support conscientious objection in defense of anti-militarism.

However, Eren refused to bring together his gay activism with the politics of *HADEP*, the political party with close ties with PKK. On the contrary, when some people took down the flag of Turkey in the congress of HADEP, Eren harshly criticized fellow LGBT activists whom he thought to have toxified the LGBT struggle with separatism. Moreover, according to Kandiyoti, "a leading male gay activist" (likely to be Eren himself) hung a flag of Turkey at the door of Claudia Roth, the representative of the German Green Party in Istanbul, also famous for her LGBT activism alongside her ties to HADEP (Kandiyoti 2002:289). Arguably, this act was intended to convey that Roth must not act as an undercover imperialist whose aim would not be the well-being of LGBT people but the dissolution of Turkey. Eren's project failed, since the members of the community could not meet on a common ground ("Bütün Lubunyalar Toplandık: Ali" 2013:152; Cingöz and Erdem 2013:225).

Despite their awareness of the repercussions of this historical baggage, neither the MP candidates nor those other LGBT people who applied for candidacy criticized one another as members of rival parties. Instead, they publicly expressed their appreciation for seeing other openly LGBT candidates. If only because none of these candidates had a realistic chance of being elected—i.e., given their standings on the party lists—they were there primarily to strengthen the visible representation of LGBT activism. For the same reason, they did not distinguish between the few political parties inviting them. For example, Özenen was an HDP candidate for a municipal assembly in 2014, a year before she became an MP candidate for CHP. When they are under the watchful eyes of others, such as those times in which they find an opportunity to express themselves on the mainstream media channels, the activists continue to follow the policy of focusing on their common denominators.

That said, the fractured left-wing politics in which the LGBT activists have obtained some agency is not likely to open more room for these activists without transferring its own existential crisis onto them. This crisis partly relates to these movements' confusion with the hegemonic culture, with which they must deal from the inside. Amidst this fundamental crisis,

98   *LGBT and the Entertainment Sector*

those LGBT activists who "waste time" by campaigning for the issues of "secondary" importance (e.g., gender-neutral toilets) have often been criticized by the other left-wing activists as they arguably mask the "primary struggle." Meanwhile, in broader public debates, LGBT individuals join different camps that cut the community vertically. Those who respect and despise Atatürk's legacy and disagree on the acceptable ways to challenge workplace rules challenge one another (*see* "Mecdelli" 2021; "Defne" 2022).

In the elections of June 2015, HDP and CHP had LGBT candidates. However, this diversity was relatively circumscribed in the subsequent polls because the decision-makers of these parties concluded that the LGBT candidates were likely to be a deterrent factor in the eyes of the "conservative electorate." Indeed, here comes the social significance of value surveys. In snap elections in November 2015, neither HDP nor CHP had any openly LGBT candidates. Some have speculated that criticism of PKK leader Cemil Bayık diverted the policy of HDP ("HDP, Eşcinsel" 2015). Beyond pure speculation, empirical evidence can be found that HDP limited its promotion of LGBT activism to the metropolitan areas, with a few exceptions in the rural South-East where "conservative Kurds" are in the majority (Lıcalı 2015). This situation may have resulted from a calculation by HDP to keep its "conservative Kurdish" voter base, on whom the AKP and South-Eastern Islamists *Hüda-Par* played as well. For example, in 2016 in Diyarbakır, the HDP-led panel on "LGBT" was eventually canceled by the organizers due to a mass campaign against the panel on social media ("Karaman'da Ensar'ın" 2016; "Sahabeler Şehrinin" 2016).

After a similar process of strategic calculation, the decision-makers of CHP concluded that the Erdoğan government only gains power when "the culture of shopkeepers" is in dispute. Instead, CHP firstly decided to prioritize its propaganda against the economic aspect of this culture and then withdrew its objection altogether. Though both parties kept their LGBT members in some of their city organizations, they have doubts about the strategic usefulness of uncompromising visibility. In 2018, the two parties removed some critical sections from their election bulletins that previously included the word "LGBT" (Erol 2018b). In their campaigns for the presidential elections, neither the CHP candidate Muharrem Ince nor the HDP candidate Selahattin Demirtaş sent a message explicitly to "LGBT" people. While re-orienting part of their visibility, the first thing to hide was "LGBT" as a single marker of identity. Let alone challenging "the culture of shopkeepers" for the sake of diversity on the street, the CHP leader Kılıçdaroğlu promised to establish a ministry led by "shopkeepers" upon coming to power in the 2023 elections.

Despite such constraints, LGBT activists have become integral to the opposition dynamics. They are active, trying to transfer their knowledge to like-minded others. They share their concerns and priorities in the panels, meetings, and marches organized by these opposition parties, as well as various university clubs and civil society associations. None of these organizations are secure in the era of the presidential decrees in the force of

LGBT and the Entertainment Sector   99

law (tr. KHK). Still, LGBT activists contribute to a much broader political community that shares their insecurities. On the flip side, just like the LGBT activists who problematized discrimination as a part of left-wing politics, Bülent Ersoy could share her primary concerns in government circles as Erdoğan's anti-Gezi role model. On one occasion, she even told then PM Erdoğan, "I am a person who travels a lot. We want the artists to be able to use the VIP [facilities at the airports]" ("Bülent Ersoy'dan şaşırtan" 2010). While these concerns starkly differ, their carriers have managed to integrate themselves into the broad ideological spectrum of Turkey. They have established some vital social links, likely to be missed by the studies focusing on them merely as an isolated sub-culture.

Notes

1 The note that they wore traditional women's clothes, however, does not finalize the answer to the question of whether they desired to represent women.
2 See Avcı (2017), Ze'Evi (2006), and Ezber (2014) for the parallel histories of the ban against the köçek practice, starting from the 16th century (also see "Bir Hatunda," 2014:35).
3 Alongside Müren and Ersoy, they watched Funda Lisa, Serbülent Sultan, and some others.
   see the memories of Ahu, Belgin, Bennu, and Demet in "80'lerde Lubunya Olmak" (2012:18, 24, 59–61, 95, 130).
4 A historic street in Istanbul, where a large group of travesties lived as a sub-cultural community for some years. In 1996, they were forcefully displaced from the street.
5 There is a remarkably similar story about the köçek dance of a travesti, nick-named Öküz Bakışlı Mehmet, with legendary folk musician from Kırşehir, Neşet Ertaş, sometime before Ertaş became well-known ("80'lerde" 2012:175).
6 See Gürel (2017) for a scrutinization of the debate over Kayhanmete's identity.
7 The inspector made this argument because the gay police officer was well-known for his religious personality.
8 Based on Dursunoğlu's female impersonation, some defined his performances as that of a travesti instead of a zenne.
9 See also the conversation between Çağla Akalın, Esmeray, Didem Soylu, and Buse Kılıçkaya in Öner (2018:25).
10 Kadir Gecesi is the night when the verses of Quran were revealed to Prophet Muhammad.
11 "Ayol abla" may be described as a stereotypically ultra-feminine way of address-ing people. In English, it literally means "hey sister!"
12 When the clerkship examination of the Ministry of Justice included the question of when Ersoy had her surgery, she commented: "of course it can be asked. I am a senior artist, who performs art inside and outside the borders of Turkey, and, I am one whose knowledge cannot be replaced" (Capa 2012).
13 The humorous variations of the Rumi quote emphasize the authority behind: "I am not Rumi, so you don't come"; "If Rumi saw these people, he would say 'you don't come'."
14 Ersoy reiterated this argument in her response to Ertuğrul Günay.
15 This was written on a placard prepared for the LGBT Pride Day: "İbne Dönme El Ele, Ahlaksız Devrime." Many LGBT individuals embraced the two Turkish words "ibne" [en. homosexual] and "dönme" [en. trans], which have defamatory or libelous connotations elsewhere.

100   LGBT and the Entertainment Sector

16 The wording of the survey was entirely under the local context. The survey included many keywords that an LGBT outside the context of Istanbul would have difficulty in understanding.

17 Marika described her and her friend, in Turkish, pejoratively as "yan sanayi kadın."

18 Among them are Toplumsal Araştırmalar Vakfı (TAV), Özgürlük ve Dayanışma Partisi (ÖDP) led by Ufuk Uras; İnsan Hakları Derneği (IHD); İbrahim Eren's club Yeşil Bizans, and Eren's political party Radikal Demokrat Yeşiller Partisi (en. Green Party), HADEP ("Bütün Lubunyalar Toplandık: Öner" 2013:118–19, 130; "Bütün Lubunyalar Toplandık: Mine" 2013:137; "80'lerde" 2012:135–36).

19 As an illustration, see the range of social issues taken into account by the Lambda-Istanbul members ("Bütün Lubunyalar Toplandık: Öner" 2013:125).

References

"1962'nin 2. Cinayetini de Bir Cinsi Sapık İşledi." 1962. *Cumhuriyet,* February 3.

"2015 Middle East Tour." 2015. *Boston Gay Men's Chorus.* Retrieved February 19, 2019 (https://www.bgmc.org/2015/07/01/2015-middle-east-tour/).

"2'si Kardeş, 3 Kaatil." 1971. *Milliyet*, January 31.

80'lerde Lubunya Olmak. 2012. İzmir: Siyah Pembe Üçgen.

Açıkgöz, Esra. 2013. "Müslüman Da Eşcinsel Olabilir…" *Gazete Vatan*, October 20.

"Acun Ilıcalı eleştirilere cevap verdi!" 2011. *Habertürk.* Retrieved August 15, 2022 (https://www.haberturk.com/medya/haber/683643-acun-ilicali-elestirilere-cevap-verdi).

"Acun Ilıcalı'ya dansöz şoku." 2016. *Yenisöz Gazetesi*, May 21.

"Acun Rekor Cezadan Sonra Soluğu RTÜKte Aldı!" 2013. *Posta.* Retrieved February 19, 2019 (https://www.posta.com.tr/acun-rekor-cezadan-sonra-solugu-rtukte-aldi-207973).

Akkaya, Fatih. 2010. "Peki Bu Ne?" *Habervaktim*, August 14.

Akpınar, Ömer. 2015. "Trans Kadına Sallamalı Saldırı: Kafayı Kolla Kızım!" *Kaos GL Haber Portalı.* Retrieved February 11, 2022 (https://kaosgl.org/haber/trans-kadina-sallamali-saldiri-kafayi-kolla-kizim).

Albayrak, Özlem. 2008a. "Sinan Çetin, Cemil İpekçi, AK Parti." *Yeni Şafak*, January 26.

Albayrak, Özlem. 2008b. "Bülent Ersoy ve Bam Telleri." *Yeni Şafak*, March 1.

Alphan, Melis. 2016. "Değişim (Fatih Ürek)." *Hürriyet Kelebek*, June 22.

Altan, Çetin. 1960. "Vampirler ve Ötesi." *Milliyet*, February 16, 2.

Altınay, Rüstem Ertuğ. 2008. "Reconstructing the Transgendered Self as a Muslim, Nationalist, Upper-Class Woman: The Case of Bulent Ersoy." *WSQ: Women's Studies Quarterly* 36(3):210–29.

Anayasa Mahkemesi [Constitutional Court]. 2014a. Ahmet Şancı case 2012/29.

Anayasa Mahkemesi [Constitutional Court]. 2014b. Şahin Karaman case 2012/1205.

Anayasa Mahkemesi [Constitutional Court]. 2014c. Sinem Hun case 2013/5356.

Anayasa Mahkemesi [Constitutional Court]. 2015. Mehmet Fatih Yiğit and others case 2014/16838.

Anayasa Mahkemesi [Constitutional Court]. 2017. Z.A. case 2013/2928 (https://kararlarbilgibankasi.anayasa.gov.tr/Basvurular/tr/pdf/2013-2928.pdf).

And, Metin. 1968. "Çengiler ve Köçekler." *Hayat Tarih Mecmuası* (2):25–29.

Andrews, Walter G., and Mehmet Kalpaklı. 2005. *The Age of Beloveds: Love and the Beloved in Early-Modern Ottoman and European Culture and Society.* Durham: Duke University Press.

LGBT and the Entertainment Sector 101

Ankebut Sayfası. n.d. *Akit TV, Fetö ve Güncel Konular.* Retrieved February 19, 2019 (https://www.youtube.com/watch?v=xlM-f-5RnZM).

Arıkan, Fahir. 2005. "Bülent Ersoy'un söyledikleri kuyruklu değil hormonlu yalan." *Hürriyet*, September 7.

Arman, Ayse. 2016. "Trans Olduğu Için Mi!" *Hürriyet*, August 16.

Avcı, Mustafa. 2017. "Shifts in Sexual Desire: Bans on Dancing Boys (Köçeks) throughout Ottoman Modernity (1800s–1920s)." *Middle Eastern Studies* 53(5):762–81. doi: 10.1080/00263206.2017.1291425.

Avşar, Helin. 2009. "Cinsel tercihim yüzünden kovuldum." *Habertürk*. Retrieved August 25, 2022 (https://www.haberturk.com/medya/haber/191140-cinsel-tercihim-yuzunden-kovuldum).

Aydın, Oya. 2006. "'Eşcinsel Olma' Işten Haklı Çıkarma Sebebi Değil." *Bianet.Org*. Retrieved (https://bianet.org/bianet/siyaset/86816-calisma-hayatinda-escinsellik).

"Barbaros Şansal (@barbarosansalfn) on Twitter: 'O muhafazakar, ben ise devrimci eşcinselim'." 2018. *Twitter*. Retrieved February 19, 2019.

Bardakçı, Ilhan. 1983. "Harem ve Kadına Dair." *İktibas*, February 12.

Bardakçı, Murat. 2005. "Çenginame." P. 243 in *Osmanlı'da Seks*. Istanbul: İnkılap.

Baştürk, Onur. 1998. "Ekranda Post Köçek Trendi!" *Negatif* 43:27–29.

Bayramoğlu, Yener. 2009. "Fatih Ürek ve Aydın'ın Cinsiyet Performansı." *Bianet*. Retrieved February 19, 2019 (http://www.bianet.org/biamag/toplumsal-cinsiyet/115785-fatih-urek-ve-aydin-in-cinsiyet-performansi).

"BDP ve CHP, Anayasada eşcinsellere eşit hak istedi." 2012. *T24*. Retrieved February 20, 2019 (https://t24.com.tr/haber/bdp-ve-chp-anayasada-escinsellere-esit-hak-istedi, 203845).

Beki, Akif. 2016. "Bülent Ersoy'lu Iftarı Çözdünüz Mü?" *Hürriyet*, June 21.

Beki, Akif. 2019. "Netflix, Akit'e Hak Verdiriyor!" *Karar Gazetesi*, July 25.

Bereket, Tarik, and Barry D. Adam. 2008. "Navigating Islam and Same-Sex Liaisons Among Men in Turkey." *Journal of Homosexuality* 55(2):204–22. doi: 10.1080/00918360802129428.

Beyaz TV. 2014. *Erkan Tan'dan dindar ve muhafazakar kesime Bülent Ersoy çıkışı.*

"Bir Cinayet Aydınlandı." 1957. *Milliyet*, June 19, 1.

"Bir Cinsî Sapık Feci Şekilde Öldürüldü." 1963. *Cumhuriyet*, March 10, 1–7.

"Bir Hatunda 1 Şeytan, Bir Oğlanda 18 Şeytan Var." 2014. *#tarih Dergi* (4):35.

"Bir Kaatil Yakalandı." 1968. *Cumhuriyet*, September 12, 5.

"Bir Kahveci Odasında Ölü Bulundu." 1953. *Cumhuriyet*, August 27.

"Boğaziçi'li Öğrencilerden Sapkın Gruba Protesto." 2015. *Hayder.Org.Tr*. Retrieved August 3, 2022 (https://www.haksozhaber.net/bogazicili-ogrencilerden-sapkin-gruba-protesto-62447h.htm).

"Boğaziçi, sapkın gruba kucak açtı." 2015. *Yeni Akit*. Retrieved February 19, 2019 (https://www.yeniakit.com.tr/haber/bogazici-sapkin-gruba-kucak-acti-75529.html).

Bulaç, Ali. 2012. "Eşcinseller." Pp. 132–38 in *Din ve Modernizm*. İstanbul: Çıra Yayınları.

"Bülent Arınç:'Güpegündüzçırılçıplak hale gelip…'" 2015. *CNN Türk*. Retrieved February 19, 2019 (https://www.cnnturk.com/video/turkiye/bulent-arinc-gupegunduz-cirilciplak-hale-gelip).

"Bülent Ersoy hapishaneyi anlatıyor." 1982. *Bulvar*. Retrieved August 25, 2022 (http://web.archive.org/web/20161104180246/http://www.zamantika.com/1980ler/bulent-ersoy-hapishanede-1982).

102 LGBT and the Entertainment Sector

"Bülent Ersoy'un Kadın Olmadığına Karar Verildi." 1982. *Cumhuriyet*, September 7.

"Bülent Ersoy, Ertuğrul Günay'ı istifaya çağırdı." 2009. *Beşiktaş Postası*. Retrieved February 19, 2019 (https://www.besiktaspostasi.com/bulent-ersoy-ertugrul-gunayi-istifaya-cagirdi/).

"Bülent Ersoy'a bir gay olarak hakkımı helal etmiyorum." 2010. *T24*. Retrieved February 19, 2019 (https://t24.com.tr/haber/bulent-ersoya-bir-gay-olarak-hakkimi-helal-etmiyorum, 111615).

"Bülent Ersoy'dan şaşırtan talep." 2010. *Habertürk*. Retrieved February 20, 2019 (https://www.haberturk.com/polemik/haber/208489-bulent-ersoydan-sasirtan-talep).

"Bülent Ersoy Intikam Istiyor!" 2012. *Internethaber.Com*. Retrieved February 19, 2019 (https://www.internethaber.com/bulent-ersoy-intikam-istiyor-464866h.htm).

"Bülent Ersoy'dan Gezi Parkı çıkışı." 2013. *Haber7*. Retrieved February 19, 2019 (http://www.haber7.com/guncel/haber/1038331-bulent-ersoydan-gezi-parki-cikisi).

"Bülent Ersoy'dan Ömür Gedik'e." 2016. *Gazete Vatan*, March 1.

"Bütün Lubunyalar Toplandık: Ali." 2013. *90'larda Lubunya Olmak*. Izmir: Siyah Pembe Üçgen.

"Bütün Lubunyalar Toplandık: Mine." 2013. *90'larda Lubunya Olmak*. Izmir: Siyah Pembe Üçgen.

"Bütün Lubunyalar Toplandık: Öner." 2013. *90'larda Lubunya Olmak*. Izmir: Siyah Pembe Üçgen.

"Bütün Lubunyalar Toplandık: Şevval." 2013. *90'larda Lubunya Olmak*. Izmir: Siyah Pembe Üçgen.

"Büyükada'da Ağaca Asılı Bulunan Cesetlerin Kimlikleri." 1972. *Cumhuriyet*, July 10.

Çabuk, Vahit. 1977. "Osmanlı Haremi." *Milli Gençlik* 2(20).

"Çağlar Cilara on Twitter: 'Madem böyle bir şey yapacaktınız benim başımı niye yediniz." 2019. *Twitter*. Retrieved March 20, 2022 (https://twitter.com/caglarcilara/status/1108278857055027201).

Çağlayan, Armagan. 2015. "Benim Gibi Ahlaklısı Var Mı?" *Radikal*, June 21.

Çakır, Ruşen. 2014. "Cemil Bayık İle Söyleşi." Retrieved March 8, 2019 (http://rusencakir.com/Cemil-Bayik-ile-soylesi-20-Agustos-2014-Tam-metin/2839).

Cantek, Funda. 2013. "Herhangi Bir Toplumsal Kesimin Özgür Olmadığı Bir Toplumda Aslında Hiç Kimse Özgür Değildir." *Mülkiye Dergisi* 37(4):223–30.

Capa, Izzet. 2012. "Bülent Ersoy, İzzet Çapa'ya konuştu." *Habertürk*, January 3.

Capa, Izzet. 2017. "Bülent Ersoy Röportajının Hiçbir Yerde Yayınlanmamış Bölümleri." *Gecce*. Retrieved February 19, 2019 (https://www.gecce.com.tr/yazarlar/izzet-capa/bulent-ersoy-roportajinin-hicbir-yerde-yayinlanmamis-bolumleri).

Çapın, Halit. 1966a. "Gece Kulüpleri." *Milliyet Haftasonu İlavesi*, May 29, 1.

Çapın, Halit. 1966b. "Garibhaneler." *Milliyet Haftasonu İlavesi*, June 12.

Çapın, Halit. 1966c. "Polis Baskın Yapınca Yerli Caroussel Revüsü Dağıldı." *Milliyet Sanat Eğlence*, October 14, 6.

Çavuşoğlu, Can. 2014. "Bülent Ersoy'a Var Da Bize Yok Mu?" *Kaos GL*. Retrieved August 25, 2022 (https://kaosgl.org/gokkusagi-forumu-kose-yazisi/bulent-ersoyrsquoa-var-da-bize-yok-mu).

Cingöz, Yavuz, and Erdem Gürsu, eds. 2013. "İktidarın Sopası: İlker." *90'larda Lubunya Olmak*. Izmir: Siyah Pembe Üçgen.

"Cinsi Sapık Yankesici Dün Tevkif Edildi." 1958. *Milliyet*, May 2, 2.

CNN Türk. 2018. *Acun Ilıcalı'dan Cumhurbaşkanı Erdoğan Sorusuna Cevap.*

LGBT and the Entertainment Sector   103

"Çorum'da Silahlı Saldırıya Uğrayan Trans Seks İşçisine Barodan Ayrımcılık!".
2014. *Kaos GL Haber Portalı*. (https://kaosgl.org/haber/corumrsquoda-silahli-
saldiriya-ugrayan-trans-seks-iscisine-barodan-ayrimcilik).
"Cumhuriyet'in Bülent Ersoy takıntısı." 2018. *Yeni Akit*. Retrieved February 19, 2019
(https://www.yeniakit.com.tr/haber/cumhuriyetin-bulent-ersoy-takintisi-446049.
html).
"Çumra Canavarının Dördüncü Kurbanı Da Bulundu." 1967. *Cumhuriyet*, April 1.
Dağlar, Ali. 2010. "Bizde gay yok." *Hürriyet*, August 14.
"Daily Sabah'tan Ilginç Bülent Ersoy Haberi." 2016. *Habervaktim*. Retrieved
February 19, 2019 (https://www.habervaktim.com/haber/474300/daily-sabahtan-
ilginc-bulent-ersoy-haberi.html).
Danıştay 12. Daire [12th Chamber of the Council of State]. 2014. 2014/7169. (http://
kazanci.com.tr/gunluk/12d-2011-750.htm).
"Defne on Twitter." 2022. *Twitter*, April 8. Retrieved August 26, 2022 (https://twitter.
com/VenusianVirgo/status/1512523094396702723).
Demir, Yunus Emre. 2016. "Kerimcan Durmaz'a Dair..." *Kaos GL*. Retrieved
February 19, 2019 (http://kaosgl.org/sayfa.php?id=22606).
Dikmen, Kerem. 2022. *Cinsel Yönelim ve Cinsiyet Kimliği Temelli İnsan Hakları
İzleme Raporu 2021*. Ankara: Kaos GL.
Doksat, Recep. 1958. "Transvestitismus." *Milliyet*, April 29.
"Dolmabahçe Cinayeti." 1952. *Milliyet*, October 23, 7.
Dörtkardeş, Ihsan. 2017. "CHP'nin Ilk Trans Delegesi." *Hürriyet*, October 10.
Dümen, Haydar. 1965. "Kişisel ve Toplumsal Yönden Zararlı." *Milliyet*, December 19.
Düzgören, Koray. 1998. "Çatışma Kışkırtıcılığında Medya 'Rezalet'leri!..."
Sözleşme, May.
Eğin, Oray. 2018. "Bir köşede yalnız." *Habertürk*, May 22.
Elbaşı, Zeynep Ekim. 2013. "'Görünürlük çok arttı ama halen edinilmiş hiçbir
hakkımız yok.'" *Agos*. Retrieved August 20, 2022 (http://www.agos.com.tr/tr/
yazi/5228/gorunurluk-cok-artti-ama-halen-edinilmis-hicbir-hakkimiz-yok).
Emiroğlu, Ünal. 1997. "Eşcinsellerin Katılımı ve Laiklik Söylemi." *Yörünge*,
July 13, 10.
"En harbi erkek, Fatih Ürek!" 2008. *Medyafaresi.com*. Retrieved February 19,
2019 (http://www.medyafaresi.com/haber/en-harbi-erkek-fatih-urek-iste-unlu-
sarkicinin-yeni-sakalli/17351).
Engindeniz, Idil. 2011. "80'lerden Günümüze Eşcinsel Hareketin Medyayla İlişkisi."
Kaos GL. Retrieved February 20, 2019 (http://kaosgl.org/sayfa.php?id=9906).
Erdem, Tuna. 2011. "Feminizm ve Queer Düşmanlığı." *Lubunya* (8): 32–4.
"Erdoğan: Beyoğlu'ndaki marjinaller." 2018. *Cumhuriyet*, March 23.
"Erdoğan, Bülent Ersoy'u Da Örnek Gösterdi." 2013. *HaberFedai*.
Retrieved February 19, 2019 (http://www.haberfedai.com/haber/116/erdogan-
bulent-ersoyu-da-ornek-gosterdi).
Erol, Ali. 2018a. "Nefret Söylemine Maruz Kalıyorlarmış." *Kaos GL Haber Portalı*.
Retrieved February 19, 2019 (http://www.kaosgl.org/sayfa.php?id=27113).
Erol, Ali. 2018b. "CHP ve HDP: Nefret Suçları Cezasız Kalmayacak." *Kaos GL Haber
Portalı*. Retrieved February 20, 2019 (http://kaosgl.org/sayfa.php?id=25945).
Ertur, Basak, and Alisa Lebow. 2014. "Coup de Genre: The Trials and Tribulations
of Bülent Ersoy." *Theory & Event* 17(1).
"Eşcinsel Şarkıcılar Hakkındaki Takibat Sürüyor." 1981. *Cumhuriyet*, June 16.
"Eşcinsel Şarkıcıların Hiçbiri Sahneye Çıkmayacak." 1981. *Cumhuriyet*, June 13.

104 LGBT and the Entertainment Sector

"Eşcinseller Ayrımcılığa Karşı Yürüdü." 2007. *Lambdaistanbul.* Retrieved February 20, 2019 (http://www.lambdaistanbul.org/s/medya/escinseller-ayrimciliga-karsi-yurudu/).

"Eşcinseller Taleplerini Meclis'e Taşıdı." 2004. *Hürriyet,* May 24.

Eyüboğlu, Ali. 2007. "RTÜK, Huysuz Virjin'i Nasıl Seyfi Bey Yaptı?" *Milliyet,* November 2.

Ezber, Gokcen. 2014. "Edebiyatımızdan Geçen LGBTT." *Gokcenezber.Com.* Retrieved (http://www.gokcenezber.com/2014/08/edebiyatimizdan-gecen-lgbtt).

"Fatih neden eski haline döndü anlamadım." 2008. *Habertürk.* Retrieved February 19, 2019 (https://www.haberturk.com/haber/haber/105054-fatih-neden-eski-haline-dondu-anlamadim).

"Fatih Ürek çok kırgın." 2009. *Mynet Haber.* Retrieved August 25, 2022 (https://www.mynet.com/fatih-urek-cok-kirgin-110100463626).

"Fatih Ürek'i erkeksileştiren modacı." 2009. *Habertürk.* Retrieved February 19, 2019 (https://www.haberturk.com/haber/haber/162638-fatih-urekierkeksilestiren-modaci).

"Fatih Ürek imajını da değiştirdi." 2015. *Ensonhaber.* Retrieved February 19, 2019 (https://www.ensonhaber.com/fatih-urek-imajini-da-degistirdi-2015-07-15.html).

"Fatih Ürek'ten 'cinsiyet' açıklaması." 2016. *Habertürk,* August 15.

"Federal Almanya'da Ahlak Buhranı." 1973. *Yeniden Milli Mücadele* 4(169):2.

Flash TV. 2013. *Eşcinsellik Hastalık Mıdır.* Retrieved August 25, 2022 (https://www.dailymotion.com/video/xuo4pw).

Gani Met. 2012. "Dağınık Düşüncelerim." *Lubunya* 10:33–36.

"Gay karakteri oynadı, TRT'den atıldı." 2010. *Radikal.* Retrieved August 25, 2022 (https://www.internethaber.com/gay-karakteri-oynadi-trtden-atildi-260469h.htm).

Gence, Hakan. 2017. "Tek rakibim Türk Hava Yolları!" *Hürriyet Kelebek,* December 13.

Göregenli, Melek. 2018. *Türkiye'de Kamu Çalışanı Lezbiyen, Gey, Biseksüel, Trans ve İntersekslerin Durumu 2017.* Ankara: Kaos GL.

Günçıkan, Berat. 2006. "Eğer İHD Olmasaydı..." *Cumhuriyet Pazar,* July 16.

Güner, Umut. 2014. "Bülent Ersoy'un mirasına dikel!" *Kaos GL.* Retrieved August 10, 2022 (https://kaosgl.org/haber/bulent-ersoyrsquoun-mirasina-dikel).

Güner, Umut. 2016. "'İşyerinde Açılmamak Tercih Değil Zorunluluk.'" *Kaos GL Haber Portalı.* Retrieved February 19, 2019 (http://www.kaosgl.org/sayfa.php?id=20869).

Gürel, Perin E. 2017. *The Limits of Westernization: A Cultural History of America in Turkey.* New York: Columbia University Press.

Haynes, Brittany Giselle. 2014. "Performing Modernity in Turkey: Conflicts of Masculinity, Sexuality, and the Köçek Dancer." MA Thesis, CUNY.

"HDP'den PKK'lı Cemil Bayık'a 'Marjinal' Tepkisi." 2014. *Haberler.com.* Retrieved February 20, 2019 (https://www.haberler.com/hdp-den-pkk-li-cemil-bayik-a-marjinal-6411012-haberi/?utm_source=facebook&utm_campaign=tavsiye_et&utm_medium=detay).

"HDP, Eşcinsel Adaylardan Neden Vazgeçti?" 2015. *Haberler.com.* Retrieved February 20, 2019 (https://www.haberler.com/hdp-escinsel-adaylardan-neden-vazgecti-7709485-haberi/).

Hiçyılmaz, Ergun. 1991. *Çengiler, Köçekler, Dönmeler, Lez'olar...* İstanbul: Cep Kitapları.

"Homoseksüel gangster: İstanbul Polisi Pusuda." 1969. *Cumhuriyet,* August 13, 7.

LGBT and the Entertainment Sector 105

"Ilk ve Orta Tedrisat Muallimleri Hakkında [...]." 1930. Turkish Grand National Assembly [TBMM]. (https://www.tbmm.gov.tr/tutanaklar/TUTANAK/TBMM/d03/c020/tbmm03020074ss0243.pdf).

Ilkkaracan, Pinar. 2016. *Deconstructing Sexuality in the Middle East: Challenges and Discourses.* London: Routledge.

Inglehart, Ronald, and Christian Welzel. 2005. *Modernization, Cultural Change, and Democracy: The Human Development Sequence.* Cambridge: Cambridge University Press.

"İptal Edilen Boston Gay Korosu Konserinin Perde Arkası." 2015. *Diken.* Retrieved February 19, 2019 (http://www.diken.com.tr/zorlunun-iptal-ettigi-boston-gay-korosu-konserinin-perde-arkasi-erdogan-boyle-istedi/).

"İt iti ısırmaz: Bir Alan Araştırması." 2010. *Lambdaİstanbul.*

"İzmir'de 2 Faili Meçhul Cinayet Dün Aydınlandı." 1966. *Cumhuriyet*, August 24, 7.

"Kan Çekti." 1959. *Milliyet*, May 26.

Kandiyoti, Deniz. 2002. "Pink Card Blues: Trouble and Strife at the Crossroads of Gender." Pp. 277–93 in *Fragments of Culture: The Everyday of Modern Turkey*, edited by D. Kandiyoti and A. Saktanber. London: I.B. Tauris.

Kandok, Halil. 2014. "'Bülent Ersoy'un Kolay Seçimi.'" *Radikal.* Retrieved (http://blog.radikal.com.tr/lgbt/bulent-ersoyun-kolay-secimi-82123).

Kaos GL. 2016a. *Cinsel Yönelim ve Cinsiyet Kimliği Temelli İnsan Hakları İzleme Raporu 2015.* Ankara: Kaos GL Derneği.

Kaos GL. 2016b. *Cinsel Yönelim ve Cinsiyet Kimliği Temelli İnsan Hakları İzleme Raporu 2016.* Ankara: Kaos GL Derneği.

Kaos GL. 2018. "İşçilerin Eşcinselliğini, Eşcinsellerin İşçiliğini Saklamak Zorunda Kalmayacağı bir Çalışma ve Sosyal Hayatı Hedefliyoruz." *Mesleki Sağlık ve Güvenlik Dergisi (MSG)* 17(65):35–37.

Karakaş, Burcu. 2014. "'Beni İfşa Ettiler, Allah Da Onların Açıklarını İfşa Etsin.'" *Milliyet*, March 9.

Karaman, Hayrettin. 2017. "Eşcinsele iyi (hoşgörülü) bakamayız." *Yeni Şafak*, July 6.

Karaman, Hayrettin. n.d. "Soru Cevap (485): Eşcinsellik Hakkında." *Hayrettinkaraman.Net.* Retrieved August 25, 2022 (http://www.hayrettinkaraman.net/sc/00485.htm).

"Karaman'da Ensar'ın Önüne Yatanlar Diyarbakır'da Ahlak Bekçisi!" 2016. *ABCgazetesi*, April 9. Retrieved February 20, 2019 (https://www.abcgazetesi.com/guncel/karamanda-ensarin-onune-yatanlar-diyarbakirda-ahlak-bekcisi-12834h/haber-12834).

"Kavramlar: Lûtilik". 1993. *İktibas* 11(178).

Kayacan, Nevin. 1990. "Dinsizliğin Ektiği Eşcinsellerle Söyleşi." *Mektup* (70).

Kemal, Mehmed. 1981. "Eşcinsel Şarkıcılar." *Cumhuriyet*, August 14.

"Kerimcan Durmaz Canlı Yayına Bağlandı, Erhan Nacar İle Yüzleşti!" 2018. *Söylemezsem Olmaz.*

"Kerimcan Durmaz Samsun'daki Saldırı Sonrasında Ilk Kez Açıklama Yaptı." 2016. *Sözcü*, December 14.

"Kerimcan Durmaz'dan Cumhurbaşkanı Erdoğan'a kutlama mesajı!" 2018. *superhabertv.* Retrieved February 19, 2019 (https://www.superhaber.tv/kerimcan-durmazdan-cumhurbaskani-erdogana-kutlama-mesaji-haber-96395).

"Kerimcan Durmaz'ın Aylık Kazancı Şaşırttı." 2017. *CNN Türk.* Retrieved August 25, 2022 (https://www.cnnturk.com/magazin/kerimcan-durmazin-aylik-kazanci-sasirtti?page=2).

Kılıçarslan, İsmail. 2015. "Zor, çok zor bir yazı." *Yeni Şafak*, June 30.

106 *LGBT and the Entertainment Sector*

Kılıçarslan, İsmail. 2019. "K-Pop, BTS, army ve Z kuşağının halleri." *Yeni Şafak*, February 12.

Kılıçkaya, Buse. 2010. "3 Mart Dünya Seks İşçileri Günü." *Lubunya* 5:18.

Kılıçkaya, Buse. 2011. "LGBT Aktivistlere Sorduk." *Lubunya*, November.

Kırbaş, Hayat. 2009. "İki Bacağımın Arasındaki Apak Namus." *Lubunya* 4:1.

Kocaer, Soner. 2011. "Ağaca bağlayıp tecavüz ettiler." *Hürriyet*, April 15.

Koçu, Reşad Ekrem. 2002. *Eski İstanbul'da Meyhaneler ve Meyhane Köçekleri*. İstanbul: Doğan Kitap.

Koseku. 2016. "Eşcinsel Biri Memuriyetten Atılır Mı?" *Memurlar.Net*. Retrieved February 19, 2019 (https://forum.memurlar.net/konu/2173018/).

Kurbanoğlu, Elçin. 2011. "Bu Naz'a, Derya'ya, Ya Da Buse'ye Yönelik Bir Saldırı Değil." *Lubunya* 8:38.

"KuşumAydın:Televizyonkariyerimbitti."2018.*CNN Türk*.RetrievedAugust15,2022 (https://www.cnnturk.com/magazin/kusum-aydin-televizyon-kariyerim-bitti).

"LGBT: Altan Tan bayraklarımızı gördükten sonra yüzünü bize dönmedi." 2015. *Radikal*. Retrieved February 20, 2019 (http://www.radikal.com.tr/turkiye/lgbt_altan_tan_bayraklarimizi_gordukten_sonra_yuzunu_bize_donmedi-1321354/).

"LGBT Dernek Temsilcileri CHP Ile Görüştü." 2012. *Kaos GL Haber Portalı*. Retrieved February 20, 2019 (http://kaosgl.org/sayfa.php?id=10337).

"LGBTİ Aday Neden HDP'de Siyaset Yaptığını Anlattı." 2015. *CNN Türk*. Retrieved February 20, 2019 (https://www.cnnturk.com/turkiye/lgbti-aday-neden-hdpde-siyaset-yaptigini-anlatti).

"LGBTT Örgütleri Vakit Hakkında Suç Duyurusu Yaptı." 2010. *Bianet*. Retrieved February 18, 2019 (https://www.bianet.org/bianet/toplumsal-cinsiyet/121376-lgbtt-orgutleri-vakit-hakkinda-suc-duyurusu-yapti).

Lıcalı, Mahmut. 2015. "Mahalle Baskısı… HDP'de LGBT Aday Yok." *Cumhuriyet*, September 20.

"M. İhsan Karaman on Twitter[1]: 'Gaylerin sponsoru KİM?'" 2015. *Twitter*. Retrieved February 19, 2019 (https://twitter.com/mikaraman/status/609739080092491776).

"M. İhsan Karaman on Twitter [2]: 'Boğaziçi Üniversitesinde ücretsiz gay korosu konseri!'" 2015. *Twitter*. Retrieved February 19, 2019 (https://twitter.com/mikaraman/status/609739080092491776).

Magazin Burada. 2019. *Kerimcan Durmaz Skandal Videoyu Kabul Ederek Sessizliğini Bozdu*.

"Maltepe'deki Transfobik Saldırılara Protesto." 2012. *Kaos GL Haber Portalı*. Retrieved February 11, 2019 (https://kaosgl.org/haber/maltepersquodeki-transfobik-saldirilara-protesto).

"Mecdelli Zeytin on Twitter." 2021. *Twitter*, September 14. Retrieved August 26, 2022 (https://twitter.com/kadikadan/status/1437680520385736704).

"Medyanın Lanetlileri: Esmeray." 2013. *90'larda Lubunya Olmak*. Izmir: Siyah Pembe Üçgen.

"Medyanın Lanetlileri: İlkim." 2013. *90'larda Lubunya Olmak*. Izmir: Siyah Pembe Üçgen.

Mehmet Halife. 1986. *Tarih-i Gılmani*. Ankara: Kültür ve Turizm Bakanlığı.

Melek, Z. 1953. "Eski Devirlerde Köçekler ve Çengiler." *Resimli Tarih Mecmuası* 4(47):2705–29.

"Merhaba." 2007. *Pembe Hayat* 2:1.

"Namaz Kılıp Oruç Tutuyorum." 2016. *Sabah*. Retrieved February 19, 2019 (https://www.sabah.com.tr/magazin/2016/10/25/kerimcan-durmaz-gercek-hayatimi-yansitsam-yer-yerinden-oynar?paging=2).

LGBT and the Entertainment Sector 107

Nil, Mahmut Şefik. 2003. "Bu Kültürde Eşcinsel Olmak." *KAOS GL*, March, 13.

"*Nil Makaracı: Demet Evgar Beni Susturmaya Çalıştı*." 2018. *Özgürüz (Youtube Channel)*. Retreived on 3 Aug 2022 (https://www.youtube.com/watch?v=3F--pj_VIV0).

Öğünç, Pinar. 2007a. "'Michael Jackson Ne Kadar Siyahsa Bülent Ersoy o Kadar Transeksüel.'" *Kaos GL*. Retrieved February 19, 2019 (http://kaosgl.org/sayfa.php?id=1307).

Öğünç, Pınar. 2007b. "Fevkaladenin Fevkinde Bir Trans Öyküsü." *Lubunya* 1:1.

Oktay, Tülay Demir. 2017. "Fatih Ürek: Kerimcan'ı ilk gördüğümde 'Bu ne ya' dedim." *Hürriyet Kelebek*, November 6.

"Öldürülen 'Travesti'yse, Mahkeme'den Ceza İndirimi." 2014. *Kaos GL Haber Portalı*. Retrieved November 30, 2021 (https://kaosgl.org/haber/oldurulen-quottravestiquotse-mahkemersquoden-ceza-indirimi).

Öner, Aysun. 2015. *Beyaz Yakalı Eşcinseller: İşyerinde Cinsel Yönelim Ayrımcılığı ve Mücadele Stratejileri*. İstanbul: İletişim Yayınları.

Öner, Aysun. 2017. "Beyaz Yakalı Lezbiyen ve Gey Bireylerin İş Yerinde Karşılaştıkları Cinsel Yönelim Ayrımcılığının Etkileri." *Mesleki Sağlık ve Güvenlik Dergisi (MSG)* 17(64):29–37.

Öner, Aysun. 2018. "Türkiye'de Trans Oyuncu Olmak." *KAOS GL* 160:23–30.

Övür, Mahmut. 2014. "Herkesin Türkiye'sine doğru." *Sabah*. Retrieved February 19, 2019 (https://www.sabah.com.tr/yazarlar/ovur/2014/07/13/herkesin-turkiyesine-dogru).

Öz, Yasemin. 2019. *Cinsel Yönelim ve Cinsiyet Kimliği Temelli İnsan Hakları İzleme Raporu 2016*. Ankara: Kaos GL.

Öz, Yasemin. 2020. *Cinsel Yönelim ve Cinsiyet Kimliği Temelli İnsan Hakları İzleme Raporu 2016*. Ankara: Kaos GL.

Özen, Saadet. 2000. "Feleğin Dansçıları." *Atlas* 93:88–96.

Özgenç, Meltem. 2018. "Manevi danışmanların hizmet kuralları." *Hürriyet*, September 12.

Öztop, Nevin. 2009. *Kadın Olma Halleri*. Ankara: Kaos GL.

"Paris Saatiyle Oruç Açtı." 2007. *Hürriyet Kelebek*, September 18.

"Peki bu yaptığın feminizme ne kadar uygun." 2022. *Twitter*. March 9. Retrieved August 12, 2022 (https://twitter.com/azginazinlikk/status/1503131501604429824).

Pembe Hayat, and Kaos GL. 2017. "Cinsel Yönelim ve Cinsiyet Kimliği Temelli İnsan Hakları İzleme Raporu 2013-2014-2015-2016-2017." Ankara: Ayrıntı Basımevi.

Phelan, Peggy. 1993. *Unmarked: The Politics of Performance*. London: Routledge.

"PSM'deki Boston Gay Men's Chorus Konseri Iptal Edilsin." 2015. *Change. Org*. Retrieved February 19, 2019 (https://www.change.org/p/e%C5%9Fcinselli%C4%9Fi-me%C5%9Frula%C5%9Ft%C4%B1rmak-ve-yaymak-i%C3%A7in-yap%C4%B1lacak-27-haziran-20-00da-zorlu-psm-deki-boston-gay-men-s-chorus-konseri-iptal-edilsin%20%E2%80%93%20http://www.yenisafak.com/hayat/zorludaki-gay-konseri-iptal-edildi-2135248).

"RTÜK'ten 'Huysuz Virjin'e darbe." 2007. *Haber7*. Retrieved February 19, 2022 (http://www.haber7.com/medya/haber/277922-rtukten-huysuz-virjine-darbe).

"Rüzgar Erkoçlar: 'Kadına Güvenilmez'" 2017. *Sözcü*. Retrieved February 19, 2019 (https://www.sozcu.com.tr/hayatim-haberleri/ruzgar-erkoclar-kadina-guvenilmez/).

Safa, Peyami. 1955. "Mânevi Savunma Refleksi." *Milliyet*, February 16.

Safa, Peyami. 1956. "Allah Korkusu Kalmayınca..." *Milliyet*, January 17.

"Sahabeler Şehrinin ağır tepkisi LGBT panelini iptal mi ettirdi?" 2016. *Diyarbakır Söz*. Retrieved February 20, 2019 (http://www.diyarbakirsoz.com/diyarbakir/sahabeler-sehri-agir-tepkisi-lgbt-panelini-iptal-mi-ettirdi-151250).

108 LGBT and the Entertainment Sector

Salik, Rüya. 2018. "Nil Makaracı, Cinsel Yönelimi Sebebiyle Diziden Kovulduğunu Iddia Etti." *Milliyet Molatik*. Retrieved February 19, 2019 (http://www.milliyet. com.tr/Nil-Makaraci--cinsel-yonelimi-sebebiyle-diziden-kovuldugunu-iddia-etti-molatik-7390/).

Şansal, Barbaros. 2014. "'Gelin Ulan Buraya i...Ler.'" *#tarih Dergi* (4):52–53.

Saygun, Semen Yönsel. 2017. "Sınıfımıza Gökkuşağının Bütün Renklerini Sokmanın Zamanıdır." *KAOS GL* 155:10–11.

Selçuk, Ilhan. 1981. "Eşcinsel?" *Cumhuriyet*, November 1.

Selek, Pınar. 2014. *Maskeler Süvariler Gacılar. Ülker Sokak: Bir Alt Kültürün Dışlanma Mekanı*. Istanbul: Ayizi Kitap.

Selvi, Abdulkadir. 2008. "Bülent Ersoy'un Rejime Ikinci Müdahalesi." *Yeni Şafak*, February 27.

Semercioğlu, Cengiz. 2017. "Selin Ciğerci Ile Gökhan Çıra Merak Edilenleri Anlattı." *Hürriyet Kelebek*, December 16.

Şenlikoğlu, Emine. 1996. "Osmanlı'da Harem ve '8 Mart Kadınlar Günü.'" *Mektup*, April.

Şenlikoğlu, Emine. 2013. "Eşcinselliğin Bilinmeyen Yüzü." Retrieved February 19, 2019 (http://www.eminesenlikoglu.org/14904_Escinselligin-bilinmeyen-yuzu. html).

Sevengil, Refik Ahmet. 1985. "Şehevi Raks - Köçekler - Tavşan Oğlanlar." P. 71 in *İstanbul Nasıl Eğleniyordu?* İstanbul: İletişim Yayınları.

Sever, Şirin. 2010. "Herkesin Hayran Olduğu Insanlar Bana Hayran - Röportaj Haberleri." *Sabah*, March 28.

"'Şizofreni' Bahane, Transfobi Şahane." 2014. *Kaos GL Haber Portalı*. Retrieved February 11, 2022 (https://kaosgl.org/haber/lsquosizofrenirsquo-bahane-transfobi-sahane).

Som, Deniz. 1981. "Eşcinsel Şarkıcılar Avrupa Hazırlığı Yapıyor." *Cumhuriyet*, June 14.

SPoD Sosyal Politikalar Cinsiyet Kimliği ve Cinsel Yönelim Çalışmaları Derneği. 2012. *LGBT Davaları: AIHM, Yargıtay ve Danıştay İçtihatları*. Istanbul: SPoD.

Star TV. 2006. *Popstar'da Bülent Ersoy ve Ebru Gündeş'in Kavgası*. Retrieved August 25, 2022 (https://www.youtube.com/watch?v=FeQA28bXlzo).

Tahaoğlu, Cicek. 2015. "LGBTİ Aktivistine Evinde Saldırı: 'Nasılsa Serbest Kalırız, Sen Düşün.'" *Kaos GL Haber Portalı*. Retrieved February 11, 2019 (http://www. kaosgl.org/sayfa.php?id=19802).

Tar, Yıldız. 2014. "Açlık Grevindeki Trans Mahpus: Ölmek İstemiyorum!" *Kaos GL Haber Portalı*. Retrieved (https://kaosgl.org/haber/aclik-grevindeki-trans-mahpus-olmek-istemiyorum).

Tar, Yıldız. 2016a. "Trans Kadına Gaspa 12'şer Yıl Hapis Cezası." *Kaos GL Haber Portalı*. Retrieved February 11, 2019 (https://kaosgl.org/haber/ trans-kadina-gaspa-12rsquoser-yil-hapis-cezasi).

Tar, Yıldız. 2016b. "Kemal Ördek'e Cinsel Saldırı Davasında Hapis Cezası." *Kaos GL Haber Portalı*. Retrieved February 11, 2019 (http://www.kaosgl.org/sayfa. php?id=22523).

"Taşkışla Civarı Soyguncuların Karargâhı Oldu." 1963. *Cumhuriyet*, August 7, 5.

Tezel, Mevlüt. 2016. "Erdoğan'ın iftarına katılmak linç sebebi oldu." *Sabah*, June 24.

"'TMM' Trans Murder Monitoring Archives." 2021. *TvT*. Retrieved July 27, 2022 (https://transrespect.org/en/research/tmm/).

LGBT and the Entertainment Sector 109

"Trans Kadına İşkence Yapan Saldırgana 16 Yıl Hapis." 2015. *Kaos GL Haber Portalı.* Retrieved February 11, 2022 (https://kaosgl.org/haber/trans-kadina-iskence-yapan-saldirgana-16-yil-hapis).

"Transları Hedef Alan Gaspçılar Tutuklandı." 2017. *Kaos GL Haber Portalı.* Retrieved February 11, 2022 (https://kaosgl.org/haber/translari-hedef-alan-gaspcilar-tutuklandi).

"Transsexual Singer Bülent Ersoy Attends Iftar Dinner Hosted by President Erdoğan." 2016. *Daily Sabah.* Retrieved February 19, 2019 (https://www.dailysabah.com/politics/2016/06/20/transsexual-singer-bulent-ersoy-attends-iftar-dinner-hosted-by-president-erdogan).

"Travesti Anısı Cübbeli Ahmet Hoca". 2016. *cubbeliahmethoca.tv.* Retrieved August 25, 2022 (https://www.youtube.com/watch?v=UOw3Vsbb3jc).

"Travestiyi Öldürene Ömür Boyu Hapis." 2011. *Sondakika.Com*, November 2.

Tulgar, Ahmet. 2004. "Musikiden Özür Diliyorum." *Milliyet*, May 30.

Ulusum, Ece. 2016. "Beyaz saçlı Huysuz Virjin!" *Habertürk*, April 14.

Ünlü, Ahmet Mahmut. 2017. *Eşcinsellik Günahı İle İnsan Kâfir Olmaz!* Retrieved August 25, 2022 (https://www.youtube.com/watch?v=OaeBDB-KUdc).

Vance, Carole S. 2007. "Anthropology Rediscovers Sexuality: A Theoretical Comment." Pp. 57–74 in *Culture, society and sexuality.* London: Routledge.

"Ve Hayat Akıp Giderken: Mine." 2013. *90'larda Lubunya Olmak.* Izmir: Siyah Pembe Üçgen.

Will, Michael R., and Bilge Oztan. 1993. "Hukukun Sebebiyet Verdiği Bir Acı: Transseksüellerin Hukuki Durumu." *Ankara Üniversitesi Hukuk Fakültesi Dergisi* 43(1–4):227–68.

Yargıtay 1. Ceza Dairesi [Supreme Court 1st Criminal Division]. 2012. E.N. 2011/1668, K.N. 2012/4593.

Yargıtay 2. Daire [Supreme Court 2nd Division]. 1986. No. 1986/651K. 27 March.

Yavuz, Zeliha. 1990. "Canavar Medeniyetin Çirkin Yüzü...!" *Mektup* 70:33.

Yıldırım, Celal. 1985. "Medeni Geçinen Ülkeler Nereye Gidiyor." *Müslüman Sesi* 24:477–78.

Yılmaz, Volkan. 2010. "Sosyal Vatandaşlık Etrafında: Ittifakın Olanakları Üzerine." *KAOS GL*, April, 20–21.

Yılmaz, Volkan. 2012. "LGBT Meselesinde Siyasi Tehditler ve Olanaklar." *Bianet.* Retrieved February 19, 2019 (https://m.bianet.org/bianet/diger/139812-lgbt-meselesinde-siyasi-tehditler-ve-olanaklar).

"Yılmaz'a Poşetli Dilekçe: Sisi'den." 1991. *Cumhuriyet*, July 7.

"Zaman Cinnet Zamanı: S, D, İ ve Ö Ile Söyleşi." 2009. *Lubunya* 4:11–14.

Ze'Evi, Dror. 2006. *Producing Desire: Changing Sexual Discourse in the Ottoman Middle East, 1500–1900.* Vol. 52. Berkeley, CA: University of California Press.

4 Women and Clothing

This chapter analyzes the unchaining of others' clothing rights from "our" first-order values pertaining to clothing. I argue that an exclusive feature of the current[1] debates over clothing is the ethical content which depends on the expression of a set of second-order values, concerned with managing difference instead of imposing ideal types, theological, scientistic, or other ideological truth claims. Irrespective of whether the interlocutors like to go beyond the scope of their foundational values, they realize the necessity of questioning what would be appropriate in the conduct of their relations with other value systems. In this setting, their main task is to align this ethical necessity with their foundational values. There are functional roles assigned to democracy in the performance of this task.

First, I will emphasize that clothing represented a value-laden matter of social order or development since the early Ottoman times. Accordingly, clothing patterns acted as the markers of some pre-defined social groups (e.g., religious communities in the *Millet System*). Following the Ottoman modernization process, some rival ideological representations, struggling for supremacy in the state, continued to share the notion that one's clothing marked one's identity. In other words, the wearer of an item of clothing had to carry the clear-cut personality that the authority assigned for this item. Even during Tanzimat and Meşrutiyet Reforms, the rival ideological positions agreed in making authoritative claims over clothing, despite that they clashed over the meaning of clothes.

Within this context, I demonstrate that clothing was not problematized by one hegemonic ideology or the other but shared in their shared cultural mindset—i.e., the common playing field where they operated. The Clothing Revolution challenged the value system of its past. In other words, its inventors rationalized intolerance against the intolerance of their past. It did not mean to challenge the state's value-laden take on clothing. On the contrary, in pursuit of making some "Secular national values" ascend, the state authority reproduced the mindset that one's dress would be a mirror of one's stance vis-à-vis the competing ideal types.

Upon assessing this historical baggage, I will argue that this cultural mindset, which transcends the rivalry of ideologies and changing authority

DOI: 10.4324/9781003311805-4

structures, has recently been challenged in unprecedented ways. In recent incidents and the *exploratory conversations* in them, intolerance has been rationalized almost always in reference to contextuality. Accordingly, instead of reducing their authoritative claims to essential features of clothes, the authorities have to rely on contextual elements, such as the time, place, and manners in which a dress appeared. This argumentation differs from the past knowledge claims based merely on the context-free properties of clothes. Among these past knowledge claims were the rationalization of intolerance against şapka (en. hat) on the basis that it represents "blasphemy" (tr. küfür), and the intolerance against *peçe* (en. niqab, full-face veil) on the grounds that it is a leftover from pre-modernity.

This shift implies limited yet significant cultural change. It indicates that some spaces, albeit isolated, have been left free and dedicated to others by the authority, albeit preferably under a watchful eye. In these conversations, I seek democratic change in the unprecedented calls for exiling this watchful eye that imposes a single, definitive meaning to time, place, and manners in which clothes appear.

The focal point of *evaluative conversations* will be the tension between parochial claims on morality and social context. Even though the alleged moral condition of clothes may have been somewhat well-reproduced, the carriers of the abovementioned ideological repertoires have realized cultural change in some key respects. This change includes a re-casting of Secularism in terms of recognizing (1) the agency of türban-wearers together with the burden of responsibility it loads on them; (2) the need to re-visit some elements of the ideological amalgam previously made to rationalize the head-covering ban; the re-casting of Islamism in terms of recognizing (3) the temporal element through which an item of clothing makes sense; and (4) the belief system's need for those who may refuse to follow the rules of *tesettür*, given the otherwise "disappointing" in-group practice of such foundational values. Most importantly, because these changes made it discursively possible for a "türban-wearer" to defend human rights in the "Secular" sense of the term, and a hijabi to be "immoral" in the "Islamist" sense of the term, clothing has been deposed from the position of acting as an infallible precursor of personality. I conclude that this change has implications for agents' instrumental considerations of democracy. They need democracy for the sake of preserving their foundational values.

Furthermore, concerned with a set of relevant ethical questions, the ideology makers seem to have admitted that their arguments cannot be based merely on a statement of their first-order values. Despite talking about themselves and others' foundational values, they had to go further to touch upon the necessity of managing some ties between these values and their discontents. In this vein, they rely on their understanding of a set of second-order values, such as freedom of conscience or the necessary space to be allocated for non-Muslims, which they think will ultimately promote their first-order values. In other words, they do not meet in a set of second-order

112   *Women and Clothing*

values in the name of democracy, but the divergence at this level renders their relationship different and is conducive to a democratic coexistence.

The *retroactive conversations* suggest that the women who recently faced some authoritative claims over their clothes have tried to reclaim their agency in various ways. Firstly, they have interlocutors who frequently ask their opinions (e.g., in mass media channels, public parades, or other meetings), facilitating their participation in ideology making. In these conversations, where they recalled the incidents, they staunchly defended their ways of life. More importantly, while doing so, none of them described their choice of clothing as "the true one," but a respectable one among others. They did not denounce another way of life to justify the ones they chose. They did not associate the intolerance they faced with any other identity as a whole—be it a religion or a value system. They made their rights-based positions explicit by denouncing the authoritative claim over their clothing preference and refusing to make their own definitive claims on what should be legitimate to wear in a given social setting. Therefore, they have something to say against the gatekeepers of hegemonic ideologies.

Finally, the chapter questions if this ethical content was accessible in the snapshots from a past yet relevant historical episode. With this aim, I examine the oft-recalled Ticani attacks (in the early-1950s) on women due to their allegedly open clothes. In this part, I argue that the attacked women could not participate in the ideology-making processes, as the gatekeepers did not need them as interlocutors. This exclusion is because they deemed the issue a matter of defending the ideal-type woman of alternative hegemonic imaginaries, none of which necessarily included the individual experience of those who faced an authoritative claim over their clothes. Women could have a voice so long as they purified their arguments from their unique stories. I conclude that, at the time, the clothing issue was commonly taken as a war of ideal types rather than empirical types.

Clothing as a Matter of Cultural Mindset

The studies on the "headscarf" or "türban" ban have not yet scrutinized the issue as one dimension of some further-reaching authoritative claims over the clothing. Limiting the question to the head-covering ban first risks reducing the subject to state policy, even though the state authority is not the sole determinant of such restrictions' rationalization. Secondly, this limit disconnects the ban from other restriction fields that may have been deemed relevant to the head-covering ban. In my opinion, the (de)construction of these relations in the human mind indicates some noteworthy shifts between the cultural periods I have introduced.

I find it noteworthy that conversations on the head-covering ban usually ended up being broader debates about the obstacles set against women. In such debates, a somewhat systematic overarching argument is that "open clothes" should be interfered with as a matter of public decency. In other

Women and Clothing   113

words, the public debate on the head-covering ban inevitably merged with additional limits on dressing in public, which render it a broader *clothing problem*. Yet, a more general category of clothing problem cannot be conclusively isolated from the other potential subjects either, as its usage triggers an even more expansive repertoire of communal pressures, extending towards numerous fields' logic of appropriateness. For they amalgamate some symbols which would otherwise be irrelevant to one another, I will name the outcomes of these ideological processes as *amalgams*.

Various amalgamation techniques explain why the public discussion in the 2000s was positioned on a dialectic between the legally grounded head-covering ban and the socially grounded neighborhood pressure. If one aimed to rationalize the former, s/he would often emphasize the existence of the latter. The latter was associated with the intolerance of an essentially conservative value system, whereas the former was intended to overturn this system by means of Secularism. On the one hand, the head-covering ban was to be fundamentally imposed by the state. On the other hand, some neighborhood-level dress codes were to be implemented by different micro-authorities that have a "conservative" take on public decency. However, these two conflicting claims underpinned one another by casting a fundamental role for clothing in the making of society and gender roles.

The dominant culture reproduces itself whenever this contestation surfaces, as it leaves no room for the contesters to think of challenging one another with respect to, say, gender essentialism. Instead, they constructed this common playing field mutually to contest what the ideal women wear, do, and say.[2] Considering the totality of these seemingly conflicting but essentially merging authoritative claims over clothing, I refuse to analyze intolerance merely against some isolated preferences—whether to wear skirts or scarves. Instead of developing yet another parochial vision, I will explore the shared cultural mindset that amalgamates clothing with other social life aspects. My intention was perfectly depicted in the title of Cihan Aktaş's study, "Kılık-Kıyafet ve İktidar" (en. Appearance-Dress and Rulership). That said, the content of Aktaş's study largely did not scrutinize the relationship between those I mentioned above—i.e., the seemingly conflicting but essentially merging authoritative claims. Instead, Aktaş was content with problematizing the "rulership" of the "Westernist" ideology that informed the late Ottoman modernization project and the Secularism of the Republic. Though she has a point in her terms, this focal point renders her study a parochial one. It sought the exercise of rulership only in the state authority and only as a property of a given form of modernism.

On the contrary, my starting point is that this fundamental cultural mindset is grasped only through a dialectic reading. The ruling elite's policies in the name of the Clothing Revolution (1925) directly responded to the deepseated Ottoman understanding of clothing. Though the ideology behind the revolution was closely related to the rulers' perception of "universal

114 *Women and Clothing*

modernity" and the requirements of nation-state building processes, their rationalization of intolerance—e.g., Şapka Law—was not merely imported from the West. In this vein, I will analyze some reasoning processes that the ruling elite underwent in their rationalizations of intolerance against the fez and hijab. Based on my analysis of the arguments of Falih Rıfkı Atay and Niyazi Berkes, I argue that these processes include the şapka wearers' fear of being seen as infidels in the face of the carriers of fez. The ruling elite rationalized intolerance against fez, partly because they perceived an existential threat from the markers of identity inherited from the past. In sum, the "Clothing Revolution" was not rationalized for its own sake but in response to historical baggage that some competing authoritative claims previously contributed.

By the same token, the contemporary public marches led by the women who have been interfered with for their clothing preferences can make sense concerning the 1990s and the 2000s mass debate over the role of subjectivity in headscarf usage. In this vein, as a result of my cross-temporal analysis, I will argue that public opinion did not take women's possible individual perspectives on clothing as a vital matter of agency in the early-1950s' ideological contestation.

This period is one in which some members of the *Ticani* movement were attacking women for their clothes. Contrary to this historical episode, the women in the recent cases have reclaimed their agency with a series of unique ethical arguments. They seem to have inherited a subjectivity notion from the previous mass debates on the head-covering ban. Therefore, many covered and uncovered women could come together in the new public marches, entitled "do not meddle with my outfit." These transmissions underlie the re-making of the cultural mindset, which contains but also goes beyond ideological counter-positions. Given that the opposite poles tend to pull each other onto a common playing field, the most fundamental question of cultural change shall be the extent to which this playing field shifted as the dialogue proceeded.

In the following part, based on a review of the historiography of this landscape, I initially describe this common cultural mindset as one that identified clothing as a fundamental social matter. Accordingly, dresses were more than dresses, as they had their personalities regardless of the subjective meanings attached to them by those who wear them. Therefore, many actors were present to regulate clothing: the *self*, law enforcers at public places, husband, father or mother in the family, teachers at school, or anybody who occasionally claimed such rulership in the neighborhood. Through sanctions, rewards, and enforcement mechanisms, clothing items became symbols exogenous to their wearers. I describe the fundamental aspect of this cultural mindset as the rejection of contextuality in dresses: some given dresses, be them *fez*, şapka, or *hijab*, would be forbidden for some assigned groups, be them Muslims, Christians, or the citizens of the Turkish Republic.

Clothing in the Ottoman "Millet" System: Tolerance and Its Limits

> Nor any infidel be allowed to wear fine clothes.
> *[Order to the Qadi of İstanbul, 1568]*
>
> (Lewis 1984:38)

Dresses served as an immediate marker of boundary in the Ottoman system (Barkey 2005:16). In this system, all *millet*s (i.e., religious communities) had their respective dress codes. The state ensured that the clothing traditions of each religious community would differ. In a hardly understandable way from the succeeding nation-state point of view, the authority would preserve the difference by force or agreement. Although in the 16th century, the millet system was not as clear-cut as it later became, the first well-known clothing regulation was made by Murat III (1546–1595) as a response to the increasing similarities between the dresses of Muslims and non-Muslims (Ercan 1990:118). According to the ideology behind this problematization, religious differences should be made explicit at first glance (Turan 2005:241).

In this understanding which the following rulers reproduced, the upper hand was granted to the Muslim symbols. Non-Muslim communities would wear "their own" costumes. Still, as a reflection of the regime's identity, it was forbidden for a non-Muslim to wear materials deemed higher quality, such as silk. For example, non-Muslim men were obliged to wear hats instead of turbans (tr. *sarık*), defined as a symbol of Muslimness. They were also not allowed to wear white and green colors that symbolized the status of the Muslim *tebaa*. Within such boundaries, the pre-recognized authority structures of non-Muslim communities were to determine their own rules of appropriateness. According to Zilfi, the authorities of non-Muslim communities agreed with the higher power of the state in terms of promoting some clear-cut physical differences between religious communities (Zilfi 2018:60). Therefore, for a long time, the system worked well as a system of tolerance.

Wearing clothes designated to another millet was a matter of political punishment (tr. *siyaset cezası*), a particular category in Ottoman Customary Law, including very severe punishments up to the death penalty. According to the register of important public affairs (tr. *mühimme defteri*) dated 1556, three Muslims were penalized with political punishment after being caught in theft "in qafirs' hats and clothes" (Ercan 1990:118). The crime of robbery and wearing "qafir's clothes" was not precisely separated in the judicial proceedings (Ercan 1990). However, given that political punishment was very rarely considered as an option for the crime of theft,[3] this heavy punishment may have been due primarily to the way the criminals instrumentalized *other*'s clothes in this case. A decree that Murat III issued in 1577 made clear that political punishment would be the consequence of breaching the rules about clothing (Refik 1935:51; *see also* footnote 7 in Ercan 1990).

Even during the time of political openings (e.g., the Tulip Age or the modernist re-makings of Selim III), the rulers aim to reproduce the restrictions

116 Women and Clothing

with renewed decrees. For instance, despite garnering some popularity for his lax attitude to the matter, İbrahim Pasha eventually had to interfere with the somewhat tightened clothes of women during the Tulip Age (Sevengil 1985:103). During the rule of Selim III, a decree (1791) emphasized that tailors who ignored the clothing law would be hung in front of their stores (Koçu 2003:64). Between 1815 and 1820, Governor Abdullah Pasha of Sidon—i.e., Lebanon and Palestine—was able to impose, for the first time in the history of Acre, the "traditional" Ottoman dress codes on Non-Muslims (Philipp 2001:183).

Clothing in Ottoman Modernization: A Matter of Social Order and Development

The Ottoman Modernization changed many things, but not the deterministic status of clothing in the cultural mindset. Though the state's choice of clothes changed in due course, the pre-assigned role of clothing as a social boundary marker remained. Because clothing patterns were to signify social order and development, they were to be pre-determined. If this policy failed in the short run, it was supposed to be corrected later. Some key conversations from the Tanzimat, Meşrutiyet, and post-war years suggest that many of the protagonists and the antagonists of "modernization" shared, at least, the understanding that clothing was critical to the visible representations of the *self* and the *other*. Therefore, the competing ideal types of this era included explicit references to clothes.

In the mid-19th century, the rulers began to rationalize removing some clothes that they previously considered appropriate. As a symbol of Ottoman modernization, the state-led imposition of *fez*, which replaced men's turbans (tr. *sarık*) and rounded crown caps (tr. şubara), was intended to bring some symbolic refreshment to the weakening Ottoman army (Kavas 2015:521). Because the dispute was not just about the development of the military but society as a whole, this policy justified replacing the old clothes with some new ones in civic life. Within this context, a comparison between two tailors' books of orders—one from 1854 and the other from 1873—demonstrate a rapid "Westernization" in upper-class women's dresses in İstanbul (Tezcan 1988). According to Cevdet Pasha, the Egyptian high society triggered this "decay" by taking the lead in bringing Western fashion into İstanbul (Bardakçı 2005:243). Furthermore, as a rare opportunity for the art historians who study lower classes, a similar transformation was documented through the wedding dresses of a wide social circle (Micklewright 1989).

Though the state authority itself paved the way for this broader change, it tried to keep an eye on these changes. Accordingly, the rulers of Tanzimat enabled Muslim students to go to Europe for education. However, they restricted these travels for young female students whom they deemed too immature to embrace the significance of veiling (Erdoğan 2013:12). When a type of black hijab called *zar* spread in the 1870s İstanbul, Sultan Abdülhamit II initially banned it, fearing that it would lead to Muslim women's religious assimilation to Orthodox Christian women, alongside other security risks, such as the surveillance of illegal activity (Davis 2006:219). Even though the palace initially wanted to deter Muslim women from using zar, it faced several limitations: the unaffordable price of *ferace* (Avcı 2007:9), the substitute of *zar*, and some tradesmen's attempts to convince the sultan to lift the ban on zar (Alus 1951:541). An incident in which a group of vagrants ripped off two women's feraces also attracted public attention to this matter (Davis 2006:219). Eventually, Abdülhamit II decided to ban *ferace* and instead re-legalize hijab in a different style.

That said, one shall not exaggerate the geographic scope of this instability. Historians of daily life underline that women of rural Anatolia remained indifferent to both *zar* and *ferace*, as their traditional clothes were already different from those relatively new alternatives popularized in the cosmopolitan space of İstanbul (Osman Hamdi Bey and De Launay 1999; Emiroğlu 2002:214). In the same vein, the regimenting dress codes of the state were not as visible in the heterogeneity of the Balkans, Cyprus, and the Rum Islands either (Zilfi 2018:60). Though this diversity does not suffice to argue that the state explicitly rationalized tolerance for some pre-selected cultural zones, it suggests, at the very least, that the state did not problematize clothing attitudes equally in different spaces. His decree suggests that Abdülhamit II would not have banned the hijab had he not come across these "hijabi women" while going to the mosque of Teşvikiye.

In sum, even though certain clothes appeared and disappeared inconsistently, the social role attached to clothing remained intact after the mid-19th century. Accordingly, clothing was perceived by the Ottoman rulers as a significant marker of social order and development. Different clothes came to take their place in the modern constructions of progressive or conservative social values. The Sultans struggled to manage the clothing attitudes by periodically negotiating restrictions upon them. They matched the new clothes with pre-defined social groups, just like they aimed to do with the old ones, albeit at a different scope.

Clothing as an Infallible Indicator of Personality

Meşrutiyet brought a new set of controversies concerning clothes. Though my aim is not to scrutinize these controversies, I shall refer to some key conversations of the time, which indicate the reproduction of the cultural mindset that conferred a formative role on clothing in the making of the society. While clothes were under dispute in this period, the competing ideologies took the social significance of clothing for granted. For example, the Meşrutiyet expressionism took shape predominantly around "new" clothes for a new model of society. The old zar and çarşaf (hijabs) were out-of-fashion

118 *Women and Clothing*

according to some carriers of the new *"Milli Moda"* (en. national fashion), such as Writer Zehra Hakkı of Sedat Simavi's magazine, İnci:

> [T]hen, like those [men], women should be civilized in terms of clothing as well as ideation.

(Toprak 1998:52)

Other magazines, such as *Hürriyet-i Fikriye, Serbest Fikir*, and *Sıyanet*, also propagated "Turkish women" to be "unchained" from the hijab. In response, writer Aksekili Ahmed Hamdi of *Sebilürreşad* Magazine argued that it was a slander campaign, led mainly by "Arab Christian writers" against "Muslim women" (Meliha 1914:345; Aksekili Ahmed Hamdi 2017:827–37).

According to Aksekili, those who gave up *tesettür* consisted of a small group of "free lovers." Emine Seher Ali simply called them "irreligious" in her article in the magazine *Kadınlar Dünyası* (Ali 2015:67). The other writers of *Kadınlar Dünyası* problematized the use of niqab (tr. peçe), which they thought did not have any place in Islam. According to them, a compulsory "national dress code" (tr. kıyafet-i milli) should have been determined once and for all (Çakır 2010). Fatma Aliye, one of the first feminists[4] of the post-Tanzimat era, also established many of her claims upon an ideal type, "the women of Islam."[5] In the conversations between these thinkers, ideal types were under dispute—e.g., whether "Muslim women" shall remove *tesettür* for the sake of "development."

As the use of the tags such as, among other things, "free lovers," "the woman of Islam," and "the national fashion" suggests, clothing was of utmost importance in the construction of ideal types. These ideal types were described, compared, and contrasted via the media. This typological approach remained popular during the post-war years (1918 onwards) (*see* Hafız Baki 1919:445; Hakkı 1919:453; Kazımi 1919:255; Metinsoy 2014:28). For example, the magazine *Haftalık Mecmua* conducted an extensive survey in 1927 to sketch the ideal-type woman that its already predominantly male readers would prefer to marry (Toprak 2017:148–57). None of the women described in the magazine displayed a contradiction between the different aspects of their personalities. Their clothes always matched well with the rest of their characteristic features. For example, Feriha Hanım preferred "alafranga" (i.e., European style) clothes while having a "free life" and being able to deal with multiple men. Nevire Hanım dreamed of having fancy clothes, like "actresses," so she would do anything to reach fame and fashion. Bedia Nuri Hanım was a hardworking student who spent her free time in a library or laboratory. Therefore, her clothes were so effortless that it was difficult to distinguish her from men. In all these descriptions, clothing acted as an infallible indicator of personality.

With the upper hand of the state authority, this mass debate on clothes entered a new phase in the aftermath of the foundation of the Republic of Turkey (1923), the founding ideology of which also defined clothing as a

Women and Clothing   119

pre-requisite of social development. As Baker examined it, the fez was one key example since, in less than a century, its meaning shifted from being a proclamation of "modernization" to a symbol of "orthodoxy" and "conservatism" (Baker 2013:72). This alteration in the collective memory was not an imposition of the state or the then dissidents but a shared element in their dialogue. In the 1920s' political climate, not many appeared to reclaim the fez as a symbol of modernization. It represented bigotry for the "progressive,"[6] just as it represented tradition for the "conservative."[7] Its old meaning was just not beneficial for the conflicting parties anymore.

The Rationalization of Intolerance: How to Defend a Clothing Revolution

"Clothing Revolution" acted as a long-standing knowledge claim of Kemalism: the outside of a head must demonstrate at first glance that its inside can change. A radical change in physical appearance would pave the way for the revolution of the mind.[8] In this section, I explore the social ground on which the ruling elite of the Republic rationalized intolerance against certain items of clothing.

To establish a developmental state after the technological failure of the Ottoman system, the ideology makers of the Republic aimed to trigger an all-encompassing cultural transformation, beginning with the replacement of critical symbols of the old culture. Fez was the solution of an ancient culture; şapka would be the solution of the civilization. Fez was a hat for the era of institutionalized heterogeneity. Şapka would be the hat for the generation of institutionalized homogeneity. In defense of this clothing ideology from the 1930s, the didactic National Holiday broadcastings on official radio and TV repeatedly denigrated the variety of clothes in the Ottoman past as "a noisy confusion" (tr. "kıyafet curcunası" in Demirer 1982), or "clothing inequality" (tr. "kıyafet müsavatsızlığı" in "Din Âlimleri" 1953:300). The ideological monopoly of the "secular knowledge" (Ülken 1982:17; Karpat 2013:156–64) would replace the institutional dualism of Tanzimat Modernism, which signified medreses' coexistence with modern schools (*see* the "new" national values in Ülken 1982:309; Kamacı 2000).

The ideology makers of Turkey's modern nation-state meant by Secularism the removal or disenchantment of the old religious classes. As a part of this program, they challenged the formerly institutionalized dress codes in terms of shape and substance. Accordingly, many defendants of "the clothing revolution" justified one-type-fits-all dresses as a necessary step against the compartmentalization of people based on their "non-national" (tr. "gayrimilli") and "primitive" (tr. "iptidai") identities.[9] Because people would not suddenly forget the Ottoman doctrine on perceiving dress statuses, any remaining fez or hijab would reproduce the old principle. As an illustration, şapka represented the Levantines in the late Ottoman period. Fez had to be forbidden so that şapka would be set free from its particularistic identity.

120 *Women and Clothing*

In his memoir, Falih Rıfkı Atay, who was close to the state elite throughout the 1930s, recalled that in the Ottoman times, the worst of non-Muslims were called "the infidel with şapka" (tr. şapkalı gâvur). Having kept in mind the symbolic location of şapka in the late Ottoman times, Atay recalled this connotation to imply that legalizing şapka for Muslims would not suffice to deconstruct its essentially otherized position among Muslims. Within this context, Atay referred to chronicler Lütfi Efendi to recall that people "almost lynched" the two officers who, as the Sultan ordered, wore the reformed jackets and pants in public, on a Ramadan Day in 1828 (Atay 1961:541). Atay concurrently reminded his interlocutors of how they began wearing şapka in public: "I remember it very well: [...] they began chasing us when they saw us with şapka. We also heard the compliment, 'infidels'" (Atay 1961:548).

In the same vein, Niyazi Berkes felt a need to refer to the previous Meşrutiyet controversies while justifying the succeeding clothing revolution. Accordingly, Berkes recalled that in the mid-19th century, the Turkish students who studied in Europe were labeled as infidels in the country just because they reportedly began wearing şapka (Berkes 2002:547). As these arguments of Atay and Berkes suggest, a tremendous fear of the ruling elite was that those men who started wearing şapka and those women who uncovered would seem less religious than those who may have maintained the clothes from the Ottoman past. Therefore, having obtained the necessary means of authority, the ruling elite rationalized intolerance against these clothes, albeit in different ways for hijab versus fez.

Their strategy of action concerning the hijab was more complicated than their strategy against the fez. As the examples of fez and şapka suggest, the imposition of change always began with men. That said, in both historical episodes, the focus shifted to women in a somewhat ambivalent manner. Frequently revised decrees in the Ottoman times and the thorny debates over the hijab in the late Ottoman period and the early years of the Republic suggest that policymakers were often confused with the clothes assigned for women. The peculiarity of women's status in the value system and the contested ideological prospects of future social development played a fundamental role in this ambiguity. Women's clothing represented a central moral issue, a very quickly-changing fashion, a symbol of social development, and at the same time a reflection of women's legitimate ecological environment, the limits of which the new regime problematized from scratch.

These complications in women's clothing were why, in the aftermath of the şapka revolution, intolerance towards *peçe* (en. niqab, full-face veil) and çarşaf (en. black hijab) did not rely on any strictly defined legal criteria. There was no law to ban them. Ruling Party CHP's 4th Congress concluded a set of reasons as to why—unlike fez—peçe and çarşaf were not a matter of legal prohibition: (1) neither çarşaf nor peçe was worn in the rural sphere; (2) in the urban sphere, half of the women had already "left behind" these clothes; (3) the rest will change their habits when they meet further education

(Yakut 2002:28). Skeptical of these predictions, some members of Congress embraced the relatively nuanced argument that çarşaf had economic consequences[10] and was hence tolerable. In contrast, peçe denoted an ideological tool for women's subordination and thus was intolerable. In response to such critiques, in 1935, the banning of peçe and çarşaf was encouraged with an administrative order from the Ministry of Interior, calling local authorities to open proceedings (Dikici 2014:102). However, because these proceedings did not rely on any clear legal guidelines, some very different conducts emerged (Yakut 2002:30–31).

The state did not criminalize the usage of peçe and çarşaf in public but systematically emphasized its ideal-type woman as an uncovered one. Mustafa Kemal defined women's clothing as a building block of the project of cultural transformation. He argued in his historic speech on August 25, 1925, that "a civilized nation's women" should not hide their faces and eyes or turn their back to men. In the same speech, he announced that Turkish society deserved "civilized" and "international" clothes. On September 6, 1925, the cabinet's decree with the force of law stated that "all civil servants' clothes [should be] the same as the clothes common and general in the civilized nations" (Özdemir 2007:51). This law forbade women to cover in the state offices and ordered male civil servants outside these offices to greet one another with a specified gesture, using şapka.

Clothing in Contemporary Turkey: Eyes on Women

The Clothing Revolution has been a reference point and arguably a building block of the institutionalized value system behind Secularism. Since the 1930s, "the standard of civilization" remains at the forefront of state discourse. By referring to this concept in a new fashion, court verdicts in the late-80s justified a head-covering ban in universities. Tolerance towards this period's clothes was re-cast around a definition of tradition and development.

First and foremost, the state courts began to differentiate between those women who covered themselves in rural areas "in a traditional manner" and those women who covered themselves despite that they got "enough education to uncover" (Danıştay 1983). The former was tolerable for the authority, given that "our elders" also covered their heads. However, the latter epitomized a deliberate political act against the fundamentals of Secularism. This argument led to the well-reproduced[11] contextual distinction, between "headscarf" (tr. başörtüsü) and "türban." In this dichotomy, tolerating başörtüsü was meant to suggest that Secularism was not inherently anti-religious, as long as its expression does not go beyond habits and customs.

On the other hand, türban signified a reaction against modernity and a conscious stance taken against the fundamental codes of the Republic. Using images to differentiate between "türban" and "başörtüsü" from afar, many ideology makers aimed to make a stable category out of a discursive difference. Together with its "urban" and "fashionable" visible representation,

122　Women and Clothing

türban's "needle" gave itself away. The Council of State's decision on December 20, 1983, which approved the High Board of Education ban, was based on this separation (Bilge 1984). Former PM and President Süleyman Demirel put forward the de-politicization of türban as a pre-requisite for lifting the ban: "all types of headscarves should be free at universities, but türban is different" (Ballı 1993:9). Then Deputy Chairman Yekta Güngör Özden of the Constitutional Court underlined that the state had not interfered with women's clothes on the streets, but "at state institutions such as universities," and the court would be "loyal to the laws of Revolution which regulate the clothes of Turkish women" ("Türbana" 1990:1). Common to these defenses was that the problem was not the headscarf *per se* but the context within which it appeared.

İlhan Selçuk was among those who led the distinction between them. According to him, the headscarf was of "pure belief." In contrast, türban manifested "a political ambition" (Selçuk 1999:2). The latter demonstrated a well-calculated Islamist reaction against the Republic and not a matter of individual freedom. That said, Selçuk's reasoning was circular in the sense that any demand to wear the headscarf in the public space would render it a türban. *Başörtüsü*, in this context, meant not demanding re-configuration of the public space.

These defenses of the ban bounced between Secularism as a value system and Secularism as neutrality above particular religious expressions. On the one hand, they relied on the ruling of the European Court of Human Rights that the state may be entitled to restrict the wearing of headscarves with the aim of "upholding the principles of secularism and neutrality of the civil service" (European Court of Human Rights 2006). On the other hand, they rationalized that the state should protect itself from those against "Secular Values" (tr. "Laik değerler" in Subaşı 2004:118). Though this value-laden position determined the state's approach to rights and restrictions in a vaguely defined "public space" (e.g., universities, military buildings, courts, and the parliament), the visibility of türban was pretty much untouched in the rest of the social scene.

Türban, Rosewater, Rolex: Ideology Making as the Amalgamation of Symbols

Here come the amalgamation processes. According to many pro-ban politicians, bureaucrats (Göktaş 1995:3), and academics of the time (Unat 1987:1; Koray 1990:2), the regulation of clothes was substantively inseparable from the democratic rights of women, such as inheritance and property rights, monogamy, the equality of men and women as witnesses before the court, and women's right to divorce. Therefore, the inseparability of these rights from women's clothes rendered wearing türban a challenge against the democratic rights of women.

According to this view, it was an inconsistency to wear türban while defending the equality of men and women. This amalgamation of türban

Women and Clothing 123

with many other issues was typical in the defenses of the head-covering ban. For example, Bahriye Üçok discussed "the türban issue" with particular reference to a collection of other incidents, such as (1) a student and a worker whom vagrants killed for not fasting; (2) a student whom his teacher beat for not waking up to the morning prayer; (3) an Alevi teacher whom students' parents forced to declare his sect; (4) a group of female students whom the admins did not let take physical education; and (5) the opening of praying rooms at mid-schools (Üçok 1993:11). According to Üçok, these examples suggested that it was a systematic attack against Secularism. Therefore, she insisted, the türban would not be a standalone matter of freedom.

Moreover, it was not the only clothing problem Turkey had. On the contrary, many held the türban responsible for other clothing problems. The Head of Yozgat National Education, who was "an Islamist," did not permit pop singer Merdağ Çağ to have her concert in Yozgat because she wore a "low-neck" outfit. Sevim Nur had to change her dress for the same show (Çalışlar 1997:4). The incidents in and outside Turkey occasionally became relevant to the head-covering ban. In 2003, Özdemir İnce translated news from France: "they burned the woman who wore a mini-skirt" (İnce 2004). Accordingly, the türban became responsible for the aggression against women who wore other clothes.

An assumption behind this amalgam was that one's appearance would constitute the first step for becoming an appropriate defender of women's rights. In line with this assumption, her opposition heavily criticized then PM Tansu Çiller for attending an award ceremony in which men and women sat separately in the room. Journalist Şükran Ketenci (Soner) pointed out "the contradiction" that Çiller wore some "clothes of the most modern type" but also attended an event that subordinated women (Ketenci 1993). Çiller's clothes, not matching her ideology, led to cognitive dissonance for Soner and others.

Uğur Mumcu was one of the most influential thinkers who opposed taking the head-covering ban as a standalone matter. He opposed the head-covering ban not because he saw it as a naïve demand for human rights but because the problem was much more profound (Mumcu 1988a). Mumcu argued that the threat in Turkey was led by a coalition of Saudi financial consortiums with some (1) "go-getter businessmen," (2) Western states that supported Islamization against the threat of Communism, (3) Turkish liberals whom he did not see as genuine liberals, and (4) "the so-called conservative and nationalist political addresses." Mumcu pejoratively described this network as an incoherent coalition: "Rosewater...after shave...green skullcap...Rolex watch...round-trimmed beard...[Islamic] cloak and Davidoff cigars" (Mumcu 1988a).

This perspective became one that many others would reproduce in the following years.[12] In Mumcu's arguments, his perception of contradictions played a significant role. He often made fun of "liberal pilgrims" (tr. liberal hacı), which he thought to be an oxymoron (Mumcu 1988b). As he pondered

124   *Women and Clothing*

these categories to be mutually exclusive, he asked how President Özal could be a "Kemalist," an "Islamist," and a "liberal" at the same time (Mumcu 1988c, 1988d, 1988e). Yet, another contradiction was between the commands of Islam and rights demands in the name of religious freedom. Accordingly, he argued that Islam orders not simply a headscarf but a *jilbab*, the outer garment that covers the whole body: "If the Islamic rules are to be applied, it is not enough for them to cover their heads with türban; they must go to university [...] with jilbabs" (Mumcu 1988f). The so-called headscarf freedom was nothing but a matter of religious exploitation led by "the Arabesque-Liberal" ideology that was tailored to re-design Turkey (Mumcu 1988f). Among others who had similar perspectives, Mumcu and Üçok were assassinated within a decade.[13] Their followers further reinforced the amalgams they established through a set of new theories in this conspiratorial climate. Many people tied the officially unidentified murders to their Secularism.

These amalgams prevailed in disputes over the head-covering ban. Accordingly, it was not simply about a particular item of clothing but the unfreedom it represented. For instance, Former President Süleyman Demirel argued with a group of students at Erciyes University, many of whom openly criticized his views in favor of the interpretation of high courts that limited the use of headscarves in public institutions:

- Demirel: If you want to change the constitution, this [*i.e.*, trying to enter public institutions with headscarves] is not how to do it. According to the constitution, Turkey is a secular [tr. laik] state, which was described [as] the separation of religion and state [...] Still, [other Muslim countries] have admitted that Islam is experienced at its best in Turkey.
- *Objection from some students, one of whom yells more loudly:* We cannot live our religion[...]
- Demirel: In Turkey, does anyone say anything against the one who prays five times a day?! You should not say anything against the one who does not pray either! [*applauded vociferously by other students in support of Demirel*].

(Genç Bakış 2006)

Although the subject of the discussion was delimited as "the headscarf issue," in the course of a dialogue, Demirel linked this subject to another field—i.e., freedom of *not* praying—since he perceived a connection between the two. The loud applause in his favor indicated that he was not alone in this route of argumentation. Having created such interrelationships, those who opposed the visibility of the Islamic veil in public institutions have questioned whether it would be easy to display the symbols of *other* religions in public institutions. They argued that the headscarf would not be a matter of religious freedom as long as different varieties of faith do not enjoy space.

Emphases on "other religions in public institutions" were often accompanied by suppositions: "if I were a Buddhist or a Jew, we would have a conflict."

Women and Clothing   125

These remarks signified the speaker's perception of being subject to intolerance in some other spheres of life. Hence, they serve to emancipate capabilities from parochial values. Once, writing his memory of how a Jewish man at a consulate was trying to hide his kippah under a hat, former executive director, Melih Meriç of Habertürk Newspaper, argued by the same token:

> A country where a kippah should be hidden under a hat and a türban under a wig is [...] tragic [...].

Through this line of argumentation, he implied that *all* should be free from external pressures, or *none* should be limitless. Others extended this argument further to encompass the authority structure between the majority and the minority belief systems. Mustafa Akaydın, the former director of Akdeniz University and the former mayor of Antalya from CHP, described his notion of Secularism in this context:

> It would not be a problem to allow türban if we were not a Muslim country [...] [T]o my university, a Jew should be able to enter with a kippah. Still, a Muslim should not be able to join with a türban since the latter would lead to [public] pressure in a Muslim country.
>
> ("Kipalı" 2008)

After this statement, Akaydın warned his audience so that his argument would not be manipulated: "if those who wear kippah consisted of 20% of the students, I would ban it too!"

Demirel's reference to the "freedom of not praying" came together with the emphasis on the freedom of not wearing the headscarf. Accordingly, allowing the headscarf in public institutions would pressure Muslim women to question themselves. In other words, any wearer of türban would represent a social group that defends the indispensability of the Islamic veil. Therefore, she should be held responsible for the social group to which she seems to belong. She was forced to wear a türban, or she pushes—through her visibility—the other Muslim women to wear it.

The Claims over Subjectivity in Clothing: Secularism and "Liberals"

Claiming that "türban can neither be modern nor contemporary," Uğur Mumcu refused to interpret the issue as a matter of women's agency (Mumcu 1988f). Türban had an autonomous meaning that transcends its carriers' subaltern position. From Professor Ahmet Taner Kışlalı to Former CHP MP Necla Arat, many shared the argument that the türban's objective meaning was unfreedom (Arat 1996; Tavşanoğlu 1996:1–8; Kışlalı 1997:3; Köse 1997:6; Metin 1997:2). Arat described it as a "voluntary serfdom" of those women "unconscious" of the meaning of freedom (Arat 1997:par3). Does head-covering indicate structural domination over women? With a

126   *Women and Clothing*

particular focus on the "liberal" alternative, this part scrutinizes the range of secular opinions on this question. This part will act as a background to my argument that the opposite positions eventually learned something from each other.

In Cumhuriyet Newspaper's historic defense of the head-covering ban, a hijabi woman spoke with a man's voice: "of course I decide myself what to wear." When, in 2005, then Head of the Parliament and AKP MP Bülent Arınç stated that he does not "denigrate" hijabis due to their choices, Journalist Hikmet Çetinkaya replied to Arınç that "these women" were covered by force, not by their free-will. Çetinkaya underlined that the people who denigrate women were "the ones that regard these clothes as appropriate for women" (Çetinkaya 2005:5). Researcher and Cumhuriyet Writer Oktay Ekinci (2002:6) echoed the argument that it was men who covered women at first in history.

Contrary to the arguments stated above, some others described the ban as a breach of individual subjectivity. The essence of religion was not the focal point of their views, at least because religion does not exist as an entity independent of one's experience of it. Therefore, they focused on what one makes of religion. For them, the issue was a matter of individual value-judgment (Kahramanoğlu 2008).[14] Furthermore, some of them staunchly defended a conception of secularism, alternative to the Secularism of "the secularists." Willingly or not, they were often called liberals on the political spectrum.

These ideology makers' starting point was a problematization of the supposed link between modernity and clothing.[15] Contrary to the arguments that equated pre-modernity with the Islamic veil, Nilüfer Göle (1996:3, 50) argued that "the Islamist identity" recently shaped around veiling had a peculiar relationship with "Western modernity." Using a similar vocabulary, Journalist Taha Akyol argued that the use of türban reflected a case-specific modernization process, as the wearers of türban in the urban setting wanted to leave home, get an education and obtain some kind of autonomy in public (Akyol 2008:55–62). According to Pınar Selek, through *tesettür,* the debate on women brought to the surface a deeply established social configuration that rendered women the objects of conflicting patriarchal proposals: "our bodies are still not ours" (İşeri and Açık 2007).

Let alone Islamists, many of these thinkers did not even call themselves religious conservatives. They did not claim that Islam—i.e., a given interpretation of Islam—would solve the ongoing/upcoming political problems. They did not consider the headscarf an incontestable "religious command," unlike the Islamist ideology makers like Abdurrahman Dilipak or Ali Bulaç. However, some famous figures among them tended to ally (Yayla 2008) with the Erdoğan government on a range of highly polarizing issues,[16] including opposition to the head-covering ban.

Many opposers of the Erdoğan government claimed that "liberals" were falling into the trap by defending the lifting of the head-covering ban (*see* Saylan 2001:2). Moreover, they criticized "liberals" for lobbying in the West

Women and Clothing   127

in favor of Islamism. They turned out to be a target, not only due to what they said in opposition to the head-covering ban but also due to their silence or dubiousness regarding the human rights violations led by the AKP government.

In this vein, İlhan Arsel called for the "liberal women" to raise their voices, given that the ones whose agency they respected would not even let them say "f" [i.e., the first letter of "freedom"] in the future (Arat 1997; Arsel 2002:2). Referring to a fetva from the Mufti of Bursa, which advised women to not resist their husbands in cases where their husbands beat them, Melih Pekdemir warned "the liberals" who prioritized the lifting of the head-covering ban: "as long as you are silent [...], you are not pro-freedom, but literally fools" (Pekdemir 2011). Professor Meryem Koray supported the lifting of the head-covering ban. Still, she was insistently critical of "the holy alliance" between "liberals-conservatives-Islamists [tr. dinciler]" who, she claimed, paved the way for the reign of religious communities in the state (Koray 2010).

After a decade, Mine Söğüt continued to criticize "liberals" who ignored the potentially poisonous power relations in the society, while insistently understanding the head-covering ban as a standalone matter of human rights:

> The 'carefree' liberals, who underestimated Secularism and defended those who made politics with Islamic references as though they were the defendants of human rights, were telling the 'anxious' seculars until yesterday: "what can happen, do you think they will cover your head when they come to power?" Now, nobody asks anything from one another.
>
> (Söğüt 2017)

Referring to a student who told his mother that their teacher "likes the headscarved students more," Linguist Sevgi Özel, a strong protagonist of a "Secular" education program, held the same group of liberals responsible for what happens "now" (Özel 2014).

Due to their ambivalent love/hate relationship with the AKP government, a wide range of voices has lost ground both in opposition and the government circles.[17] However, this antagonism does not mean that parts of their vocabulary did not leave residue in others' following ideology-making processes. Having been digested and de-contextualized from its previous users' past "wrongdoing," I shall argue that the vocabulary of agency matters more than ever in contemporary conversations.

Exploratory Conversations after the Lifting of the Ban

Turkey entered the AKP Government's first term with the historical baggage described above. In the latest phases of this era, the state's long-term modernist ideology has been challenged in several ways by a somewhat

128   *Women and Clothing*

"Islamist" or purportedly "Muslim Democratic" government. The ban was de-facto lifted during the third term of AKP. Even "Secularist CHP" did not oppose the lifting of the ban in the parliament. That said, the controversy over women's clothing has not been resolved. In this period, women's clothing was under contestation not only as a legacy of the state-led head-covering ban but also through a set of other incidents in which women were targeted for their clothing preferences.

The following parts will question these more recent cases of intolerance, which appeared toward the end of the third term of the AKP government in the aftermath of the de-facto lifting of the head-covering ban. I have shown in the last part that in various structures of authority, through one or the other ideological repertoire, clothing has been construed in Turkey as a fundamental matter of social order and development. Clothing attitudes breached the borders of tolerance by the time they provoked the authorities' senses of appropriateness.

The following chapter will first demonstrate that the many authorities may still appear at any level—i.e., micro, meso, or macro—at nighttime or daytime, in parks or schools or on public transportation, media, or the parliament to interfere with a woman's clothing. Having said that, the new authoritative claims have to refer to a new, albeit segregated, space for others' clothes. This necessity signifies the downgrading of first-order values in the debate over clothing rights.

Intolerance and the Context

The recent rationalizations of intolerance have been predominantly based on contextual elements, such as the time, place, and the manner in which a piece of fabric appears. A member of the security personnel of Maçka Park in İstanbul warned Çağla Köse when she left one of the public toilets ("Maçka Parkı'ndaki Kadın" 2017): "I cannot let you hang around here with these clothes." Köse reacted: "who are you to say this?!" As the people around them noticed the loud conversation, they interfered to defend Köse. Eventually, Security Personnel Savaş İ. called the police. Some days later, suspended from his work, Savaş İ. explained why he went to warn Köse. According to him, a woman with a little child had told him that "this woman" was sitting near the toilet with "her body-parts open." To them, Köse was not a good role model for children in the park.

A similar case was reported in İzmir's district of Alsancak, between a police officer and two women, Derya Kılıç and Seray Gürer, who were sexually assaulted late at night. Kılıç told the police officer, whom they saw on a street corner, that one of the two men on a motorbike touched her from behind. However, the police officer began criticizing them: "given that you wear these clothes and hang around at this time, what they did is nothing [tr. "az bile yapmışlar"]" (Ertürk 2017). Kılıç claimed that the officer also insulted them: "bitches." While Kılıç was cursing in response, the officer attacked her (Uysal 2017). In the officer's narrative, he had just told the women to go to the police station, given that he would not be able to leave his position at that moment. While explaining how Kılıç insulted him before he used force, the officer also mentioned the beer bottles that Kılıç and Gürer were carrying on the street. He was stressing this detail as a sign that the two women breached some rules of appropriateness.

Other incidents suggest that women do not have to be out late at night to face possible assault due to their clothes. The context-dependent rationalization of intolerance considers many things alongside timing. For example, Ayşegül Terzi remembers nothing about why a man she did not know kicked her on the bus. In his testimony, the perpetrator Abdullah Çakıroğlu said he could not put up with Terzi's clothing, which was "disrespectful to the others on the bus." Çakıroğlu's lawyer claimed that Terzi's garment was "suggestive" in the sense that "she sprawled out on two seats despite that she had a mini-skirt" ("Tekmeci Saldırganın" 2017). They claimed that there were customary rules to be followed in public transportation. Almost the same happened to Asena Melisa Sağlam, beaten on a minibus by a stranger, who began his insults with a question: "are you not ashamed of wearing these clothes during Ramadan?"

A high-school student, Fatma Dilara Aslıhan, was also attacked on a minibus by another woman just because she was going to school with a headscarf. While Aslıhan was talking to a retired teacher of physics about her classes, the aggressor pulled Aslıhan's headscarf from behind and ordered her not to go to school with the headscarf. The aggressor was sure that any school must have specific rules of conduct, including a dress code of its own. When Director Yadigar İzmirli banned "mini-skirts" in İstanbul Aydın University, she was relying on the symmetric opposite of this so-called procedural knowledge claim: "Just as judges wear robes because their job necessitates it, the academics should be careful with their clothes as well" ("Mini eteği" 2014). İzmirli argued that this context was irrelevant to "freedoms" in any way: they can do anything they want in their off-hours. Similarly, during a trial, Judge Mehmet Yoylu did not open the session as he thought that the skirt one of the lawyers wore was too short, and therefore "inappropriate for the practice of law." On the flip side, according to psychologist Üstün Dökmen, headscarved women shall not be allowed to work as psychiatrists, psychologists, or school counselors: "they cannot be neutral."

In Middle East Technical University (METU), two "students wearing headscarves"[18] were protested against by a group. From a very short distance—i.e., less than a meter, the protesters directed their cardboard placards, which contained a huge arrow directed at the two women, with the following note: "warning: there is Cemaat[19] here." One of the two women yelled: "can you go away?!" A protester replied: "show your ID, or you will go away!" Later on, another protester made the authoritative speech: "we do not allow religious communities (tr. cemaatler) to work at METU." Eventually, the two women left the area amidst slogans against religious obscurantism.

130 *Women and Clothing*

On their Twitter page, the protesters declared: "We have fired the *Cemaat* members, who force the newly registered students, with lies and slanders, to stay in their dormitories" (Odtuogrencileri on Twitter 2013). The group especially emphasized that their reaction was not against the two women's headscarves:

> [O]ur headscarved friends best know the fact that METU students do not have any problem with headscarves.
>
> ("Odtü'de Yalan" 2013)

The problem, for them, was that the women were agitating against the conditions of the METU dormitories. In other words, it was a manipulation to forward new students to the dormitories of a religious foundation. The protesters' argument in this context differentiated between the students as "the Cemaat members" and the students as "headscarved friends."

Gözde Kansu was dismissed from a TV project in the aftermath of Minister Hüseyin Çelik's denigration of her attire. One second after delivering the caveat, "we do not interfere with anybody's clothing," Çelik added: "but this is inappropriate!" (tr. "ama olmaz bu kardeşim ya!"). In his following speech act, the interviewer interrupted Çelik:

INTERVIEWER: Now they will say that you interfere with people's clothes.
ÇELIK: In public TV channels worldwide, there is a sensitivity over this [dress codes]. We do not interfere with anybody's clothing [*reiterated for the second time*]. But if you wear something almost like a night outfit [tr. gece kıyafeti], can you present a popular TV show? Would it be welcome? Nowhere in the world would it be welcome.

(Ne Var Ne Yok 2013)

Kansu was presenting the program on a public channel, ATV, at 20:00 on a Saturday. Right after Çelik's comment, Kansu lost her job. Though the production company declared that its decision was nothing to do with Kansu's attire or the minister's comments, it also underlined that Kansu was fired because her "manners" and "style of presentation" did not fit the project ("Gözde Kansu'yu" 2013). Before everybody else, Kansu did not believe the explanation:

> [The recording] lasted for 7 hours. Everyone [in the casting team] said "marvelous!" Director Caner Erdem said, "that's it!"
>
> (Arman 2013b)

Kansu's "night outfit" was targeted by the minister, as he thought that 8 P.M. was not late enough for her clothes to appear.

In this period, women's appearance also served as a justification for sexual abusers. Abusers often blamed their victims for their clothes at the given time or place in which sexual abuse took place. In Sağlam's case, the footage did not make clear whether the act was due to the perpetrator Ercan Kızılateş being uncomfortable with Sağlam's clothing, or whether he initially tried to molest her and then attacked her because Sağlam's response was not positive. Though both Kızılateş and Sağlam mentioned the conversation in which Kızılateş reprehends Sağlam due to her clothing on "the Ramadan day," the expert opinion, based on the camera footages, was that they did not even talk to one another before the attack. Instead, Kızılateş "caressed" Sağlam's hair ("Şortlu" 2017). It was likely that Kızılateş tried to mask his sexual harassment with a claim against Sağlam's clothing. There are many other cases where the perpetrators aimed to excuse their acts of sexual abuse with arguments centered around women's clothing ("İstanbul Esenyurt'ta" 2017; "Üniversiteli" 2018).

To sum up, in these cases, wearing a particular type of clothing could not be problematized *per se*. Wearing this item at this hour, in this manner, on this street/park, or late-night/prime-time became the focal point of the intervening ideology. Intolerance in these cases differs from the intolerance against *peçe* on the basis that it represents pre-modernity; or the intolerance against şapka on the grounds that it means blasphemy. The recent arguments instead resemble the 1990s' and the 2000s' relatively unpopular procedural opinion that the headscarf would be tolerable as long as it does not appear on the head of a doctor who would be obliged to wear a surgical balaclava.

As long as it was a "night outfit" for the night—i.e., not an outfit for prime-time on TV, an item of clothing with a "cleavage" seemed tolerable even for the seasoned member of Islamist parties. This reasoning was why Minister Çelik kept repeating that they do not interfere with anybody's clothing—i.e., one second before he interfered. This authoritative claim is identical to those who censor billboards ("Yıldız" 2013) and dummies ("İç giyim" 2017) by arguing that the public appearance of "women's underwear" would threaten public decency.

The cultural change described here is neither based on a shift in the moral standards that a given clothing item is believed to represent nor on the ultimately value-based understanding of "public decency." Change lies in the implicit acknowledgment that a clothing item, no matter the extent to which it is valued or despised, should have a right to appear in a specific field that it is appropriate for. Those who proclaim authority have to justify giving space, albeit limited and contested, for the existence of difference. As such, the clash emanates from the imposition of parochial values in the name of common rules of appropriateness.

Ethical Concerns in the Re-making of Secularism

In the previous part, I analyzed the most recent cases where intolerance was rationalized, communicated, and put into practice. Intolerance in these cases was based on a set of conditions through which this item appears. These

132   *Women and Clothing*

arguments imply that a zone of freedom has been acknowledged for others' dresses to appear. In this part, I analyze some contestations over this zone that, many ideology makers agree, has to go beyond one's first-order values.

Agency Brings Responsibility

During the session on lifting the head-covering ban for MPs (late-2013), the opposition party, CHP, did not reproduce Secularism in the form of opposition to the lifting of the ban. The decision resulted from strategic calculations (i.e., AKP would exploit it in the aftermath of the Gezi Protests) and ideological ambivalence (i.e., alternative arguments between CHP members over the way to define and defend Secularism). Within this context, the defense of Secularism was re-cast by CHP MP Şafak Pavey in a historic parliamentary speech. In her statements, Pavey reassessed Secularism by admitting the agency of MPs with türban, which many ideology makers of Secularism previously denied türban wearers. That said, alongside recognizing their agency, her Secularism held them responsible:

> Indeed, I have great concerns about the future of Secularism in my country, but my concern is not in the symbols squeezed between a lipstick and a türban. [...] I have great expectations from MPs with türban. I expect them to explain to me why my country is the 120th in terms of women's rights.
>
> (Şafak Pavey TBMM 2013)

In short, the agency brings responsibility. The türban-wearing MPs shall be held responsible for the failures in which they take part. Describing women with türban as "victims but not innocents" (Held 2016), this ideology developed a way of recognizing the agency behind headscarf, without romanticizing its relevance to human rights.

Accordingly, "an MP with a headscarf" should be questioned, for instance, on whether she defends others' rights as she once defended one's headscarf. As such, Pavey could keep some of the amalgams that were made in the name of Secularism in the past. Accordingly, she described her identity by means of these amalgams: "we are the ones who were burned in Sivas,[20] shot in Gezi, [and the ones] whose houses are marked. We are the ones who are punished for one's way of life." Pavey explained why, within this social context, she directly referred to "MPs with headscarves":

> I talk to you as a person who was obliged to wear türban for many years, in geographies that you did not go even as tourists: Afghanistan, Yemen, Iran. [...] I talk to you as a woman deputy, who was hindered, by a male deputy, from wearing pants in Parliament [...] I speak to you as a woman, whose non-existing legs [*Pavey is disabled*] has been turned by men into a political conversation.

Pavey did not put forward her own values in the name of Secularism. She defined Secularism as an instrument to prevent the hegemony of any value system over the other. Instead of targeting the isolated first-order values of her interlocutors, she focused on the coexistence of different value systems in broader, shared social spaces. She was not afraid of the türban on the head of a police officer, but "the future of violence that the police promise me."

Secularism Devoid of Parochial Values

Pavey was the first of many others who would later follow the same line of argumentation, concerned *not* with values of one's own and others but with the possibility of making them coexist in a shared space. For example, Writer and Actress Gülse Birsel wrote an open letter to Minister Kaya, whom Birsel called her "sister and schoolmate." In this open letter, Birsel asked the minister to stop the government members' denigration of "women's clothing and laughter." Instead, Birsel asked them to focus on some "common" problems that she believed the government should have been busy with: "Violence against women has reached its peak [...] early-marriages are encouraged [...] [and] students have been left to the dormitories of illegal foundations" ("Gülse Birsel'den" 2016). Based on anecdotal evidence, Birsel argued that the narratives over the clash of "covered" and "uncovered" were nothing but a "huge balloon" (Birsel 2016).

This approach focuses on the question of how to manage the social ties between different values. At this moment, one talks about one's own and others' values and beliefs; yet s/he always has to further touch upon the mutual social setting in which they all share a joint responsibility. In this vein, CHP MP Zeynep Altıok Akatlı underlined her position towards the head-covering ban on adults:

> Even though I think türban is the most fundamental icon of gender discrimination, [I] defend and respect the freedom of clothing and thought for every individual who turns 18.
>
> (Altıok Akatlı 2014)[21]

Altıok's perspective was akin to that of Pavey, which accepted that a female police officer should be able to wear türban since the problem is not what a police officer wears but what this officer may force others to do. After all, male police officers never had to clothe themselves in a particular manner to prove that they defend an oppressive ideology. After disintegrating the representations of oppression from clothes, Secularism's plain and straight-forward concern became oppression.

Despite keeping many previously made amalgams, this interpretation of Secularism was not appreciated by some who reproduced the old-school, value-laden arguments. The objection came about primarily because Pavey denied judging a personality based on the person's choice of a "lipstick" or

134   *Women and Clothing*

"turban." In other words, she attempted to deconstruct the long-standing claim that the outside of a head reflects the inside of it (*recall* the arguments of Atay and Berkes). In response, seasoned journalist Işık Kansu of Cumhuriyet Newspaper criticized Pavey for ignoring the symbols that Secularism previously deemed dangerous (Kansu 2017). In this context, Kansu was disturbed by Pavey's defense of female police officers' right to wear türban.

Işık Kansu also criticized Pavey for referring to Secularism with the word "sekülarizm" instead of "laiklik." It has been a recent debate among the students of Secularism that the Anglo-model secularism would be called "sekülarizm," whereas the French model is to be called "laiklik" (fr. Laicite). Using the word sekülarizm may be inferred as a rejection of the long-standing defense of *laiklik* in Turkey. In the repertoire, "sekülarizm" meant non-interference with religion, whereas "laiklik" was the name for the state control and regulation of the religious sphere, deemed potentially dangerous. According to her in-group critiques, Pavey had sold out *laiklik* by using the word *sekülarizm*.

Secularism "to protect headscarves too"

As she stopped reflecting on Secularism as a representation of her first-order values, Pavey's speech also included a reference to how Secularism would also protect a covered girl who kisses her boyfriend in the park. She clearly mentioned this girl as someone who does something wrong in accordance with her own value system.[22] In this context, she revisited Secularism as a promise of protection for those carriers of contradiction. Like all the other arguments I examined above, this argument also challenged the determinism of one's parochial values in the conversation over others' rights.

Pavey was not the only member of CHP who re-cast Secularism in this manner. CHP MP Tuncay Özkan, who led "Republic Protests" (tr. Cumhuriyet Mitingleri) in which millions of people participated, recently reviewed his former statements in favor of the head-covering ban:

> But I watched my speeches later on. I realized that I was so harsh [...] Now I am more mature that I could say I am sorry if I frightened the conservative people [...] Thank God everyone in this country does not share the same ideas.
>
> ("Tuncay" 2016)

This series of evaluations continued with the CHP leadership's exclusion of Former MPs who had previously taken an uncompromising position against lifting the head-covering ban. Among these MPs were Necla Arat, Canan Arıtman, and Nur Serter, who led "the rooms of persuasion"—i.e., where the headscarved students were interrogated and "convinced" to open their hair in universities. In addition to the party members who began to criticize them for distancing CHP to the "real problems" of Turkey, and

Women and Clothing   135

hence underpinning the hegemony of the Erdoğan regime, the head of CHP Kılıçdaroğlu re-evaluated the previous policies: "in the past, there were mistakes in our language" ("Kılıçdaroğlu" 2019). In 2022, Kılıçdaroğlu started a "helalleşme" campaign, an Islamic jargon meaning writing off each other's debts. As part of this campaign, Kılıçdaroğlu expressed his apologies to headscarved women: "If I'm going to have a legacy, it will be reconciling the people of this country with each other." After a decade-long contestation over the true definition of Secularism, recent snapshots suggest that most contesters have become accustomed to the once polarizing publicity of headscarves.[23]

Six years after the Republic Protests, a distinctive feature of the Gezi Protests was the symbol of "secular students" holding umbrellas for "the conservative protesters" so that they could pray under the rain. On the public forums, the participants in the Gezi Protests staunchly defended "those participants with türban" against the ones who saw a contradiction in this snapshot ("taksim gezi parkı" 2013). Challenging the pro-ban propensity to amalgamate "türban" with the violation of women's democratic rights, the new argument is that wearing a headscarf would not necessarily symbolize turning a blind eye to human rights issues. In the scope of this argument, distinguishing the headscarf from the türban has also become meaningless.

On the other hand, "the Kabataş Case" of the Gezi Protests has become a toxic subject. Journalist Elif Çakır wrote it as a case of harassment enacted by some "half-nude men" against "a headscarved woman with her baby." Relying on a forensic report, Erdoğan repeatedly referred to this incident to denigrate the protests as anti-religious. However, the video footage of the incident aroused mass controversy concerning the validity of the incident. In response to the publicly expressed doubts prompted by the footage, Elif Çakır declared that it was not her task to prove that the incident occurred. Çakır's lawyer later argued that the so-called victim Zehra Develioğlu exaggerated a reciprocal taunt up to the level of an unrealistic story of harassment ("Elif" 2015). When a pro-government journalist, Cem Küçük, noted that it was "a mismanaged fabrication," another pro-government journalist, Abdülkadir Selvi, bashed Küçük for calling Erdoğan a liar indirectly ("Abdülkadir" 2015).

Apart from the highly contested case of Kabataş, head-covering was not problematized in any way during Gezi Protests. On the contrary, "the anti-capitalist Muslims" in particular turned out to be a symbol of the protests, as they crystallized the alternative argument that "neighborhood pressure" hides beneath social classes in the neighborhood. In other words, their appearance recalled the left-wing view that the real tension was not between "Islamic bourgeoisie" and "Secular bourgeoisie" (Şimşek 2009; Göçmen 2010). Nearly a decade after its historic propaganda against the lifting of the ban, on May 1, 2018, Cumhuriyet Newspaper presented the Labor Day Celebrations in Ankara with the photo of a covered woman, holding a flag of the Socialist Party of the Proletariat (SEP).

136   *Women and Clothing*

Amid the debates on whether "Islamism" established its cultural hegemony, Cumhuriyet writer Deniz Yıldırım asked why the pro-government media ignored the protests led by the makeup company Flormar's workers, "most of whom are headscarved." Yıldırım answered his own question:

> [I]t is because, in the "culture" [of the government], there is no place for a headscarved worker who seeks justice.
>
> (Yıldırım 2018)

In the 2019 municipal elections, both the Turkish Communist Party (TKP) and CHP had headscarved candidates whom, indeed, the parties did not label as "headscarved." Accordingly, Fatma Akın was a "textile worker," and Hilal Ülkü Türedi was "the 18-year-old daughter of a farmer." The leaders of both parties justified their unprecedented decisions by emphasizing that one's identity is not exhausted by one's headscarf. Contrary to the previous authoritative claims, these narratives did not take clothing as an all-encompassing indication of personality.

Back in 2016, a police raid into Cumhuriyet Newspaper was protested against by the newspaper's readers. Yeni Akit Newspaper, never polite towards any non-Islamist and most other Islamists, called it "a theatre" when Cumhuriyet published a photo of some "covered" old women among protesters ("Cumhuriyet'in" 2016). Contrary to my argument in this part, one may contend that this new perspective was of some relevance to the changes in the administrative structure of the newspaper. In 2014, the management of Cumhuriyet Newspaper was taken over by some so-called "liberals" led by Journalist Murat Sabuncu. Critiques of this transition said the "Kemalist" Cumhuriyet of İlhan Selçuk and Mustafa Balbay was captured by "liberals"—hence, the shift in its narrative on the headscarf. That said, my argument is that the sympathy towards the image of *covered women opposing the government* was not entirely explainable by the "liberal" directors of Cumhuriyet. On the contrary, Balbay himself mentioned the shift in his own words:

> In the past, we gave our türban-wearing sisters the pip; now, we give them our hands.
>
> (Kocaaslan 2015)

This revision was in congruence with that of famous journalist Mehmet Ali Birand who, back in 2012, was sure that the headscarf had become ordinary in the media landscape (Tufan 2012).

Last but not least, headscarved women have been more than welcome in the recent parades entitled "don't meddle with my outfit" (tr. kıyafetime karışma). They have been invited to stand in the photo frames, as their participation would challenge the perception that the parades consisted of defending a particular set of clothes. A similar approach has been embraced

Women and Clothing   137

by a newly founded platform, *Yalnız Yürümeyeceksin* (en. "You will not walk alone"), which aims to help women who cannot remove their headscarves due to family pressure. In response to the assumption that they support the head-covering ban, the platform members declared: "No, we are also against the policies of removing headscarves through force" (Vurdu 2018). As this common theme of opposition to interference suggests, these organizations have been meant to form a shared voice for women irrespective of their different first-order values. For sure, this new capacity-building discourse has implications for feminism's historical tension between holding responsible for the *culture* versus the *nature* of patriarchy.

Ethical Concerns in the Re-making of Islamism

The state that Erdoğan calls "New Turkey" invests in cultural projects that correspond with a set of parochial values. The government stopped funding some spheres of activity (e.g., cultural events, educational programs) associated with the rival value systems, such as "Kemalism," or broadly, modernism. However, in the course of this war of supremacy, the ideology makers behind Islamism have also been pushed to re-evaluate the tolerance question, primarily for reasons that relate to the management of their parochial values. Accordingly, the re-making of Islamism has been driven by sociological changes that these gatekeepers admittedly could not manipulate in accordance with a perfectionist sense of their value system.

Revisiting Tolerance in Family

The wedding of preacher Ahmet Mahmut Ünlü's daughter has given a hint as to how a "proper" Islamist may react, when one's first-order values are challenged by those to whom one has inescapable ties. When Ünlü's daughter appeared at the wedding with a somewhat "stylish" wedding dress, many, including the fellow members of the İsmailağa Religious Community, criticized Ahmet Mahmut Ünlü for letting his daughter, first, lead a mixed-sex wedding gathering, and second, wear a "religiously prohibited" dress for the wedding. Ünlü did not explicitly problematize the wedding ritual during the ceremony. On the contrary, he made a short speech at the ceremony, which Erdoğan and some ministers also attended.

However, after the wedding, he declared that he disapproved of his daughter Yüsra's clothing choice. He underlined that even some of the most outstanding teachers of religion could not educate their children; and that they, the teachers of religion, could not make the society fully embrace the hijab. Nevertheless, most importantly, Ünlü underlined that it is ultimately the responsibility of his daughter to behave by her religious values. On the one hand, Ahmet Mahmut Ünlü did not interfere with his daughter's clothing preference; on the other, Yüsra Ünlü did not raise her voice against her father's public argumentation against her practice. In this exchange, Ünlü

138   *Women and Clothing*

tolerated his daughter through non-interference, just as his daughter was publicly silent towards the possibly reprehensible terms of tolerance she faced. Generally speaking, the authoritative voices behind Islamism[24] seem to have agreed that women should comply with their husbands'/parents' preferences within the confines of tesettür. This was a principle that Ahmet Mahmut Ünlü explicitly defended in his speech after the wedding, though he admittedly could not educate his daughter in this respect.

The timely ethical question that appears in this context is what to do in case one's addressee does not comply with one's instructions about tesettür. In their evaluative conversations on this question, the preachers of the mainstream religious communities have come to agree that "pressure," in the sense of interfering with one's will, failed as a means of resolving such disagreements. Instead, they set forward that the value system indicates a set of "legitimate" ways for the discontents to exit its confines. The question that ultimately arises is whether the government's value-laden political statements are an obstacle to this.

Süleymaniye Foundation's fetva website laid down that Muslims should continue to inform their close social circles about the commands of Islam regarding tesettür. That said, on conveying the message, the fetva underlined that force must not be an option because religion cannot be practiced without intent ("Eşime" 2009). At the micro-level, many conservative families began to share the same understanding. For example, a woman who eventually removed her headscarf described the way her "radical Islamic family" had approached her so that she could embrace hijab:

> Let us not put so much pressure on her so that she does not end up opening her head.
>
> (Cebeci 2018:par38)

In the same vein, having argued that Islam does not prescribe a legal punishment for most moral issues, Mustafa İslamoğlu described the breach of tesettür as a matter of "morality," hence not reversible by means of enforcement (İslamoğlu 2013:48).

Ahmet Mahmut Ünlü calls for men to "be extremely patient" before "beating their wives," which he describes as the last resort in the face of highly exceptional cases, such as "breaches of honor" (Cengiz 2015). According to him, "brute force" is not the way to react towards "most disagreements" over the clothing. As he explained in the context of his daughter's wedding, Ünlü's reaction consisted of turning his back to her during the ceremony. He claimed to show Allah's command with this act, utilizing certain gestures. Also, through words, he reminded people of his own "proper" wedding. Moreover, he publicly prayed for those like his daughter so that they eventually embrace the hijab.

In cases where the disagreement over clothing persists in a family, Nureddin Yıldız advises men to consider divorce. Because Yıldız interprets divorce as a unilateral option for men, he criticizes the civil code for rendering it very difficult (Yıldız 2013). He implies that these "difficult" conditions encourage men to cheat on their wives. Having mentioned religious divorce as a solution, Abdülaziz Bayındır made the caveat that divorce under Islamic Law is not easy for men either, due to "the heavy obligations" it imposes on them (Bayındır 2009). Whereas Nihat Hatipoğlu equates religious and official divorce, others strongly disagree with this argument (Köse 2012). Despite the differences in this respect, their ideas merged on the point that the value system indicates a route of exit for those unwilling to stay in its confines. Divorce is one of the many ways to *otherize* those who had previously been mistaken as the *self.*

Tolerance Towards Others

Beyond family, the timely question is whether Muslims have a duty to exercise physical force over a stranger due to her clothing. The media channels where many self-proclaimed Islamists write—e.g., Star, Sabah, Yeni Şafak, and Yeni Akit—commonly refer to the aggressors, whom I have mentioned throughout the exploratory conversations, as mentally ill people. They published without redaction interior Minister Süleyman Soylu's statement that "violence against a woman" is unjustifiable, no matter she wears "a headscarf or a mini-skirt" ("Soylu" 2017). In the same vein, they did not problematize Judge Mehmet Yoylu's suspension from work following his reaction to the lawyer for her "mini-skirt." Moreover, they also shared the minister of justice Abdülhamit Gül's criticism of Yoylu: "it is unacceptable that [...] the judge is busy with the lawyer's clothing instead of the legal case" ("Bakan" 2019). They dismissed the representative quality of the cases of violence that was well-documented. In other words, according to them, these acts were just individual cases that do not represent Islam's true authoritative claims on the subject matter.

In case the records of an incident were not fully clear, they sought to falsify them. For example, some of those speakers called the Maçka incident bogus, because they claimed no one would interfere with a woman's open-clothes in Maçka, next to Nişantaşı "where every second person wears shorts" (Albayrak 2017; Kökçe 2017:par2). Having claimed that most of these incidents were just fabricated or exaggerated, they focused on how these incidents may have been used to provoke mass protests and upheavals against the religious circles, "just as in the time of Ticanis" (Çiftçi 2006; "Yalan" 2006; "Öğrenciye" 2008; Kaya 2015; Battal 2017; Say 2017). To prove how tolerant Islamists are, journalist İsmail Kılıçarslan of Yeni Şafak, who worked for ten years in the "Milli Görüş" TV channel named Kanal 7, recalled that he managed to have colleagues who wore "mini-skirts" alongside those others—i.e., "Alevis," "Kurds," and "even Christians and Atheists" (Kılıçarslan 2015). Kılıçarslan asked if any covered woman, other than the cleaning ladies, was employed in the Secularist camp.

140   *Women and Clothing*

Intentionally or not, Kılıçarslan's story summarizes the flow of culture for the members of the Nakshibendi and the Nur orders, who accommodated some differences while struggling to be influential bankers, statesmen, tradesmen, and media patrons (Bulut 1997; Mardin 2006:261–97). Even Dilipak, who explicitly calls himself "intolerant" concerning this matter, noted that his team in Kanal D consisted of women. His policy in this environment was to not stay in the same room with his women colleagues: "even if it is wintertime, I do not close my door. If they close the door, I will open it and leave the room" (Avşar 2009). During his interview with Helin Avşar, Dilipak appreciated Avşar's choice of attire. If she wore a "low-neck" dress, Dilipak would either refuse to stay in the same environment or ask Avşar to cover her body.

These strategies of partial accommodation are based on some pre-defined categories of otherness (e.g., "uncovered women," "Alevis," "Christians," etc.). Under these categories, the speakers, as mentioned earlier, agree that Muslims should warn one another about the commands of their religion. Nevertheless, they acknowledge that they must not interfere with the clothing preferences of others, as long as the latter does not symbolize a "threat"—i.e., obviously, yet another matter of speculation. In this vein, then Prime Minister Binali Yıldırım made his authoritative speech while evaluating the mental state of Çakıroğlu, who kicked Terzi:

> What he did is not what a normal person would do. You may not like [the way somebody is dressed]. Then you [normally] mutter... If this man's previous record is scrutinized, the fact that he has [mental] problems will surface.
>
> ("Hoşuna gitmeyebilir" 2016)

Binali Yıldırım admits that one does not have to appreciate others' clothes, though he also implies that one is not obliged to turn a blind eye to others' clothes. Taken together, he just corrects what he would do if he were Çakıroğlu on that bus. If he were Çakıroğlu, he would mutter.

With the same line of argument, they dismissed the association of Islamism with ISIS' new-year's-eve attack at Reina Nightclub. After campaigning for a couple of weeks with the slogan, "Muslims should not celebrate Noel," the opponents of the new-year celebrations claimed that they were wholeheartedly against this attack. In the aftermath of the attack, they made it public that their aim was not to interfere but to remind what a Muslim must (not) do. Ali Karahasanoğlu (2017) from Yeni Akit argues that what "we" do is nothing beyond saying, "Hey mate, if you take alcohol, your health will be worsened. Also, taking alcohol is forbidden according to our religion! But it is up to you!" They aimed to convey their message in the form of muttering or talking to "a mate," whereas the ISIS's particular way of giving its message was different.

According to Ahmet Mahmut Ünlü, there was no difference between attacking a "place of worship" and a "place of entertainment." In this

Women and Clothing 141

instance, Ünlü recalled his dialogue with a pious man who desired to attack a bar. When Ünlü asked him how long he had been righteous, the man counted: "approximately ten years." Ünlü responded to the man: "so, according to your understanding, somebody should have killed you 11 years ago." In his Friday preaches, Ünlü repeatedly told his followers that they "cannot despise" women who do not follow the rules of tesettür: "the hijabi may end up undressing, whereas the nude may end up repenting" (Teşvikçi 1997). He advised his listeners to focus on where they end up in terms of their relationship with religion.

All ideology makers mentioned above support a set of responses to those who do not wear proper clothes. Some defended warning them, whereas others defended mumbling and muttering about them or making some passive aggression felt. The mainstream current of Islamism just opposes going beyond these measures, though these measures are likely to be denounced as "neighborhood pressure" by others. What more can be done for the sake of the belief system remains an open question, given that many others oppose "correcting" themselves after muttering.

Trade-Off: The Imposition of Practice, or Sincere Belief

Reiterating the argument that a Muslim has a duty to warn others for their misconduct, the ideology makers of Islamism seem to have kept their long-standing claims about what an "ideal" Islamic setting would constitute. Es'ad Coşan preached long ago that Muslims should interfere to stop "the sinners" if those who do *not* sin are in the majority in a given setting (Coşan 1993). Some decades later (2012), Özlem Albayrak argued that the dualism between "shorts" and "headscarves" was nothing but a consequence of the political climate created by the head-covering ban (Albayrak 2012). Albayrak underlined that, in this period, Islamists had to "borrow liberal arguments" to defend freedom for all on equal footing.

However, the conditions have changed as the ban has finally been lifted. Concerning the dress codes of high schools, Albayrak later stressed that "balanced" arguments should be challenged "if necessary"—i.e., in accordance with the conservative values of the government (tr. "serde muhafazakarlık var") (Albayrak 2012). According to Albayrak, for the time being, both shorts and headscarves should be permitted in high schools, given that the only feasible alternative is to forbid both. Therefore, she hypothetically suggests that others' clothes may be restricted without negotiation if they breach the authority's sense of appropriateness. This argument resembles the way the microcosmic authorities of some neighborhoods proclaim the conservative identity of "our" neighborhoods. Accordingly, women should pay attention to what they wear, should they visit these areas.

Because these proposals would unmoor one's conduct from one's belief, some thinkers construed them as a threat to the belief system. Despite emphasizing that Islam does not allow anyone to claim, "my body & my

142   *Women and Clothing*

choice" (i.e., given that the body belongs to Allah), Mustafa İslamoğlu underlined that it would be "a cruelty" to interfere with people's clothes through law enforcement. According to him, the issue is one of the belief systems, and as such, relevant to "conscience" instead of "police" (İslamoğlu 2008).

A recipe with these ingredients—i.e., an essentialist categorical approach and the need to accommodate difference—would set free the conscience of non-believers, lapsed believers among traditional Muslims, and "bad" Muslims who are aware of their sins. This notion of tolerance would require each group to recognize its own status vis-à-vis the terms of reference pre-defined by the authority, the utmost desire of which is to have a monopoly over the definition and the operationalization of Islam. In this context, it should be noted that the ideology makers such as Abdülaziz Bayındır, Mustafa İslamoğlu, and Hayrettin Karaman define the precondition of an "Islamic State" to be its character as a safe space for "non-believers" as well as believers. Hayrettin Karaman describes an Islamic State as a model in which non-Muslims should have a right "to keep" their clothes. That said, it should be strictly forbidden for them to imitate Muslims, and vice versa (Karaman 2018). This is a rationalization of tolerance without relativism, which, these ideology makers assume, will protect both the belief system and the "legitimate" free space for divergent social practices of others.

The Temporality of Clothes

This idea of tolerance tends to miss the tricky question of what counts as imitation (tr. teşebbüh, taklit). This question has turned out to be an open dispute that challenges the clear-cut categories regarding the self and the others. For example, Abdulmuizz Fida, the teacher of Islam in a web-based religious community, re-evaluated the changing status of wedding dresses as follows:

> Even though Women's white wedding dresses came from Christianity, it no longer makes you look like an infidel. It is because most Muslim women wear it now [...] Wearing şapka in the early Republican Era was a sign of being an infidel. Now, although it is still not appreciated, it won't face *tekfir*.
>
> (Fida 2010)

The sources of the İskenderpaşa Religious Community also argue that şapka has turned out to be a customary practice, hence not a matter of imitation anymore ("Tesettür ve" 2014:par23). A similar take on "customs" justifies women's opening of their hair in some public settings ("Baş Açık" 2014). As this line of argumentation suggests, the status of a clothing item is situated in the inevitably changing social circumstances.

The Refah and the successive AKP cadres had to make the same argument to rationalize the peace they had with the tie (tr. kravat).[25] After some decades of being accustomed to a tie, Erdoğan, who ended up being a conservative of ties, gave a tie to PM Alexis Tsipras of Greece as "a present," just because Tsipras did not fulfill his "task" of wearing one in a formal setting.[26] At a time (2008) when Gülenists' arguments were public, popular, and authoritative, Fethullah Gülen preached that a Muslim who dresses like a non-Muslim would *not* necessarily turn out to be an infidel. However, according to Gülen, the intention to look alike would signify *küfür* (en. blasphemy) *per se* ("Gülen'den" 2008). Female Preacher Emine Gümüş Böke of the İstanbul Mufti Office described this red line as the intention to carry "the symbols of other religions" (Böke 2017:27). These sources merge on the point that Islam does not dictate a specific type of clothing, as the styles are made and re-made in relationship with a set of temporal and spatial settings.

As a timely precaution against imitation, many have recently developed ways to differentiate their dress in a socially recognizable way from that of others—i.e., non-Muslims or Muslims who are not considered devout enough. Many Islamic fashion shows have begun to serve this cause by claiming to design "appropriately stylish" clothes, such as the so-called Islamic wedding dresses. With the condition that they do not "commercialize" clothing in a manner that would "breach the borders of religion," Karaman (2005) defended these attempts to put together more likable clothes appropriate to the compelling new conditions. Having acknowledged that there may be mixed weddings where one "has to" attend, Karaman states that women should comply with "the rules of tesettür" at these gatherings (Karaman 2004). He did not specify any category of wedding dresses, as he thinks there is room for free choice within the borders of tesettür. In this case, even though the definition of tesettür is deemed time-independent, it has been the temporal element that prevails in one's evaluation of whether a certain piece of clothing fits into the rules of appropriateness. Accordingly, these guidelines connote that a clothing item may not always be what it used to be.

Recently, however, this inescapable temporal dimension paved the way for a mass social change in the conduct of tesettür—i.e., an unwanted change for many. Throughout the 2000s, many "conservative" publications, from those of Yeni Şafak to Zaman, contained articles that aimed at guiding "conservative women" about the alternative ways to combine their clothes in a "stylish way" (Cömert 2007; Olgun 2007a, 2007b, 2007c; Haşema 2008). In the meantime, Islamist cloth designers became unprecedentedly vocal in discussing one another's approach to tesettür while producing new clothes for "the conservative women" (Kübra and Büşra 2011).

At this point, the conversation turned out to empty some of the abovementioned claims against relativism. This is because it remains undefinable where the authority lies to develop the clear-cut authoritative allegations that, on the one hand, will define the terms of imitation, adjustment, and threat, and on the other hand, will resolve the tensions over the flow of culture that pushes for a re-definition of clothing patterns. Who decides what has become customary?

144   *Women and Clothing*

Saving the Belief System

Never mind managing others' clothes, these circles admittedly lost control of the differing conservative motives behind clothing. Some leading figures dismissed the attempts to make Islamic fashion and style, as the aim of tesettür is to cover oneself against all kinds of public attraction (Tosun 2017). Crucially, Yeni Akit published the following note in one of its reports on the subject:

> With their style, the second-generation headscarved women drew a rebuff from the first generation.
>
> ("İşte" 2015)

This publication pessimistically admitted that the old argument about "the nudes of the high society" has turned out to be popular in the mass public: "we saw so many of those who wear hijab but also do embarrassing things" ("İşte" 2015:par55). On the flip side, many women who seem to follow the tesettür rules join the social media debates to support others, arguing that they are also subject to sexual harassment and harassment is not about clothing. This new social condition deposed clothing from the position of acting as an infallible precursor of personality.

In the meantime, Yeni Akit referred to a series of news to criticize some 'seemingly conservative' women for their inappropriate activities, such as a headscarved woman who received a marriage proposal in a nightclub ("Başörtüsüne Zulüm" 2018). In the same period, many others wrote about the recent generation of "conservative men" getting married to "uncovered women" and the current generation of "headscarved women" who do not very much like the narrow-mindedness of "conservative men." In line with these "pessimistic" scenarios, psychiatrist Sefa Saygılı and Diyanet member Ülfet Görgülü were concerned with the ways through which "conservatives" became "sexualized" in the urban life. This life, according to Saygılı, has led people to escape from "small towns' neighborhood pressure" (Tayman 2008; "Mahremiyet" 2015:5).

Moreover, the neighborhoods that carried a conservative identity diverged from each other regarding their clothing preferences. For example, the upper-middle-class Çukurambar district of Ankara demonstrated how the AKP MPs, conservative bureaucrats, and the government's favorite building contractors came together to form a zone of "conservative" high culture, full of meeting points for like-minded people—e.g., cafés, restaurants, mosques, helal houses, bookstores, and the AKP headquarters. Though the conservative image of Çukurambar has been displayed *among other things* by cafés that refuse to sell alcoholic beverages, these cafés also began to exhibit a new public space in which upper-middle-class conservative women began putting together headscarf and fashion. A tesettür shop in Çukurambar advertises: "this year, the unicolored combinations are especially trendy" (Akçaoğlu 2018:111, 44, 72–80). According to Al Jazeera, Turkey is the biggest spender of the global market of "Islamic fashion," which, by 2023, is expected to reach $361 billion (Navlakha 2019).

Emine Şenlikoğlu, a seasoned protagonist of tesettür in "the first-generation," argues that a woman must not cover her head if she also "wears pants," "crosses her legs in a café [...] with a cigarette in her hand" ("Emine Şenlikoğlu'ndan" 2015). Having underlined that "nobody forces" these women to cover, Şenlikoğlu asked them why they "pretend." She also repeatedly criticized "the conservative media" for censoring what she calls full-tesettür. According to her, "the conservatives do not like women with real tesettür" ("Emine Şenlikoğlu" 2017). During a conversation between two well-known women who write on the sociology of Islam, Fatma Barbarosoğlu explained to Nazife Şişman how the "Muslim TV channels" of the 1990s paved the way for this differentiated approach to tesettür. Accordingly, the headscarved presenters, who began to appear on the screen daily, had started to feel the need to wear a new attire every other day (Barbarosoğlu 2015:114).

The transformed images of these "conservative women" influenced many housewives. Abdurrahman Dilipak noted that "these deformations" were led by the explosion in the use of the headscarf ("Dandik" 2010). Dilipak added:

When I see them, I tell [myself] that I wish they either gave up on this [contradictory] state or gave up on the headscarf.

(Özvarış 2013)

Having described tesettür as "the prioritization of women's personality over their femininity" (İslamoğlu 2013:15–19), Mustafa İslamoğlu argued that "this issue of headscarf" has been diluted, not by the pro-ban "non-Muslim Turks" (İslamoğlu 2013:111–14), but by the carriers of "tradition" who promoted tesettür as men's protection from women (İslamoğlu 2013:37). In a manner deserving of İslamoğlu's criticism, member Metin Balkanlıoğlu of İsmailağa Religious Community was mediatized due to his rude reaction to the covered women who breach "the honor of tesettür":

Cover yourself properly! Don't play with my religion!

("İsmailağacı" 2017)

The Association of Furkan published articles to warn Muslims with the argument that their usage of "trendy" headscarves has turned out to be a matter of culture at the expense of belief. Amidst "this toxic fashion" among religious people, "the hijab has turned out to be the black wreath at the door of Capitalism" (Kibritçi 2011).

The Islamist Magazine of Vuslat went further, explicitly criticizing Tayyip Erdoğan's wife Emine Erdoğan and Abdullah Gül's wife Hayrünnisa Gül for deforming tesettür ("Modanın" 2013). Referring to the AKP Ministers'

146 *Women and Clothing*

wives, who once felt obliged to make up for their public appearances, Hidayet Şefkatli Tuksal noted that this obligation might have finally turned into an embrace. However, as opposed to the pessimism depicted in Vuslat, Tuksal concluded from within the Islamist community: "the community has relaxed with all these things. I don't think Erdoğan would [criticize] make-up anymore" (Özvarış 2015). Among others, Vuslat writers were not as optimistic as Tuksal about this relaxation.

Despite their wide-ranging criticisms, the critics could offer little strategy other than expressing their obligation "to make the youth learn religion properly"—setting aside the disagreements on who knows religion properly. A study conducted by sociologist Özlem Avcı suggested that it would be an arduous task, given that there are "76 different types of covering" in a single religious community: "[we] do not criticize them, but they criticize one another" (İnce 2012; *see also* Avcı 2012). In 2017, President Tayyip Erdoğan expressed a similar concern, though it was probably not the same as that of Vuslat's criticism of the Erdoğan family:

> Our generation is the latest witness of [...] local values [tr. mahalli değerler]. A significant portion of new generations has been deprived of this richness. Based on one's clothing, one's shoes, one's hat [and] one's body posture, if we cannot figure out which culture one belongs to, it means that we are in the clutches of cultural drought.
>
> ("Cumhurbaşkanı" 2017)

This quote was followed by Erdoğan's manifesto for his "2023 vision," which he described as a project of cultural reconstruction. Operationally, there was not much of substance in his speech, beyond making "the youth" listen to "the artisan" for "real art and science"; struggling against the toxic effects of the internet, TV, and especially social media; investing in new TV projects and to lesser extent literature; and developing cultural centers such as Yunus Emre Institute and Turkish Maarif Foundation. In this speech, the question left unanswered was how this project would manage to overcome a wide range of disappointments with one monolithic cultural imagination.

In conclusion, ideology making has been triggered by the new, unsettling trends in the (mis)conduct of the values that Islamists consider Islam's exclusive content. According to the sources I have referred, these first-order values should be re-operationalized in many ways. In the meantime, they had to emphasize that the carriers of these values must refrain from pushing others to imitation. The solution is quite the contrary: to look different from those who do not align themselves with these values. However, for this task to be successful, some breathing space must be given to the others to not have to play the Islamist to get a job, win a tender, or walk on the street. For the sake of securing the value system, the clothing rights of others should be disconnected from the foundational values of the self.

Women and Clothing 147

In this struggle to secure the value system, a confusing question is how to re-order the very different claims on Islam. Among these claims are that of (1) the Erdoğan government, which bases its discourse on value-laden claims; (2) those that have injected some kind of "fashion" into the conservative dress-codes; (3) those that oppose some or all segments of this fashion; (4) and those that oppose anything other than their own proposals. In this vein, it should not be seen as a coincidence that many religious communities have already begun to disagree with this Islamist government, which they wholeheartedly supported in the recent past. Today, they half-heartedly continue to support the government, as they do not want "Secularists" to return to power.

The Question of Agency: "why bother with someone else's clothing?"

Although the label "ideology maker" might have so far referred misleadingly to a very influential, somewhat famous, and well-heard class of elites, I describe ideology making as a mental process in which everyone participates. This part will go further by demonstrating how significant some previously unheard voices might become in the ideology-making processes of hegemonic ideologies. As such, this section examines a set of arguments through which the women whose clothing an authority has intervened to alter have defended themselves. After reviewing how they evaluate their objectification, I will examine how they aim to reclaim their agency by talking to the hegemonic ideologies. Finally, I will question if their arguments were remarkable in a previous episode of Turkey's democratization experience.

Terzi, who was kicked by the stranger on the bus, evaluated what she later heard from others:

> According to what I heard from the witnesses, he said, "she is a devil, she has to die" [...]Why would you want to kill somebody you do not know, [...] [and] with whom you did not argue or fight in any way?

The perpetrator Abdullah Çakıroğlu knew her through his own ideology. He did not have to know Terzi in person, as his ideology informed him of who Terzi was. Having claimed that everything happened per the Islamic Law, Çakıroğlu rationalized his act:

> She had a short skirt [...] I lost myself, as I thought that she trampled on the values of our society and the country we live in [...] My moral side overweighted.

> ("Tekmecinin" 2016)

In his defense, he oscillated between rationalizing his action and declaring some symptoms of his mental illness. He and his lawyer were keen to

148   *Women and Clothing*

convince others that he was mentally ill but also that Terzi behaved against public decency. In other words, he emphasized that he should have refrained from attacking Terzi, but it was not because Terzi did not deserve a warning.

In Fatma Dilara Aslıhan's case, it was certain that she was attacked not as a stranger but as an "Islamist," which was the only feature she had in the eyes of the aggressor. Soon after she entered the minibus on the Kadıköy-Kartal line (İstanbul), her headscarf was pulled by another woman sitting in the back row. After removing Aslıhan's headscarf, the woman continued yelling:

> This is the reality [...] you are terrorists [...] you and your green capital killed all these enlightened people [tr. aydınlar].

Aslıhan was the embodiment of Islamism, rather than an individual or a high-school student who would have neither enough time nor maturity to comprehend the gravity of these issues. Puzzled by how many things a headscarf might mean, Aslıhan's mother asked: "can anybody be judged only with this [showing her own headscarf]? I just condemn it" (Beyaz TV 2017).

In these cases, the aggressors' ideology, often in collaboration with the silence of bystanders, defined the meaning of the given clothing items. In other words, the outstanding authority which appeared out of nowhere objectified the meaning of clothes by symbolic or physical force. In Maçka Park, as the indictment of the prosecutor verified, the security personnel member Savaş İ. reproached Köse with the following words:

> [People like] you wear these clothes and then blame the security personnel when somebody rapes them.
>
> ("Maçka Parkı'ndaki Kıyafet" 2017)

This reference to "the people like Köse" had nothing to do with Köse as an individual, but with the way Savaş İ. perceived a social type by means of Köse's clothing preference. To Köse, it was an act of discrimination and a breach of freedom of belief and thought. To the crowd gathered there to defend Köse, Savaş İ. should have been punished. One guy yelled at the others who supported Köse, "don't be so naïve! As long as you don't crush their heads, they will bedevil you [tr. sonra çıkıyorlar tepenize]" (Her Telden 2017).

Terzi was not as lucky as Köse, who was at least defended by the crowd around her. She blamed all the people who witnessed Çakıroğlu's attack: "I want to call so many people to account." Aslıhan, whose headscarf was pulled off, also blamed the people on the minibus since they did not do anything to stop the aggressor. Asena Melisa Sağlam recalled that the passengers on the minibus even defended the aggressor when he began accusing Sağlam of the dress she chose for the Ramadan day (DHA 2017). In these

Women and Clothing 149

cases, the people around them were somewhat complicit in the meaning imposed by the aggressors on the clothes of Terzi and Sağlam.

It is not just the owners of these authoritative claims who believe that the other loses personality at a certain point. Such incidents may easily convince the victims to believe that they themselves lack subjectivity. Ipek Atcan, kicked by a stranger for crossing her legs with a skirt at a metro station, later said:

> I am angry with myself before all else. "You should not have kept quiet," I tell myself [...] Then I am mad at those who surrounded me. But what could they have done when I was silent?
>
> (Atcan 2016)

Realizing the moment that her agency is in danger, Atcan made the first step to reclaim it by publicizing those words. All of the women mentioned above made their stories public, sooner or later. They raised their voices in the broader community and gave confidence to many other women who share a similar fate. Their self-conscious efforts and the support gathered around them indicate a noteworthy cultural change that the next part will explore.

Women Who Reclaim Their Agency

With the attendance of Köse, a public march was organized in Maçka Park. A foundation named "Progressive Women" (tr. İlerici Kadınlar) defined the ideology behind this incident as the one that masked child abuse in a pro-government religious foundation: "this is the Islamist [tr. dinci], reactionary and Jihadist mentality" ("Maçka Parkı'ndaki Özel" 2017). CHP MP Selina Doğan evaluated the incident as the targeting of "the secular fraction [of the society]" (Şen 2017). Though Köse was there to listen to all these speeches, their reference to a broader ideological struggle may or may not have reflected Köse's narrative of the problem.

In her speech, Köse made a straightforward argument that prevailed in the march: "hands off my body," "my clothing is not your concern." In her short speech, Köse did not describe her choice of clothing as the true one, but a respectable one among others. She did not denounce another way of life to justify her preferences. She did not associate any other identity with the incident—be it a religion, a value system, or a political ideology. In her speech, she instead challenged the authorities with a personal statement: "Neither police nor anybody else, no one can interfere with anything of mine." She also made the following caveat: "I cannot either interfere with anybody else's clothing." Köse not only denounced the authoritative claim over her clothing but also refused to make her own authoritative claim as to what is suitable to wear. Sharing her suspicion that she may have been interfered with because she is a lesbian, she concluded her speech: "Lesbians will not be silent."

150   *Women and Clothing*

Fatma Dilara Aslıhan, whose headscarf was pulled off by a stranger, also developed an ethical argument, notwithstanding that she was not even an adult in legal terms:

> My message to society is that they should value each person really equally, without making any discrimination, between the covered, the uncovered, the hijabi, the very-open-clothed. [...] Is not it a mission of humanity? I have intense feelings right now [tr. "şu an gerçekten çok değişiğim"], seriously, I am sorry [asks for the interview to be ended].

Aslıhan also used her social media account to share more of these statements: "you will learn in this country how to respect beliefs and unbelief, covers and openness" ("Fatmadilaraygt" 2017). In the same vein, Ayşegül Terzi reacted against Çakıroğlu's authoritative claim:

> He says, "I kick if I see any open part in a woman's body." Who are you? What is your status [tr. ne sıfatın var]?
>
> ("Otobüste Darp" 2016)

Gözde Kansu, fired from ATV after Minister Çelik's comments on her attire, described how it is always women who are targeted by the authorities and sacrificed by the observers:

> Nobody wanted to behave in contradiction with the political will [of the government]. This is so clear. The easiest [option] was to victimize me. Again, a woman.
>
> (Arman 2013a)

Asena Melisa Sağlam and Ayşegül Terzi continued to criticize the officers who were supposed to defend them. Sağlam finally understood why "reality shows" on TV were so popular:

> The justice system, the police, the law does not protect them. They try to solve their problems on their own.
>
> ("Masenasaglam" 2017)

Terzi was angry since her father had to find and submit the footage from the camera on the bus to the police: "you [the police] have the car, go check yourself!" Both Terzi and Sağlam reported that they got angry when the officers repeatedly asked them if they have a complaint against the perpetrators.

While reclaiming their agency, they did not necessarily go against the senses of appropriateness they assigned to society. Köse, for example, underlined that she knew what the standard was:

> Am I a maniac that I would open my breasts in front of people?
>
> ("Maçka Parkı'ndaki Kadın" 2017)

Ayşegül Terzi stated that she does not have a problem with the publicity of religious norms. Reading some offensive messages that she received on social media after the incident, Terzi blamed Çakıroğlu and the others for instrumentalizing religion: "I really wonder if they read anything about it." Asena Melisa Sağlam could not easily decide whether she should care about the normative aspect of her clothes on the Ramadan day:

> [My jumpsuit] had cleavage in front, but my bag was hung there. Would he be disturbed... [*she cuts off the sentence*] But also, who would think if their clothing bothers someone else?
>
> ("Darp edilen" 2017)

Sağlam forced herself to stop her calculation as to the moral condition of her clothes. Gözde Kansu was sure that there was no discrepancy between any social norm and her cloth. She first responded to Çelik: "He calls my attire a night outfit. Of course it is! Should I have presented it with a pair of jeans and a t-shirt?" Then, she added:

> I am a young person in my 30s, and I dress myself this way. And I think there is no abnormality in that. I will continue dressing myself this way. Even defending [myself like that] looks weird to me. In my opinion, debating the cleavage of somebody else's clothing is embarrassing.
>
> (Arman 2013b)

As she promised, Kansu continued wearing clothes she liked. She could also continue working in the same industry, at least because authoritative claims based on contextual elements also lead to randomness. Deciding whether the interaction between a clothing item and its carrier's manner and timing fit together tolerably is not a mechanical process. As she agreed in her conversation with Journalist Ayşe Arman, there have been so many presenters with arguably "more open"[27] clothes on TV, but Kansu was somehow randomly targeted in Minister Çelik's arbitrary choice.

Even though she was fired from the abovementioned show at ATV, Kansu continued to participate in other TV projects. One of the latest of those projects, in 2018, retook place in ATV, which remains a media source loyal to the government. In April 2018, Journalist Oğuzhan Toracı of Sabah Newspaper, also led by the owner of ATV, conducted an interview with Kansu that focused primarily on her personality traits, recent projects, but also on "violence against women." Concerning the latter, she noted that she "experienced psychological and verbal violence," without providing any further details.

Neither Kansu nor Toracı mentioned the previous authoritative claim over Kansu's "low-neck" outfit. In case it is relevant for anyone, the photos of the interview depicted Kansu in a shirt with the top two buttons left open (Toracı 2018). Silently, Kansu reclaimed her agency, at least in part. After five years, she spoke about psychological and verbal violence against women. She spoke on the very same media channel that had interfered with her dress.

152   *Women and Clothing*

Just like Kansu, Sağlam insisted that she would continue wearing her skirts: "we must not fear, we must not hesitate" ("BBC 100" 2017). Pop music singer Gülşen did precisely the same when the presenter warned her about her socks during a concert in Ordu. Having noted their conversation during the show, Gülşen advised the mayor of Ordu, among the participants, not to work with this presenter anymore ("Gülşen" 2018). Addressing the women who joined others to judge her clothing, she narrativized the broader issue as "patriarchy" turning women against each other. In the same vein, pop music singer Hadise protested the censorship implemented by the Radio and Television Supreme Council (tr. RTÜK) of her music video due to her costume. Wearing the same clothing in her next concert, Hadise declared:

> If Turkey is a democracy, my video should not be censored [...] I do not fear anything. I am a free artist.
>
> ("Ben" 2018)

Aslıhan also declared that nobody would be able to remove her headscarf. On the other hand, Terzi publicly expressed her hesitancy to wear shorts anymore. Though most of these women could manage to do so, one's return to one's clothes is arguably the most challenging step in regaining agency. Based on an examination of the Ticani attacks of the early-1950s, the following part will seek the agency of the women attacked in a previous episode.

Back to the 1950s: Where Were "the Women" during Ticani Attacks?

The Ticani sect in Turkey, led by Mehmet Kemal Pilavoğlu, faced a series of accusations. The primary allegation was the breaking of the statues of Atatürk. Among other charges were allegations that they attacked women whom they thought appeared in inappropriate clothes. Ticanis had some blatant propaganda over clothing. In their in-group meetings, preachers labeled the wearers of şapka as "infidels" ("Denizli'de" 1952:3). In his court defense, Sadık Demirtepe, a sect affiliate, summarized their goal as "giving religion to those without one and giving underpants to those without one [tr. Dinsizlere din, donsuzlara don]" ("Bir Ticani" 1952:1). In this period, aggressors randomly appeared in parts of Ankara (Ulus, Yenişehir) and İstanbul (Şehzadebaşı) to throw razors on the arms or legs of women whom they saw with "open-clothes," such as blouses and skirts. Clothing prevailed in the Ticani discourse in such a way that in this period, journalist Fahri Nevruzoğlu (1952:3) had begun labeling them as "an underpants sect" (tr. don mezhebi).

In this part, I argue that the women who were attacked by Ticanis, or who were suspected to be sect members, were not vocal through their own voice but a given repertoire of ideal-type women. First and foremost, I shall question the perceived significance of the Ticani aggression towards women

Women and Clothing 153

at the time, especially in comparison with other acts they committed. I take the national press of the time to be the most important source in seeking an answer to this question.[28] For example, a well-detailed chronology (1965) prepared by the editorial board of Cumhuriyet Newspaper on "[Religious] Reactionist Movements" (tr. Gericilik Hareketleri) did not touch upon Ticanis' attacks on women in this period. In this chronology, the early 1950s consisted of the Ticanis who broke the statues of Atatürk, the Ticani members who were caught conducting rituals or secret meetings, and others who attempted to assassinate journalist Ahmet Emin Yalman ("Gericilik" 1965:1, 7). In this period, many public marches were organized in the cities where Atatürk statues were targeted ("Gençlik" 1951; "Heykele" 1951). The news coverage of the Ticani activities was predominantly based on these attacks on statues.

Having examined this period and its immediate aftermath in mainstream newspapers and magazines of any mainstream ideological orientation, in women's magazines, in political party meetings, and in public marches, I was unable to find a statement made by any of the women directly attacked by Ticanis. On the flip side, it was relatively easy to trace the messages of statue-makers, how they saw the Ticani threat, whether they thought their profession could have a future, and even how they interpreted nudity in statues ("Röportaj" 1953:2).

Because the absence of evidence is not the evidence of absence, I shall underline that these women's silence does not suffice to suggest that their victimization was not considered a significant matter. Therefore, I examined some complementary data in which the significance of such incidents was touched upon. As a result of this analysis, I argue that these emphases were made when an ideal clothing style was to be defended. The women who were attacked did not speak for themselves, but many others—i.e., those in various positions of ideology making and spreading in the media, civil society, and parliament—articulated in the name of these women. First and foremost, it was the Union of Turkish Women (tr. Türk Kadınlar Birliği) that produced an ideological discourse in the name of the women:

> From the newspapers, we have been following outrageously that they want women to cover themselves with hijab and confine themselves in the house, men to wear fez instead of şapka, [and] tekkes and medreses be re-opened. Turkish women believe that Turkish Reforms (tr. "Türk inkılabları") would bring our nation to the standard of civilized nations [...]
>
> ("Kadınlar" 1951:1–5)

This declaration ended with the statement that the Union is "convinced this statement is a translation of the feelings of all Turkish women." In such representations, women were taken as a monolithic body of political discourse, with no room for individual experience. Therefore, it was an ideal type that

154 *Women and Clothing*

prevailed within this context. This ideal type of woman did not just have a claim as to the right clothes. She also made claims on the places of worship, the mediums of education, and the roots of Turkish reforms.

In defense of women's clothing freedom, many raised their voices. These voices, however, were purified of the unique statements of individuals. This de-emphasis was at least because the attacks were not considered to target individuals but the Republic's ideals. Before all else, then minister of interior Halil İbrahim Özyörük standardized "the meaning" (tr. manâ) of these activities: "[it is] the preservation of our reforms (tr. inkılap) that made us reach the level of a civilized society" ("İnkılap" 1951:3). These voices would have realized an imagined woman for a civilized society. In this frame, the ideal type represented a collective voice of "youth," "our daughters," or "our women workers."

One key illustration of these narratives was a series of interviews conducted by Cemaleddin Bildik (1951:3–4) in Akşam, entitled with the question "what do our daughters say?" In these interviews, young students in a female student dormitory were asked their thoughts about claims against their clothing in general, and particularly the shorts they were about to wear during National Holiday Celebrations. In reaction, none of the students had an individual approach. Instead, they had broader claims over what would be the ideal item of clothing for women:

BILDIK: What would you say? What would you do if you were hindered from going out uncovered, with short skirts and open legs?
STUDENT 1: It is over! One of the Atatürk Reforms is sparing women from the state of bogeyman (tr. umacı vaziyet), and dressing them in civilized clothes [...] Replacing these clothes [...] with baggy-trousers (tr. şalvarlar) that cover our legs [...] would be the acceptance of backwardness [...]
STUDENT 2: If the ones [who wanted us to cover ourselves] asked first the opinions of their wives, and if they have, their daughters. Unarguably, neither his daughter nor his wife would embrace [the idea].
STUDENT 3: If he were single, he would never say his desire [...]
B: Why?
S3: So simple! It is because he would not be able to find any woman to agree with him, and he would remain single!

The "umacı vaziyet" of hijab, which was transmitted to students as a tag, was well-repeated at the time, from religious knowledge claims (Çağatay 1956:8–9) to political slogans. In this climate, Ticani attacks were denoted as a revolt against the ideals of the Clothing Revolution. They were considered the symmetric opposite of the Revolution's authoritative claim on ideal clothing.

The denigration of the hijab often accompanied the claim to defend the representation of women attacked by the Ticanis. In this vein, alongside the

Women and Clothing   155

convicted men's beards and hats, the black hijabs worn by the women on trial were cherry-picked in the media reports ("Adliye'de" 1951:1–5; "Atatürk Düşmanlarına" 1951:3; "Cezaevindeki" 1951:1). With reference to their dyed, round-trimmed beards and black hijabs, the alleged members of the Ticani movement were described in some media coverages to have a "weird appearance" ("Ticanilerin Duruşması" 1951:1).

Associating the appearance of the hijab, fez, and sarık (en. men's turban) with the Ticani ideology also caused misunderstandings. For example, in Mahmutpaşa, a group of university students ordered two men with sarık— i.e., an old man and a teenager—to remove their sarıks. When the old man, Mohammad, refused to follow this command, the university students ripped off their sarıks based on the preconception that they were Ticani members. The aggressors calmed down only after Mohammad yelled that they were Syrians ("Bir Suriyeli" 1951:2). Almost the same happened to the brother of former president Husni al-Za'im of Syria, Salahâddin Al-Za'im. He was arrested as a Ticani suspect in Ankara for breaching the Şapka Law ("Hüsnü Zaim'in" 1951:3). In another instance, a round-trimmed bearded man and a hijabi woman were caught when they got close to a statue of Atatürk ("Şehrimizde" 1951:3). The analytical distinction between Ticanis and the other religious organizations, such as the members of Büyük Doğu, was rarely emphasized in the mainstream media ("Ticaniler Hakkında" 1951:3). Any breach of the Şapka Law was likely to be classified under the umbrella of Ticani activities ("Şapka Kanununa" 1951:1–2).

In the intellectual landscape of this period, "the educated women" were expected to fit certain ideological criteria determined by the ideal type. From Şevket Rado—i.e., the director of one of the first women's magazines (*Resimli Hayat*) in the history of Republic—to Vâlâ Nurettin—i.e., a consistent advocate of the enlightenment paradigm in the media, an ideology maker who often touched upon the role of women in society, and a writer who used female names for some of his pieces[29]—the ideology makers of this period emphasized Secularism's expectations of women.

Vâlâ Nurettin argued that Turkish women should be more strongly indoctrinated with the principles of the Revolution. Because women did not have enough education in Turkey, the young generations were transmitted a corrupt notion of how women should be:

> Women should not pollute our national landscape with hijabs [...]
> Whereas the women of other nations further develop their houses and works, Eastern Women with the hijab move back and forth in a clumsy manner in all aspects of life [tr. her sahada bilgisizlik, beceriksizlik ediyor].
>
> (Nurettin 1956:2)

Having rationalized the argument that women could wear anything but "the symbols of backwardness," Nurettin underlined that this argument

156 *Women and Clothing*

did not contain any pressure. According to him, any more toleration would be exploited by "the *hacıağa*,"[30] who wants to enjoy *harem* life with "four birdbrained women" (Nurettin 1956:par7). Nurettin also shared the disappointment of "honest Muslims" with "a hijabi woman" selling a religious newspaper on a bridge in İstanbul. He concluded that the "Turkish womanhood" did not deserve being reinstated as a "black bogey" (Nurettin 1951). Last but not least, Vâlâ Nurettin reproduced the construct of symmetric opposition between the hijab and the clothes Ticanis attacked. In response to the Yeni Sabah writer Kadircan Kaflı (1954:2), who criticized Nurettin for "provoking intellectuals" against hijabi women, Nurettin referred to the Ticani attack on women. He asked the likes of Kaflı not to encourage those who want to interfere with civilized women (Nurettin 1954:2).

Şevket Rado had a different approach to the intolerance rationalized by the Clothing Revolution. To him, the most critical question was not whether people wore şapka or fez. What was of utmost importance was whether people had the economic means to purchase these clothes (Rado 1951b:2). That said, Rado himself was a reproducer of the enlightenment paradigm and Secularism's ideal-type woman. For example, he caricaturized the critics of the Clothing Revolution with the following statement in irony:

> Atatürk made a mistake! By taking out our red fez and making us wear şapka, he made us look like Europeans. But there are people among us who want to look ridiculous. Why would you rectify those who want to look ridiculous?
>
> (Rado 1951a:2)

Contrasting Egyptian and Turkish women—i.e., the former struggling to get their political rights recognized and the latter already having these rights— Şevket Rado stated his disappointment with "some [women in Turkey] who have a desire to go backward by not giving the civilization the credit it deserves" (Rado 1951c:2). Rado's magazine for women, *Resimli Hayat*, did not touch upon any of these ideological contestations, as it took the appearance of a civilized woman to be a settled one. Ignoring the flawed illustrations of women, *Resimli Hayat* wrote about the images of the ideal type.

None of these arguments were outliers at the moment they were made. Editor Nadir Nadi of Cumhuriyet Newspaper reported during his visit to the Aegean that "many women covered their faces with the niqab because their clothes were interfered [by reactionists]" (Nadi 1951b:3). Despite making the caveat that these were "individual cases," Nadi argued that they should still have been taken seriously by the Menderes Government so that Ticanis would not dare to cover more women. Nadi also examined Ticanis' attacks on women within the context of the Clothing Revolution. Accordingly, it was not enough to put into force a law on the protection of the memory of Atatürk [i.e., to protect the statues]; on the contrary, the state should have empowered its implementation of the Clothing Law alongside the Law on the Alphabet (Nadi 1951a:3).

Women and Clothing   157

Reproducing the argument that Turkish women were not yet educated in the ideal sense of the term, Bedii Faik called on the women to wake up against the Ticani threat:

> Where are you? Why don't you defend the reforms that gave rights to womanhood?

Referring to some cases of sexual harassment that targeted women for their clothes, *Her Gün* Editor in Chief Mehmet Faruk Gürtunca addressed women:

> True that the state is the guard of Reforms. However, you, Turkish house women, you [should] be the guard of Reforms as well.

In a similar vein, Burhan Felek argued that it was due to neglect on the part of the pro-revolutionary forces if Ticanis were still in favor of the veil (Felek 1951:3).

Responding to a similar wave of criticism regarding the government's soft measures against breach of these laws, Prime Minister Menderes asked public opinion to help sustain freedom of belief and accordingly have faith in popular support for the principles of Secularism ("İrtica" 1951:1–2). In this speech, Menderes described democracy as a regime of tolerance (tr. tahammül rejimi). Whereas Yeni Sabah Editor in Chief Sefa Kılıçlıoğlu backed Menderes' take on tolerance, Akşam and Cumhuriyet writers, as well as the members of the National Union of Turkish Students (tr. Milli Türk Talebe Birliği), criticized Menderes for underestimating the gravity of these "religious reactionist" threats. According to them, this was not a matter of tolerance but a conflict to define the ascendant ideals of the society.

From Eşref Edip to Necip Fazıl Kısakürek, many Islamist thinkers of the time also refused to interpret this episode as a matter of tolerance. They rather construed it as a conflict over who would shape the society. To begin with, the Islamist Magazine of Sebilürreşad, in which Eşref Edip had the primary role, described the abovementioned acts of social hostility as a product of some "insane" people (tr. meczup) ("Hadiseler" 1951:94). Having suspected that Ticanis in Ankara may not have followed the obligations set by Tijanis in Morocco, which the magazine was interested in exploring ("Ticani Tarikatının" 1950:218), Sebilürreşad refused to enter the controversy between the critics of the Democratic Party versus the likes of Zafer Newspaper which aimed to uncover "the secret ties" between the Ticani leader and the CHP leadership.

Instead, what Sebilürreşad problematized was the propaganda against hijab. Accordingly, the magazine published an open letter that condemned Cumhuriyet Newspaper for its survey project that described hijab as a matter of "ignorance" (tr. cahil) and "bigotry" (tr. yobaz, örümcek kafalı) (Dövez 1956:287). Based on its counter-claim that "95%" of Turkish society

158 *Women and Clothing*

was Muslim, Sebilürreşad repeatedly asked how a minority could rule over the majority in a democracy ("Sözün Özü" 1948:67). Accordingly, in the previous era (tr. "devr-i sabık"), the CHP governments used Secularism as antagonism against the religious institutions of Muslims ("Millete" 1951:51). As such, Secularism made the society lose its cultural essence.

In a similar vein, in his visits to Anatolian cities, Necip Fazıl Kısakürek often mentioned that the first generation of the Republic was brought up "rootless" (tr. köksüz) in a manner "lacking personality" (tr. şahsiyetsiz) (Kısakürek 1950a:19). To him, the roots of the society were cut off by the Kemalist ideology, leaving the youth's mind captive (Kısakürek 1951:46). Beginning with the early Ottoman period, he classified history into four ages. The last two were the periods of "imitation," referring to the Ottoman modernization, and the Republican period of "total impersonality and the era of captivity to the West" (Kısakürek 2004:189). His definition of the *Büyük Doğu* Islamist struggle was to re-construct "the gold mine of our soul," which he claimed the Republic's founders made rusty and turned into a tinplate (Kısakürek 1950b:34).

The Magazine of Hareket shared the same pessimism about, for example, (1) Cahid Okurer's description of the "insincere" city-life, where "this woman" who holds one's hand will end up in the bed of somebody else she will soon meet (Okurer 1952); (2) Nurettin Topçu's analyses of how the enemies of Muslim values "captured" the youth step by step, leading the society to lose its essence (Topçu 1952, 1953). Cevat Rifat Atilhan described the agency that "undressed our girls" as "the hands of the invisible enemy" (Atilhan 1950:1). The shared element in these narratives was the positioning of the individual as a passive carrier of grand ideologies. Under such conditions, it did not make sense to set aside the competing ideal-type women and ask the empirical women what they thought about the issue.

Notes

1 My reference to "current" refers to the aftermath of the de-facto lifting of the head-covering ban.
2 Historically, secularism in the West has a more complicated relationship with gender essentialism and inequality than often assumed (Scott 2018).
3 Exceptionally, thieves were penalized with political punishment only if they committed theft multiple times (see Aydın 1993:480).
4 Fatma Aliye was not a self-proclaimed feminist, as she rejected the Eurocentrism of the dominant first-wave feminism. However, Aliye's efforts in the field of women's studies may well be considered under the historical trajectory of feminism.
5 Though Fatma Aliye also wrote about the real-world problems of women between "tradition" and "faith," she constructed ideal-type characters in response to Western feminists and "francophone Turks," whom she claimed to lack the knowledge of true Islam. Among her "women of Islam" were happy concubines (tr. cariye) and hijabi women who, thanks to their hijab, could freely have conversations with men in public (see Aliye 2009:9, 16, 39, 51; Karaca 2011:93).
6 Atatürk used in Nutuk the words "ignorance" (tr. cehil), "heedlessness" (tr. gaflet), and "fanaticism" (tr. taassup) for fez.

Women and Clothing 159

7 See Sebilürreşad's defense of şapka ban for Muslims, together with its defense of fez against the claim that fez belongs to the Rum millet (Sebilürreşâd 1924).

8 In Atay's words (1961), it is not a matter of hat but a matter of head ["bu başlık değil, baş davası idi"]. Similarly, Niyazi Berkes (2002:547–48) argued that a key step in leading to a revolution in the people's minds was to prove the ability to change the accessories they wear on their heads. The description of the şapka law was as follows when introduced by Koraltan in 1925 (Özkaya 1989): "Though not having any significance [in the rest of the world], the hat problem is of special value for Turkey, determined to join the family of civilized nations." Many years later, Erksan (1997:2), an intellectual, quoted the following statement from Atatürk: "nothing will change as long as the inside of a head remains the same."

9 The adjective "non-national" (tr. gayrimilli) was as popular as the adjective "primitive" (tr. iptidai). Their opposites were defined as "civilized" (tr. asrî), "national" (tr. milli), and "international" (tr. beynelmilel). See Turhan (2015:167) for the particularistic identity that fez was believed to connote.

10 Recall the tradesmen's previously discussed dialogue with Sultan Abdülhamid.

11 See Bayram (2009) for the reproduction of the term at two critical junctures, 1997 and 2002.

12 See Güldal Okuducu making the same argument a decade after Mumcu (Köse 1997).

13 Bahriye Üçok, Uğur Mumcu, Turan Dursun, and Ahmet Taner Kışlalı, who were known for their strong opinions on the Islamization of Turkey, were assassinated within a decade.

14 See a debate on this difference between writers Etyen Mahcupyan and Ali Bulaç (Koray 2011).

15 One of the first examples of this approach is in Öymen (1986).

16 Among them were the Referendum of 2010, and the handling of the Ergenekon and Sledgehammer Cases.

17 My argument is based on the disappearance of their voices from the mainstream public debates. My claim may be exemplified by (1) the disappearance of once pro-government liberal organizations such as "Young Civilians" (tr. Genç Siviller); (2) the opposition leaders' only half-hearted support for the release of jailed "liberals" such as Ahmet Altan and Nazlı Ilıcak; (3) the in-group controversy over Cumhuriyet Newspaper's publication of Altan's article in August 2018; (4) a mass controversy which led to the firing of Nuray Mert from the same newspaper; (5) the narrative as to how Cengiz Çandar ended up leaving Turkey after spending a decade defending the AKP government's "democratizing" moves.

18 This is the description of the media that criticized the protest. For the protesting students, whether they were students was unclear.

19 The word cemaat (en. Jamaat, literally, "religious community") was often used to refer to the Gülenists in this period.

20 In 1993, a mob in the city of Sivas staged an arson attack on a hotel and killed 35 people, most of whom were artists and thinkers known for their Alevi identities.

21 However, against the lifting of the ban in mid-schools, Altıok (2014:par12) refused to set aside her first-order values.

22 The speakers of contesting value systems seem very similar when it comes to expressing antipathy towards contradictions—e.g., this woman who wears jeans together with a headscarf, that hijabi who holds her boyfriend's hand in public, another woman that combines the türban with heavy make-up or high-heels, a Muslim who celebrates the new year on January 1, takes alcohol for 11 months but Ramadan, covers her hair only in graveyards or holy shrines. None of these empirical types fit into the ideals of hegemonic ideologies with which they are identified.

23 The decade I describe in that section started with former CHP Leader Baykal's well-disputed "hijab opening" ("Çarşafa" 2008).

160 *Women and Clothing*

24 I refer to both the former ideology makers, such as Mehmed Zahid Kotku, Mahmud Es'ad Coşan, and Süleyman Hilmi Tunahan, and the more recent ones, such as Ahmet Mahmut Ünlü, Nureddin Yıldız, Abdülaziz Bayındır, and Hayrettin Karaman.
25 See the evaluation of a religiously conservative politician, Abdullah Gürsoy, in Doğan (2016:173).
26 Because Tsipras did not wear this tie in their following meeting, Erdoğan asked him where his tie was.
27 Indeed, I do not employ measurement unit like that of the "clothing police." However, Arman's evaluation makes sense within the given context.
28 See Başgil (1966:190) for the ways newspapers could shape mass politics in the 1950s.
29 One of the names he used was Hatice Süreyya. Another name close to Nurettin is Nihal Karamağralı, one of the first woman scriptwriters in the Republic, who either co-authored her work Casuslar with Vâlâ Nurettin, or she was simply Nurettin with yet another nickname ("Kadın Eli" 2006).
30 A pejorative statement referring to a graceless and imprudent man who begins to spend a fortune after moving to a large city from his small town.

References

"Abdülkadir Selvi'den 'Kabataş Kurguydu' Diyen Cem Küçük'e" 2015. *T24*. Retrieved August 18, 2018 (http://t24.com.tr/haber/abdulkadir-selviden-kabatas-kurguydu-diyen-cem-kucuke-kurgulari-erdogan-mi-yapti, 314320).
"Adliye'de Yeni Bir Ticani Hadisesi." 1951. *Milliyet*, March 18, 1–5.
Akçaoğlu, Aksu. 2018. *Zarif ve Dinen Makbûl: Muhafazakâr Üst-Orta Sınıf Habitusu*. İstanbul: İletişim Yayınları.
Aksekili Ahmed Hamdi. 2017. "Bilinmesi Elzem Hakikatler." Pp. 827–37 in *Türkiye'de İslamcılık Düşüncesi 2*, edited by *İsmail Kara*. İstanbul: Dergah Yayınları.
Akyol, Taha. 2008. *Modernleşme Sürecinde Türban*. İstanbul: Nesil Yayınları.
Albayrak, Levent. 2017. "Parkta Kirli Oyun." *Akşam*, August 6.
Albayrak, Özlem. 2012. "Kılık-kıyafet, başörtüsü, şort!" *Yeni Şafak*. Retrieved August 19, 2018 (https://www.yenisafak.com/yazarlar/ozlemalbayrak/kilik-kiyafet-baortusu-ort-35183).
Ali, Emine Seher. 2015. "Tesettür Meselesi (12 Mar 1329 [1914], Kadınlar Dünyası No.39)." P. 67 in *Feminizm Kitabı: Osmanlı'dan 21. Yüzyıla Seçme Metinler ed. Hülya Osmanağaoğlu*. Ankara: Dipnot Yayınları.
Aliye, Fatma. 2009. *Nisvan-ı İslam (1309) [İslam Kadınları (1892)]*. İstanbul: İnkılab Basım Yayım.
Altıok Akatlı, Zeynep. 2014. "Çocukluk." *Sosyal Demokrat Dergi*. Retrieved September 3, 2018 (http://www.sosyaldemokratdergi.org/zeynep-altiok-akatli-cocukluk/).
Alus, Sermet Muhtar. 1951. "II. Abdülhamid Devrinde Kadın Kıyafetleri." *Resimli Tarih Mecmuası* 2(13):544–47.
Arat, Necla. 1996. "Türbanlı Demokrasi'ye Doğru." *Bizim Gazete*, November 18.
Arat, Necla. 1997. "Değişmeyen Öz." *Bizim Gazete*, February 3, 2.
Arman, Ayse. 2013a. "Kovulan sunucu Kansu" *T24*. Retrieved August 7, 2019 (https://t24.com.tr/haber/dekolteli-sunucu-gozde-kansu-kurban-olarak-beni-sectiler-yine-bir-kadini, 241591).
Arman, Ayşe. 2013b. "Kurban olarak beni seçtiler." *Hürriyet*, October 10.
Arsel, Ilhan. 2002. "Susan Kadınlarımız..." *Cumhuriyet*, May 9, 2.

Women and Clothing 161

"Atatürk Düşmanlarına Karşı Gençliğin Asil İnfiali." 1951. *Milliyet*, June 26, 3.

Atay, Falih Rıfkı. 1961. *Çankaya: Atatürk Devri Hatıraları*. Vol. 1. İstanbul: Dünya Yayınları.

Atcan, Ipek. 2016. "Metrodaki Olaya İstinaden." *Günün İçinden Bıdılar*. (http://gununicindenbidilar.com/2016/11/28/metrodaki-olaya-istinaden).

Atilhan, Cevat Rıfat. 1950. "Kızlarımızı Çırılçıplak Teşhir Medeniyet Değil Vahşetin En Bayağısıdır!" *Hür Adam* 1(16):1.

Avcı, Özlem. 2012. İki Dünya Arasında: İstanbul'da Dindar Üniversite Gençliği. İstanbul: İletişim.

Avcı, Yasemin. 2007. "Osmanlı Devleti'nde Tanzimat Döneminde 'Otoriter Modernleşme' ve Kadının Özgürleşmesi Meselesi:'Authoritarian Modernity' in the Ottoman Empire in the Tanzimat Period and the Question of Women's Liber." *Osmanlı Tarihi Araştırma ve Uygulama Merkezi Dergisi OTAM* 21(21):001–018.

Avşar, Helin. 2009. "Seninle odada yalnız kalmam." *Habertürk*. Retrieved December 10, 2018 (https://www.haberturk.com/polemik/haber/176836-seninle-odada-yalniz-kalmam).

Aydın, Mehmet Akif. 1993. "Ceza." Pp. 478–82 in *İslam Ansiklopedisi*. İstanbul: Türk Diyanet Vakfı İslam Araştırmaları Merkezi.

"Bakan Gül tepki göstermişti." 2019. *Haber7*. Retrieved July 30, 2019 (http://www.haber7.com/guncel/haber/2865001-bakan-gul-tepki-gostermisti-o-hakim-gorevden-uzaklastirildi).

Baker, Patricia L. 2013. "The Fez in Turkey: A Symbol of Modernization?" *Costume* 20:72–85. doi: 10.1179/cos.1986.20.1.72.

Ballı, Refet. 1993. "Türban Sorunu." *Milliyet*, March 23, 9.

Barbarosoğlu, Fatma. 2015. *Kamusal Alanda Başörtülüler*. İstanbul: Profil.

Bardakçı, Murat. 2005. "Ahlâkı Kim Bozdu?" P. 243 in *Osmanlı'da Seks*. İstanbul: İnkılap.

Barkey, Karen. 2005. "Islam and Toleration: Studying the Ottoman Imperial Model." *International Journal of Politics, Culture, and Society* 19(1–2):5–19.

"Baş Açık Olarak Gezmek Caiz Midir?" 2014. *İskenderpaşa*. Retrieved September 4, 2018 (http://www.iskenderpasa.com/27B6E20E-0454-41A4-8E76-98E99716C992.aspx).

Başgil, Ali Fuat. 1966. *27 Mayis ihtilali ve sebepleri*. İstanbul: Kubbealtı Yayınları.

"Başörtüsüne Zulüm!." 2018. *Yeni Akit*, November 15.

Battal, Burak. 2017. "Yalancılara boyun eğmeyiz." *Yeni Akit*. Retrieved August 25, 2018 (https://www.yeniakit.com.tr/haber/yalancilara-boyun-egmeyiz-379728.html).

Bayındır, Abdülaziz. 2009. "Günümüzde Karı-Koca İhtilafının Sebepleri." *Süleymaniye Vakfı*. Retrieved August 19, 2018 (http://www.suleymaniyevakfi.org/arastirmalar/gunumuzde-kari-koca-ihtilafinin-sebepleri.html).

Bayram, Salih. 2009. "Reporting Hijab in Turkey: Shifts in the Pro- and Anti-Ban Discourses." *Turkish Studies* 10(4):511–38. doi: 10.1080/14683840903141590.

"BBC 100 Women on Twitter." 2017. *Twitter*, October 16. Retrieved May 25, 2019 (https://twitter.com/BBC100women/status/919896539346194432).

"Ben Atatürk çocuğuyum." 2018. *odatv.com*. Retrieved September 17, 2018 (https://odatv.com/rtuk-ceza-verirse-verir-19031819.html).

Berkes, Niyazi. 2002. *Türkiye'de Çağdaşlaşma*. İstanbul: Yapı Kredi Yayınları.

Beyaz TV. 2017. *Fatma Dilara Aslıhan Yiğit'in Annesi Konuştu*, February 16.

Bildik, Cemaleddin. 1951. "Kızlarımız Ne Diyorlar?" *Akşam*, May 2, 3–4.

Bilge, Necip. 1984. "Üniversitelerde Modern Başörtüsü." *Cumhuriyet*, June 25.

162 Women and Clothing

"Bir Suriyeli Hoca Yanlışlığa Kurban Gidiyordu." 1951. *Milliyet*, June 30, 2.
"Bir Ticani Mahkemede Yeni Bir Hadise Çıkardı." 1952. *Milliyet*, March 28, 1.
Birsel, Gülse. 2016. "Aynı Fotoğrafta Birlikte Gülümsemek." *Hürriyet*, August 30.
Böke, Emine Gumus. 2017. "İslam Hukuku'nda Kıyafet-Örtünme ve Kıyafetler Üzerindeki Resim ve Yazıların Durumu." *The Journal of Kırıkkale Islamic Sciences Faculty* 2(3):27.
Bulut, Faik. 1997. *Tarikat Sermayesinin Yükselişi.* Ankara: Doruk Yayınları.
Çağatay, Neset. 1956. "Kadının Örtünmesi (Tesettür)." *Din Yolu* 1(3):8–9.
Çakır, Serpil. 2010. "Kadınlar Dünyası'nda Giyim." Pp. 249–61 in *Osmanlı Kadın Hareketi*. İstanbul: Metis Yayınları.
Çalışlar, Oral. 1997. "Milli Eğitim Müdürü Karakelle." *Cumhuriyet*, May 29, 4.
"Çarşafa Rozet Takanlara." 2008. *SoL Haber Portalı*. Retrieved September 1, 2018 (http://haber.sol.org.tr/sabah-sabah/carsafa-rozet-takanlara-haberi-231).
Cebeci, Büşra. 2018. "Babam Açıldığımı Duyarsa, Kardeşimi de Üniversiteye Göndermez." *Bianet.Org*.
Cengiz, Mehmet. 2015. *Cübbeli Ahmet Hoca Karı Koca Hakları Sohbeti*. Retrieved 27 Aug 2022 (https://www.youtube.com/watch?v=kQHiVLrHS5k).
Çetinkaya, Hikmet. 2005. "1 Mayıs'ın Ardından." *Cumhuriyet*, May 3.
"Cezaevindeki Ticanilerin Sakalları Kesildi." 1951. *Akşam*, August 4, 1.
Çiftçi, Zeynep. 2006. "Tesettür Faciası Değil 'yalan Haber' Faciası." *Yeni Şafak*, December 18.
Cömert, Yusuf Ziya. 2007. "Erkekler şık olabilir kadınlar dursun hele." *Yeni Şafak*. Retrieved August 18, 2018 (https://www.yenisafak.com/yerel/erkekler-sik-olabilir-kadinlar-dursun-hele-28101).
Coşan, Mahmud Esad. 1993. *Cuma Sohbeti - İyiliği Emretme, Kötülüğü Engelleme Görevi*. Akra. (http://www.esadcosankulliyati.com/arsiv/cuma/c930331.html).
"Cumhurbaşkanı Erdoğan 3. Milli Kültür Şurası'na katıldı." 2017. *Yeni Şafak*. Retrieved August 26, 2018 (https://www.yenisafak.com/hayat/cumhurbaskani-erdogan-3-milli-kultur-surasina-katildi-2622567).
"Cumhuriyet'in 'başörtü' tiyatrosu." 2016. *Yeni Akit*. Retrieved August 10, 2018 (https://www.yeniakit.com.tr/haber/cumhuriyetin-basortu-tiyatrosu-229459.html).
"Dandik tesettür'e İslami kesimden tepkiler." 2010. *Haber7*. Retrieved August 25, 2018 (http://www.haber7.com/yasam/haber/590957-dandik-tesetture-islami-kesimden-tepkiler).
Danıştay [Council of State]. 1983. *142/2788*, December 20.
"Darp Edilen Üniversiteli Kız Konuştu." 2017. *Hürriyet*, June 21.
Davis, Fanny. 2006. *Osmanlı Hanımı: 1718'den 1918'e Bir Toplumsal Tarih*. İstanbul: Yapı Kredi Yayınları.
Demirer, Kemal. 1982. "Kılık Kıyafet." TRT Arşiv.
"Denizli'de Ticani Ayini Yapanlar." 1952. *Milliyet*, March 24, 3.
DHA. 2017. *Asena Melisa Sağlam Röportajı*, June 21.
Dikici, Ali. 2014. "II. Meşrutiyet'ten Cumhuriyete Miras Kalan İç Güvenlik Anlayışı ve Türk Polis Teşkilatı." *Türk İdare Dergisi* 86(479):91–122.
"Din Âlimleri Yetiştirmek: Dinî Kisve Yasağı." 1953. *Sebilürreşâd* 6(144):300.
Doğan, Sevinc. 2016. *Mahalledeki AKP: Parti İşleyişi, Taban Mobilizasyonu ve Siyasal Yabancılaşma*. İstanbul: İletişim Yayınları.
Dövez, Mustafa. 1956. "Çarşaf Meselesi: Cumhuriyet Gazetesi'nin Tuttuğu Hatalı Yol." *Sebilürreşâd* 9(218):287.

Women and Clothing 163

Ekinci, Oktay. 2002. "Türbanı Kadınlara Erkekler Taktı." *Cumhuriyet*, November 27, 6.

"Elif Çakır'ın avukatı Fidel Okan." 2015. *Radikal*. Retrieved August 17, 2018 (http://www.radikal.com.tr/turkiye/elif_cakirin_avukati_fidel_okan_kabatas_olayi_kurgu_ve_duzmece-1302431/).

"Emine Şenlikoğlu: Gerçek tesettürlüyü muhafazakarlar istemiyor." 2017. *Milli Gazete*. Retrieved August 25, 2018 (https://www.milligazete.com.tr/haber/1429667/emine-senlikoglu-gercek-tesetturluyu-muhafazakarlar-istemiyor).

"Emine Şenlikoğlu'ndan tesettür tepkisi." 2015. *Yeni Akit*. Retrieved August 25, 2018 (http://www.yeniakit.com.tr/video/emine-senlikoglundan-tesettur-tepkisi-1730.html).

Emiroğlu, Kudret. 2002. *Gündelik Hayatımızın Tarihi*. Türkiye İş Bankası Kültür Yayınları.

Ercan, Yavuz. 1990. "Osmanlı İmparatorluğunda Gayrimüslimlerin Giyim, Mesken ve Davranış Hukuku." *Osmanlı Tarihi Araştırma ve Uygulama Merkezi Dergisi OTAM* 1(01):117–25.

Erdoğan, Aynur. 2013. "Tanzimat Döneminde Modern Bilim Algısı." *Sosyoloji Dergisi* 3(26):1–31.

Erksan, Metin. 1997. "Fötr Şapka ve Kasket." *Cumhuriyet*, July 22, 2.

Ertürk, Ali Ekber. 2017. "İzmir'deki 'Kadınlara Polis Yumruğu' Skandalında Yeni Gelişme." *Sözcü*, August 12.

"Eşime ve çocuklarıma dini yaşamaları için baskı yapabilir miyim?" 2009. *Fetva.net*. Retrieved August 19, 2018 (http://www.fetva.net/yazili-fetvalar/esime-ve-cocuklarima-dini-yasamalari-icin-baski-yapabilir-miyim.html).

"European Court of Human Rights." 2006. *Kurtulmuş v. Turkey*, January 24.

"Fatmadilaraygt on Twitter: 'Bu ülkede inançlara, inançsızlığa, başörtüsüne ya da açıklığa saygı duymayı öğreneceksiniz.'" 2017. *Twitter*. Retrieved February 19, 2019.

Felek, Burhan. 1951. "Traş." *Cumhuriyet*, August 7.

Fida, Abdulmuizz. 2010. "Gelinlik Giymek Caiz Mi?" *Kur'an ve Sünnetten Delillerle Soru - Cevab*. (https://www.islam-tr.net/konu/gelinlik-giymek-caiz-mi.16078/).

Genç Bakış. 2006. *Süleyman Demirel Başörtüsü Sorusu*. Kanal D. (https://www.youtube.com/watch?v=i52dQaQ9Ick).

"Gençlik, Heykele Yapılan Tecavüzü Heyecanla Tel'in Etti." 1951. *Akşam*, March 6, 2.

"Gericilik Hareketleri." 1965. *Cumhuriyet*, January 18, 1–7.

Göçmen, Aylin. 2010. "Bana paradoksunu söyle..." *BirGün*. Retrieved August 10, 2018 (https://www.birgun.net/haber-detay/bana-paradoksunu-soyle-4125.html).

Göktaş, Evin. 1995. "Halk Eğitimi Merkezinde Başörtü Skandalı." *Milliyet*, February 19, 3.

Göle, Nilufer. 1996. *The Forbidden Modern: Civilization and Veiling*. University of Michigan Press.

"Gözde Kansu'yu Neden Kovduk." 2013. *Hürriyet*, October 10.

"Gülen'den Kılık Kıyafet Uyarısı!" 2008. *Milliyet*, June 13.

"Gülse Birsel'den Aile Bakanı Kaya'ya: Kız kardeşim..." 2016. *BirGün*. Retrieved September 3, 2018 (https://www.birgun.net/haber-detay/gulse-birsel-den-aile-bakani-kaya-ya-kiz-kardesim-113434.html).

"Gülşen Sunucuya Sinirlendi." 2018. *Milliyet*, July 26.

"Hadiseler: Ticanî Meselesi." 1951. *Sebilürreşâd* 5(106):94.

Hafız Baki. 1919. "Mağlubiyetimizi Dinsizlik ve Adem-i Tesettürde Aramalıyız." *İtisâm* 41:445.

164 Women and Clothing

Hakkı, Emin. 1919. "Tesettür, Fuhuş ve Esbab-ı Fuhuş." *İtisâm* 42:453.
"Haşema, bu yaz plajlara damga vuracak." 2008. *Yeni Şafak*. Retrieved August 19, 2018 (https://www.yenisafak.com/yenisafakpazar/hasema-bu-yaz-plajlara-damga-vuracak-125791).
Held, Deniz Alan. 2016. "Mağdur Ama Masum Değil." *Indigo*.
Her Telden. 2017. *Maçka Parkı'nda Kıyafet Gerginliği*, July 30. (http://www.youtube.com/watch?v=Zf3ArchBvVA&feature=youtu.be).
"Heykele Tecavüz: Konya'da Büyük Bir Miting Yapıldı." 1951. *Akşam*, March 10.
"Hoşuna Gitmeyebilir, Mırıldanırsın." 2016. *T24*, September 22.
"Hüsnü Zaim'in Kardeşi Ankara'da Ticani Zanniyle Emniyete Götürüldü." 1951. *Milliyet*, August 7, 3.
"İç giyim mağazasının cansız mankenlerini protesto edecek." 2017. *CNN Türk*. Retrieved September 16, 2018 (https://www.cnnturk.com/turkiye/ic-giyim-magazasinin-cansiz-mankenlerini-protesto-edecek).
İnce, Barış. 2012. "Dindar nesil yetiştirme konusunda cemaatle AKP arasında kriz çıkacak." *BirGün*. Retrieved September 1, 2018 (https://www.birgun.net/haber-detay/dindar-nesil-yetistirme-konusunda-cemaatle-akp-arasinda-kriz-cikacak-60721.html).
İnce, Özdemir. 2004. "Evet, mini etekli kızı yaktılar!" *Hürriyet*, April 20.
"İnkılap Düşmanı Ticanilik Kökünden Tasfiye Edilecek." 1951. *Milliyet*, July 17, 3.
"İrtica Hareketleri." 1951. *Akşam*, March 18, 1–2.
İşeri, Gülşen, and Tacım Açık. 2007. "Kadın Hakları Açısından Zor Konu." *Birgün*, August 25.
İslamoğlu, Mustafa. 2008. "Maksada Gelelim." *Mustafaislamoglu.Com*. (https://mustafaislamoglu.com/maksada-gelelim/).
İslamoğlu, Mustafa. 2013. *Tesettür Yazıları*. İstanbul: Düşün Yayıncılık.
"İsmailağacı Vali Kardeşinin Seviyesi" 2017. *Diken*. Retrieved August 25, 2018 (http://www.diken.com.tr/ismailagaci-vali-kardesinin-seviyesi-boyle-mi-olmali-tesettur-gelen-opsun-giden-yalasin/).
"İstanbul Esenyurt'ta taciz etti, dövdü!" 2017. *Yeni Akit*, August 17.
"İşte günümüzdeki 'çeyrek tesettür' anlayışı!" 2015. *Yeni Akit*. Retrieved August 23, 2018 (http://web.archive.org/web/20180309150622/http://www.yeniakit.com.tr/foto-galeri/iste-gunumuzdeki-ceyrek-tesettur-anlayisi-1084).
"Kadın Eli Değmiş Polisiyeler." 2006. *Radikal*, March 31.
"Kadınlar Birliğinin Beyannamesi." 1951. *Cumhuriyet*, March 20, 1–5.
Kaflı, Kadircan. 1954. "Camide Tüllü Kadın." *Yeni Sabah*, July 10, 2.
Kahramanoğlu, Kürşad. 2008. "Türban insan hakkı mı?" *BirGün*. Retrieved September 1, 2018 (https://www.birgun.net/haber-detay/turban-insan-hakki-mi-13437.html).
Kamacı, İpek. 2000. "The Cultural Policies of Turkish Republic during the Establishment of Nation State (1923–1938)." PhD Thesis, Bilkent University.
Kansu, Işık. 2017. "Şükürler Olsun!" *Cumhuriyet*, August 12.
Karaca, Şahika. 2011. "Fatma Âliye Hanim'in Türk Kadin Haklarinin Düsünsel Temellerine Katkilari." *Karadeniz Arastirmalari* (31):93.
Karahasanoğlu, Ali. 2017. "'Hayat tarzı...' Paranoyak iseniz, biz ne yapalım?" *Yeni Akit*. Retrieved August 25, 2018 (https://www.yeniakit.com.tr/yazarlar/ali-karahasanoglu/hayat-tarzi-hayat-tarzi-paranoyak-iseniz-biz-ne-yapalim-17789.html).
Karaman, Hayrettin. 2004. "(076) Dinimize Göre Düğün Nasıl Olmalıdır?" Retrieved August 10, 2018 (http://www.hayrettinkaraman.net/sc/00076.htm).

Women and Clothing 165

Karaman, Hayrettin. 2005. "Tesettür ve Kıyâfet." Retrieved August 15, 2018 (http://www.hayrettinkaraman.net/yazi/hayat/0487.htm).

Karaman, Hayrettin. 2018. "İslâm Ülkesinde Gayr-i Müslim Vatandaşlar (Ehlü'z-Zimmeh)." *Yeni Şafak*, August 5.

Karpat, Kemal. 2013. "Modern Eğitim ve Toplumsal-Felsefi Değişim." Pp. 156–64 in *İslam'ın Siyasallaşması*. Timaş Yayınları.

Kavas, Serap. 2015. "'Wardrobe Modernity': Western Attire as a Tool of Modernization in Turkey." *Middle Eastern Studies* 51(4):515–39. doi: 10.1080/00263206.2014.979802.

Kaya, Sinan. 2015. "Müdire Hanım'a kirli kumpas." *Yeni Akit*, February 21.

Kazımi, Halide Nusret. 1919. "Müslüman Kadını Nasıl Olmalı?" *İtisâm* 29:255.

Ketenci, Şükran. 1993. "Çiller-Kadın-Demokrasi." *Cumhuriyet*, August 31.

Kılıçarslan, İsmail. 2015. "Maçı nerde kaybediyoruz?" *Yeni Şafak*. Retrieved August 23, 2018 (https://www.yenisafak.com/yazarlar/ismailkilicarslan/maci-nerde-kaybediyoruz-2015845).

"Kılıçdaroğlu: CHP'de Başörtülü Milletvekili Neden Olmasın." 2019. *16punto*. Retrieved July 30, 2019 (https://web.archive.org/web/20190509024557/https://16punto.com/kilicdaroglu-basortu-yasagi-dogru-degildi-chpde-basortulu-vekil-neden-olmasin).

Kısakürek, Necip Fazıl. 1950a. "Büyük Doğu Cemiyeti Kayseri Şubesinin Açılış Hitabesi." In *Büyük Doğu Cemiyeti*. İstanbul: Büyük Doğu Yayınları.

Kısakürek, Necip Fazıl. 1950b. "Tavşanlı'da Verilen Açılış Hitabesi." In *Büyük Doğu Cemiyeti*. İstanbul: Büyük Doğu Yayınları.

Kısakürek, Necip Fazıl. 1951. "Kütahya Hitabesi." In *Büyük Doğu Cemiyeti*. İstanbul: Büyük Doğu Yayınları.

Kısakürek, Necip Fazıl. 2004. "İzmit'in Büyük Doğu Cemiyeti." In *Büyük Doğu Cemiyeti*. İstanbul: Büyük Doğu Yayınları.

Kışlalı, Ahmet Taner. 1997. "RP Rejimin Neresinde?" *Cumhuriyet*, February 19, 3.

Kibritçi, Abdullah. 2011. "Çarşaf Karşıtı Dindar?" *Furkan Derneği*. Retrieved August 19, 2018 (http://furkandernegi.blogspot.com/2011/01/carsaf-karsiti-dindar.html).

"Kipalı Da Girer, Başörtülüler Asla." 2008. *Haber 7*, February 5.

Kocaaslan, Nur Banu. 2015. "CHP'li Balbay" *Diken*. Retrieved September 9, 2018 (http://www.diken.com.tr/chpli-balbay-eskiden-turbanli-kardeslerimizin-canini-sikiyorduk-simdi-elini/).

Koçu, Resat Ekrem. 2003. *Tarihimizde Garip Vakalar*. İstanbul: Doğan Kitap.

Kökçe, Halime. 2017. "Ticaniler, Aczimendiler...Ama Artık Yemezler." *Star*, August 3.

Koray, Meryem. 1990. "Acınası Bir Özgürlük Çağrısı." *Cumhuriyet*, February 12, 2.

Koray, Meryem. 2010. "Türban-kadın-eşitlik." *BirGün*. Retrieved September 1, 2018 (https://www.birgun.net/haber-detay/turban-kadin-esitlik-15492.html).

Koray, Meryem. 2011. "Caanım kadınlar..." *BirGün*. Retrieved September 3, 2018 (https://www.birgun.net/haber-detay/caanim-kadinlar-15555.html).

Köse, Faruk. 2012. "Nihat Hatipoğlu'nun talak fetvası üzerine..." *Habervaktim*. Retrieved August 15, 2018 (https://www.habervaktim.com/yazar/52991/nihat-hatipoglunun-talak-fetvasi-uzerine.html).

Köse, Türey. 1997. "Ülkede Mini [...]." *Cumhuriyet*, January 11.

Kübra and Büşra. 2011. "'Pantolon giyme' dediğim için müşteriyi kaçırdım." *Yeni Şafak*. Retrieved August 19, 2018 (https://www.yenisafak.com/yenisafakpazar/pantolon-giyme-dedigim-icin-musteriyi-kacirdim-324010).

166 Women and Clothing

Lewis, Bernard. 1984. *The Jews of Islam*. 1st ed. London: Routledge.

"Maçka Parkı'ndaki Kadın Konuştu." 2017. *CNN Türk*, July 30.

"Maçka Parkı'ndaki Kıyafet Davasında Genç Kadın İçin Şok Karar". 2017. *Hürriyet*, October 6.

"Maçka Parkı'ndaki Özel Güvenlik Tacizine İlerici Kadınlar'dan Tepki (Video)." 2017. *Cumhuriyet*, July 30. (http://www.cumhuriyet.com.tr/video/video/792639/ Macka_Parki_ndaki_ozel_guvenlik_tacizine_ilerici_Kadinlar_dan_tepki.html).

"Mahremiyet ve Aile." 2015. *Diyanet Aylık Dergi*, January.

Mardin, Serif. 2006. "Islam in the Nineteenth and Twentieth Century in Turkey." Pp. 261–97 in *Religion, Society, and Modernity in Turkey*. Syracuse University Press.

"Masenasaglam on Twitter: 'Birlik olalım, duyarlı olalım!'" 2017. *Twitter*. Retrieved February 19, 2019.

Meliha, Ayse. 1914. "Müslüman Kadını Hürdür ve Mesuttur." *Sebilürreşâd* 11(282):345.

Metin, Hulusi. 1997. "Başörtüsü Bahane." *Cumhuriyet*, January 3.

Metinsoy, Elif Mahir. 2014. *Mütareke Dönemi İstanbulu'nda Moda ve Kadın 1918–1923*. Libra Kitapçılık ve Yayıncılık.

Micklewright, Nancy. 1989. "Late-Nineteenth-Century Ottoman Wedding Costumes as Indicators of Social Change." *Muqarnas* 6:161–74.

"Millete İtap Etmeyiniz." 1951. *Sebilürreşâd* 5(104):51.

"Mini Eteği Yasaklayan Rektör: Akademisyen Öğrenciye Örnek Olmalı." 2014. *Cumhuriyet*, December 22.

"Modanın Kurbanı Tesettür." 2013. *Vuslat* 146:1.

Mumcu, Uğur. 1988a. "Türban Yasası." *Cumhuriyet*, November 20.

Mumcu, Uğur. 1988b. "Liberal Hacı!" *Cumhuriyet*, July 22.

Mumcu, Uğur. 1988c. "Renkler." *Cumhuriyet*, July 24.

Mumcu, Uğur. 1988d. "O Gün." *Cumhuriyet*, July 28.

Mumcu, Uğur. 1988e. "Panzehir." *Cumhuriyet*, September 11.

Mumcu, Uğur. 1988f. "Türban ve Cilbab." *Cumhuriyet*, December 6.

Nadi, Nadir. 1951a. "Atatürk Kanunu." *Cumhuriyet*, July 17, 3.

Nadi, Nadir. 1951b. "Var Mı Yok Mu?" *Cumhuriyet*, March 24, 3.

Navlakha, Meera. 2019. "Why Muslim Fashion Is Taking Over the Luxury World." *Vice. Retrieved* July 30, 2019 (https://www.vice.com/en_in/article/evyejj/ why-muslim-fashion-is-taking-over-the-luxury-world).

Ne Var Ne Yok. 2013. Beyaz TV. Retrieved 26 Aug 2022 (https://www.dailymotion. com/video/x15s82h).

Nevruzoğlu, Fahri. 1952. "Bir Yobazın Hezeyanları." *Milliyet*, March 29, 3.

Nurettin, Vâlâ. 1951. "Bu Bid'atler Kimsenin Hoşuna Gitmiyor." *Akşam*, April 23, 3.

Nurettin, Vâlâ. 1954. "İrticaa 'hınk!' Dememeli!" *Cumhuriyet*, July 13, 2.

Nurettin, Vâlâ. 1956. "Şanlı Mevkiimizi Kazanmağa Yeni Bir Fırsat." *Cumhuriyet*, March 21, 2.

"ODTÜ'de Yalan ve Provakasyon Tutmayacak!" 2013. *Muhalefet*. Retrieved August 5, 2019 (http://muhalefet.org/haber-odtude-yalan-ve-provakasyon-tutmayacak-12-7572.aspx#).

Odtuogrencileri on Twitter. 2013. "Yeni kayıt olan öğrencileri iftiralarla[...]." *Twitter*. Retrieved February 19, 2019.

"Öğrenciye kezzap yalan çıktı." 2008. *Yeni Şafak*, February 14.

Okurer, Cahid. 1952. "Samimiyetini Kaybeden Şehir." *Hareket*, December 1.

Women and Clothing 167

Olgun, Ayşe. 2007a. "Alsak Alsak Ne Alsak?" *Yeni Şafak*. Retrieved August 18, 2018 (https://www.yenisafak.com/yenisafakpazar/alsak-alsak-ne-alsak-45070).

Olgun, Ayşe. 2007b. "Genç nesil tesettür." *Yeni Şafak*. Retrieved August 18, 2018 (https://www.yenisafak.com/yenisafakpazar/genc-nesil-tesettur-daha-ozgur-daha-spor-26773).

Olgun, Ayşe. 2007c. "Ortadoğu'nun gözü pardösülerimizde." *Yeni Şafak*. Retrieved August 18, 2018 (https://www.yenisafak.com/yenisafakpazar/ortadogunun-gozu-pardosulerimizde-42863).

Osman Hamdi Bey, and Marie De Launay. 1999. *1873 Yılında Türkiye'de Halk Giysileri: Elbise-i Osmaniyye*. Sabancı Üniversitesi.

"Otobüste Darp Edilen Ayşegül Terzi İlk Kez Konuştu." 2016. *CNN Türk*, September 27.

Öymen, Orsan. 1986. "Çağdaş Uygarlık ve Barbarlık." *Milliyet*, June 7.

Özdemir, Kamuran. 2007. "Cumhuriyet Döneminde Şapka Devrimi ve Tepkiler." *Unpublished MA Thesis, Anadolu Üniversitesi Sosyal Bilimler Enstitüsü*.

Özel, Sevgi. 2014. "Laik Eğitim Neden Gerekli?" *Cumhuriyet*, June 20.

Özkaya, Yücel. 1989. "Atatürk Biyografisinden Sayfalar: 1923–1928." *Atatürk Araştırma Merkezi Dergisi* 6(16):93–153.

Özvarış, Hazal. 2013. "Dilipak: Keşke Bu Halden Veya Başörtülerinden Vazgeçseler..." *T24.Com.Tr*. Retrieved August 27, 2018 (http://t24.com.tr/haber/hayrunnisa-gul-tesetturun-icini-bosaltti-emine-erdoganin-kiyafeti-yozlasti/236698).

Özvarış, Hazal. 2015. "AKP'li Kadınlar Erdoğan'ı Masal Dinler Gibi Dinliyor." *T24*. Retrieved September 5, 2018 (http://t24.com.tr/haber/17-25-aralik-cemaatin-hukumeti-devirme-girisimi-tapeler-dogru-teror-orgutu-suclamasi-agir, 288335).

Pekdemir, Melih. 2011. "Kadınların dayak yeme özgürlüğü..." *BirGün*. Retrieved September 1, 2018 (https://www.birgun.net/haber-detay/kadinlarin-dayak-yeme-ozgurlugu-14998.html).

Philipp, Thomas. 2001. *Acre: The Rise and Fall of a Palestinian City, 1730–1831*. New York: Columbia University Press.

Rado, Şevket. 1951a. "Atatürk'ün Hataları." *Akşam*, March 16, 2.

Rado, Şevket. 1951b. "Politika Bir Kenarda Dursun." *Akşam*, March 27, 2.

Rado, Şevket. 1951c. "Sözün Gelişi: İleri-Geri." *Akşam*, 2.

Refik, Ahmet. 1935. *On Altıncı Asırda İstanbul Hayatı*. İstanbul: Devlet Basımevi.

"Röportaj: Türkiye'de Heykelleri Döken Tek Sanatkâr." 1953. *Milliyet*, March 13, 2.

Şafak Pavey TBMM. 2013. *CHP TV*, June 25.

"Şapka Kanununa Aykırı Hareket Edenler." 1951. *Akşam*, March 9, 1–2.

Say, Zekeriya. 2017. "'Beyoğlu'nu geri alacağız!' dansı..." *Yeni Akit*. Retrieved August 19, 2018 (https://www.yeniakit.com.tr/yazarlar/zekeriya-say/beyoglunu-geri-alacagiz-dansi-20480.html).

Saylan, Turkan. 2001. "Laiklik ve Terör." *Cumhuriyet*, October 8, 2.

Scott, Joan Wallach. 2018. *Sex and Secularism*. Princeton University Press.

Sebilürreşâd. 1924. No 24(616):1340.

"Şehrimizde Alınan Tertibat." 1951. *Milliyet*, July 1, 3.

Selçuk, İlhan. 1999. "Başörtüsü ve Türban." *Cumhuriyet*, May 5.

Şen, Dilek. 2017. "Kadınlardan Tacize Büyük Tepki." *Cumhuriyet*, July 30.

Sevengil, Refik Ahmet. 1985. "Lâle Devrinde Kadınların Giyim ve İncelikleri." Pp. 103–5 in *İstanbul Nasıl Eğleniyordu?* İstanbul: İletişim Yayınları.

Şimşek, Ali. 2009. "Hayat Tarzı Ihbarcılığı Ya Da Mahalledeki Sınıfı Unutmak." *BirGün*, July 17.

168 Women and Clothing

Söğüt, Mine. 2017. "Pembe Bir Otobüs Nereye Gider?" *Cumhuriyet*, September 20.
"Şortlu Kadına Minibüste Saldıran Ercan Kızılateş Hakkında Karar Verildi." 2017. *Cumhuriyet*, September 12.
"Soylu: Kadına şiddet kabul edilemez." 2017. *Yeni Şafak.* Retrieved August 19, 2018 (https://www.yenisafak.com/gundem/soylu-kadina-siddet-kabul-edilemez-2622317).
"Sözün Özü." 1948. *Sebilürreşâd* 1(5):67.
Subaşı, Necdet. 2004. "On Religious School(er)s: The Modern Resources of Theological Heritage." *Değerler Eğitimi Dergisi* 2(6):116–32.
"taksim gezi parkı işgaline katılan türbanlı kız." 2013. *ekşi sözlük*, May 31. Retrieved September 3, 2018 (https://eksisozluk.com/taksim-gezi-parki-isgaline-katilan-turbanli-kiz--3853231?a=nice&p=2).
Tavşanoğlu, Leyla. 1996. "Üniversiteler Şeriat Kıskacında." *Cumhuriyet*, September 29.
Tayman, Enis. 2008. "Artık Tesettürlü Eşler de Aldatıyor!" *Tempo*, May 3.
"Tekmeci Saldırganın Avukatından Küstah Savunma." 2017. *Hürriyet*, October 13.
"Tekmecinin ifadesi!" 2016. *Yeni Akit*, September 21.
"Tesettür ve Mahremiyetle Ilgili Konular." 2014. *İskenderpaşa.* Retrieved September 4, 2018 (http://www.iskenderpasa.com/27B6E20E-0454-41A4-8E76-98E99716C992.aspx).
Teşvikçi. 1997. *Kadının Başı Açık Diye Onu Da Hakir Göremezsin.* Retrieved (https://www.youtube.com/watch?v=8VHm4lG4Unk&ab_channel=Te%C5%9F-vik%C3%A7i).
Tezcan, Hülya. 1988. "Osmanlı İmparatorluğu'nun Son Yüzyılında Kadın Kıyafetlerinde Batılılaşma." *Sanat Dünyamız* 14(37):44–52.
"Ticani Tarikatinin Esasları." 1950. *Sebilürreşâd* 4(89):218.
"Ticaniler Hakkında İzmir Savcısının Beyanatı." 1951. *Milliyet*, June 29, 3.
"Ticanilerin Duruşması." 1951. *Milliyet*, August 24, 1.
Topçu, Nurettin. 1952. "Mesuliyet Hareketi." *Hareket* 8–9.
Topçu, Nurettin. 1953. "Şahsiyet." *Hareket* 3.
Toprak, Zafer. 1998. "Tesettürden Telebbüse." *Tombak* 19:52–63.
Toprak, Zafer. 2017. *Türkiye'de Yeni Hayat-İnkılap ve Travma 1908–1928.* İstanbul: Doğan Kitap.
Toracı, Oguzhan. 2018. "Gözde Kansu: Hayat Bana Yokuşta Stiletto Ile Koşmayı Öğretti." April 22.
Tosun, Resul. 2017. "Başörtüsü Tek Ölçü Değildir." *Star.Com.Tr.* Retrieved August 19, 2018 (http://www.star.com.tr/yazar/basortusu-tek-olcu-degildir-yazi-1245632/).
Tufan, Erkam. 2012. *M.A. Birand Ile Özgürlükler ve Başörtüsü Üzerine.* Bugün TV. Retrieved August 27, 2022 (https://www.youtube.com/watch?v=yJoPpxt-jGs&ab_channel=ErkamTufan).
"Tuncay Özkan: 'Çıktığım günden beri o insanlardan özür diliyorum.'" 2016. *Oda Tv.* Retrieved August 10, 2018 (https://odatv.com/ciktigim-gunden-beri-o-insanlardan-ozur-diliyorum-0603161200.html).
Turan, Namık Sinan. 2005. "16. Yüzyıldan 19. Yüzyılın Sonuna Dek Osmanlı Devletinde Gayri Müslimlerin Kılık Kıyafetlerine Dair Düzenlemeler." *Ankara Üniversitesi SBF Dergisi* 60(4):239–67. doi: 10.16987/ausbf.64444.
"Türbana İzin Yok." 1990. *Cumhuriyet*, November 1, 1.
Turhan, Mümtaz. 2015. "Fasıl VIII: Kültür Değişmelerinin Umumi Bir Tahlili." P. 167 in *Kültür Değişmeleri: Sosyal Psikolojik Bakımdan Bir Tetkik.* İstanbul: Doğan Kardeş Yayınları

Women and Clothing 169

Üçok, Bahriye. 1993. "Adım Adım İlerleyen Kara Tehlike." *Milliyet*, March 1, 11.

Ülken, Hilmi Ziya. 1982. *Türk Tefekkürü Tarihi*. İstanbul: Yapı Kredi Yayınları.

Unat, Abadan. 1987. "Başörtü: Eşitsizlik İçin Baskı." *Cumhuriyet*, January 6, 1.

"Üniversiteli Kadını Tacizden Tutuklanan Adamın Yakınları [...]." 2018. *Diken*, January 30.

Uysal, Gözde Naz. 2017. "Yardım Istediği Polisten Dayak Yedi." *Hürriyet*, August 13.

Vurdu, Buse. 2018. "Başörtülerini çıkaran kadınların hikayesi." *Evrensel*. Retrieved December 10, 2018 (https://www.evrensel.net/haber/361882/basortulerini-cikaran-kadinlarin-hikayesi-yalniz-yurumeyeceksin).

Yakut, Kemal. 2002. "Tek Parti Döneminde Peçe ve Çarşaf." *Tarih ve Toplum* 220:23–32.

"Yalan haberin belgesi." 2006. *Yeni Şafak*. Retrieved August 20, 2018 (https://www.yenisafak.com/gundem/yalan-haberin-belgesi-20255).

Yayla, Atilla. 2008. "AK Parti'nin Liberallerle Zor Ama Zorunlu İlişkisi." *Liberal. Org.Tr*. (http://www.liberal.org.tr/sayfa/ak-partinin-liberallerle-zor-ama-zorunlu-iliskisi-atilla-yayla, 340.php).

Yıldırım, Deniz. 2018. "Kültürel Iktidar." *Cumhuriyet*. Retrieved December 26, 2018 (http://www.cumhuriyet.com.tr/koseyazisi/1181658/Kulturel_iktidar.html).

Yıldız, Nureddin. 2013. *Kadının Giyimine Kocası Karışabilir Mi?* Fetva Meclisi. Retrieved August 27, 2022 (https://www.fetvameclisi.com/fetva-kadinin-giyimine-kocasi-karisabilir-mi-31487.html).

"Yıldız Teknik Üniversitesi'nde reklam sansürü." 2013. *Hürriyet*. Retrieved September 16, 2018 (http://www.hurriyet.com.tr/gundem/yildiz-teknik-universitesinde-reklam-sansuru-23397693).

Zilfi, Madeline C. 2018. *Osmanlı İmparatorluğu'nda Kölelik ve Kadınlar (1700–1840)*. İstanbul: Türkiye İş Bankası Kültür Yayınları.

5 Alevis and Funerals

This chapter examines a relatively new rationalization of intolerance, which brings together the politics of recognition and assimilation against some syncretic religious traditions developed within Alevilik. While the recognition and assimilation ideas have been in conflict since the 1980s identity turn, their opposite poles have begun to make similar claims against the syncretic rituals many Alevis acculturated after urbanization. By examining the problems Alevis have recently encountered during their funerals, I will question where "our" history of sectarianism has reached.

Both sides have occasionally disdained the untidy flow of urbanization. In doing so, they tend to challenge one another based on *essentialism*, which obliges both to have an exclusive claim on what Alevilik is: a sect of Islam, a separate religion, a communal religious culture, or philosophy. Funeral practices have become particularly significant since they reveal the shared essentialist grounds of the contention. Accordingly, syncretic funeral rituals serve non-recognition—i.e., "assimilation" for the politicians of difference—or introduce heterodoxy—i.e., "heresy" for the orthodox.

Before scrutinizing cultural change in the landscape of funerals, I will briefly describe *salâ* as a matter of Turkish Islamic tradition instead of the theological corpus of Islam.[1] Having become a part of this tradition after their mass migration to urban centers, the Alevi communities followed a somewhat immature mixture of the politics of recognition and tolerance. However, after the identity turn of the 1980s, they had explicit in-group cleavages over the alternative forms of recognition that they were to demand. Among these options are the representation of Alevilik within Diyanet as a sect of Islam, the abolition of Diyanet for a "true" Secularism, and the institutionalization of Alevilik as the symmetric opposite of Diyanet. Amid disagreements, many ideology makers blamed the politics of tolerance, claiming that it led to the assimilation of the urbanized generations.

Based on this historical baggage, I will analyze the recorded incidents relating to Alevis' funerals, in which some Alevis felt offended, and explain why. While examining the *exploratory conversations* in each incident, I will divide them into two groups. These are the incidents in which Alevi citizens (1) encountered problems while having the funeral salâ read from

DOI: 10.4324/9781003311805-5

mosques and (2) became the objects of a state funeral ceremony organized per Diyanet's interpretation of (Sunni) Islam. In these incidents, Alevis have manifested some distinctive forms of religiosity.

Those in the first group have taken a syncretic approach to religious and cultural institutions by combining two attitudes that were never connected before. Despite the imams' averseness, they maintained that the funeral salâ should be read from a mosque in their neighborhood. On the other hand, they insisted that their funerals would take place at a cemevi, instead of a mosque. Officials have responded to this attitude in two ways. Firstly, the religious personnel was ordered by Diyanet to read the salâ. Secondly, however, they were also called by Diyanet to refuse to use the word "cemevi" during the relevant address section accompanying the salâ. In sum, Diyanet's religious personnel read the salâ for Alevis; but they do so without fully announcing where their funerals will take place. Within this context, I will argue that the knowledge claim, "salâ is not read for Alevis," meant different things throughout the Alevis' transgenerational funeral experience.

As regards the second group of cases, I will demonstrate that almost all Alevi families who were asked to hold a state funeral ceremony preferred to have their funerals at a cemevi, regardless of the disincentives such as the lack of state-level participation in cemevi funerals. That said, most of these families also consented to have a second funeral in the form of an official ceremony at a mosque or another central place where Diyanet's personnel were supposed to perform the funeral prayer. The state representatives, who tend to disappear during cemevi funerals, became visible in these official ceremonies.

In *evaluative conversations,* I examine several debates concerning funerals, primarily among the ideology makers of Alevism. This part demonstrates that a new tension between the religious identity and the religious doctrine lays the groundwork for clashing views on the changing funeral cultures of Alevis. Accordingly, the refusal to conduct mosque funerals has been justified primarily in terms of identity politics instead of the belief system. In this context, Alevis have a fundamental disagreement on the extent to which identity politics shall prevail over the belief. The state-led assimilationist policies, such as building mosques in Alevi villages, have triggered an unsettled cultural period in the Alevi communities. This alertness against assimilation feeds the identity politics, arguably at the expense of certain practices justified in the belief system.

On the flip side, I will also touch upon some critical conversations between these ideology makers, the government, and other anti-recognition actors, such as some popular teachers and theologists of Islam who oppose the recognition of Alevilik for various reasons. These actors push the Alevi associations to come up with a clear-cut definition of Alevilik. Their arguments imply that cemevi can be recognized as a place of worship only if Alevis "admit" their religion does not have anything to do with Islam. In this context, they oppose all syncretic approaches, either by calling for assimilation

172 *Alevis and Funerals*

(i.e., Alevilik as a temporary and faulty cultural representation of Islam) or by calling for total separation (i.e., Alevilik as a separate religion). Bringing them together, I argue that the clash between the politics of assimilation and recognition merges in a common framework of essentialism. In this framework, the conflict has been based on totalistic claims over "what Alevilik is" as an innately existing category on a timeless ground.

In the third and last section, which is composed of what I call *retroactive conversations*, I analyze conversations between (1) the Alevis who requested salâ from mosques; (2) the Alevis who consented to have two funerals; and (3) their critics who often blamed them for serving the project of assimilation. The essentialist framework makes clear marks on the retroactive conversations. Alevis who requested salâ from mosques have been criticized from a two-way essentialist standpoint. From this standpoint, Alevis should not demand anything from mosques, given that they are either not Muslims or never pray at mosques. Also, those Alevis who go to mosques serve the assimilation of Alevis, supporting the enemies of "the genuine Alevilik" that struggles against non-recognition. After presenting these claims, I will conclude that tolerance will remain relevant amid these cultural contestations, even if a form of the politics of recognition succeeds.

The Changing Scenery of Funerals

The massacres of Kahramanmaraş in 1978 and Çorum in 1980 were triggered by the slogans, "the funeral prayer cannot be conducted for Alevis/Communists,"[2] and "the salâ is not (to be) read for Alevis/Communists."[3] Commemorating these massacres yearly, many recall these slogans to indicate the intolerance against Alevis. As such, Alevis' funerals represent the stillness of sectarian tensions. Starting with them, I shall discuss some stark differences between this landscape's old and new snapshots.

The literature on this matter focuses mainly on four relational processes: Alevis' relationship with the state, with one another, with religion, and with the other social forces. Through the conjunction of these relational processes, Alevis found themselves in new social contexts and acted accordingly. These transgenerational processes have been summarized in the academic literature under the headings of urbanization (Karpat 1976; Ayata 2008), secularization (Dressler 2008), Europeanization (Özyürek 2009; Kaya 2013; Ulusoy 2013), politicization (Erman and Göker 2000), and revitalization (Van Bruinessen 1996; Çamuroglu 1998).

While offering new opportunities, these processes also imposed further restrictions. Alevis began migrating to the urban centers in Turkey or Europe in large groups—often in larger groups than the Sunni migrants since Alevis did not feel secure when dispersed (Çubukçu 1966). After the beginning of mass migration in the 1960s, they either stopped their ritualistic cem-meetings altogether or kept them secret (Karpat 1976:225–30). This secrecy was not just a product of fear but also a reproducer of the already distorted image of Alevilik outside their social circles.[4] Before urbanization, Alevis had to conduct their cem-meetings with great caution in many parts of the country. For example, among the neighboring Sunni villages, the inhabitants of an Alevi village in Kozak Downhill, close to Izmir's Bergama district, held cem-meetings in great secrecy by keeping watch on the borders of the town (*see* Harmancı 2012).

Amid similar constraints, millions of Alevis migrated to the urban centers. Immigration was a general trend beyond this particularistic explanation. That said, Alevis' immigration was particularly noteworthy because the rural cities with large Alevi populations, such as Sivas, Kars, Erzincan, and Tunceli, were "the champions of migration" by 1990 (Ballı 1990:18). This mass migration also explains why Alevis had some influential political figures in the large cities, such as Istanbul and Ankara, and why they later had their most well-organized ideology-making associations in these large cities, alongside the European capitals.

The new urban context deeply affected Alevis' cem-meetings and funeral preparations. Having fewer cem-meetings meant that many Alevis left their worship environments behind. Lacking the environmental means to conduct their funerals as they did in the rural past, many Alevis began to have their funerals at mosques. Some had funerals in front of their apartments. Compared to the traditional village houses, the limitations of these medium-rise buildings pushed many Alevi groups to carry their funerals back to their hometowns (Büyükokutan 2007:69). For those who lost such ties, there was no convenient option but a mosque funeral.

Leaving the environment of worship behind meant rapid secularization as well. In time, many Alevis forgot their rituals. The succeeding generation was not born into a practicing culture ("Aleviliğe" 1987). Relatedly, their religious leaders, *ocak dedes*, faced the danger of extinction in time because fewer *dedesoylu* candidates appeared to undertake the duties of a dede.[5] The Alevi communities did not have sufficient means to educate Alevis in accordance with the strict traditional hierarchy of the institution of *dedelik*.

Embracing Alevis in the multi-party system, the political ideology of Secularism also underpinned the sociological process of secularization. In the Ottoman times, Alevis relied on the institution of dedelik to resolve their internal disputes since they did not want to be judged by Qadis—i.e., the magistrates of Shari'a Courts. However, a few decades after the foundation of the Republic, the courts of Secularism, which were supposed to consider them equal citizens, became legitimate in their eyes (Görmüş, Öztürk, and Özberki 1987:30–31). Finally, their leftism during the cold war disillusioned many from the traditional hierarchies in Alevilik.[6]

Intolerance as the Old Problem of Mosque Funerals

Starting with the period discussed above, Alevis' mosque funerals contextualize their cross-generational problems with Diyanet. They were often insulted during preaches ("İmam Alevilere" 1965:6). Sometimes, their

174 *Alevis and Funerals*

bodies were not washed before the funeral ("Hoca, Alevi" 1968:3). As an illustration of their shared fate with Marxists, some Diyanet personnel and connected ideological fractions opposed reading or listening to their salâ (Öztürk 2010). In many cases, a funeral prayer was also not performed (Ateş 1976:7; Demirtaş 1990:16). Many funerals were held without Alevis informing the imam about the religious orientation of their deceased family member (Adlı 2016). So as not to be exposed and alienated, many of them hid their identities.

Hiding one's identity during the funeral was not always enough to go unnoticed. In some cases, it was the religious personnel who detected some signs of Alevilik. One example was the funeral of Bektaş Akkol in Malatya ("Hoca, Alevi" 1968:3). In this case, the religious personnel of the hospital explicitly asked if the deceased was an Alevi or Sunni because he was suspicious of the name of the dead: "Bektaş." This case is indicative of why for many years, Alevi parents frequently gave their children names that do not signify Alevilik (Toprak et al. 2009:54). Additionally, the deceased's hometown was also a factor that an imam occasionally took into account (Tol 2005:38).

Right after the massacre of Maraş, former Minister and MP Turan Güneş of CHP mentioned his disappointment in the following words: "In our country today, even our funeral ceremonies are made separately" ("Güneş'in" 1978:9). According to Güneş, shared funeral ceremonies represented the value of coexistence. After four decades, it is difficult to find a problematization of separate funeral ceremonies in Turkey. Even though some ideas of recognition were apparent—albeit immature—at the time (*see* "Anayasa'nın" 1961:5), Alevis demanded tolerance during funerals, given that they did not see any problem with mosque funerals in terms of their belief system. In other words, they desired their funerals to be held in the same as could be demanded by Sunni citizens.

The funeral salâ was a particular question from the point of view of Sunni Islam. As they do today, many theologians of the period kept claiming that it was just a tradition based on Turkish religious music: neither a sacred duty (tr. farz) nor an obligation (tr. vacip). The relatively deculturated Islamists claimed more openly that salâ is not based on the sunnah of Prophet Muhammed. Beyond Alevis, the carriers of the Sufi tradition were offended when some theologians defined salâ as an illicit novelty (tr. haram bid'at). And yet, it remained a vital element of the *settled* Anatolian culture of Islam in a manner that transcends sectarian boundaries. According to its Sunni supporters, salâ was not a harmful tradition, even though it did not exist at the time of the Prophet. Its main aim was to make announcements in the neighborhood—e.g., about funeral dates or the eternal love for Prophet Muhammed. Bizarrely, refusing to read the salâ for Alevis meant not conducting a ritual, which was disputable in terms of Sunni Islam, for a group on the basis that they were not Sunni Muslims.

For some decades after mass urbanization, the mosque became a given for many Alevi citizens, as they had already begun to have their funerals at

Alevis and Funerals 175

mosques within the social setting of urban life. There was no standard place of worship for Alevis in the urban centers, and their hometown was often too far away to transport a funeral. Even when building mosques became a state policy in their villages, Alevis did not necessarily problematize the mosque funerals. Instead, they questioned the authority of Diyanet and its role in the denigration of Alevis' relationship with the faith. For example, the villagers of Izmir's village of Bademler, among those villages in which the post-1980-coup governments planned to build a mosque, protested against the plan with the following words:

> We do not want a mosque. If it is built, nobody will go there except for the funeral prayers.
>
> ("Bademler'in" 1987:33)

After the 1980s' identity turn, the state policy of building mosques in the Alevi villages and the organization of the first cemevis in urban settings shifted the focus from tolerance to assimilation, difference, and recognition.

Assimilation as the New Problem of Mosque Funerals

Since the 1980s, Alevis have re-considered their relationship with the politics of social class and cultural identity (Vorhoff 1998; Göner 2005). Even though the class dimension did not entirely disappear in the post-cold-war period, it was re-shaped concerning the question of ethnocultural and religious identities (Erman and Göker 2000). For example, "Kurdish Alevis" claimed their intersectional identity, as opposed to the former identity constructions based on locality (tr. *hemşehrilik*) (Van Bruinessen 1997; Çelik 2003:143). The European Alevi communities, in particular, played a key role in this transformation from political activism to cultural reclamation. With such newly established networks, Alevilik has been re-made as a public religion (Şahin 2005). The shift from the 1960s to the identity turn of the 1980s was not a linear process. By the late 1990s, many public figures reported that the political efforts were disillusioning for Alevis (Çakır and Yılmaz 2001; Cem TV 2016). As a building block of cultural reclamation against assimilationism, they re-configured their worship environment in the urban setting, establishing the first cemevi buildings in large or essential cities.

In due course, the authority structures of Alevilik changed under the ideology-making processes of "Alevism" (Massicard 2007:21–22). The rituals in the cemevis, the differentiated duties of the new *cemevi dedes* (Sökefeld 2002; Dressler 2014), and the relationship of cemevis with, on the one hand, the religious institutions of *ocaks*, and on the other, the civil society organizations, foundations, associations, and federations became matters of in-group contestation (Yaman 2003). This polarization had its repercussions for Alevis' differentiated defense of Secularism. Should Alevis be represented in Diyanet, or should Diyanet be abolished altogether? Must Alevis

176   *Alevis and Funerals*

demand recognition in the name of Secularism, in which Diyanet has played a crucial role, or must they defend another kind of secularism? How should Alevilik be positioned with the official Islam in Turkey? After the identity turn, the disagreements over these questions became more explicit.

State funeral ceremonies, as the representations of the 'official Islam' in Turkey, were also problematized for the first time in the 21st century. The chronological record of state funerals suggests that before the foundation and the spread of cemevis, the sectarian dimension of state funeral ceremonies was not problematized in public. Common sense necessitated having these ceremonies at a mosque, chosen per the neighborhood where the deceased's family lives.[7] The mosque was a given for all funerals—except for that of the believers of other Abrahamic religions, who are much less likely to be an object of state funeral ceremonies, given that so few of them, if any, served as soldiers or politicians.[8]

Before the foundation of cemevis, Alevis' main problem with state funeral ceremonies was the other participants' use of certain symbols. Among them were the right-wing anti-communist marks (e.g., the grey-wolf hand gestures) and the somewhat politically-poisoned religious slogans, such as "ya Allah Bismillah, Allah-u Ekber" [tr. Tekbir]. The problem was that Alevis saw and heard these symbols when attacked as well (Tamer 2006:6). Approximately a decade after the spread of cemevi funerals, the criticism towards state funeral ceremonies shifted to more fundamental issues. These issues include the role of Diyanet in the official ceremonies and the incompetence of Alevis in conducting an official ceremony at cemevis. In this vein, the funeral of Murat Taş in 2009 became the first publicly problematized state funeral ceremony. Afterward, the content of state funerals would not be isolated from the broader claims of the Alevi communities, which began to complicate mosque funerals, be they ordinary or official ceremonies.

Even though deep disagreements surfaced over re-configuring religious and cultural institutions, Alevis commonly agreed that they should not remain an isolated cultural group (Şener 1995:23; Kehl-Bodrogi, Heinkele, and Beaujean 1997). For they decided that the current and the past crises signify some successive chapters of the same problem, repeating well-known phrases—e.g., "salâ is not to be read for Alevis"—have continued to play a crucial role in anchoring today's problems with the past episodes. Although many leaders of this politics of recognition refuse to demand salâ from mosques, the expression continues to serve their ideology as a meaningful way of carrying the baggage of collective memory.

In this period, the bureaucrats of Diyanet insistently claimed to read salâ for the funerals of "all Muslims," which is intended by Diyanet to include Alevis as well as Sunnis. However, the core issue to be inquired is as follows: if the Alevis' expectations from a funeral proceeding have fundamentally differed since the 1990s, to what extent could it be possible for their complaint about Diyanet to reproduce the same story? Being deprived of the funeral salâ is something that Alevis problematized before and after

Alevis and Funerals 177

Alevi revivalism. The meaning of not reading the salâ has shifted with the revivalist strand. Before, it was a problem of intolerance. Then, it has become a problem of assimilation.

Repeating the Same, Meaning Another: "Salâ is not to be read for Alevis"

In the following exploratory conversations, I scrutinize the cases in which Alevi citizens had problems with official religious personnel about their funeral organizations. Even though the seemingly timeless expression, "salâ is not to be read for Alevis," has been well-repeated within the specific context of these cases, I claim that the acts this expression signifies have gradually changed after the normalization of cemevi funerals among Alevis. In this vein, I firstly clarify that in the recent cases, salâ was read one way or another, notwithstanding several implications of discrimination during this process. Nonetheless, the religious personnel have drawn the borderline of tolerance around the use of the word "cemevi" during the salâ. Furthermore, the families were particularly offended by the aversion of the religious personnel while reading the salâ. In response, they have combined two attitudes that were never connected before: (1) they insisted that a salâ should be read; (2) they still had their funerals at a cemevi.

These features of the incidents determine the flow of conversations in specific ways. Firstly, such requests from mosques seem contradictory to the claims made on behalf of Alevi revivalism. Therefore, the Alevis who still request a ritualistic performance from mosques have been condemned by many other Alevis, including some of the most influential organizations of Alevi communities. Secondly, however, these requests do not mean these people are "assimilated." On the contrary, the Alevis in these cases were keen to have their funerals at cemevis, as opposed to the undoubtedly assimilated Alevis who only go to mosques. These two points will constitute my analysis of the following parts, which are evaluative and retroactive conversations.

The relatives of Nurten Mirzeler in the city of Adana wanted her death to be announced with a *salâ*. For the funeral, Mirzeler was brought back to Adana from Germany. However, after meeting with Imam Musa Oğuz Tarhan of the Camii Şerifi Mosque, the family claimed that the imam refused to read the salâ because it is "not to be read for Alevis." Soon after this argument, the imam faced a group of neighbors at the lodging building of the mosque. He told them that he read the salâ in the morning—i.e., when the neighbors "may have been sleeping." The deceased's sister asked the imam: "can you swear on God that you read it?"—she reported that the imam preferred silence ("Adana'da" 2015). Eventually, rejecting the allegations of discrimination, the imam read the salâ "once again." "Some circles from outside our neighborhood want to drag me into a political field," the imam told the press when this incident was publicized ("İmam: Alevilerin" 2015). Later, a woman from the neighborhood claimed that the same imam did not read the funeral

178   *Alevis and Funerals*

salâ for her Alevi husband either: "this imam is discriminatory. Eventually, we found another imam" ("İmam: Alevilerin" 2015).

The other similar incidents suggest that more has been at play than the personal attributes of the imams. The religious personnel follow a Diyanet order while limiting the salâ. In Izmir, the imam of the Bilali Habeşi Mosque accepted the request for the salâ to be read for an Alevi citizen. With the salâ, the family wanted the funeral place to be heard. The funeral was to take place at a cemevi. Nevertheless, the imam made the caveat that the order from Diyanet had forbidden using the word cemevi during salâ. The deceased's relative asked three different mosques, but he got the same answer from all of them ("Diyanet, İmamlara" 2016). He explained what eventually happened: "we had to go from door to door to tell everyone where the funeral would take place" ("Ölen" 2016).

In an anonymous case, a woman whose grandmother had passed away explained their experience in similar words:

> The imam told [my father] that he would announce, "the funeral will take place from the *house*" [i.e., using the word 'ev' without uttering 'cem']. My father replied, "you will tell this, and everybody will come to our house, and then they will have to go back to the cemevi. Our house is in the opposite direction of the cemevi". [...] The imam insisted [...], and my father eventually said, "then do not read the salâ. I don't want it."
>
> (Erdemir et al. 2010:229)

Just as Külekçi reported from three different mosques, similar incidents were recorded at various mosques. Upon 21-year-old Çağrı Türker's death in Nazilli's Pınarbaşı neighborhood, his uncle asked the imam of the Hacışerif Mosque, İbrahim Hoca, to read salâ for the deceased. The imam replied, "if the funeral takes place at the cemevi, you have to go to the municipality for the announcement. It is not about us, not about the mosque" (Savaş 2016). Disagreeing with the imam, Türker's uncle went to the müftü[9] to ask for the justification for this policy. He reported müftü's words cautiously:

> I do not want to accuse him wrongly, but he literally said, "not necessary, the sala is not important."
>
> (Savaş 2016)

Türker's uncle asked the müftü if he would say the same had his child died. After leaving the müftü's office, the imam called him back and said he would read the salâ for Türker. However, the imam refused to announce that the funeral would take place in "the cemevi of Pınarbaşı." Instead, he suggested: "let us say only that the funeral will take place in Pınarbaşı." As a result, he read the salâ without referring to where the funeral would take place.

Alevis and Funerals   179

The müftü of Izmir, Necati Topaloğlu, explained the policy of *Diyanet*:

> According to Islam, cemevi is not a place of worship but a house of culture. According to our culture and tradition, also in our history [...], the places of worship are the mosques. All the rest are the centers of culture. [...] Our policy is not something specific against them [*i.e.*, cemevi]. So, it is not that we do not read the salâ.

This argument repeats what Former President Mehmet Nuri Yılmaz of Diyanet said in 1995: Alevilik is a culture—neither a sect nor a religion (Çakır 1995:23). Clearly, this statement reduces cemevi to the official position of Nakshibendi and Nur lodges. Ali Bardakoğlu, the former president of Diyanet between 2003 and 2010, also defined cemevis as places of a mystical culture: "neither playing *ney*, nor the rite of whirling, nor the rite of cem, [...] they cannot be counted equal to prayer (tr. namaz)" (Yılmaz 2005:18).

One month later, another imam, Harun Gür, was claimed to have refused to read the salâ for V.T. with the following argument: "V.T. never came to the mosque. Salâ is not read for Alevis"—because they do not pray at the mosque ("İzmir'de İmam" 2016). Özgür Aydın from ANF News reported that this argument between the relatives of V.T. and the imam followed the imam's refusal of a written application made by the relatives. This report was denied very quickly, not only by the imam but also by Diyanet. Supporting its personnel, Diyanet declared that, instead of the imam, a "voluntary officer" read the salâ. The practice was documented in the security cameras of the mosque (Diyanet İşleri Başkanlığı 2016). According to the imam, the real reason was that he was not at the mosque at the time of the delivery of the request: "eventually the salâ was read [by someone else]. A salâ does not have to be read by the imams" (Oğuz 2016). Many of V.T.'s relatives did not hear the salâ, including his neighbor Cevdet Doğan, who was the person that went to the mosque to request V.T.'s salâ:

> They say that the salâ was read only once, very shortly and with many of its parts missing. Nobody heard it, including me.
>
> (Oğuz 2016)

The voluntary officer, a vendor of bird seeds in the bazaar, said that he missed some parts of the salâ due to haste. As a part of the salâ, he did not announce that the funeral would take place at the cemevi. Moreover, he also "forgot" to say, "may God rest his soul" [tr. Allah rahmet eylesin].

The Mayor of Çiğli, who has also been an Alevi, described this as "the mentality that says 'salâ is not to be read for Alevis'":

> They use our taxes for the expenditure of mosques, but they do not even read a salâ for us.
>
> ("İzmir'de İmam" 2016)

180 *Alevis and Funerals*

In all these cases, the salâ was read one way or another. However, in none of them was the word cemevi used. In all these cases, even though the religious personnel (imams and müftüs) did not seem enthusiastic about reading it, they read the salâ when the families insisted. The families' insistence partly explains why these incidents were well-publicized. To demonstrate its stance, Diyanet opened an investigation into the case of Mirzeler in Adana and the case of V.T. in Izmir. These investigations reiterated that the salâ of Alevis should be read from mosques. Correspondingly, in these cases, Diyanet aimed to make clear that the salâ was eventually read. The Müftü of Adana, Arif Gökçe, introduced this investigation by underlining that "an Imam must be insane to say 'salâ is not read for Alevis'" ("Alevilerin selası" 2015). Referring to V.T.'s funeral, Diyanet declared, "the claim that a citizen's salâ was not read because he was an Alevi is not true at all" (Diyanet İşleri Başkanlığı 2016). According to the organization, these claims were nothing more than lies that aimed to polarize society. After all, the institution concluded these investigations in favor of its personnel.

However, despite the official position of Diyanet, these conversations between Alevis and imams suggest that the Diyanet personnel tend to look for excuses not to read the salâ for Alevis. In the cases of Türker, Mirzeler, and V.T., the Diyanet personnel initially problematized the idea of practicing salâ. The latter denied only a part of these conversations. Even though they may not have rejected the demand, they always made some arguments that irritated the families, even after reading the salâ. For example, having been called back by the imam after he met with the müftü, Türker's uncle guessed that the imam changed his policy of not reading the salâ, "probably because he was ordered by the *müftü*" (Savaş 2016). In other words, he maintained his criticism, "given that" the policy change was due to pressure instead of the imam's sense of self-responsibility.

Similarly, in Mirzeler's case, the sister of Mirzeler noted that the imam later came to their house to ask for his apology to be accepted. However, Mirzeler's sister was disturbed about how the imam made excuses, even during his apology. For example, he said that he was not obliged to read the salâ because the day of the request was his day off. Therefore, he noted, he wanted to read the salâ just as part of his own "*charity*" [tr. *hayrına*], and not out of any duty ("İmam: 'Alevilerin'" 2015). In V.T.'s case, the imam's excuse for not reading the salâ was that he was not at the mosque. On the one hand, the personalized content of these justifications, once again, suggests that Diyanet ordered the imams to have the salâ read. On the other hand, it is also clear that the families were offended when they saw the reluctance of the religious personnel in proceeding to read the funeral salâ. They want to be welcome, not just for a salâ to be read.

An incident in the little district of Havza revealed this element of averseness, which all the other cases implied. In this case, the imam asked the deceased's neighbor to wait with the dead for about an hour until he would join them to hold the funeral. In this period, the deceased's neighbor saw,

Alevis and Funerals 181

just by chance, the imam while entering the müftü's office. He decided to listen to the conversation "secretly" from the doorway. In this meeting, the imam asked if he should hold the funeral of "a Kızılbaş" (i.e., Alevi, highly derogatory for some). In response, the müftü ordered the imam to check if the neighborhood would "revolt" in case he refused to hold the funeral ("Havza'da" 2005:33–34). Should he feel that the neighbors would raise their voices, he should keep the funeral. On the other hand, if they seemed silent enough, then the imam would not hold the funeral. Furthermore, the müftü ordered the imam not to perform a funeral prayer in any case, even though he implemented the other funeral procedures. Having felt offended, the deceased's neighbor told the imam not to hold the funeral.

In all these cases, it was apparent that the families insisted that a salâ should be read, while the neighborhood reacted if this demand was refused. Taken together, these incidents suggest that the neighborhood's reaction may have decided how the religious personnel eventually behaved. Though they feel the social costs, many Alevis keep some mosque rituals without sacrificing cemevis in urban settings. They are neither assimilated nor deculturated—by deculturation, I mean the efforts to purify rituals from the marks of the recent cultural experience.

State Funeral Ceremonies: "Do you bear witness that he was a Muslim?"

The following exploratory conversations involve individuals who had two separate funerals instead of one as usual. The Alevis who reportedly had two funerals (i.e., one at a cemevi and one at a mosque) are likely to be state personnel for whom the Council of Ministers decided to organize a state ceremony. According to the procedure, the deceased is transported to the site of the state funeral ceremony. For Alevis, just as Sunnis, this place is likely to be a mosque. For some Alevi martyrs, the ceremony site was chosen as another location, such as a major square or a governorship building. In these cases, one argument for the second funeral ceremony outside the cemevi is that cemevis are not officially recognized places of worship. A second argument, which does not necessarily cohere with the first, is that this second gathering is not a religious ritual but an official ceremony that is supposed to take place at an officially recognized site. Both arguments are empirically false, as I will demonstrate.

Before proceeding with this task, I am primarily interested in the basis for this procedure's problematization. To my records, an official funeral ceremony at a cemevi is a rare instance, with the only examples being Gendarmerie Private Ozan Aslan's and Private Berkay Işık's funerals. These two cases are exceptions among others. For example, as a soldier in the Turkish Armed Forces (TAF), Murat Taş was killed by PKK in Eruh, in 2009. Since he was an Alevi, his family brought the body of Taş to the Istanbul Alibeyköy Cemevi for the funeral. By the time the *dede* of the cemevi

182 *Alevis and Funerals*

finished his introductory speech to begin the funeral prayer, a person who introduced himself as a lieutenant-colonel reportedly approached the family and told them that "the official ceremony" would take place in the Ataköy Mosque. The family did not question the plan.

In 2012, Lieutenant-colonel Ali Tatar, who committed suicide after being (re)arrested having been accused of being a member of a terrorist organization called "Ergenekon" in the military, also had two funerals. His body was brought first to the Karacaahmet Cemevi in Istanbul and the following day to the Kocatepe Mosque in Ankara for the official ceremony. The funerals of Özkan Ateşli, who died in Foça in 2012 in a PKK bomb attack, took place first at the Haramidere Cemevi in Istanbul and then at the Ataköy Mosque. After the funeral prayer at the cemevi, Ateşli's relatives told the dede that Ateşli would be carried to the mosque by the soldiers. In his words, the dede "did not have a status to say anything against it" ("Alevi Şehide İki" 2012).

The state institutions other than TAF are not talkative on this matter. However, when they do so, they produce two contradictory arguments in favor of this policy. The first argument has been that official ceremonies are not religious activities. Accordingly, the religious ritual in these cases takes place at a cemevi, and the official ceremony later takes place somewhere else as a non-religious act. The conversational records demonstrate that this argument is empirically false since it ignores that funeral prayer is performed during these official ceremonies. Furthermore, this argument disregards how Sunni state personnel can combine the state funeral ceremony with their religious duties. If the state funeral ceremony were not taken simultaneously as a religious activity, they would also have a separate state funeral ceremony upon their funerals at mosques.

The second argument is that cemevis are not officially recognized places of worship, so a state funeral ceremony cannot take place at these places. This argument is also empirically false. The officials initially offer a mosque for these ceremonies, but alternatively, they can forward them to other sites such as major squares, especially when families oppose going to a mosque. Uğur Sağdıç's funeral took place at the Turhal Square of the Republic in Tokat, after the "unofficial" funeral at the Yavşanlı Cemevi. Under Diyanet's understanding of a proper funeral, Sağdıç's funeral prayer was performed in the square which, obviously, has not been a place of worship. Similarly, Kenan Ceylan's official ceremony occurred before the district governorship, following the other funeral at the Zile Cemevi. In front of the governorship, Ahmet Erdem, the müftü of Tokat, performed a funeral prayer. The religious personnel of Diyanet do not have any problem conducting a funeral prayer in places that are not officially recognized as worship places.

During the conversations, the critics repeatedly noted that official ceremonies occur in the form of religious rituals. At Sağdıç's funeral, the funeral prayer was performed on the square, in the way it is performed at any mosque. Alongside hundreds of participants, several high-level state officials and AKP MPs were there to pray for Sağdıç. Opposing this practice

Alevis and Funerals   183

there, CHP MP and Former Chief Public Prosecutor Ilhan Cihaner, who was one of the few participants in both funerals, described this moment as the surfacing of "the contradiction between the state and Secularism":

> If you make the official ceremony at the square of Municipality, how come do you perform a funeral prayer? Is not prayer a religious ritual?
> (Cihaner 2012; *see also* "Cihaner" 2012)

These ceremonies manifested that Diyanet has been deeply embedded in the regulation of state funeral ceremonies. No matter the place of the official ceremony, it included a religious practice that the state found appropriate.

Another problematized aspect of these cases is the lack of state-level participation in cemevi funerals. State officials prefer to participate in official ceremonies rather than in cemevi funerals. Various cases suggest that government representatives are reluctant to go to cemevis, at least because they have been afraid of protests. This reluctance has already been apparent for some Alevi prisoners whose cemevi funerals the police do not attend. Crucially, however, the martyrs' families suffer from similar problems. For Uğur Sağdıç, state-level participation at the cemevi was little to none: only the governor of Tokat was there on behalf of the government, though many participants looked for an elected member of the government. After this funeral, Sağdıç was brought to the Turhal Municipality Square for a state funeral ceremony. As opposed to the cemevi funeral, the mayors and several district governors were present alongside several MPs. Exceptionally, Gendarmerie Private Ozan Aslan's family insisted that the state funeral ceremony for Aslan should take place at the Kadıköy Cemevi. As the officers eventually followed the order of the family, Aslan's funeral became the first state funeral ceremony organized at a cemevi. However, only the military personnel attended it on behalf of the state. A few years later, Private Berkay Işık's officially held cemevi funeral aroused controversy for the same reason: "No one from the top of the state attended the ceremony" (Uludağ 2020).

Regarding the funeral of Oktay Durak, killed in an ISIS attack, the head of Alevi Culture Associations Doğan Demir conveyed that the officials of District Gendarmerie Command asked Durak's family if it would be possible for the funeral to be conducted at the command building, instead of Durak's hometown. They made this request because Durak's hometown, Yozgat's Çukurören village, was "an Alevi village," where the officials would be afraid of protests against the government ("Şehit Olan Alevi" 2016). As the family did not accept this excuse, the funeral took place in the village square in Çukurören.

This perception that the Alevi population has been more critical of the government also had consequences in the funeral of Gendarmerie Lieutenant Ali Alkan. Even though Ali Alkan and his family were "Sunni Muslims," they were labeled Alevis because Ali's brother Mehmet Alkan, also serving in the military as a lieutenant colonel, criticized President Erdoğan during

184 *Alevis and Funerals*

the funeral.[10] The Alkan family not only declared they were Sunnis but also underlined that these claims were nothing more than disrespect to the Alevi people. In this conversation, the family felt pushed to declare their sect.

After Özkan Ateşli's funeral, CHP MP Ali Serindağ submitted a parliamentary question. He wondered the reason for the lack of state-level participation at the cemevi funeral. Minister Ismet Yılmaz of National Defense responded that the Garrison Command participated in the cemevi funeral on behalf of the state (İçgen 2012). However, participation at the mosque funeral of Ateşli went far beyond that: President Abdullah Gül sent a wreath to the mosque, and many high-level officials were present at the mosque. Among them were then Minister for EU Affairs Egemen Bağış, Governor Hüseyin Avni and Mayor Kadir Topbaş of Istanbul, Chief Hüseyin Çapkın of Police, and Admiral Bülent Bostanoğlu of the Fleet. Inevitably, many speakers compared the participation in these soldiers' funerals at cemevis and mosques.

With an official statement, TAF declared that, being "loyal to Article 2 of the constitution" (i.e., Secular State), it "took the consent of the [Ateşli] family" for the second funeral at the mosque ("TSK: Camide" 2012). Even though the family's consent was a key factor, the criticism was made regardless of the family's permission, given that the families were under severe constraints. The first criticism was that the state dared to ask the family if it would be possible to organize a ceremony at the mosque. This act manifested the state's official religion beneath its claim over Secularism. Even though the family did not oppose the authorities' proposal, this case triggered a problematization of the authorities' understanding of Secularism. Secondly, the participation of the Garrison Command was not enough to represent the state, at least because the problematized course of funerals provoked comparisons between the participation at cemevis and mosques. Ateşli's funeral at a cemevi was not attended by any high-level state officials, including Ateşli's high commander, Navy Admiral Bülent Bostanoğlu.

The funeral of Neşet Ertaş, a master of Anatolian folk music, aroused a similar controversy. Ertaş, who practiced the Abdal musical tradition of Alevilik, had a mosque funeral in which many high-ranking state representatives competed against each other to be visible in the front row. PM Erdoğan and other ministers were among the participants in the funeral, which became a state ceremony in practice. A security cordon was set up between the statesmen and others. Despite having refused the "honorary" title of *state artist* because he was singing with the society, Ertaş had a funeral organized for the state protocol.

Ertaş never described the kind of funeral he preferred, just as he never spoke in a self-centric manner throughout his life. That said, the government made its position clear against those who claimed he should have had his funeral at a cemevi. Amid this tension, before conducting his funeral prayer, the imam asked the community an unprecedented question that surprised theologians before all else: "do you bear witness that he was a Muslim?"

Alevis' Expressions of Cultural Change

Considering the exploratory conversations, my aim in this part is to capture some key ideology-making processes. First and foremost, I analyze the ideology makers' evaluative conversations over cemevi funerals. Secondly, I will examine the implications of the contested position of Alevilik vis-à-vis Islam. These debates take place within the Alevi communities, as well as between the Alevi communities and the government, Diyanet, and other Sunni teachers of Islam who oppose the recognition of Alevilik.

The current ideology-making processes are led primarily by members of organizations that Alevis established for their politics of recognition. Some of these ideology makers prioritize the inherited religious institutions of Alevilik, such as the ocaks, whereas others prioritize cemevis led primarily by civil society organizations, associations, or federations. Though they all support a politics of recognition, these institutions are not necessarily in line with one another. On the contrary, they have severe disagreements. Their conversations have been pivotal due to their widened representative quality after the identity turn. The largest of these organizations is the Alevi-Bektashi Federation (ABF) and the Federation of Alevi Foundations (AVF). Under their umbrellas, many foundations have been active; among them are the Pir Sultan Abdal Cultural Association (i.e., under the umbrella of ABF) and the CEM Foundation (i.e., under the umbrella of AVF).

My sources here will be a series of conversations grounded on direct (i.e., dialogical) or indirect (i.e., dialectical) encounters. The dialogical encounter is a television debate on CNN Türk (Payzın 2016), where a discussion about funerals took place between the head of AVF Doğan Bermek, the head of ABF Baki Düzgün, dede Hüseyin Dedekargınoğlu of the Ocak of Dede Garkın, and research scholar Ayşe Acar, who was also the then executive editor of CEM Radio of CEM Foundation. At the same time, I will also focus on the previous interviews of President İzzettin Doğan of the CEM Foundation, the publications of the organizations mentioned above, and the academics and research scholars who discussed the changing landscape of funerals.

Regarding Alevis' departure from mosques, the ideology makers diverge on the ideological relationship they see between their collective identity and religious doctrine. Even though the speakers tend to share a consensus on the essential role of identity in the politics of recognition, some argued that identity politics should not redefine the theological foundation of Alevilik. Others, however, push for some radical revisions in the belief system, hand in hand with their understanding of the requirements of recognition. Though all agree that cemevis are Alevis' worship places, the CEM Foundation (and AVF) also approves of the practice of having funerals at mosques. Crucially, the latter justify cemevi funerals explicitly in reference to identitarianism rather than the belief system. The representatives of this position, such as İzzettin Doğan, argued that cemevi funerals would not be needed when the sociological dynamics that justify identity politics cease to exist.

186   *Alevis and Funerals*

The members of ABF staunchly oppose Doğan's argument. Many defendants of the recognition politics have become antagonistic towards the idea of mosque funerals for Alevis, as they think any request made of mosques ends up underpinning the decades-long assimilation project. The anti-recognition speakers, such as the governments, Diyanet, and some leading ideology makers of Islamism, have exploited this polarization in several ways ("Alevi Aydınları" 1991). Firstly, as a precondition for recognizing Alevilik, they pressure the Alevi organizations to *precisely* define what Alevilik is—i.e., as a single monolith. Moreover, by referring to the contestations within Alevilik, they tend to de-legitimize the demands of these organizations. All these conversations over recognition and assimilation have been made on the grounds of essentialism.

Religious Identity or Religious Doctrine?

In a TV debate on CNN Türk, the dede of the *Ocak* of Dede Garkın, Hüseyin Dedekargınoğlu explained his understanding of the cultural change behind Alevi funerals:

> In essence, a funeral takes place neither at a mosque nor a cemevi. The funeral takes place on the *musalla* stone.[11] But we, Alevis, bring them to our cemevis since our identities are rejected, and we are ignored. It is the surfacing of an identity. Otherwise, a cem prayer is not conducted around a deceased person.

Dedekargınoğlu recognized the social construction of a new ideological relationship between religious identity and religious doctrine throughout his argumentation. By amalgamating the alienation of the Alevi identity with the re-configuration of funerary rituals, Dedekargınoğlu made the caveat that this move does not have a theological basis.

Similar arguments have been made by the members of the CEM Foundation. During his conversation with journalist Mustafa Karaalioğlu, President İzzettin Doğan's evaluation was in line with Dedekargınoğlu. According to Doğan, this cultural change was *only* due to the problems Alevis experience in mosques:

> I was so neutral towards the issue of holding funerals at cemevis. [I was saying,] "there are mosques here!" [tr. "yahu camiler var!"] [...] They said, "there are imams who do not hold our funerals." Imams sometimes say, "firstly, learn how to pray [before asking me to pray for you]."
> (Karaalioğlu 2001)

Dedekargınoğlu and Doğan share the argument that holding funerals at cemevis is not an obligation: the funerals can also take place at mosques since mosques have a *musalla* stone, which should be enough for a funeral.

Both speakers recognized that the problems Alevis face at mosques push them to have their funerals at cemevis.

This mutual feeling of alienation brings together the Alevis of different political orientations, even though the extension of their arguments contradicts. HDP MP and Researcher Ali Kenanoğlu referred to some of these acts of hostility, from the imams' refusal to hold their funerals to insults during funerals. Among these traumatic examples is the unplugging of the fridge that the deceased's body was to be placed inside. Based on this conspiracy, the enemies of Alevis tried to make popular the stories of how non-Muslim bodies rust after death. Kenanoğlu concluded:

> [We are glad that] cemevis have been built, and we have been saved from this humiliation.
>
> (Kenanoğlu 2013)

Based on a similar experience, Ergin Doğru, Former Provincial Head of the Party of Democratic Regions (DBP), suggested that Alevilik should develop a new model by its "essence" (Doğru 2013). This call for the re-designing of cemevi rituals was made in 1997 by Derviş Tur, the former head of Dedes Assembly of the European Federation of Alevi Communities. Himself being a migrant in Germany, Tur reported that "they" realized in 1985 that many young Turks were jailed in Germany:

> We have realized that most of them were Alevis. We said among us, 'the Sunnis built their mosques, the Jews have their synagogues, and the Christians have their churches. Where will [our] children go?' [...] Then we decided to act urgently.
>
> (Ercan 1997:4)

Throughout the 1980s, this was a popular argument among Alevi dedes. Dede Baki Dalak from Sivas often underlined that "in the past"—i.e., the period in which Alevis were born into a practicing culture—there was "no single bit of crime" in the villages where Alevis lived. According to him, crime rates have increased since Alevis forgot the essence of Alevilik ("Geçmiş" 1987:28). By emphasizing similar problems Alevis face in public, many ideology makers proposed their own essentialist programs to revise the cultural institutions of Alevilik.

Competing Essentialisms

In the TV channel founded by the European Alevi Unions Confederation (AABK), Yol TV, speakers insistently invited Alevis to do things self-consciously "in an Alevi way." On behalf of the Austria-based Federation of Alevi Communities, Dede Ercan Sinci stated that they actively work to remove the "non-Alevi components" from funeral rituals ("AABF" 2014).

188   *Alevis and Funerals*

Denmark-based Federation of Alevi Communities called on Alevis not to request anything from mosques:

> Most [imams] [tr. *"hocalar"*] refused to wash the deceased bodies of Alevis by saying, "you do not come when you are alive, but you bring your dead," whereas some saw [our mosque funerals] as a source of income or a way to assimilate Alevis. This problem lasted until the foundation of the Alevi associations, and in some regions, it persists. As of now, our Alevi institutions should make the service of funerals on their own. [Our] funerals should take place under the Alevi propriety, and should not be handed over to mosques [and] imams.
>
> ("Alevi-Bektaşi" n.d.)

Alongside this argumentation, dede Hüseyin Gazi Metin from the Federation prepared a guide on managing funerals in accordance with the "Alevi propriety" [tr. Alevi erkanı]. These attempts to re-model Alevilik also triggered a reaction against some cemevis performing funeral ceremonies differently. The Alevi Cultural Center of Basel, among others, warned other cemevis that Alevilik would be assimilated into Sunni Islam if they continued to turn their back on the "essence" of Alevilik while conducting their funerals ("Anadolu Aleviliğinde" n.d.).

A more radical expression of essentialism was the "movement of returning to the essence," introduced by Co-Chair Barış Aydın of the Union of Revolutionary Alevis. The movement did not just strictly forbid the option of mosque funerals for Alevis but also, in a straightforward way, set out what to do in cemevis to return to the essence (Aydın 2016a). Among these "necessary steps" was removing pictures of Ali and Atatürk from cemevis, since the former introduced Shari'a Law, and the latter banned the Alevi lodges. In the same declaration, Alevis were called on to stop reading Quran in cemevi funerals. They would also have to standardize the color of the cloth laid on coffins: red instead of green, "given" that green resembles Shari'a. Finally, the coffin should not face towards the *kıble*, the direction of Mecca, but towards the participants.

For many, these attempts are a strategic necessity—i.e., in how the concept has been used in post-colonialism. Correspondingly, strategic essentialism may act as an antidote of assimilation. According to their almost identical expressions of the context of assimilation, the process began when Alevis had to hide their identities in public. The process deepened when, in the urban centers, they were pressured to attend Friday prayers, fast in Ramadan just as Sunnis do, take compulsory religion courses under Diyanet's monopoly over religion, and indeed, hold funerals in the way Sunnis did.[12]

The agents behind these projects explicitly recognized that their agenda was politically-driven, and rightly so. However, a polarizing subject among the ideology makers is the extent to which religious rituals, such as those

Alevis and Funerals 189

that occur during funerals should be politicized. In the televized debate on CNN Türk, even though all Alevi leaders admitted that political activism was needed alongside the practice of faith, they fundamentally disagreed on the limit of politics in cemevis. Former chairman of AVF, and head of the Ocak of Alevi Thought, Doğan Bermek, emphasized the point that politics should never enter cemevis:

> I cannot let politics leak into my faith; otherwise, it is Emevism.[13]

Together with Dedekargınoğlu and Bermek, Ayşe Acar from the Ocak of Baba Mansur defended a strict separation between the political field, where Alevi associations struggle to get their identities recognized, and the theological area where the institution of *dedelik* works in its traditional hierarchy. In this context, Acar introduced a caveat: "the sociology of these issues should not be confused with the tradition of faith." Dedekargınoğlu concluded that politics must not penetrate cemevis.

In the dialogical setting of this debate, their interlocutor was Baki Düzgün, the president of the Alevi-Bektashi Federation and a member of the Ocak of Baba Mansur. Düzgün reacted *angrily*—in a manner condemned by other participants—against the contextualization of these arguments about cemevi funerals. According to Düzgün, cemevi funerals should not be regarded as a politicization of religious ritual:

> When people hold their funerals at mosques, nobody puts it into question [by labeling it as a political act]; but when we have our funerals at cemevis, it is bad that even an Alevi [e.g., Acar, Bermek, and Dedekargınoğlu] puts it into question.

Here, Düzgün constructed a symmetry between mosque and cemevi funerals: both are political, or none should be labeled as politically driven acts. The other participants' rejection of this argument was closely related to their interpretation of Secularism. According to them, the separation between politics and religion should also apply to a funeral's landscape. Düzgün had a claim over Secularism as well, but he refused to see cemevi funerals as a political activity. Instead, he implied that cemevi funerals must eventually enter a period of settled culture—i.e., accustomed and undisputed.

Dedekargınoğlu opposed the symmetry that Düzgün assumed between the ritual forms in mosques and cemevis:

> [In Alevilik] dedes never deal with the burial procedure of a deceased. Imposing this procedure on dedes is a result of urbanization, [...] [and it mistakenly] equates the dede with a mosque [imam] [tr. "hoca"]. An ocak dede in Alevilik is not an equivalent of a mosque imam [...]. Each ocak's dede is [in principle] equal to the president of Diyanet.

190   *Alevis and Funerals*

This causal claim between urbanization and the mistaken symmetry has removed many of the once "heterodoxic" properties of Alevilik. In response to the likes of Dedekargınoğlu, some ideology makers claim that urbanization necessitates the re-configuration of religious practices. For example, according to Fuat Bozkurt, the duties of dedes cannot remain untouched in the urban social setting. At the least, this is because dedes no more meet the needs of urbanized Alevis:

> The old tales and legends hold no interest for modern Alevi youth, who regard them as mere superstitious fabrications.
>
> (Bozkurt 2005:101)

Therefore, Bozkurt has been interested in what kind of revised education dedes should take so that they would not only conduct congregational meetings but also "be capable of conducting marriage and funeral services" (Bozkurt 2005:102).

Referring to this approach in an article, Dedekargınoğlu underlines that the executives of Alevi foundations, who are the ones that regulate cemevis, aim to replace *ocak dedes* with *cemevi dedes*. Dedekargınoğlu continues:

> Even though they do not know much about the Alevi belief system [...] these executives claim that ocak dedes are uneducated and ignorant.
>
> (Dedekargınoğlu 2010:204)

The hierarchical structure of Alevilik has been put into question on many occasions. Beginning in the late 1960s, the young generations of Alevis rejected the traditional hierarchy utilizing the ideological repertoire of Marxism. As late as 2006, the division was clear when Veliyettin Ulusoy declared himself as the *postnişin*[14] of Dervish Lodge of Hacıbektaş, on account that he descends from Hacıbektaş. Some Alevis described this act as a "Shari'a-minded" one, as they thought this hierarchy resembled the religious communities of Nur, or more specifically, the Gülen movement (Hasan 2006:16). Finally, a clash between *ocak dedes* and *cemevi dedes* has been triggered due to the re-organization processes.

On the politicization of funerals, another critical question is whose funeral should be held at cemevis. Acar, Dedekargınoğlu, and Bermek criticized some political groups' flag-carrying in cemevis, whereas Düzgün emphasized that everybody who demands a cemevi funeral should be able to have it. Acar warns that among these political groups are organizations that are officially designated as terrorist organizations, such as DHKP-C. Referring to Berkin Elvan's funeral, who died at 13 with a rubber bullet fired by a police officer during the Gezi Protests, she offers an account of how terrorists tried to dominate the funeral process, at Okmeydanı Cemevi, with their political rituals. She asked Alevis to be careful about such activities, as political opponents instrumentalize these incidents against Alevis.[15] In this way, Acar justifies the temporary decision made by the police to prevent Elvan's funeral from taking place at the Okmeydanı Cemevi. In contrast, Baki Düzgün was antagonistic to any kind of state involvement in the 'internal' processes of Alevilik. Unexpectedly, Düzgün criticized his interlocutors for being "the Alevis of the state."

Following the crisis over VT's funeral, president Elif Bakır of the Foundation of Karabağlar Pir Sultan Abdal declared, "even the existence of Diyanet shows that this state is not democratic and secular" (Aydın 2016b:par4) Bakır called on the Alevi organizations to "unrecognize the state" just as it does not recognize Alevilik. Süleyman Deprem, the dede of the ocak of Sinemili, also reacted:

> This state is not our state. Alevis must establish a system and a life that fits their path [tr. yol] and propriety [tr. erkan].
>
> (Aydın 2016b:par5)

Head Ismet Erbulak of Izmir Democratic Alevi Association asked all Alevis to question "what Alevis are still doing in this state" (Aydın 2016b:par6).

Previously, İzzettin Doğan mentioned his wonderment over why "politically motivated funerals" kept coming from all over the country, especially from prisons, to some specific cemevis, such as Gazi and Okmeydanı cemevis. During his interview with Journalist Mustafa Karaalioğlu in 2001, his description of the ambiguity was as follows:

> Perhaps some of these people [who had been brought] were Sunni; but eventually, most were Atheists. An Atheist cannot be Sunni or Alevi.

Doğan claimed that these funerals might have been sent to further alienate Alevis from the broader society by depicting them as criminals. Doğan's desire for integration contradicted the politics of difference practiced by others. That said, just as Baki Düzgün argued, İzzettin Doğan admitted that those who want to have a funeral organization at a cemevi should be able to do so, no matter their religion or political status. The fundamental difference between their arguments is that Doğan called on the security institutions to investigate why some militant groups "politicize cemevis." However, as the following section explains, even AVF doubted how reliable the security institutions are at some critical junctures.

The Military and Secularism: An Interrelationship to be Deconstructed?

In the first stages of the two-funeral procedure, the disagreement between the parties involved incognizance on both sides. Those querying the situation did not know why they were supposed to hold another funeral apart from their cemevi funerals. The regulations were vague, and the government

192 *Alevis and Funerals*

was out of reach. Following the funeral of Murat Taş (2009), several Alevi associations asked the Turkish Armed Forces (TAF) to explain the reasons behind this implementation. AVF wrote a letter to the Turkish Armed Forces, asking if the problem emanates from lacking official recognition.

In this letter, the Federation made it clear that it was ready to blame the other government departments rather than TAF. TAF replied that the Garrison Commands undertake the organization of *only* the military activity during state funeral ceremonies, leaving "all religious aspects of the funeral to the family" ("Genelkurmay'dan" 2009). TAF did not mention any other government institutions in making official ceremonies. In the aftermath of this conversation, AVF declared that the answer of TAF was satisfactory to them. In a nutshell, AVF read the TAF response as approval of having the following funerals at cemevis, provided that the families prefer it that way.

However, the procedure was not that simple, as the amendment of the regulation on state funeral ceremonies made clear in 2013. In time, the flow of the conversations reflected more ideological thinking on the subject, with clearer counter-positioning of interlocutors. As such, those querying the situation were no longer curious but openly critical. The government made its position apparent in opposition to the critics by amending the regulation on state funeral ceremonies.

With the 2013 amendment, the AKP government handled the problem in its own exclusionary way. Accordingly, Diyanet was appointed as the new member of the organizational committee of state funerals ("Devlet Cenaze" 2013). The amendment was justified on the grounds that it would help consider "the religious sensitivities" in state funerals (Hasan 2013). This amendment clarified the actor behind the "religious aspects" of funerals. It would not be the families who determine the religious aspects of official ceremonies. The problem with the involvement of Diyanet has been that the institution was not designed to represent a religious sensitivity other than its own: from the era of Diyanet's former president Elmalı to today, Alevis have had fundamental problems with the institution. This regulation amendment was meant to unmask a previously implicit religious particularism behind official ceremonies.

A comparison between the two TAF declarations (i.e., after the funerals of Murat Taş in 2009 and Kenan Ceylan in 2015) reveals the subtle transformation in the self-identity of TAF vis-à-vis the issue. The declaration after Ceylan's funeral is different from the previous response sent to the Federation of Alevi Associations. The answer previously made by TAF spoke on behalf of the state and underlined that the religious aspects of funerals would only be decided by the family. On the contrary, in the later declaration, TAF no longer addressed why there could not be a single state funeral ceremony at a cemevi. On this occasion, TAF only aimed to exonerate its institutional credibility: it made clear that it had its officials at both ceremonies as it sees both ceremonies as equally valid. Contrary to the first declaration, which implied that the whole problem was a misunderstanding, the

Alevis and Funerals   193

second declaration did not deny the existence of the problem but rejected the alleged complicity of TAF in it: "TAF attends the cemevi funerals."

Even before the 2013 amendment made by the government, the regulation was not simply between the garrisons' military roles and the families' religious desires. The previous regulation had stipulated the collaboration of several institutions in the making of the funeral ceremonies. Under the presidency of the Ministry of Foreign Affairs Directorate General of Protocol, these institutions were the Garrison Commands of TAF, the Ministry of Interior, Governorships, and Municipalities where the funeral would occur ("Devlet Cenaze" 2006). Even though the role of TAF included military activity, the regulation did not clarify how the religious aspect of ceremonies would be determined. In a nutshell, the pre-2013 regulation did not consider the matter clearly because no one problematized the (then implicit) ideological codes of state funeral ceremonies before Murat Taş's funeral.

Bureaucratic Value Politics: The Military's Values, among Other State Institutions

This process has challenged a deep-seated relationship many Alevi ideologues saw between Secularism and TAF's value carriership. After the problems, some ideology makers argued that they should no longer rely on the military for "the preservation of Secularism." Sometime after Taş's family informed the dede of the cemevi that his body would be carried to the mosque, dede Hüseyin Güzelgüz articulated the reproach:

> Given that even the military behaves like this, the sincerity [behind "the Alevi opening"[16]] should be questioned.
>
> ("Alevi Şehide Sünni" 2009)

The dede's emphasis, "even the military," was due to the institution's identity as a vanguard of Turkey's Secularism and a force against sectarianism. In the same vein, in the aftermath of Özkan Ateşli's cemevi funeral, admiral Bülent Bostanoğlu, who did not attend Ateşli's cemevi funeral, was harshly criticized. Among these critics, journalist Nedim Şener wrote that admiral Bostanoğlu left behind a soldier under his command (Şener 2012).

According to Şener, this negligence was proof that the state-led "Alevi opening" was stillborn. Former President Murtaza Demir of ABF described the mosque funeral of Kenan Ceylan as a "heartbreaking" moment. In his open letter to the military commanders, Demir was critical:

> If you ask me, you should have opposed the impact of sectarianism on the military posts. Your precious [tr. "Sizin sarı öküzünüz"] was the concept of secularism. [...] [But] given that you could not stand up against pressures, while embracing the rally for building mosques at the military barracks, you at least should have said, "let us build a couple

194   *Alevis and Funerals*

of cemevis as well; let us not produce separatism and discrimination." During the process of "Ramadan feasts," have you ever remembered the Alevi soldiers who had Muharrem Fast? [H]ave you ever joined them to break a fast?

The critics were reproachful of the military, not in the form of a reaction to the other, but in the form of expressing some feelings of disappointment and disillusionment towards a partner. The behavior of other state institutions was not surprising to them, but the military's complicity was far more noteworthy—i.e., in Demir's terms, "heartbreaking."

Following Kenan Ceylan's funeral, the TAF made a more comprehensive statement about its interpretation of these funerals:

As TAF, we never see our children as Turkish, Circassian, Bosnian, Kurdish, Alevi, Sunni, or non-Muslim, and we never tolerate seeing them as such [...] Such an understanding, approach, or order cannot exist in TAF. The funerals of [...] [our] martyrs are organized [...] at the places that they demand, no matter what their religious beliefs are. For our martyr [...] Kenan Ceylan, the first ceremony was made at 11:30 at the cemevi with the participation of military officials, and the second ceremony was made at 12:45 at the Government House. The statement in the news that the TAF officials did not attend the funeral at the cemevi is inappropriate and incorrect.

(Ergan 2015)

This declaration did not respond to all the criticisms, firstly because TAF preferred to make it not on behalf of the state but only in the name of its own institution. In this context, it is clear that, like the critics, TAF differentiated itself from other state institutions. Therefore, it preferred not to discuss the government's approach towards cemevi funerals. Because TAF refrained from speaking on behalf of the state, its explanation did not cover why the high-level state officers do not participate in martyrs' funerals at cemevis.

Essentialism and Its Discontents

The essentialist framework has clear marks on some retroactive conversations between Alevis. This section firstly demonstrates that the Alevis who requested the funeral salâ from mosques have been criticized from an essentialist standpoint. One party in the interlocution makes the following claims: (1) Alevis should not demand anything from mosques, given that they are either not Muslims or never pray at mosques, (2) Alevis who go to mosques serve a project of assimilation; and (3) Alevis who see cemevis as a place of worship must sever their ties, not just with mosques but also with Islam. After presenting the essentialist contours of intolerance, I argue that essentialism fights the idea of a heterodoxic culture in flow, which inevitably contradicts the language of authorities.

Sinan Işık, who sued Turkey in the ECtHR because he was not allowed to change the religion section in his identity card from "Islam" to "Alevi," has rationalized intolerance against the syncretic approaches among Alevis. Following the funeral of Mirzeler in Adana, Sinan Işık reacted against the Mirzeler family by defending the imam:

> The attitude of the imam is eminently Islamic. If you are an Alevi, what are you doing at a mosque? I wish all imams did the same thing! I am sure all the Islamist assimilators will take advantage of this incident; they will condemn the imam vigorously, say that Alevis are sincere Muslims, and maybe as a lesson to all, they will even pay the imam off.
>
> (Işık 2015)

It is not difficult to find a similar line of argumentation elsewhere. For example, in response to V.T.'s case, dede Mustafa Aslan of Narlıdere Cemevi in Izmir said that "it is wrong for Alevi people to demand anything from mosques," even though he also emphasized that the mosque should have met this demand no matter what (Aydın 2016b:par6). Kemal Mutlu, the head of the Association of People from Dersim, noted that it is "out of the question" that Alevis are not supposed to go to mosques (Aydın 2016b:par7). After the same funeral, dede Baki Güngör of Kırklar Cemevi called on Alevi people not to demand anything from mosques:

> The [imam] is doing what is necessary in his belief [...] Every single Alevi who goes to the mosque is who is to behave with Sunni-Hanefi beliefs. Every single Alevi who goes to the mosque is who is to settle for all insults against Alevi people till today, given that s/he is subject to the [imam] there. We, Alevis, do not pray behind Sunni [imams].
>
> (Güngör 2016)

None of these speakers would deny that Alevis had mosque funerals for many decades in urban settings. While seeing this activity as a manifestation of assimilation and alienation, some like Güngör offered Alevis alternative rituals like those they acculturated from Sunni Islam. In contrast, others like the AABK leadership labeled both alternatives as assimilationism. They lament that the components of mosque funerals have been settled in Alevilik. Accordingly, all Alevis should have problematized these practices after the foundation of cemevis. When the mayor of the Maltepe district of Istanbul, Ali Kılıç, also a CHP member, declared that he combines the Friday prayers at mosques with the cem-meetings at cemevis, he was heavily criticized for the same reason: "his comment constitutes a step to assimilation" (Saçlı 2016).

196 *Alevis and Funerals*

A cross-temporal comparison suggests that these arguments make a misplaced claim on anti-assimilationism. As the speakers commonly mention, Alevis' experience of assimilationist policies has been based on several pillars. The first pillar was that Alevis lost their ties with their worship environment. Connectedly, in the urban centers, many Alevis had to follow the rituals of Sunni Islam so as not to be alienated in their new social settings. Throughout the 1980s, the state complemented this activity by intensifying its policy of building mosques in Alevis' villages. Many Alevis either converted to Sunni Islam in due course (Öktem 2000) or have forgotten their rituals. Since then, the members of both ABF and the AVF tend to report their discomfort with fellow believers' "lack of knowledge" about their religion (Alemdar and Çorbacıoğlu 2012:121).

These characteristic features of the assimilation process do not suffice to explain any of the demands denigrated by the speakers mentioned above. First and foremost, from the funeral of Mirzeler to that of V.T., none of these cases were mosque funerals. On the contrary, they were cemevi funerals that the Alevi citizens wanted to be announced from a mosque with the funeral salâ. Therefore, it is not that these Alevis lost contact with the developments concerning the re-organization of cemevis. Instead, they mixed some mosque rituals with their cemevi rituals, both of which they evaluated just as the Alevi associations evaluate collectively. By integrating their past cultural experiences with their current life, they complemented their cemevi funerals with the salâ, which is not a theological property of Sunni Islam but a tradition of Turkish religious music. This interest of Alevis may not be a coincidence, given that the makam [en. the system of melody] of the funeral salâ is *hüseynî*, which is the tonic that represents a building block of the Alevi-Bektashi musical culture in Anatolia (Yöre 2011). By requesting the salâ, they did not "pray behind a Sunni imam." They did not part company with the broader Alevi community.

The reasons behind their demands vary. Some of them see the salâ as a valuable cultural performance. For example, following the müftü's claim that "salâ is not important," Türker's uncle asked the müftü if he would say the same if his child died. With this question, he did not differentiate between the müftü being a Sunni and himself being an Alevi. Some others, on the other hand, saw the salâ as a means of informing the neighborhood about the news and the details about a funeral. In their ecological environment in the urban centers, Alevis have contact with the Sunni population. For this reason, the salâ has become a way to inform the neighbors. For their Sunni neighbors to hear them, some Alevis ask the municipalities to announce the details of funerals. In contrast, others request the neighborhood mosques to make this announcement as a religious musical expression.

For the same reason, it was not always the relatives of the deceased, but occasionally the Sunni neighbors who themselves asked the religious personnel to read the salâ. This was a way of showing their respect for the deceased. In V.T.'s case, his neighbors insisted that the salâ should be read.

Alevis and Funerals 197

From this point of view, it does not matter if the deceased is a Sunni, an Alevi, or a Jew. In an incident that writer Yılmaz Özdil described (Özdil 2016), the community of the Hisarönü Mosque in İzmir requested the imam to announce the death of their neighbor, Basmacı Yusuf. Basmacı Yusuf was a Jewish citizen who put cartons in front of his store across from the mosque so that the people could use them in case the mosque was packed. It was why, in time, Yusuf had so many friends in the mosque community. Their request for the announcement, however, was refused by Diyanet on account that he was not a Muslim. With this request, the mosque community did not mean to assimilate Yusuf into a religious belief he did not share. Neither did they try to dilute the theological corpus of Islam. By relying on a religious tradition, they simply wanted to pay their respects to Yusuf.

The families of Alevi state personnel who had two funerals also manifested a syncretic approach. According to the conversations available to us, only Durak's family insisted that the funeral should take place in the village square. The authorities eventually accepted their demand. In all the other cases, the families accepted the officers' proposals. After Özkan Ateşli's funeral, his family reacted to speculation that questioned their consent to transfer Ateşli's body to the mosque after the cemevi funeral. Here, the claims of Ali Kenanoğlu, the chairman of the Hubyar Sultan Alevi Cultural Association, were responded to by the members of Ateşli family. Upon speaking with the dede of the cemevi, Kenanoğlu stated that the family wanted the official ceremony to take place in the cemevi, and yet the soldiers did not accept:

[N]either did the family nor did us have consent, but there was nothing we could do.

("Alevi Şehide Camide" 2012)

This claim was denied by the brother of Ateşli, who underlined that the two-funeral program was made the day before, with the consent of the family:

The mosque is the house of God, just as the cemevi is [...] The decision was not taken by force. They told us that [the official ceremony] would take place here [at the mosque], and we accepted.

("Alevi Şehide İki" 2012)

In conclusion, what should be underlined is the difference between the assimilationism that has become a state policy and the multiple identities and sense-makings that Türker's uncle or Ateşli's brother manifests alongside many others. Whereas the former aims to isolate cemevi as a cultural institution, the latter sees cemevi as a worship place. The former dismisses the religious doctrine that cemevi is based upon, whereas the latter embraces it. While assimilationism is happy to read the funeral salâ for an Alevi only if s/he has a mosque funeral, syncretism introduces the word cemevi in the funeral salâ at a mosque. Whereas essentialism is keen to categorize

198 Alevis and Funerals

Alevilik—employing the language of orthodoxy—either as a separate religion or just an imperfect cultural form of Islam, syncretism practices religion without fitting into any clear-cut categories.

These syncretic practices also differ from the potentially hegemonic projects, such as the "mosque-cemevi project," which Fethullah Gülen patronized with the collaboration of the head of CEM Foundation, Izzettin Doğan. The plan was to build a single place that includes a mosque and a cemevi, separated only by a public soup kitchen. Although this project was presented as a defense of Anatolian syncretism, the building was, in fact, located in an Alevi neighborhood, Tuzluçayır. Therefore, its appeal to the Sunni population was "nearly unthinkable" (Göner 2017:181). In other words, the project was not meant to consider, for example, Sunni students who prefer cemevi courses of the traditional music instrument, named *saz* or *bağlama*, which Alevis use in their religious rituals. As such, the "mosque-cemevi" resembled Alevis' experience of assimilationism, given that many Alevi villages already had mosques in the last couple of decades, whereas so few of the Sunni-majority neighborhoods had a cemevi.[17] Undeniably, Gülen's previous speeches against certain Alevi groups also underpinned these negative impressions.

In summary, the syncretic practices of Alevi citizens, not to be confused with the policies and the projects imposed from above, turn the question "what is Alevilik" upside down. The question is wrong. As long as essentialism rules over the contestations between recognition and assimilation, both solutions will bring their own crises into the life of Alevis. As Pınar Ecevitoğlu (2011) argued, the language of the state or other authorities manifesting a passion for defining inevitably contradicts the language of heterodoxy.

Notes

1 Salâ is a form in Turkish religious music (Özcan 2009:15–16). It shall not be confused with the Arabic word, salaat, which means prayer (tr. namaz). Following a musical expression, a funeral salâ includes an announcement as to the details of the funeral, such as the address and the time of the funeral.
2 Tr. "Alevi'nin cenaze namazı kılınmaz."
3 Tr. "Alevi'nin salâsı okunmaz."
4 See in Balkanlı (1953:2) a conversation between a dede and a journalist, which reflects this distorted image.
5 Dedes are the spiritual leader of Alevis. An Ocak denotes an institutionalized family line in Alevilik.
6 Also published in 1972, Kaftancıoğlu (2003) narrativizes the de-legitimizing interpretation of Hakullah, a fee paid to the traveling dedes when they visit a village. Similarly, Aşık Mahzuni Şerif, a very influential "ashik" in both Alevi and left-wing political circles, criticized the "backward" traditions of his community (Otyam 1963:7).
7 These funerals take place primarily in Istanbul or Ankara. For example, in Istanbul, if the person is located on the Anatolian side, his/her funeral takes place in the Selimiye Mosque in Üsküdar, or Erenköy Galip Paşa Mosque. On the European side, it either takes place in the Ataköy 5. Kısım Mosque, or the Levent Mosque.

8 The three state funeral ceremonies held recently are: (a) at the Hagia Yorgi Church for Ilya Banogo, a Turkish Korean war veteran of Rum descent, (b) at the Virgin Mary Armenian Church for Arut Köse, a Turkish Korean war veteran of Armenian descent, and (c) at Mor Abraham Monastery in Mardin for Yusuf Kurt, a Syriac "civilian martyr."

9 A müftü is a Muslim legal expert appointed to certain places by Diyanet to give rulings on religious matters.

10 What triggered these speculations was also on social media. A Twitter hashtag, "#Lieutenant Colonel is Alevi" [tr. Yarbay Alevi], quickly turned out to be the top trend on Twitter. Eventually, the family had to deny the allegations.

11 Musalla stone is placed in the courtyard of mosques and cemevis. It is a shared element at these places of worship. On the basis that the stone is never placed inside the buildings but outside them, it may be argued that funerals are actually not taking place at mosques or cemevis.

12 "Gelin Canlar" (2005) includes a thousand Alevi citizens' expressions of assimilation and alienation. Another investigation that addresses such perceptions is "Türkiye'de Alevilere" (2008:338–69).

13 The term "Emevism" (tr. Emevicilik) is popular in the ideological repertoire of Secularism in Turkey since it signifies the poisoning of religion with political ambitions. Therefore, Emevism is often equated with Islamism.

14 The central authority of a religious lodge.

15 See also the debate between Former Minister of Health Osman Durmuş and then President of ABF Ali Balkız in "İbretle İzliyoruz" (2001:7).

16 "Alevi Opening" is a label used by the AKP government as a statement of its political will to alleviate the problems that Alevis face in Turkey.

17 An exception was the village Çankaya in Erzincan. The village, which had 300 Alevi and 700 Sunni inhabitants, finally had its cemevi in 1998 ("Cami ve" 1998).

References

"AABF 9. Olağan Genel Kurulu Gerçekleşti." 2014. *Aleviten Österreich*, April 26.

"Adana'da Sela Krizi." 2015. *Günaydın Gazetesi*, March 10.

Adlı, Ayşe. 2016. "Hüseyin Elmas ile sözlü tarih görüşmesi." *Bilim ve Sanat Vakfı (BISAV) and İstanbul Kalkınma Ajansı (İSTKA)*.

Alemdar, Zeynep, and Rana Birden Çorbacıoğlu. 2012. "Alevis and the Turkish State." *Turkish Policy Quarterly* 10(4):117–24.

"Alevi Aydınları Patladı: Diyanet Bizi Bölmeye Çalışıyor." 1991. *Nokta*.

"Alevi-Bektaşi İnancında Cenaze Hizmetleri." n.d. *Danimarka Alevi Birlikleri Federasyonu*.

"Alevi Şehide Camide Zoraki Tören İddiası." 2012. *İnternet Haber*. (http://www.internethaber.com/alevi-sehide-camide-zoraki-toren-iddiasi-450732h.htm).

"Alevi Şehide İki Tören." 2012. *Radikal*, August 11.

"Alevi Şehide Sünni Tören." 2009. *T24*, September 13.

"Alevilerin selası okunur mu?" 2015. *Cumhuriyet*, March 9.

"Aleviliğe Ne Oluyor?" 1987. *Yeni Gündem*, August 23.

"Anadolu Aleviliğinde Cenaze ve Kırk Lokması." n.d. *Basel ve Çevresi Alevi Kültür Merkezi*.

"Anayasa'nın Birinci Müzakeresi Bitti." 1961. *Milliyet*, April 26.

Ateş, Cafer. 1976. "Diyanet İşleri Başkanına Açık Mektup." *Cumhuriyet*, July 12, 7.

Ayata, Sencer. 2008. "Migrants and Changing Urban Periphery: Social Relations, Cultural Diversity and the Public Space in Istanbul's New Neighbourhoods." *International Migration* 46(3):27–64.

200 Alevis and Funerals

Aydın, Barış. 2016a. "Aleviler Özüne Dönmeli." *Anadolu Işığı,* June 23. Retrieved January 5, 2017 (https://web.archive.org/web/20170105163254/http://www.anadoluisigi.org/alevilik/aleviler-ozune-donmeli).

Aydın, Özgür. 2016b. "İzmir Alevi Kurumları." *ANF News,* January 26.

"Bademler'in Camisi Yok, Tiyatrosu Var." 1987. *Nokta,* September 27.

Balkanlı, Hüsniye. 1953. "Hacı Bektaş Köyünde Görüp İşittiklerim." *Milliyet,* December 13, 2.

Ballı, Refet. 1990. "İstanbul'u Doğu Yönetiyor." *Milliyet,* October 6, 18.

Bozkurt, Fuat. 2005. "State-Community Relations in the Restructuring of Alevism." Pp.100–13 in *Alevi Identity: Cultural, Religious and Social Perspectives,* edited by T. Olsson, E. Ozdalga, and C. Raudvere. London: Routledge.

Büyükokutan, Aslı. 2007. "Muğla Yöresi Alevî Türkmenlerinde Ölümle İlgili İnanç ve Pratikler." *Türklük Bilimi Araştırmaları* 21(21):63–86.

"Cami ve Cemevi Birarada." 1998. *Hürriyet,* August 26.

Cem TV. 2016. *Prof Dr İzzettin Doğan Aihm Basın Açıklaması,* May 3.

Cihaner, İlhan. 2012. "Namaz Dini Bir Ritüel Değil Mi?" *CHP Arşiv.* Retrieved October 19, 2017 (http://arsiv.chp.org.tr/?p=84493).

"Cihaner: 'Ölüme Yolladığınızda Dinini Sordunuz Mu?" 2012. *BirGün,* September 6.

Çakır, Ruşen. 1995. "Değişim Sürecinde Alevi Hareketi." *Milliyet,* July 12, 23.

Çakır, Ruşen, and İhsan Yılmaz. 2001. "Siyasetten Kopuyorlar." *Milliyet,* August 19.

Çamuroglu, Reha. 1998. "Alevi Revivalism in Turkey." Pp.79–84 in *Alevi Identity: Cultural, Religious and Social Perspectives,* edited by T. Olsson, E. Ozdalga, and C. Raudvere. London: Routledge.

Çelik, Ayşe Betül. 2003. "Alevis, Kurds and Hemşehris: Alevi Kurdish Revival in the Nineties." Pp.141–57 in *The Alevi Enigma: A Comprehensive Overview.* Leiden: Brill.

Çubukçu, Ibrahim Agah. 1966. "Sünnilere Kapalılık." *Milliyet,* June 19, 2.

Dedekargınoğlu, Hüseyin. 2010. "Dedelik Kurumu ve Sürek Anlayışı." Pp.193–205 in *II. Uluslararası Tarihten Bugüne Alevilik Sempozyumu,* edited by A. Erdemir, M. Ersal, A. Tasgin, and A. Yaman. Ankara: Cem Vakfı.

Demirtaş, Nurcan. 1990. "Haksızlığa İsyan." *Milliyet,* November 20, 16.

"Devlet Cenaze Törenleri Yönetmeliği." 2006. *Resmi Gazete [Official Gazette of the Republic of Turkey],* December 2. Catalogue Number 26364.

"Devlet Cenaze Törenleri Yönetmeliğinde Değişiklik Yapılmasına Dair Yönetmelik." 2013. *Resmi Gazete [Official Gazette of the Republic of Turkey],* August 2. Catalogue Number 28726. (http://www.resmigazete.gov.tr/eskiler/2013/08/20130802-2.htm).

"'Diyanet, İmamlara Sela Verirken Cemevi Demeyin Talimatı Verdi' Iddiası." 2016. *T24,* June 26.

Diyanet İşleri Başkanlığı. 2016. *Basın Açıklaması,* January 23. Retrieved August 16, 2016 (https://web.archive.org/web/20160412205949/http://www.diyanet.gov.tr/tr/icerik/basin-aciklamasi/30475).

Doğru, Ergin. 2013. "Kentleşen Aleviliğin Sorunları." *Radikal.* (http://blog.radikal.com.tr/din/kentlesen-aleviligin-sorunlari-37768).

Dressler, Markus. 2008. "Religio-Secular Metamorphoses: The Re-Making of Turkish Alevism." *Journal of the American Academy of Religion* 76(2):280–311.

Dressler, Markus. 2014. "The Modern Dede: Changing Parameters for Religious Authority in Contemporary Turkish Alevism." Pp. 269–94 in *Speaking for Islam, Religious Authorities in Muslim Societies,* edited by G. Kramer and M. Sökefeld. Leiden: Brill.

Alevis and Funerals 201

Ecevitoğlu, Pınar. 2011. "Aleviliği Tanımlamanın Dayanılmaz Siyasal Cazibesi." *Ankara Üniversitesi SBF Dergisi* 66(03):137–56.

Ercan, Özcan. 1997. "Yeni Nesil Uğruna." *Milliyet*, October 28, 4.

Erdemir, Aykan, Cahit Korkmaz, Halil Karacali, Muharrem Erdem, Theresa Weitzhofer, and Umut Bespinar. 2010. *Türkiye'de Alevi Olmak*. Ankara: *Alevi Kültür Dernekleri & Alevi Enstitüsü*.

Ergan, Ugur. 2015. "Genelkurmay'dan Açıklama." *Hürriyet*, August 27.

Erman, Tahire, and Emrah Göker. 2000. "Alevi Politics in Contemporary Turkey." *Middle Eastern Studies* 36(4):99–118.

"Geçmiş Artık Masal Gibi." 1987. *Nokta*, September 27.

Gelin Canlar Bir Olalım: Alevilerin Dilinden Ayrımcılık Hikayeleri. 2005. Pir Sultan Abdal Kültür Derneği.

"Genelkurmay'dan Alevi Açılımı." 2009. *Oda Tv*. (http://odatv.com/genelkurmaydan-alevi-acilimi-0810091200.html).

Göner, Özlem. 2005. "The Transformation of the Alevi Collective Identity." *Cultural Dynamics* 17(2):107–34.

Göner, Özlem. 2017. *Turkish National Identity and Its Outsiders: Memories of State Violence in Dersim*. London: Routledge.

Görmüş, Alper, Serhat Öztürk, and Ayşe Özberki. 1987. "Alevilik Tarihe Karışıyor: Cem Ayinleri Mahzun..." *Nokta*, September 27, 30–31.

"Güneş'in Konuşması." 1978. *Milliyet*, December 27, 9.

Güngör, Baki. 2016. *Alevilerin Selası Okunmaz Diyen Cami Hocasına Verilen Cevap*.

Harmancı, Hasan. 2012. "İnsan Yiyen Aleviler." *HasanHarmanci*. Retrieved September 1, 2019 (http://hasanharmanci.blogcu.com/insan-yiyen-aleviler/11717097).

Hasan, Aydın. 2006. "Aleviler Arasında 'Pir' Tartışması Başladı." *Milliyet*, August 19, 16.

Hasan, Aydın. 2013. "Devlet Cenaze Törenine Dini Ayar." *Milliyet*, August 2.

"Havza'da Yaşanan Bir Cenaze Vakası." 2005. *Alevi Olmak: Alevilerin Dilinden Ayrımcılık Hikayeleri*. Ankara: Pir Sultan Abdal Kültür Derneği.

"Hoca, Alevi İşçinin Cenazesini Yıkamadı." 1968. *Milliyet*, January 31, 3.

"İbretle İzliyoruz." 2001. *Cumhuriyet*, January 28, 7.

İçgen, Levent. 2012. "TSK Cemevindeki Törene Katılmış." *Vatan*, December 3.

"İmam Alevilere Hakaret Yüzünden Linç Ediliyordu." 1965. *Cumhuriyet*, June 14, 6.

"İmam: 'Alevilerin Selası Mı Olur?' Şeklinde Bir Söz Sarfetmedim." 2015. *Haberler*, March 9.

Işık, Sinan. 2015. "Tüm Duyarlı Aleviler Bu Imama Destek Olmalı."

"İzmir'de İmam Ölen Kişinin Alevi Diye Selasını Okumadı." 2016. *Cumhuriyet*, January 22.

Kaftancıoğlu, Ümit. 2003. "Hakullah: Bektaşiliğin Gölgesinde Sömürü." *Su Yayınları*.

Karaalioğlu, Mustafa. 2001. "İzzettin Doğan: 'Derdimizi Siyasilere Anlatamadık.'" *Yeni Şafak*, January 17.

Karpat, Kemal. 1976. *The Gecekondu: Rural Migration and Urbanization*. Cambridge: Cambridge University Press.

Kaya, Ayhan. 2013. *Europeanization and Tolerance in Turkey: The Myth of Toleration*. Basingstoke: Palgrave Macmillan.

Kehl-Bodrogi, Krisztina, Barbara Kellner Heinkele, and Anke Otter Beaujean. 1997. *Syncretistic Religious Communities in the Near East: Collected Papers Od the International Symposium "Alevism in Turkey and Comparable Syncretistic*

202 *Alevis and Funerals*

Religious Communities in the Near East in the Past and Present" Berlin, 14–17 *April 1955.* Leiden: Brill.

Kenanoğlu, Ali. 2013. "Alevi Cenazesi." *Evrensel*, January 17.

Massicard, Elise. 2007. "Alevi Hareketinin Siyasallaşması." *İstanbul: İletişim Yayınları.*

Oğuz, Mustafa. 2016. "İzmir'de Sela Krizi." *Hürriyet*, January 23.

Öktem, Alper. 2000. "Burdur'a Yerleşmiş Senirkent Alevileri." *Tarih ve Toplum* (196):43–49.

"Ölen Alevi Kadın Için Imamdan Cemevsiz Sela." 2016. *Kazete: Özgür Kadının Sesi*, June 26.

Otyam, Fikret. 1963. "Hu Dost: 'Sana Cevabımdır'..." *Cumhuriyet*, October 18, 7.

Özcan, Nuri. 2009. "Salâ الصلا." *İslam Ansiklopedisi* 36:15–16.

Özdil, Yilmaz. 2016. "Cenazede Şopen Mi Çalsak Itri Mi?" *Sözcü*, April 20.

Öztürk, Erhan. 2010. "'Müslüman Değil' Diye Salasını Okumadılar." *Sabah*, April 24.

Özyürek, Esra. 2009. "'The Light of the Alevi Fire Was Lit in Germany and Then Spread to Turkey': A Transnational Debate on the Boundaries of Islam." *Turkish Studies* 10(2):233–53.

Payzın, Şirin. 2016. *Ne Oluyor: Alevilerin Talepleri*. CNN Türk, January 21. (https://www.cnnturk.com/tv-cnn-turk/arsiv/ne-oluyor/alevilerin-talepleri).

Saçlı, Ismail. 2016. "Hem Camiye, Hem Cemevine Gidilir Mi?" *Habercem*, May 20.

Şahin, Şehriban. 2005. "The Rise of Alevism as a Public Religion." *Current Sociology* 53(3):465–85. doi: 10.1177/0011392105051336.

Savaş, Erdal. 2016. "Alevi Gencin Cenazesi Tartışma Doğurdu." *Nazilli*, December 13.

"Şehit Olan Alevi Askerin Cenazesi Ile Ilgili Açıklama." 2016. *Koz: Aylık Haber Aktüel Dergisi*, December 23.

Şener, Cemal. 1995. "Çoksesli Rönesans." *Milliyet*, July 4, 23.

Şener, Nedim. 2012. "Alevi Açılımının Ruhuna Fatiha." *Posta*, August 15.

Sökefeld, Martin. 2002. "Alevi Dedes in the German Diaspora: The Transformation of a Religious Institution." *Zeitschrift Für Ethnologie* 127(2):163–86.

Tamer, Meral. 2006. "Şehit Ailelerini Dinlemeliyiz." *Milliyet*, September 12, 6.

Tol, Ugraş Ulaş. 2005. "Alevi Olmak: Alevilerin Dilinden Ayrımcılık Hikayeleri." Ankara: *Pir Sultan Abdal Kültür Derneği.*

Toprak, Binnaz, İrfan Bozan, Tan Morgül, and Nedim Şener. 2009. *Din ve Muhafazakarlık Ekseninde Ötekileştirilenler. İstanbul: Metis Yayınları.*

"TSK: Camide Tören Için Ailenin 'olur'unu Aldık." 2012. *NTV*, August 13.

"Türkiye'de Alevilere Yönelik Dini Ayrımcılık Hakkında Beyanlar." 2008. *Türkiye'de Dini Ayrımcılık Raporu.* Mazlumder.

Uludağ, Alican. 2020. "'Alevi askerin cenazesine devlet zirvesi ve Genelkurmay katılmadı' iddiası." *Cumhuriyet*, January 3. (https://halktv.com.tr/gundem/alevi-askerin-cenazesine-devlet-zirvesi-ve-genelkurmay-katilmadi-iddiasi-415367h).

Ulusoy, Kivanc. 2013. "The 'Europeanization' of the Religious Cleavage in Turkey: The Case of the Alevis." *Mediterranean Politics* 18(2):294–310. doi: 10.1080/13629395.2013.799346.

Van Bruinessen, Martin. 1996. "Kurds, Turks and the Alevi Revival in Turkey." *Middle East Report* 200:7–10.

Van Bruinessen, Martin. 1997. "'Aslini Inkar Eden Haramzadedir': The Debate on the Ethnic Identity of the Kurdish Alevis." Pp.1–23 in *Syncretistic Religious Communities in the Near East.* Leiden: Brill.

Alevis and Funerals 203

Vorhoff, Karin. 1998. "'Let's Reclaim Our History and Culture!'-Imagining Alevi Community in Contemporary Turkey." *Welt Des Islams* 38:220–52.

Yaman, Ali. 2003. "Anadolu Alevileri'nde Otoritenin El Değiştirmesi: Dedelik Kurumundan Kültürel Organizasyonlara." Pp. 331–56 in *Bilgi Toplumunda Alevilik*. Bielefeld: Bielefeld Alevi Kültür Merkezi,

Yılmaz, Önder. 2005. "Prof. Bardakoğlu: Alevilerin Talebi Siyasi." *Milliyet*, November 6, 18.

Yöre, Seyit. 2011. "The Musical Codes of Alevi-Bektashi Culture." *Türk Kültürü ve Hacı Bektaş Velî Araştırma Dergisi* 60:234.

6 Conclusions

Democracy, the regime of popular self-government where alert and talkative citizenry protects rights and freedoms, may not require agreement on values. From the micro to macro level, the dialectical encounters covered in this book suggest that the first constructive step is likely to be acknowledging the disagreement over values before negotiating rights, freedoms, capabilities, and duties. Through the traces of conversational texts, the book has focused on several unique ways in which the cultural resources, including but not exhaustive of values, and their functions in ideology-making might change.

Despite their uniqueness, these routes are not alien to other country contexts with value plurality. The Islamists' "our values, our democracy" project resembles the Western right-wing populists' reduction of democratic values into the construct of Judeo-Christianity. In the context of value demonstrativeness, both particularisms adjoin the universalist currents of the same value-based approach, exemplified nowadays by the construct of the French republican values. Islamic democracy has become an unfruitful search that results from the depiction of democratic culture as a parochial value system. Applied without a sustainable tolerance regime, it fails for the same reason that value monopolism puts Western democracies at risk.

Value demonstrativeness has become a transnational political climate. In this climate, interlocutors tend to claim survival by differentiating their value expressions, even when their value orientations are negotiable. The question left unanswered for this era is not which values democracy is established on but how democracy may be anticipated within a plurality of value expressions. Demonstrating that value expressions say little (or, at least, not all) about the culture in flow is a starting point to approach this question. This book aimed to take this first step.

An essential part of the literature I have problematized tends to take cultures as *entities*. Instead, this book took them as *processes*. The contemporary narrative on cultural clashes relies on a notion of clear-cut, monolithic culture zones that meet one another only to remain the same—i.e., destroy the *other* or vanish. Contrary to this understanding, I contend that the medium

DOI: 10.4324/9781003311805-6

of a conversation is capable of projecting collective playing fields where seemingly different worlds operate in interaction. Conversations appear not only in making confrontations but also in sharing common spaces in which intended and unintended transmissions occur. As such, confrontation may often serve as a process of accommodation, and consequently, it may lead to recasting some seemingly persistent cultural resources. Instead of examining a cultural resource in isolation, such as values *per se*, I scrutinized how they are translated into different cultural periods.

Different periods trigger specific uses of the cultural resources. These shifts cannot be detected utilizing value surveys, primarily due to the survey technique's reliance on exogenously imposed social contexts, limited speech acts, and the explicit expression of cultural resources prior to social action. Even in cases of an overarching value consensus, the values may be expressed so differently that their complication will not be reducible to the preset catchphrases used in survey contents. Therefore, focusing on the dialogues unexpected to their participants and overhearers, including researchers, becomes an essential enterprise. In conclusion, I shall summarize and integrate the book's empirical findings while focusing on the broader disputes over the role of values in democracy and the merits and limits of tolerance.

The Re-Operationalization of Values

The common theme in my case studies was the re-operationalization of values in ideology-making processes. For example, I examined how Alevis evaluated the meaning of mosque funerals, the values a funeral symbolizes, and the success of the current practices in meeting these values. At the outset of this process, they developed a new identity consciousness in line with their politics of recognition. The state authority is tactically open to the possibility of recognizing a non-Muslim Alevi religion, but strictly against recognizing multiple trajectories or the idea of an Islamic sect with a worship place other than a mosque. Meanwhile, the same authority gets along well with a form of Alevilik that could be assimilated into "Islam"—i.e., one that defines the mosque as its only place of worship. It is no more fashionable to curse Alevilik as the Elmalılı administration did in the 1960s. The new custom is juxtaposing the kinds of Alevilik and then cursing the dissidents.

Similarly, the mainstream currents of Islamism have come to rationalize an implicit tolerance towards LGBT people who do not threaten their value politics even if these individuals contradict the values by showing their deviant identity markers. These decisions to accept the hitherto unacceptable go hand in hand with the development of a broader left-wing opposition, in which the LGBT activists have begun to participate, against the cultural hegemony of conservative "aggression" and "bigotry." Once this door has been opened, the makers of Islamism are calculating how to keep religiously

206 *Conclusions*

conservative LGBT individuals away from the rival repertoire. Meanwhile, employing the other tools given by their value system, some Islamists feel dissonance in being able to get along only with the "rich" and "neoliberal" visible representations of LGBT.

In the funeral and entertainment landscapes, the *other* is embraced depending on its affirmation of and contribution to the parochial values of the *self*. Although this change gives the *others* in these landscapes ("Alevis" and "LGBT" people) a space to choose what they stand for, it does not go too far in materializing a threat to the amalgam between the authorities' first-order values and others' rights and freedoms. In this vein, Alevis could not make the state recognize their places of worship since they did not come up with a single definition of Alevilik that meets the state's value-laden criteria. Similarly, the authorities' parochial values determine their approach to a gay employee in the public sector, a murdered sex worker, or a transgender entertainer whose visibility is under investigation. Many will not consent to be bound by an agreement in which they will be tolerated as objects of pity. On the contrary, their struggle is to be recognized as equal rights holders, if not revolutionize the landscape. Meanwhile, their out-group calls for equal rights translate into new in-group debates on value plurality.

In the clothing landscape, I claimed that values have been re-operationalized more comprehensively by going beyond the domination of such parochial values. An authority—e.g., a minister, a court, one's parents, a teacher, or a random stranger—may still raise its voice to interfere with women's clothing preferences. It may rationalize its action in the name of a hegemonic ideology, be that "Islamism" or "Secularism." On the other hand, as I have also demonstrated, the identical ideological repertoires have acquired a new dimension where many narrators conclude that intervening in others' clothes based on one's parochial values would be counterproductive. The ethical arguments of the women who aim to reclaim their agency after experiencing intervention are also in line with this cultural change. Moreover, my comparative analysis of the Ticani case suggests that the individual voices of these women are better heard in ideology-making processes. In a nutshell, those arguments pave the way for constructing a common awareness regarding the distinction between one's first-order values and others' rights and freedoms.

The re-makers of these contested ideologies claim to have inherited the values they consider foundational—e.g., the cases of Ahmet Mahmut Ünlü and Şafak Pavey, among others. Nonetheless, at the same time, they rationalize the need for a limited tolerance—i.e., one without relativism. This restricted tolerance does not necessarily stop dialogue but renders it meaningful primarily as a matter of second-order values. Therefore, a theological claim of the *self* is not likely to be respected by the *other*, whereas a claim based upon the acknowledgment of their different values has the ability to trigger new and potentially productive discussions.

Democracy beyond Shared Values

Openly acknowledging the disagreement tends to be more productive in the setting where relativism is unachievable. Therefore, the flow of the conversations in Turkey encourages the interlocutors to problematize even the most subtle impositions of others' first-order values in the name of appropriateness rules. Within the incidents I have examined, some rules were set forward and imposed in various ways, but they also were disputed and challenged when they did not pass the test of parochiality in shared spaces. The boundary moments, such as the disputed incidents and the ensuing debates over them, as I have examined, are a step toward decontaminating standard rules from parochial values. The separation between them seems necessary to imagine building a democratic system of rights, freedoms, and duties.

Amid the ongoing contestations, a shared lesson in Turkey is that attempts to reject the *other*'s difference may end up being worse for one's foundational values. A clear repercussion of this idea is the adverse reaction of the new generation of Secularists towards the former defenders of the head-covering ban. Another repercussion is the lamentation of the previous generation Islamists about the "fake" new carriers of their value system. Finally, the women whose clothes were interfered with have agreed that neither they nor others deserve interference. While denouncing the authoritative claims over their clothing, they refused to generalize their authoritative claims regarding what is suitable to wear. These agents try to save their parochial values by going beyond them, but also without giving them up.

Second-order values are linked to first-order values in the sense that an ideology maker will not sacrifice the latter for the sake of the former. The second-order value expressions that generate tolerance to others originate from the foundational values of the *self*, which define the *other*'s otherness. Hence, the second-order values are not likely to be produced together with the *other* who does not represent the value system. Contrary to the value-based imaginations of democracy, common ground cannot be established by trying to construct an allegedly neutral, higher value standard. Proposals based on this approach to democratic culture fall short of imagining heterogeneity in the form of different and even conflicting ways to agree. Rights may eventually become common values, but not necessarily.

Blurred Boundaries

The book argued that some dialectical encounters can still blur the putatively clear-cut boundaries between clashing identities. Those blurred boundaries signify a step to breaking the social segregation between the *self* and the *other*. In other words, new discursive possibilities have appeared to shift the polarization dynamics. For example, by adopting a new language of intersectionality, the "left-wing" parties decided to have a few headscarved candidates as "workers" and "farmers" without sacrificing their defense of

208   *Conclusions*

Secularism. In reaction, Erdoğan's government seems to have turned a blind eye to its "headscarved sisters," especially if they acted as workers who prioritized their labor rights (e.g., the Flormar case).

Given that clothing seems to have lost its position of acting as the infallible precursor of personality, further research is needed to test whether the meetings between different clothing items have less likelihood of being taken by their carriers as an outright contestation between the *self* and the *other*. This moment may be the last stage before reaching a *settled* cultural period. However, this reconciliation comes with another *unsettled* cultural period, where the quality of the garments, instead of their shape, will create new meanings for the in-group and out-group.

The boundaries have also become fuzzy in the other landscapes discussed in the book. Even though the ideology makers of Islamism repeat their antagonism against "LGBT," many of them have begun to distinguish clearly between the visible representations of LGBT identity that contradict and fit into their social project. In line with this cleavage, the visible representations have diversified unprecedentedly in terms of alternative politics of recognition, visibility, and approaches to "common values." Subject-centered identity building (e.g., the LGBT community) seems to have lost its analytical power. Because, at this stage, the critical question is not "who we are" but "what we are against," LGBT individuals—activist or not—will have a say as part of the broader ideological struggles.

Another illustration of how dialectical encounters blurred the boundaries is the re-configuration of *cemevi* and *mosque* in the eyes of Alevis. By founding cemevis, the Alevi communities adjusted their relationship with mosque communities, which they entered after they migrated to the urban centers. While embracing cemevi in urban settings, however, a group retained elements that they acculturated during their engagement with the mosque activities. Combining the rituals of mosque and cemevi is at odds with the ways in which the Alevi belief system is being recast elsewhere. The politics of assimilation and recognition shape Alevilik together in accordance with their clashing interests, whereas the Alevis who keep carrying the marks of heterodoxy are being forced into a subaltern position.

Recognition without Tolerance

Well-established in the state bureaucracy and the pro-government ideological repertoire, the language of orthodoxy pushes Alevis to solidify the authority structure of Alevilik. According to the government, this is a pre-condition of recognition. In this project, the newly founded Alevi associations—or the triumphant among them—are supposed to not only manage the flow of the culture of Alevis but also define and freeze the relationship between Islam, the Alevi identity, and the cultural institutions that operationalize this identity. Tolerance is possible with inaction or disregard, whereas, in such a relationship, recognition might tie the future of Alevilik

Conclusions 209

to the affirmation of the state authority. Recognition constitutes the core of the necessary acknowledgment of disagreement on values. It also has other merits, such as underpinning self-esteem and mutual legal personalities. Nevertheless, it does not necessarily escape the hierarchy problem for which liberal thinkers criticize the idea of tolerance.

I have kept track of the double-sided rationalization of intolerance against some syncretic Alevi traditions on the landscape of funerals. The rule of essentialism will not resolve many Alevis' problems, for it falls short of considering how cultural practices might be reshaped by a multitude of factors, such as neighborly relations, identity politics, or religious doctrine. Cemevi acts as a worship place for Alevis who are not assimilated, whereas it acts as a culture center for Sunni students who prefer cemevi courses on the folk (musical) instrument, *saz*. The Alevi traditions constitute a crucial part of these students' cultural resources, notwithstanding their different religious sects.

While being a place of worship for many, a mosque might act as a center of culture for an Alevi citizen requesting the funeral salâ, as a traditional religious musical expression, to be read so that one's Sunni neighbors hear the details of a funeral. Neglecting this differentiated integration of the components of "our" culture will lead to an imposition of false conditions on recognition. Amid such multifaceted cultural practices, which cannot be defined once and for all, the concept of tolerance will remain relevant.

Other's Familiarity and the New Migration Question

While emphasizing the necessity to acknowledge value disagreements for democratization, the book left the prerequisites of such acknowledgment out of its scope. The analytical framework I offered to study the conversations, structures, and agents has at least one implication: the interlocutors have to speak the same language and familiarize each other. Agreement in disagreement is unlikely to develop in the fear of the unknown. This foundational question has become crucial, given that Turkey has become a stock of migrants from Syria, Afghanistan, and many others within a decade. Lacking Turkey's memory, the settlement of these societies has turned into a time bomb with the impact of resource scarcity and the economic crisis. Whether and when these newcomers can participate in the public debate depends on a series of factors that requires research, first and foremost, with capability approaches. Such an enterprise will require developing new knowledge generation and political economy perspectives.

Beyond, all ideologies will have to situate themselves in this new reality. Many ideology makers of Islamism, including various religious communities and the government party, frame migration from the perspective of religious brotherhood. Placing the migrants as "Muslim brothers" in the public debate renders them a part of the already tense ideological contestations. Meanwhile, migration means importing other religious traditions, as well as

210 *Conclusions*

the deculturating global imaginations of Islam. Especially the Salafi strands of Islamism, previously weak in Turkey where the traditional Islam is rooted in Sufism, will challenge the balance of power in the religious communities.

The Turkish-Islam synthesis faces the question of whether threats to the religion are synonymous with threats to the nation. Meanwhile, the nationalist vein of Secularism claims ascendance by zooming in on the image of "Afghan" immigrants disturbing "Turkish" women on the street. Shorts and veils remain hot topics in this landscape, whereas the "rich Arab" and the "Almancı" (i.e., Turkish-origin German) who exploit the depreciating Turkish lira enter the scene. With the increasing visibility of wealthy immigrants, a new class consciousness takes heart from the native-migrant classification. New ideological equations are on the horizon to liquefy the current rigidities and render the near past distant.

Index

Note: *Italic* page numbers refer to figures; page numbers followed by "n" denote endnotes.

Abdülhamit II 117, 159n10
Abrahamic religions 25, 176
AKP 2, 8, 25, 33, 38, 56–57, 69, 74, 78, 80, 82–83, 88, 93, 94, 98, 126–28, 132, 142, 144–45, 159n17, 182, 192, 199n16
Alevi-Bektashi Federation (ABF) 185–87, 193, 196, 199n15
Alevi Foundations 185, 189–92, 196
amalgamation 5, 39, 113, 122, 186
antagonistic democracy 23
anti-capitalist Muslims 7, 135
assimilation 11–12, 25, 117, 170–72, 175–77, 186, 188, 194–98, 199n12, 208
Atatürk, Mustafa Kemal 121, 152–56, 158n6, 159n8, 188
authority structure 7, 38–39, 43, 90, 98, 115, 125, 175, 208

Bakhtin, Mikhail 14, 36, 46n15
Berkes, Niyazi 114, 120, 134, 159n8
blasphemy 111, 131, 143
Boston Gay Men's Chorus 56, 69–71
Bourdieu, Pierre 15, 35
Buber, Martin 36

Calvinists 24
case: Ergenekon 68, 159n16, 182; Sledgehammer 68, 159n16
Catholic 1, 24
Cemevi 11–12, 42, 171, 175–98, 199n10, 199n11, 199n17, 208–9
çengi 5, 59–60
CHP 10, 88, 94–98, 120, 125, 128, 132–36, 149, 157–58, 159n23, 174, 183–84, 195

Christian 24, 46n5, 114, 117–18, 139–40, 142, 187
civic culture 29, 46n1
civilization 36, 119–21, 156
civilized 118, 121, 153–56, 159n8, 159n9
classes: lower 60, 116; religion 4; religious 119; social 7, 135
clothing revolution 6, 11, 110, 113, 119–21, 154–56
comparative 26–27, 30, 42, 206
comparisons: cross-cultural 30; cross-temporal 17, 37, 42, 196
conversation: evaluative 17, 37, 43–46, 56, 93, 111, 138, 171, 177, 185; exploratory 17, 37, 43–46, 55–56, 61, 69, 111, 127, 139, 170, 177, 181, 185; micro-level 18, 43–46; retroactive 17, 37, 43, 56, 64, 81, 112, 172, 177, 194; *see also* conversational texts
conversational texts 35–43, 204
Council: of Ministers 181; Radio and Television Supreme 72–74, 91–92, 152; of State 66, 122; UN Human Rights 67
countries: authoritarian 40; Middle Eastern 40; Muslim 30, 124
court: of Cassation 63–64, 82, 93, 96; Constitutional 66–67, 122; decision 64–66; of Human Rights 122; proceedings 55, 61–63; records 37–43; Shari'a 173
Cübbeli Ahmet Hoca *see* Ünlü, Ahmet Mahmut
cultural: exceptionalism 26; experts 31; period 1, 12–15, 38–39, 112, 171, 205,

212   Index

208; resources 1, 12–17, 29–33, 43, 65, 204, 209; variables 26–27; zone 36, 117, 207
culture: democratic 1, 26–30, 46n7, 204, 207; of shopkeepers 54–57, 93, 98; wars 36; zones 204; *see also* settled culture; unsettled culture

Dede: cemevi 175, 181–97; ocak 173, 185–97
Deleuze, Gilles 13, 16
Demirel, Süleyman 39, 122–25
democratization 1–3, 17, 22–27, 47n16
dervish 3, 15, 74
dialectic 12, 17, 36, 44, 46n15, 113, 185, 204–7
Dilipak, Abdurrahman 126, 140, 145
Dink, Hrant 85, 96
Diyanet 11, 18n14, 42, 76–79, 144, 170–92, 197, 199n9
Doğan, İzzettin 185–86, 191, 198
Durmaz, Kerimcan 69, 74–75, 86–87

Eco, Umberto 13
Emevism 189, 199n13
Erdoğan, Recep Tayyip 2, 6–8, 25, 41, 70, 74, 76–77, 79–82, 86, 88, 90, 98–99, 126, 135, 137, 143, 145–47, 160n26, 183–84, 208
Ersoy, Bülent 7–8, 42, 60, 70, 76–85, 88, 89–91, 93–94, 99, 99n3, 99n12, 99n14
essentialism 113, 142, 158n2, 170–72, 186–88, 194–98, 209
Eurocentrism 30, 158n4; *see also* Westernist
European: Alevi communities 175; Alevi Unions Confederation 187, 195; capitals 173; Convention on Human Rights 67; Court of Human Rights 67, 122, 195; Federation of Alevi Communities 187
event-based approach 17, 37–40

fez 114, 116, 119–20, 153, 155–56, 158n6, 159n7, 159n9
Foucault, Michel 14
freedom 3, 6, 17, 23–24, 82, 88, 122–32, 207; for all 141; of belief 148, 157; of clothing 133; of conscience 111; of expression 24; to not pray 39; of not praying 124–25; of not wearing the headscarf 125; of religion 39; *see also* unfreedom

Gaza spirit 15–16
gender equality 1, 24–25, 29–31, 122
gender justice 25
Gezi Protests 77, 90, 95, 132, 135, 190
Giddens, Anthony 15
Gramscian 8
Gül, Abdullah 145, 184
Gülen, Fethullah 68, 143, 159n19, 190, 198

Habermas, Jürgen 25, 28
habit 12–15, 41, 120–21; *see also* habitual; habitus
habitual cultural periods 14–15
habitus 15
hammam 54, 59, 61; *see also* köçek, çengi
head-covering ban 6, 10, 38–39, 44–45, 111–14, 121, 123–28, 132–34, 137, 141, 158n1, 207
headscarf 10, 18n7, 76, 112, 114, 121–26, 129, 131, 132, 135–36, 138–39, 144–45, 148–50, 152, 159n22
hegemonic: culture 97; ideology 4, 7–8, 10, 58, 78, 110, 112, 147, 159n22, 206; imaginaries 112; projects 198
heterodox 5, 170, 190, 195, 198, 208
hijab 6, 9, 81, 111, 114, 117–20, 126, 137–38, 141, 144–45, 150, 153–58, 158n5, 159n22, 159n23
homosexuality 18n10, 29–30, 35, 46n9, 58–60, 67, 79, 87
Huysuz Virjin 69, 72

ideology-making 3, 12, 16, 34, 37, 39, 45, 64, 112, 127, 147, 173, 175, 185, 204–6
Ilıcalı, Acun 74–75
Imam Hatip 79
Inglehart, Ronald 1, 18n10, 28–30, 46n7
İpekçi, Cemil 70, 91
Islamic culture 1
Islamic societies 18n10, 31, 76
Islamism 2, 7, 18n16, 34, 47n17, 56, 76, 78, 81, 88, 96, 111, 127, 136–38, 140–41, 148, 186, 199n13, 205, 206, 208–10
Islamist 2, 6–8, 15, 24–25, 33–34, 38, 43, 45, 47n17, 56, 69, 76–77, 93, 98, 111, 122–24, 126–28, 131, 136–37, 139, 141, 143, 145–49, 157–58, 174, 195, 204, 206–7
Islam question 22, 24
Ismailağa religious community 9, 33–34, 46n12, 46n13, 78, 137, 145

Index   213

Jewish 125, 197
Jihad 24
Jihadist 45, 149
John, Elton 69–72
Judeo-Christian 204

Karaman, Hayrettin 18n11, 33, 46n4, 78,
    86, 142, 160n24
Kemalism 54, 119, 137
Kemalist 124, 136, 158
Kılıçarslan, İsmail 79, 139–40
kippah 125
Kısakürek, Necip Fazıl 157–58
Kızılbaş 5, 181
köçek 5, 45, 59–61, 99n2, 99n5
Kurdish: Alevis 175; political movement
    96; Problem 96; separatists 97; song
    74; trans 96; voter 98

Laclau, Ernesto 25–26
LGBT: activism 5, 56–57, 75, 80, 84, 93,
    96–98; activist 57, 64, 80–81, 84–85,
    93–99, 205; association 63–64, 79–80,
    82, 86–87, 90, 92, 94–97; community
    55, 80–81, 97, 208; employee 8, 66–68,
    89–90; flag 70, 79, 95; identity 5–6, 8,
    38, 41, 45, 54, 56, 61, 68–69, 71, 89,
    208; individuals 25, 46n9, 98, 99n15,
    206, 208; lobbies 96; magazines 38;
    Movement 87; people 2, 5, 7–8, 38, 55,
    63, 65, 69, 70–71, 74, 79, 85, 87–94,
    97–98, 205–6; person 8, 55–56, 62,
    67, 78, 86, 90–91; Pride 7–8, 42, 76,
    79, 88, 94–95, 99n15; propaganda 77;
    public officers 65; representations 56,
    58; rights 25; sex workers 55; sinners
    79, 86, 93; struggle 97; visibility 68, 75;
    voters 78
liberal: argument 39, 141; culture
    26; democracy 28; democrats 1;
    ideology 124; jihad 24; Muslims 24;
    nationalists 25; neoliberal 57, 78, 206;
    organizations 159n17; pilgrims 123;
    postmodernism 95–96; sex workers 95;
    thinkers 209; values 24; women 127;
    zealotry 25

Marxism 5, 54, 93, 190
Marxist 95, 174
Meşrutiyet 110, 116–17, 120
Middle East 25, 40–41, 69, 71
Middle eastern: countries 34, 40; cultural
    exceptionalism 26

migration 170, 172–73, 209
millet system 6, 11, 110, 115
modernism 6, 113, 119, 137; see also
    postmodernist
modernization 110, 113, 116, 119, 126, 158
mosque 4–5, 11–12, 18n13, 42, 45–46,
    78, 117, 144, 171–89, 193–98, 198n7,
    199n11, 205, 208–9
Mouffe, Chantal 23, 26
Mumcu, Uğur 123–25, 159n12
Müren, Zeki 60, 84, 99n3
Muslim Brotherhood 25, 209

Nakşibendi 34
national dress code 118
nationalism 18n16, 85, 91
nationalist 25, 85, 123, 210
Nationalist Action Party 16
Neşet Ertaş 46, 99n5, 184

Özal, Turgut 81–82, 91, 124

Pavey, Şafak 10, 95, 132–34, 206
Pir Sultan Abdal Cultural Association
    185, 191
populism 24–25
populist 22–24, 80, 204
post-industrial democracies 22
postmodernist 36
post-secularity 28

Ramadan 7, 18n8, 69–71, 76–77, 84, 120,
    129, 131, 148, 151
rational-choice theories 27
recognition 4, 6, 8, 11–12, 17, 19n16, 57,
    68–69, 82, 170–72, 174–76, 185–86,
    192, 198, 205, 208–9
Refah: cadres 142; Party 88; tradition 88
reflexive 14–16, 19n17
rights: activist 96; in the ballot box
    90–91; based positions 112; demands
    124; of LGBT individuals 25; of the
    other Abrahamic religions 25; of
    others 146; and restrictions 122; in the
    "Secular" sense of term 111; through
    peaceful negotiation 91; violations
    127; of women 122; see also LGBT
    rights
Rorty, Richard 25
Rumi 3, 83, 99n13

Safa, Peyami 60
Safavid 16

214 Index

Salâ 11–12, 18n13, 42, 170–72, 174, 176–81, 194, 196–97, 198n1, 198n3, 209
Salaat 198
Şansal, Barbaros 87, 91
şapka 111, 114, 119–21, 131, 142, 152–53, 155–56, 159n7, 159n8
sectarianism 5, 15, 34–35, 170, 193
Secularism (with capital S) 2–3, 5–6, 10–11, 39, 44–45, 58, 60, 93–95, 111, 113, 119, 121–27, 131–35, 155–58, 170, 173, 175–76, 183–84, 189, 191, 193, 199n13, 206, 208, 210
secularism (with small s) 18n4, 45, 93, 122, 126, 134, 158, 176, 193
Selçuk, İlhan 60, 122, 136
Şenlikoğlu, Emine 60, 79, 145
settled culture (cultural period) 12–13, 15, 39, 59, 189, 208; *see also* culture and unsettled cultural period
Seyyid (Battal) Gazi 15, 19n18
Sharia Courts 173, 188, 190
Shia 15–16, 34
silence 8, 17, 37, 40–42, 127, 148, 153, 177
social context 3–4, 9–10, 13, 17, 19n17, 30–33, 35–36, 38, 111, 132, 172, 205
Social Hostilities Index 39, *41*
state funeral 4, 171, 176, 181–83, 192–93, 199n8
structural variables 27
Sufism 210
Sufi tradition 174
Sunni 4–5, 11, 15–16, 25, 34, 91, 171–74, 176, 181–85, 187–88, 191, 194–98, 199n17, 209
Swidler, Ann 12–13, 18n3, 35–36
syncretism 197–98

Tanzimat 110, 116, 118–19
tesettür 9–10, 111, 118, 126, 138, 141–45
Ticani 42–43, 112, 114, 139, 152–57, 206
tolerance 59, 65, 68–71, 73, 76–80, 82–84, 110–15, 117, 119–21, 125, 128–29, 131, 137–40, 142, 156–57, 170, 172–77, 194–95, 204–9

trans-exclusionary feminism 54
turban 6, 18n7, 111–12, 115–16, 121–26, 132–36, 155, 159n22
Turkish Armed Forces (TAF) 181–82, 184, 192–95
Turkish Employment Agency (İŞKUR) 55, 65, 92
Turkish Religious Foundation (Türk Diyanet Vakfı) 77, 84
Turk-Islam synthesis 2

Üçok, Bahriye 123–24, 159n13
unfreedom 124–25
Union of Turkish Women (Türk Kadınlar Birliği) 153, 157
United Nations 67
Ünlü, Ahmet Mahmut 9–11, 33
unsettled culture (cultural period) 38, 171, 208
Ürek, Fatih 60, 69, 72–75

value survey 1, 4, 8, 16–17, 22–23, 30–35, 46n9, 76, 98, 205
values: common 1, 54–57, 83–84, 89, 207–8; first-order 8–10, 23, 57, 110–11, 128–34, 137, 146, 159n21, 206–7; foundational 8–9, 17, 23, 29, 110–11, 146, 207–9; French republican 24, 204; liberal 24; second-order 23, 29, 110–11, 206–7; self-expression 28–30, 46n7; shared 1, 26, 75, 84–85, 89, 207; substantive 25; survival 28; traditional 28

Western: consciousness 14; contexts 46n10; culture 14; democracies 28, 204; fashion 116; feminists 158n5; -ist ideology 113; -ization 116; -ized 26; modernity 126; right-wing populists 204; secular society 28; states 123
Westernist 113
worker 5, 7, 38, 45, 55, 61–63, 64, 66–67, 75, 80, 84, 91, 95, 104, 123, 136, 154, 206–8
World Values Survey 18n10, 28–30, 35